MY AMERICAN CENTURY

OTHER BOOKS BY STUDS TERKEL

American Dreams: Lost and Found

Chicago

Coming of Age:
The Story of Our Century by Those Who've Lived It

Division Street: America

Giants of Jazz

The "Good War": An Oral History of World War II

The Great Divide:
Second Thoughts on the American Dream

Hard Times: An Oral History of the Great Depression

Race: How Blacks and Whites Think and Feel
About the American Obsession

Talking to Myself: A Memoir of My Times

Working: People Talk About What They Do All Day
and How They Feel About What They Do

MY AMERICAN CENTURY

Studs Terkel

THE NEW PRESS

NEW YORK

Library of Congress Cataloging-in-Publication Data
Terkel, Studs.
My American century / Studs Terkel
p.   cm.
ISBN 1-56584-365-7 (HC)
1. United States—Biography. 2. Interviews—United States.
3. National characteristics, American. 4. United States—Social conditions—
1933–1945. 5. United States—Social conditions—1945–   . I. Title.
CT220.T43   1997
920.073—dc21   96-52779
[B]   CIP
Published in the United States by The New Press, New York
Distributed by W. W. Norton & Company, Inc., New York

Established in 1990 as a major alternative to the large, commercial publishing
houses, The New Press is the first full-scale nonprofit American book publisher
outside of the university presses. The Press is operated editorially in the public
interest, rather than for private gain; it is committed to publishing in innovative
ways works of educational, cultural, and community value that, despite their
intellectual merits, might not normally be commercially viable. The New Press's
editorial offices are located at the City University of New York.

Production management by Kim Waymer
Printed in the United States of America
97 98 99 9 8 7 6 5 4 3

to

ANDRÉ SCHIFFRIN

editor and publisher

In memory, we find the most complete release from the narrowness of presented time and place.... The picture is one of human beings confronted by a world in which they can be masters only as they discover ways of escape from the complete sway of immediate circumstances.

—F.C. BARTLETT, *Remembering*

CONTENTS:

CONTENTS

CONTENTS

CONTENTS

FOREWORD

The title of this book tells of a happy convergence—a writing observer's destiny to have lived in a nation whose recent fate has granted it a worldwide ascendancy. Studs Terkel was born during the early adolescence of this century, the second decade, when we emerged as a great power, the nation whose belated entrance into the First World War decisively hastened its conclusion. Thereafter, gradually (and reluctantly and even fearfully), America became first among nations, its economic and military potential a looming presence even in the 1930s, when (like other capitalist countries) it lay perilously wounded. But the Great Depression, here and abroad, ended with the Second World War—indeed, Hitler had shown the world in the middle 1930s what military preparedness can do for a stagnant, even prostrate economy: a huge shot in the arm. By the early 1940s, to quote President Roosevelt, the United States had become a great "arsenal of democracy"—millions of men and women, hitherto jobless or only marginally employed, now working full-time (often overtime) at a halfway decent wage.

Not that bliss had once and for all arrived in the lives of America's working people. The Wagner Labor Relations Act, which had at last strengthened the right of labor unions to organize and bargain with employers, had been enacted only in the late 1930s; and even after the Second World War had ended, unions across the country would have to struggle long and hard on behalf of their members. But the country would not again in the twentieth century slip into the kind of major collapse experienced in the 1930s. For decades, from 1950 to the late 1980s, we fought another kind of war, called *cold*—funneling billions of dollars into the defense industry and, as a consequence, providing a continuing stimulus to our industrial life. Still, for many millions of our people (for the substantial majority, actually), a reasonably stable economy has meant no end to worries about work and wages. Today, most of our citizens are barely able to stay ahead of their various creditors and, of course and alas, can all too easily lose their jobs and thereby the everyday sense of self-respect that goes with having a paycheck to cash or deposit every week. Such a vulnerability informs the life of even those lucky to be hard at work, as anyone interested in talking with ordinary working people will soon enough learn. But precisely who has had such an interest? To be sure, some earnest, determined journalists have insisted on talking with factory workers or office workers and have reported on what they saw or heard. Certain social scientists have likewise tried to understand how our "common folk" have managed—and done so not through distanced conceptual assertion but through fieldwork, efforts to learn firsthand from artisans or farmhands, from those who wear blue collars or white collars, how their lives go, how they manage (against what odds) in the course of their daily lives. Yet, anthropologists, as Margaret Mead long ago lamented, avoid their native lands in favor of natives in distant continents; and sociologists increasingly rely upon survey research, quantitative data enabled by the increasingly intricate technology of computers, and so cannot be counted on for individual interviews of any length and depth with particular men and women.

How lucky, then, for all of us, that Studs Terkel has been with us these many years. He has sought us out, sat with us, posed questions to us, wondered about us, asked of us what we have to say, got it all down on his tape recorder. Thereupon, he has returned to his own workplace (after visiting us in ours or in our homes) so that he can hear us yet again, consider what we have said, sift and sort those many words and sentences, and finally, give his own editor's shaping sense to our statements, which, in turn, have become available to any of us fortunate enough to be his readers and really, thereby, his students. We learn through his work about our fellow Americans, how their various lives go, depending on who it is (living where, doing what) Mr. Terkel has managed to get to know.

This kind of person-to-person acquaintance becomes over time (as a consequence of keen listening, questioning, sharply sensitive editing) a form of idiosyncratic social inquiry, but not of a kind that is without precedent. Now in his eighties, Terkel graces us in these pages with a look back at his serious and important interviewing initiatives, his stories of lives, his oral histories, his attempts to understand abstractions such as "race" or "class" or "old age" through the personal accounts of his fellow twentieth-century citizens. We can perhaps best honor him not only by reading and rereading his books (or, if we live within listening distance of his Chicago radio program), by tuning in to his interviews, his music, his lively, original-minded, pointed comments, but also by trying to place him in a cultural and intellectual tradition. He has demonstrated an extraordinary capacity to place us, as it were, to help us locate where we are in our country's (social, economic, political, racial) scheme of things, and of course, to take a particular place, such as Division Street in the Chicago he knows and loves so much and explore it mightily, find in it (to call upon the words of the Book of Common Prayer) "all sorts and conditions" of people, who become, finally, a lively and instructive cast of characters in a closely observed drama whose action a talented playwright (let us now call him, one of many roles he brilliantly manages) has chosen to evoke. Yet, as the psychoanalyst and historian Erik H. Erikson once reminded the participants in a seminar of his, "even the most creative among the gifted, even a genius, has ancestors and antecedents, both." He was talking to us about Freud, but he was urging on each of us in the seminar, because of one or another biographical interest, a careful, considered examination of who and what preceded the person and time we were studying.

In that historical spirit, one seeks a home even for this exceptionally talented person, Studs Terkel, whose singularity of imagination and mode of work and manner of being are evident and impressive. Over 150 years ago, actually, Ralph Waldo Emerson was encouraging his listeners and readers to turn their backs on Europe, not in envy or an ignorant refusal of erudition and sophistication, but out of a necessary self-respect, a self-interest that would be a prelude, he knew, to a young nation's growing achievement in the arts and letters. He dared take on university curricula that gave no regard to moral matters ("Character is higher than intellect"), and he spoke of "representative man," an effort to look beyond the self-regarding, if not self-important, high-and-mighty ones in the academic and commercial worlds to whom, he knew, writers like himself can sometimes become almost beholden. He applauded Thoreau and Whitman, individuals who dared to go their own way and to give voice to ideas and values other than those favored by many professors or people of prosperity. Thoreau sought a humble life, one appreciatively tied to nature. Whitman celebrated ordinary people, working hard to stay afloat, their expended energy, he knew, the mainstay of a nation's daily life. He immersed himself eagerly in the rough-and-tumble of a country's growing urban scene; took in its sights, smells, sounds without anxiety or fear; sang of sweat and brawn, of polyglot energy become a new kind of national community.

Not that certain nineteenth-century European writers were not also responsive to ordinary people, obscure and of modest means or quite impoverished, who lived in the countryside or the important cities of that powerful continent. Dickens had grown up poor, had even spent part of his childhood in debtor's prison with his family, and for all his eventual prominence and success, would never turn his back on those who toiled hard to scrimp by. In novel after novel, he created characters meant to stay with us, teach us how it goes for those who do work different from that done by many of us who read his books. Zola in France and Dostoyevsky and Chekhov in

Russia tried to evoke with sympathy and detailed care how people of humble circumstances managed to make do. Even Tolstoy, whose *War and Peace* and *Anna Karenina* mainly probed a world of wealth, of ballrooms and country estates, turned his back on all that during his well-known spiritual crisis in middle age and began to regard closely, respectfully, the way his own serfs lived and, too, those who shared their lives, the villagers whom heretofore he had ignored in favor of the nobility and the *haute bourgeoisie.* His moral fables, his tales of spiritual conflict, feature servants and agricultural workers and people barely getting by in out-of-the-way places—a big distance traveled from the czar's entourage, residing in St. Petersburg or Moscow. This shift, so we learn in his *Confession,* was of enormous moral significance to him. He found in the poor a quiet, unassuming dignity earned daily through their hard labor; and he kept remembering, in that regard, the proclaimed righteousness of the Hebrew prophets and of Jesus, their insistent interest in "the last" rather than "the first," and their wish, through parables, to remind us of moral virtues that can accompany a harsh, menial life.

Certain writers of fiction were not alone in their desire to explore so-called plain folk. In particular, mid-eighteenth-century England was graced with a master of social observation and writing, Henry Mayhew. His newspaper articles, in their sum, amounted to an enormously thorough and suggestive investigation, *London Labour and the London Poor.* He gave careful, considerate attention to a great capital city's shopworkers and needlewomen, its tailors and boot and shoe makers, its tanners and milliners and toy makers and woodworkers and weavers and hatters and brewery workers, its carpenters and merchant seamen, and not least, those who hawked wares, sold food, ran errands, hustled their way through long and marginally lived days. "As a class," he once observed, "I must say that the work people that I have seen appear remarkably truthful, patient, and generous; indeed, every day teaches me that their virtues are wholly unknown to the world." He continues in that reflective vein at some length (echoes of the older Tolstoy, of George Eliot in *Middlemarch,* of Thomas Hardy in *Jude the Obscure*)—a compassionate witness to the struggles of those he has come to know, but also a writer anxious that his readers begin to question their own assumptions even as they learn about those that inform the lives of others with whom they share a nationality and a residence in a particular city, if little else.

Although Mayhew was careful to give us, now and then, the actual voices of those he met and to offer the substance of conversations he had with various men and women, he is, inevitably, the main character in his journalism. Put differently, his London people come to us through his narrative voice; he uses the third person to chronicle their stories, to describe their work. Novelists, of course, "make up" their stories; though surely Dickens or Eliot called upon their powers of attention, perception, memory, worked into their fictional explorations of urban or rural nineteenth-century England words and ways of behavior heard and seen in "real life," thereby turning the imagined reality of a short story or a longer piece of fiction into its very own distillation of truth.

Today, we have the tape recorder, so it is easier for someone of Henry Mayhew's ambition, energy, and sensibility (and Studs Terkel is our twentieth-century Mayhew) to do the kind of work that was done over one hundred years ago in such a way that our era's various men and women—met, watched, assessed, and heard—can speak for themselves. Now, hours and hours of conversations can be recorded, transcribed, edited, made available to those who want to read (or, yes, themselves listen). Yet, over ninety years ago, in 1906, a book appeared in which autobiographies alone figure, under the title of *The Life Stories of Undistinguished Americans as Told by Themselves:* first-person accounts of how it went in turn-of-the-century America for people still identified by their country of origin—"The Life Story of a Lithuanian" and similar accounts of "a Greek Reader," "a Polish Sweatshop Girl," "an Italian Bootblack," "an Irish Cook," or others identified as a "Florida Sponge Fisherman," "a Southern White Woman," "a Southern Colored Woman," "a Farmer's Wife," "an Itinerant Minister." All those stories were originally sought by Hamilton Holt, the editor of the *Independent,* a journal published in New York City in the last decade of the nineteenth century and the early years of this one. Some of those accounts were self-initiated by men and women who felt they had something to say and wanted to do so; others were the result of interviews, which were written up by reporters and then shown to the person who had told the story.

The editors of the *Independent* obviously did not just stumble into these hard-pressed, uneducated, newly arrived Americans. A search had to be made, and before that, an idea entertained, honed down to its essentials, handed over to reporters and writers for implementation. In a sense, the reporters or interviewers had to learn to get along with, understand, and earn the trust of those whose lives were to be self-described, as it were—a microcosm, those two individuals, of the larger kind of human connection and insight that publication in a newspaper or magazine is meant to further. When readers of the *Independent* felt themselves newly awakened and informed, courtesy of the stories offered by the magazine, they had not only the individuals "behind" the printed autobiographies to thank but those "behind" *them,* so to speak, even as Studs Terkel has made us privy to so many lives courtesy of the gifts of his own life put to such persistent and accomplished use. If other efforts to tell how it goes for the hurt and the troubled, the ordinary and the successful, the lucky and the unlucky, have preceded those of Studs Terkel, it is fair to say that his reach has been uniquely broad and deep, an achievement that has required a lifetime to realize.

We have, of course, had access to the "voices" of Americans who lived in past centuries through their diaries, letters, sermons.

Moreover, novelists such as Stephen Crane, Theodore Dreiser, Jack London, Upton Sinclair, Frank Norris, Zora Neale Hurston, Richard Wright, Ralph Ellison, and in our time, Raymond Carver and Richard Ford have used fiction to explore various kinds of American marginalities. And in a class by itself, we have the work of the poet and novelist James Agee, whose collaboration with a photographer, Walker Evans, gave us the memorable *Let Us Now Praise Famous Men*. Before Chicago gave us Terkel, it gave us the sociologist W. I. Thomas, whose *Polish Peasant in Europe and America* (1920) and, later, *The Unadjusted Girl* (1923) rendered a kind of social science—vivid, gripping, plainly spoken, yet convincingly eloquent—that is sorely missing today. Contemporaries of Terkel's have also done his kind of work in other countries, notably Ronald Blythe in his "Portrait of an English Village": a mix of authorial commentary and the voices of a community in East Anglia—a thatcher, a schoolteacher, a nurse, a gravedigger, a farmhand. In France, the novelist John Berger, working with the photographer Jean Mohr, gave us a sense of how Europe's post–World War II migrant workers live, though mostly in a third-person narration, and similarly with the social historian Charles Van Onselen, whose dramatically titled *New Babylon* and *New Nineveh* tell of the human side of the industrialization of South Africa in the early years of this century (after the discovery of gold in the Witwatersrand). His tales of liquor sellers and cab drivers and prostitutes and domestic servants and Afrikaner workers trying to hold on to decent jobs, not to mention the blacks endlessly recruited to do the hardest work for the most meager of wages, are also *about* various kinds of people, rather than a compilation of their own stories, whether spoken to another or written by themselves, handed to another.

To be sure, nowadays, the tape recorder is an almost sacrosanct part of both journalism and social science; and so reporters on a local beat carry their slim pocket-size Sonys, as do anthropologists in Africa or Asia. None of the latter, though, have equaled Oscar Lewis's exceptionally knowing use of that machine. The issue eventually becomes not the machine or even the matter of who is approached for conversation and information, but the person who comes armed with an enabling technology. Studs Terkel has done tape-recorded interviews for decades, but he has also uniquely brought to the individuals whose first-person narratives he seeks a particular mind's intentions and aspirations, its resolve, its moral energy, its mix of emotional candor and soulfulness. His has been an unflagging resourcefulness put at the service of a social conscience, not to mention a quick-witted, penetrating interest in sizing up what truly counts, in getting to the heart of things, in deferring to the opinions of others rather than mobilizing them in the service of an observer's expression.

Who else has roamed more broadly across a nation's lines of social, economic, educational, racial, cultural division, separation, and done so for so long and with such clear and striking success? What follows is, indeed, an American century as told to a devoted listener, a seeker of life's truths as they have been discovered in lives and as they are revealed in conversations at once pointed and relaxed, freewheeling and utterly precise, concentrated and to the point. Here Terkel's masterly ability to win the confidence of others ought be mentioned and saluted. A whole cohort of reporters or social scientists or essayists in search of a project or a book could agree upon a given "population" to pursue or questions to pose, even on the individuals who would best respond to such an investigation—but that is a mere beginning. Soon enough, the critical matter is at hand: Who is able to sit with whom, saying and asking what, in which manner? How well I remember Erik H. Erikson telling a group of us in a seminar ("The Study of Lives") that even as each psychoanalyst elicits somewhat different responses than those that would be offered to his or her colleagues, so it goes in other human situations. The truism, then, that we are different things to different people becomes of enormous importance as we contemplate the range of these interviews, their complexity and subtlety and candor, their directness, their instructive blend, so often, of a tone properly reserved, yet utterly forthcoming. We surely begin to realize, after a while, that these individuals, in their generous responsiveness to an extraordinarily inviting interviewer, have granted him the right to be proprietary in this book's title. Those he has met over the decades have given him what he has quite distinctively been able to invite of them.

Anyone who has heard Studs Terkel's voice, never mind met him, knows the vitality of this man, the liveliness, the humor and the largeness of spirit, the thoroughgoing attentiveness he can bring to bear on an occasion or subject matter, and needless to say, the connection he makes with a person whom he is covering. His conscientious regard for matters small and large, his inviting charm, his worldly savvy that in no way banishes from sight an almost shy, introspective side of his personality, his intellect—all of that makes him someone one wants to know, to speak with readily, honestly. In his substantial integrity and his yearning for the substantive (the details that will become in their gradual accumulation a broad and telling canvas), he becomes much more than an effective radio host or an able, astute biographical explorer who, courtesy of a machine, can capture word for word an extended spell of declarations, reservations, thoughts, and second thoughts. In truth, he is the almost magically summoning "other" of philosophy's long existentialist discussions, the one whose wholly evident interest in us makes for our moments of self-avowal: With you I will look boldly within, and to you I will say what I have learned. How else to account for what so many in the pages ahead have said (and about so much)?

In his great lyrical examination of Paterson, where the first factory in America was built, William Carlos Williams exhorted himself, let alone the rest of us, with: "outside/outside myself/there is a world,/he rumbled, subject to my incursions/—a world/(to me) at rest,/which I approach/concretely." So it has also gone with Studs Terkel. He has most certainly approached our contemporary world "concretely," enabled to do so by his quite exceptional humanity. When back in his study, of course, he has kept himself very much in touch with that world, populated by his informants, his teachers, his fellow human beings with whom he shares an American citizenship—hence the wise and gracious and magnanimous nature of his editing. These stories owe their convincing impact to the shrewd and skilled shaping of them at the hands of someone who knows how to make the words of others soar in their intent, in their deliverance of this or that message, opinion, concern, conviction. What for some would be the heavy burden of hours and hours of tapes becomes for Studs Terkel, our foremost documentarian, our leading student of American variousness as it gets embodied in human particularity, a grand opportunity. Hence his books that have, in essence, presented us to ourselves, and hence this collection of vintage moments from these books: yet another chance for us to look back at this hugely eventful century of our national life through the memories of those who lived in it and made it, in their respective ways, what it has turned out to be.

—ROBERT COLES

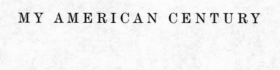

MY AMERICAN CENTURY

INTRODUCTION

In 1936, a lowly civil servant ($1,260 per annum), I occasionally appeared as an actor at the Washington Civic Theatre. My glory moment came in the role of Shad Ledue, a hired man who became the gauleiter of a New England town. The play was an adaptation of Sinclair Lewis's novel, *It Can't Happen Here.* It was a fantasy: home-grown fascism taking over.

During this time, Hitler was on the rise in Europe; there was a Great Depression here as well as there, with millions on breadlines; there was a profound discontent in the air and a nameless fear. There were dark thoughts in unexpected quarters. There were movements, too.

There were William Dudley Pelley and the Silver Shirts; Father Coughlin and his fulminatory Sunday evening sermons, reaching radio's multitudes; and there was Huey Long's warning of fascism appearing in the name of 100 percent Americanism. Ersatz populism was on the wing. And the one whose heart and mind they all courted was Shad Ledue—working like a dog, he felt, and getting nowhere. He had grievances, you bet.

Shad loathed his employer, Doremus Jessup, the town's newspaper editor and publisher. Shad was surly, a bully, a semiliterate, a loose-jawed brute. Jessup was kindly, enlightened, somewhere between a moderate conservative and the warmest kind of liberal. His way with Shad was that of a forbearing master with a sometimes unruly mutt. "I tell myself I'm doing something of a social experiment," Jessup explained, "trying to train him to be as gracious as the average Neanderthal man. Or perhaps, I'm scared of him—he's the kind of vindictive peasant that sets fire to barns."* Jessup, you see, had a great sense of humor.

---

* Sinclair Lewis, *It Can't Happen Here,* (The Sun Dial Press, 1935).

INTRODUCTION

I remember that one exhilarating instant, during the dress rehearsal, when my Corpo uniform fit so snugly, so naturally. It became me. I no longer slouched. I was ramrod straight, my hands on my hips in the manner of General MacArthur, glowering past the darkened house toward the last row of the theater in the Wardman Park Hotel. I looked beyond. Shad was miraculously *somebody*.

Sixty years later, shortly after the Oklahoma City bombing, a spiritual kinsman of Shad Ledue, Mark Koernke, in his uniform of mottled fatigues, declared the bombing a government plot. Koernke, something of an independent contractor, had broken away from the Michigan Militia and formed his own. On his nationwide shortwave radio program, he offered a suggestion: "I did some basic math the other day, using the old-style math. You can get about four politicians for about 120 feet of rope. Remember when using this stuff always try to find a willow tree. The entertainment will last longer."*

At night, he spoke his piece. During the day, he was, like Shad, a hired man at the University of Michigan. A maintenance man, he was called. As he occasionally visited the honors class to screw in a lightbulb or fix a lock on the door, was his presence ever noticed, let alone acknowledged by the distinguished professor? Perhaps these two were born-agains: one, as Shad Ledue; the other, as Doremus Jessup.

How did Shad Ledue come to be? Or Mark of Michigan, as he called himself? Was he born, like Markham's man with the hoe, "dead to rapture and despair"? There's a question seldom asked: "Whose breath blew out the light within his brain?"

Mark and his fellow militiamen had their moment of celebrity, dubious though it was, on the six o'clock news. What I have found remarkable is that there has seldom, if ever, been such commemoration of other lives, who may have had the same beginnings, the same bitterness, the same twisted longings—and yet experienced a

* James Ridgeway, *Village Voice*, April,1995.

transfiguration. They were not struck by any blinding light on the road to their Damascus. It was over a long haul of daily trials and small revelations that led to a sort of redemption and transcendence. They had discovered where the body was buried and who did what to whom.

It is these faces in the crowd that have most attracted me during my searchings.

Consider C. P. Ellis.

Some years ago, I came across a small sidebar on page twenty-something of the daily newspaper. It concerned the former Exalted Cyclops of The Ku Klux Klan, Durham, North Carolina. He had become a fervent civil rights advocate and the spokesman for a trade union, overwhelmingly black. How come? I had to track him down.

A poor white: father dead of cotton dust; sole support of mother and sister at 13; married, four kids, one blind and retarded; dead-end jobs; barely subsisting. "They say abide by the law, go to church, do right and live for the Lord and everything'll work out." It didn't. Seven days a week, twelve, fourteen hours a day. Heart attack. Dead broke. "I didn't know who to blame. I had to hate somebody. Hatin' America is too hard to do because you can't see it to hate it. I blamed it on the black people because that was easy." He joined the Klan. It was easy.

"First night was the most thrilling time of my life. Here's a guy who struggled all his life to be somethin' and here's the moment. I'll never forget it." The white robe, the hood, the illuminated cross, the oath, the applause. "For this one little ol' person, C. P. Ellis." He was *somebody.*

A time of the civil rights movement; busting picket lines with guns, billy clubs; congratulatory phone calls from the town's Respectables. However, a funny thing happened. "One day, I was walkin' downtown and a city council member saw me comin'. I had expected him to shake my hand because I had been to his home and last night he was on the phone. He crossed the street. Oh shit, I began to think, there's somethin' wrong here. That's when I began to do some serious thinkin'."

One revelatory moment after another. And now he's "butting heads with professional union busters who are college graduates. Imagine! Me and those wonderful black women, we hold our own with 'em. We're not inferior! Oh, I got a taste of it and I can't quit." Talk about being somebody.

Consider Peggy Terry.

She came out of the Ozarks, out of hard times and soup lines, out of stoop labor in the scorching fields. Out of fifth-grade schooling, she became the voice of the mountain people in the big city. "Today you're made to feel it's you're own fault. If you're poor, it's only because you're ignorant and lazy. I once hated blacks. If I really knew what changed me.... I've thought about it and thought about it. You don't get anywhere because you always see yourself as something you're not. As long as you can say I'm better than they are, then there's somebody below you can kick. But once you get over that, you see you're not any better than they are. In fact, you're worse off 'cause you're believin' a lie."

The first person I visited during these adventures, beginning in the mid-'50's, was Florence Scala. She was a young housewife trying to save her rainbow-colored neighborhood from demolition by the city's power brokers. It was here that Jane Addams had set her bucket down so many years ago. The fight was lost, but Florence experienced a sort of revelation.

"This was when I began to lose the feeling of idolatry you have about people. I so admired those nice people on the Hull House board. They were of old, highly respected families. I was later to find out these nice people could hurt you the most. I see now we have to feel equal to anyone. It's a feeling poor people don't have. You must never be afraid to say something even when it's off. Just keep at it. You're as good as they are."

She ran for the city council against the machine, the Mob, and the power brokers. The nice people looked away. She lost. "Among those who backed me were some from the far right. At first, I couldn't understand why. But there was something frustrating them. They were hurting. They felt themselves unable to count anywhere."

A few weeks later, on a rainy night, a cab picked me up. The name on the license up front read: Dennis Hart. Small talk led to the subject of Florence Scala; she had been in the news. "She was the greatest woman I've ever known. She made you feel you were really worthwhile. Working in her campaign was the greatest experience of my life—in courage."

That's why he joined the John Birch Society—"to find my courage." All his life, it had been humiliation, a sense of being nobody, and fear, a pervasive fear. "Now, I mingle with a lot of successful people. They're saying the problem is very simple. Life is complicated enough as it is. If you complicate things further, you're asking for trouble.

"I'm not worried about the Bomb. I feel this is a wilderness and I've lived in a wilderness all my life. Atheists are those most fearful of the Bomb. A man who truly believes in God doesn't run around worrying about these things. He knows there's a Hereafter."

A flash-forward, 1988; a generation later. I am in the lobby of the Willow Creek Church,* shortly before the first Sunday morning service begins. I run into Mike, Connie, and baby Jason. It

---

* "It is among the largest and fastest-growing congregations in Chicago, offering its well-scrubbed and youthful adherents an energetic blend of religious pop music, morality plays, and plain-spoken sermons by the church's founder and pastor, Bill Hybels.

"The church has a profound appeal to upwardly mobile young professionals, who faithfully negotiate their turbocharged foreign automobiles through the monumental congestion in Willow Creek's 1400-car parking lot on Sundays for a low-key taste of 'biblical principles' before lunch."

—Bruce Buursma, religion editor, *Chicago Tribune*, July 12, 1985.

appears they share Dennis Hart's vision of a sweet apocalypse. He is a computer technician. She is a "stay-at-home mom."

"Since I became a Christian," she says, "I don't worry about the Bomb. It's in God's hands. I think there will be a nuclear war, but the events leading up to it haven't happened yet…so why not have children?"

A smiling David passes by. He's in data processing. "If a nuclear war happened and my wife and I died, if we accepted the Lord as our savior, we'd be in Heaven. That's better than being on earth."

Reverend Hybels's hip sermon evokes appreciative laughter. "Next Sunday, we'll have some cameras set up. We'll be taping the service. Don't dress up too much because we don't want anybody to think this is a traditional church. So wear bare jerseys, short pants, whatever." Much laughter.

Roy Larson has observed this phenomenon from the year one, An ex-minister and journalist, he teaches at a midwestern university. "These programs have a lot of appeal, especially to young adults who have no sense of history. You don't need it. It's bland, it's inoffensive, it's fast food, it fills you up for a while. You're given answers, there's no need to reflect. The followers are what you'd call nice people, hearty, outgoing, always smiling. But the smile is not connected to the rest of the body, with feeling or thought.

"There's always been a prophetic strain within religion: against the grain. It's always been a minority. But it's the salt. The New Testament warned us about the salt that loses its savor. A religion that loses its prophetic oomph is salt-free. Bland. Tasteless."

Jean Gump is, in this sense, salty to a rare degree. A middle-class, suburban grandmother; mother of twelve; active in church and community; president of the PTA; League of Women Voters, one of the most respected citizens of her community.

Being full of that scriptural salt, she did what came naturally to her, to the dismay of her neighbors. On Good Friday, 1986, "We commemorated the crucifixion of Christ by entering a missile silo in Holden, Missouri."*

They hung a banner on the outside of the chain-link fence that read: SWORDS INTO PLOWSHARES AN ACT OF HEALING, ISAIAH 2. "You know, 'We will pound our swords into plowshares and study war no more.'" Her casual recounting of the affair was pure Gump, whimsical, often hilarious, always heartbreaking. Especially the moment when the boy soldier, young enough to be her grandchild, descended from the armored vehicle, his gun at the ready. As she lowered her hands to reach into her purse, she said to the trembling boy, "Shoot if you must, sonny, but I've got to blow my nose."

Her husband, Joe, followed suit at another missile site. He, too, was arrested and tried. There were trials, delays, deals offered—if only there were a recantation, a simple "I'm sorry." Considering the obstinate nature of the Gumps, none came forth. She was sentenced to a term of eight years in a federal pen. She became no. 03789-045 at the Correctional Institution for Women, Alderson, West Virginia. After serving a few years, she was released; so was Joe, from a Minnesota federal "college." Neither appeared repentant. A contumacious couple. Talk about salt.

Postscript: I ran into Chris Daniels, a scruffy, eighteen-year-old Clint Eastwood clone, of Appalachian stock, who had more than his share of run-ins with the cops. Apropos of nothing, he says, "I read a news story about this lady, Jean Gump. Ever heard of her? "Yeah," I reply. "She's in the same book you are."†

"Yeah? Oh, wow. We watched on TV where she went to this Minute Man missile site and beat on the thing. What turned me on to it, she's a grandmother and she risked her future for a cause. It

---

* Her fellow trespassers were four fellow Catholics, "young enough to be my children." They were members of Silo Plowshares. It hardly made the news.

† *The Great Divide: Second Thoughts on the American Dream.*

was like—wow—she did all this to get people thinkin' about what's happenin'. It was like—wow—that's pretty strange."

It may be strange, at that. Jean Gump and others of those salty ones I encountered appear to be searching for some sort of vision of a society in which, to paraphrase Dorothy Day, it would be easier for people to behave decently.

> You who thought of yourself, up to that moment, as simply a number, suddenly spring to life. You have that intoxicating feeling that you can make history, that you really count.
>
> —NICHOLAS VON HOFFMAN

George Malley knew that he counted, but springing to life and making history were something else. He was too heavily laden. When he spoke, it was with a deliberateness, almost a reluctance, as though each word were a tooth extracted. When he drove his ancient Dodge, it was at a studied pace, much to the obvious annoyance of the other motorists. I thought of the aristocratic old lady in the Queen Mary Hat, who, in the early '20s drove her electric car in the same fashion and at the same speed: "I have an instinctive fear. I dread the thought of what may happen."

I first met George Malley in the '50s. He was a craftsman of old-world values, who sensed a new species of young, rehabbing his block, gentrifying it. He was not Ibsen's middle-aged architect, fearing young knuckles rapping at the door; it was an awareness of a shift in our society's values, especially among the young.

It was not that alone which disturbed him. "My feeling about the Negro is this: I never try to think in terms of his being equal to me. I don't know and he doesn't know. The average Negro is not. I'm not saying he won't be and that he might surpass me someday. But I fear him. By and large, he represents violence."

Twenty-five years later, I paid him another visit. "During the '60s, I used to talk to my boys a lot. At the time, they took issue with me. I thought they were trying to turn the world as I knew it upside down. Now, strangely enough, I see a hell of a lot of what they had to say come about. But now my boys have taken the opposite stance. Now, they're for law and order at any price. They're for hit 'em over the head if there is no other way.

"I guess they've become adults. In our society, when you become an adult, you stake your claim. They have property now. They both have homes. They're doing fine. Once my sons called me a narrow-minded bigot. It is I who have changed most dramatically. I see things now that I didn't see then. I'm surprised at myself. I feel I could live with black people now. Yes, I still worry about violence. But I'm sure the black man has the identical worry, even more so than I have. So we're sharing something in common, see?

"For the past dozen years, my most contented moments is when I'm alone. I like to get up at four o'clock in the morning and sit in this chair and just be alone with my thoughts. I have had very little formal education, but I like to think things through, to try to understand. By myself. No TV, no radio, no newspaper. Knowledge has only real value when there's understanding. It's tremendous, it's exhilarating."

Chester Kolar, is a fellow homeowner, who, unlike the other, can't be bothered. "Over the radio comes a bulletin: so many people killed. I mean what are they trying to fire up? This poor man that's trying to get his eight hours to keep his family going—what does John Q. Public know what should happen? Let's not stick our noses into something we know nothing about."

Eva Barnes does stick her nose into things. She is a tavern keeper in a blue-collar neighborhood; an alumna of the stockyards, where she had worked since the age of twelve. Unlike most of her patrons, she saw hope in the rebellious young of the '60s. She was at one time arrested along with them, during an anti–Vietnam War gathering. "My mother had seven gold stars in the window. From the First World War, you know. Those poor Lithuanian boys who lived by our house. There's death enough. I don't like to see nobody killed. This world is beautiful to live...."

> At the end of the most extraordinary period of transformation in human affairs, old landmarks have disappeared, new ones are not yet recognized as such, and intellectual navigation across the suddenly estranged landscapes of human society becomes unusually puzzling for everyone.
>
> —ERIC HOBSBAWM

Some time ago, I arrived at the airport of a large American city. I hadn't been there in years. I didn't recognize it at all. The old landmarks that had distinguished this metropolis from others were no longer there. I saw a Golden Arch; I saw a Red Lobster; I saw a Holiday Inn; I saw a Days Inn, more modest in price. The landscape was identical to that of the city I had just left. At my assigned hotel, I was greeted by a smiling, sweet-faced young woman, a badge on her lapel: Barbara. I had been greeted at the city I had just left by a smiling, sweet-faced young man, with a badge on his lapel: Peter. Was I on a treadmill?

I left a wake-up call at the switchboard for 6:00 A.M. I added gratuitously, "I've got to be in Cleveland pretty early." The voice responded, with some concern: "Sir, you are in Cleveland."

In 1969, while exploring midwestern rural towns seeking out survivors of the Great Depression, I lost my bearings in Le Mars, Iowa (population 8,276). I couldn't find the house of a witness of a near-lynching of a judge, who, in the '30s, had relentlessly foreclosed mortgages of desperate farmers. "Where is that street?" I asked the manager of the town's supermart. He didn't know. "I'm a stranger here myself." He had recently been transferred by the company.

Jessie Binford, Jane Addams's old colleague, had returned to her hometown, Marshalltown, Iowa. Her father was one of its pioneers. Here, she came to die. "They've scattered the people. Everybody is a stranger. Even here. The human touch is going. Nothing stays the same, I know. We should have the intelligence and the courage to meet the many changes that come into the world and will always come. But what are the intrinsic values we should not give up? That's the great challenge that faces us."

Rex Winship doesn't think it's much of a challenge. Never mind the past, he deals in futures. Rex is one of the Forbes 400 richest Americans. His estimated net worth is more that $400 million. His payroll, in cities throughout the world, runs to 1,500.

"Nothing is forever. You always have to stay flexible, so you can change. Fast. The globalization of the communications market is going to be dramatic. You're going to be able to sit in your office in Chicago, look up at the wall and be in touch with the world. You want to be able to move—and fast. You want to be to send a young guy to Singapore for two years, Sydney, Australia for a year, and then back to Chicago. Today, you don't want the kid married."

In the trading room, where scores of young brokers are intently studying their quote machines, his public relations person, in the manner of a gracious hostess, guides me. "The turnover is tremendous. Two to five years with one firm and then out. The business just changes so fast. We affectionately call it the war room. You feel like you're going to battle [laughs]. Yeah." What most impressed me was the singular silence in the room.

The old-time printer bemoans the disappearance of talk in the workplace. "Today, the composing room is as silent as the editorial room. Have you been over at the city desk of any of the newspapers lately? It used to be so wild and romantic. Now it's like a tomb."

On the desks of the young reporters in the city room, as on the desks of young traders in the brokerage house, is the ubiquitous IT, through whose windows they stare in the manner of voyeurs. Each is in a private world, close by colleagues, yet planets away. It is solipsism en masse.

W. H. "Ping" Ferry, fully aware of the remarkable advances in high technology, had a bone or two to pick. "At Dartmouth, my alma mater, they got a bequest of 50 million dollars to build a new library. It's going to be full of mainframes, the apparatus at the heart of computer activity. By the time this thing is finished, a young man or woman can walk into a room in his or her freshman year and never emerge until four years later to get the degree. He can go to all his classes by computer. He can get his grub brought in by computer. He will never have to emerge." That was five years ago.

> Hanover, N. H.—Through a plug in his dorm room, Arthur Desrosiers, a Dartmouth College sophomore, pursues all his preoccupations of undergradute life without leaving his chair: He questions professors, fishes for dates, browses the library catalogue, orders pizza and engages in 2 A.M. bull sessions on the meaning of it all.
>
> Using the campus E-mail system, known as Blitzmail, he sometimes trades a series of back-and-forth messages with his two roommates—*even though they are sitting just a few feet away.*
> —TRIP GABRIEL,
> *New York Times,* November 11, 1996

Ping Ferry may not have been Nostradamus, but he came uncomfortably close. Wright Morris, thirty-five years ago, put it succinctly: "We are more and more in communications and less and less in communication."

Click. The image of Gary Bryner and the unimate came to mind. In 1970, I visited Lordstown, Ohio. It was the Vega plant of General Motors. Gary was the young president of Local 1112, UAW. The company had introduced a unimate on the assembly line. "A unimate is a welding robot. It looks just like a praying mantis. It goes from spot to spot to spot. It releases that thing and it jumps back into position, ready for the next car. They never tire, they never sweat, they never complain, they never miss work. And they never talk."

Click, click. Another image. Sixty-five years ago, I was seated in the last row of the Blackstone Theatre balcony. Or was it the Harris or the Selwyn? The play was Karel Capek's *R.U.R.* (Rossum's Universal Robots). A Theatre Guild production. Place: An island. Time: The future.

Plot: A factory has manufactured worker-robots, "living automats, without souls, desires or feelings." There are now millions. A physicist has secretly changed the formula and has created two humanized robots. The robots, who have been used, when needed, as soldiers, revolt. They overwhelm the few humans left. The factory builder is the only human left on earth. In the epilogue, he discovers the two humanized robots, a young man and a young woman. They have the touch of Adam and Eve.

As the curtain falls, we have the idea that mankind may have another go at it. It is a replay of Miranda spotting Ferdinand: "How beauteous mankind is! O brave new world, That has such people in it!"

As for that brave, new tomorrow, Moms Mabley, in another context, professes to a doubt: "Maybe so, maybe so, baby, but I ain't bettin' my gold tooth on it." Einstein expressed a similar concern, albeit in a somewhat different fashion. He worried about our twentieth-century obsession: technology *über alles*.* If Moms Mabley and Albert Einstein were worried, I'm worried.

Are we being ironically transmogrified? Having invented robots who emulate humans (i.e., the unimate), are we humans now emulating robots? Consider the young, thoroughly absorbed, staring at their terminals; the college boy impaled to his chair; the mechanized voice on the telephone increasingly replacing the human one. Will vox humana become vox *automa*? Are the somebodies becoming the somethings?

Perhaps these bleak reflections are no more than a wearisome

---

* Our entire much praised technological progress…could be compared to an axe in the hands of a pathological criminal.
—Albert Einstein from *The Other Einstein* by Albrecht Fölsins (Viking).

recitation of the Rime of the Ancient Luddite. Yet Jessie Binford's challenge still holds: What are the intrinsic values we should not give up?

My American Century is the name of this book. It is the possessive pronoun that bears emphasis. It reflects, of course, a personal point of view. In all my works, it has been so. I have tried for as much balance as possible, yet "objectivity," so often a reprise of the doctrine of the announced idea, of the official truth, has escaped me. My turf has been the arena of unofficial truth—of the noncelebrated one on the block, who is able to articulate the thoughts of his/her neighbors, inchoate, though deeply felt. I confess to never having been privy to "highly reliable sources."

James Cameron, the nonpareil of British journalists, spoke with some authority in this matter. During the darkest days of the war in Vietnam, he had visited Hanoi, the first Western journalist to do so. On coming to the United States, he brought forth the astonishing news that the North Vietnamese were humans, not unlike ourselves. He was, as a matter of course, excoriated in all our media, especially by the most respected and prestigious. "If not downright mischievous, I was certainly 'non-objective.' " He had committed the unpardonable sin of challenging official, and thus accepted, truths.

"It never occurred to me, in such a situation, to be other than subjective, and as obviously as I could manage to be. I may not have always been satisfactorily balanced; I have always tended to argue that objectivity was of less importance than the truth, and that the reporter whose technique was informed by no opinion lacked a very serious dimension."

Amen.

As we approach the end of the twentieth century, let David Brower, offer the valedictory. His instruction to his fellow elders who have experienced and lived out most of this century.

"Our young haven't lost their history. It was taken from them. We've stuffed them into a procrustean bed, to make them fit whatever its size or shape may be. You've got a file on this century, stored in your heads, that nobody else has. *There'll be nobody like you ever again* [emphasis his]. Make the most of every molecule you've got, as long as you've got a second to go. That is your assignment. That is your charge."

NOTE

This quasi-anthology of my eight oral journals is not arranged chronologically, that is, in the order of each book's publication date. Thus, *Division Street: America,* published in 1967, appears as the fourth chapter of this volume. *American Dreams: Lost and Found,* published in 1980, provides the opening sequence.

There is a chronological order of sorts. The impressions of our most telling and traumatic events are told by my elders and contemporaries who experienced them, and as I remember them.

Beginnings; the Great Depression; World War II; postwar prosperity and the Cold War; the insistent matter of race; the computer and its revolution, altering our work, our language, and—more than we at this moment may realize—our behavior; and, inevitably, less gracefully than need be, the withered face of age.

In the making of the eight books dealing with our time and place, I had visited about 1,000 people, largely those uncelebrated and unsung. Yet, it was their sense of anonymity and lack of self-indulgence that made them the ideal oral historians. Unfortunately, I had to choose but a few for this work, hardly more than fifty. It is with apologies that I salute those not included here, though appearing in the other volumes, and with profound gratitude to them and to those present in these pages.

Part I

The Dream

American Dreams:
Lost and Found
(1980)

INTRODUCTION

For the nine-year-old boy, in 1921, traveling on that day coach from New York to Chicago, it was simple. And exhilarating. Though he wasn't the proper British butler Ruggles, whose mind was boggled by images of a Wild West and equally wild Indians in multifeathered headgear, the boy envisioned a Midwest that, too, was frontier country.

It was a twenty-four-hour journey, clickety-clacketing through the outskirts of large and middle-sized Pennsylvania cities, through the main streets of small Ohio towns, of sudden appearances in the aisles of hawkers bawling out their wares, of steaming hot coffee and homemade sandwiches, of local newspapers called *The Globe, The Sun, The Star, The Planet.* Yes, *The Herald,* too, for something terribly exciting was being heralded. It was a momentous adventure, uniquely American. Out there was more: a reservoir of untapped power and new astonishments.

"One of my earliest memories was a trip across the country with my grandfather." A Chicago physician reflects in 1979. He is the grandson of the late General Robert E. Wood, who was, at the glowing time, chairman of the board of Sears, Roebuck and Company. "We were sitting in the engineer's cab. It was the Great Northern. We were going through the mountains. The steam engine was a huge one. I remember thinking how big the country was and how powerful the engine.

And being with someone as powerful and confident as my grandfa-
ther. It was about 1940. I was seven and optimistic."

The sprawl of the Chicago stockyards, whose smells on a summer
night, with a stiff breeze blowing from the south, overwhelmed the
boy. It was not at all unpleasant to him, for there was a sense of
things happening, of propitious times ahead. The condition of
those who had actually worked in *The Jungle,* revealed some fifteen
years earlier by Upton Sinclair, had caused something of a stir, but
time, benign neglect, and editorial silences had deliquesced public
indignation.

Warren Gamaliel Harding, handsome, silver-haired, genial, was
our president. Hollywood couldn't have done better. He was a cross
between Francis X. Bushman and Theodore Roberts. Normalcy
was on the wing, and the goose hung high. 1923. Came the first
political scandal in the boy's memory: Teapot Dome. It was, the
teachers told him, an aberration. Corruption was not endemic to
the American scene. Bad apples in every barrel. And our barrels,
praise God, have been a fruitful lot.

It was another story the boy heard in the lobby of his mother's
hotel. The guests were boomer firemen, journeymen carpenters,
and ex-Wobblies, as well as assorted scissorbills* and loyal company men. The cards were stacked, groused the former, between

---

* A scissorbill was the pejorative ascribed to the workingman who was pro-
 boss and anti-foreigner. A turn-of-the-century piece of doggerel was perversely dedicated to him.

> You're working for an Englishman
> You room with a French Canuck
> You board in a Swedish home
> Where a Dutchman cooks your chuck.
> You buy your clothes from a German Jew
> You buy your shoes from a Russian Pole
> You place your hopes on a dago Pope
> To save your Irish soul.

rounds of solitaire, hearts, and cribbage. If you don't like it, go to Russia, retorted the others. Inevitably, the wild political arguments became highly personal, fueled as most were by bootleg whiskey.

"The early part of the century was an exciting period in the life of the United States." The ninety-five-year-old economist taps his memory. "Almost every community had a channel of expression: city clubs, trade union central bodies, forums, Cooper Union. Speakers would go from state to state, town to town, get ten dollars here, fifty dollars there. There were thousands who would come to hear Gene Debs, myself, Clarence Darrow, crowds, crowds, filling Madison Square Garden."*

Ed Sprague and Big Ole were the two most eloquent and hot-tempered lobby performers. The others, usually full of piss and vinegar, were unusually subdued when these two had the floor. Ed was much for words, though little for food. He dined on graveyard stew, bread broken up in a bowl of hot milk. He had no teeth: they had been knocked out by vigilantes in Seattle during the general strike of 1919. In no way did it interfere with his polemics, bellowed through snuff-stained gums. It was mortal combat between himself and the devil: big business. The boy was reminded of Billy Sunday, exorcising *the* devil: "I'll stomp him, I'll punch him, I'll bite him and, by God, when my teeth are all gone, I'll *gum* him back to hell!"

Big Ole was Ed's *bête noire,* closest at hand. He defended John D. Rockefeller, J. P. Morgan, Henry Ford, and gloried in Teddy Roosevelt's credo of soft words and the big stick. He was Ed's equal in decibel power. They were wrestling, not so much for the hearts and minds of the others as for the pure hell of it. Theirs was the American yawp. Every man a king. Every man a Demosthenes. It was a fouling, gouging, no-holds-barred match: Hackenschmidt versus

---

* Scott Nearing, in his nineties, reflecting at his home, Harborside, Maine.

Frank Gotch. Along with the others, the boy was enthralled, for it was, behind the wild expletives and runaway metaphors, power they were "discussing." Of the potent few and the impotent many.

"If you listen to any president of the United States," says Nicholas Von Hoffman, " 'power' is a word he never discusses. Senators never use that word either. It gets people thinking. Who knows where your thinking might take you? It you don't talk about power, it's like not lifting the hood of the automobile. You don't know how the damn thing works."

Ed Sprague and Big Ole had three things in common. Each was singularly skilled with his hands, a craftsman. Each visited Gladys on Sunday mornings. She ran a crib along Orleans Street. It was Ed's defiance of God and Ole's show of reverence, one of the weisenheimers put it. Gladys was fond of both; she favored lively men. She favored quiet men too. Gladys was an egalitarian, and a true entrepreneur. Each wrote letters to the editor with the regularity of a railroad timepiece. When, in the course of human events, the name of one or the other would appear on the editorial page, it was an occasion for celebration.

One of the more sober and scholarly guests at the hotel turned the boy on to E. Haldeman-Julius Blue Books. They were small paperbacks, encompassing the writings of all the world's wise men—and an occasional wise woman—from the Year One. Published in Girard, Kansas, twenty such books would come to you in return for one buck plus postage. An especially fat one would go for a dime. Aristotle, Voltaire, Fabre on the life of the mason bee, a nickel apiece. All of Shakespeare's tragedies, a dime. Not a bad buy. These booklets, fitting neatly in the hip pocket, became his Dr. Eliot's Five-Foot Shelf.

It was his first acquaintance with the writings of Tom Paine. In school, he had been taught the troublemaker's words about times that try men's souls, but not his words that challenged men's minds. "As America was the only spot in the political world where the principles of human reformation could begin, so also was it the best in the natural world. The scene which that country presents to the spectator has something in it which generates and enlarges great ideas. He sees his species, not with the inhuman eye of a natural enemy, but as kindred...."

In the woods of northwest Oregon, the embattled logger neglects the breakfast the waitress has laid out before him. His thoughts are elsewhere, and his fervor. "The forest to me is an awesome and beautiful place. The young loggers were not here to see what was there before. If you've never known something, it's difficult to appreciate what's been lost. What happened to all that majestic timber? I believe that only by being in the presence of beauty and great things in the world about us can man eventually get the goddamn hatred of wanting to kill each other out of his system. The beauty is going."

The traveling singer from Idaho no longer experiences the ancestral pull toward her hometown. "Boise hardly exists for me any more. All the things I remember with pleasure have been torn down and replaced by bullshit.... Downtown Boise, all covered, is like a cattle chute for customers. It used to be like a little cup of trees. Just trees and this river. Old, old houses and a sense of community. None of that's there any more. It's all gone."

In the mid sixties, while journeying through the farm states on the prowl for depression storytellers, I came upon Marcus, Iowa, along the South Dakota border. Population: 1,263. At the supermart, the three people I encountered were unaware of the man I was seeking; his father had founded the town. The checker at the counter seemingly at home, thought "the name's familiar, but I just can't place it." For her, too, it was an estranged landscape.

A few days later, in the town of Le Mars, I was walking toward a hamburger joint. It was at night. It may have been on the outskirts of town; as I recall, there was no sidewalk. A patrol car slowed down beside me. The two policemen were curious, that's all. Nobody else was walking.

"We began pretty well here in America, didn't we?" Jessie Binford, Jane Addams's old colleague, asked herself rhetorically, as she, in 1963, returned to her hometown, Marshalltown. Her father had founded it. "When you think of all the promise in this country...I don't see how you could have found much greater promise. Or a greater beginning. Yet the commonest thing I feel in this town is fear of the unknown, of the stranger. Fear, fear. We should have the intelligence and courage to see the many changes that come into the world and will always come. But what are the intrinsic values we should not give up? That's the great challenge that faces us all."

The twenties, the time of the boy's train ride, were neither the best of times nor the worst, though innocence, like booze, brings forth its morning-after hangover. A better world was acomin', the boy felt. How could it miss? There was so much of it, so many frontiers. And what, with so much inequity, so much room for improvement.

With Bob LaFollette and George Norris, senators of independent mind, ringing the bell in the night—a warning of power in fewer and fewer hands—Americans aware of sharp truths and even sharper dangers, would respond. With the certitude of a twelve-year-old, and the roaring eloquence of the hotel guests remembered, the boy was never more certain. What he did not quite understand was that infinitely lesser men were awarded much more attention, much more printer's ink. In later years the clones of Coolidge, expertly machine-tooled and media-hyped, have done, and are doing, equally well. Ed Sprague's thunder still rolls in the boy's ear "Who owns these things? Who makes scrambled eggs of our brains? In their stately mansions, they rob us of our stately minds."

Cannot Hannah Arendt's "banality of evil" be subject to transposition: the evil of banality? In 1792, Paine observed: "The mighty objects he beholds act upon the mind by enlarging it, and he partakes of the greatness he contemplates." In 1972, the less fraudulent of our two presidential candidates, on winning the California primary, beamed over all three networks: "I can't believe I won the whole thing." Thus did an Alka-Seltzer commercial enrich our political vocabulary.

Vox populi? Is that all there is to the American Dream, as celebrated in thousands of sixty-second, thirty-second, and ten-second spots each day on all channels? A mercantile language, debased, and nothing else? Is there no other language, no other dream?

"Some people may think it's childish of me, a poor white, to have faith in the deep yearnings of my people," says a woman from the South. "They're much like the people of Mexico. If a person in their midst is identified as a poet or he can draw or play an instrument, this person has stature." (Remember the surge of pride in Pa Joad's voice as Connie picked up the guitar and sang? "That's my son-in-law.")

"It's amazing, even in the backwoods of Alabama, there's a classic tucked away in some country school. It's funny, poetry has a way of molding people. There's a buried beauty—[suddenly] Gray's Elegy *changed my life. Who knows who's buried, who could have been what? The men in power should get all the poetry out of schools, anything that touches on real beauty. It's dangerous."*

The ninety-year-old Pole who came here in 1896 and worked his livelong life in the mills still hungers. "I used to attend lectures at Hull House. The things that bothered me were so many things I couldn't understand. There was a professor from the university lecturing on relativity, Einstein. The worst of it was I didn't understand half the words he used. I never understood relativity. I guess I got too old and too tired."

Kuume is the Finnish word for fever. It was the American fever. They came early in this century and at the turn. All to the land, by nature and industry blessed. To make it, of course, and to escape, as well, the razor's edge and, in remarkably many instances, the Old Country draft. Their mothers didn't raise their boys to be soldiers, either. The manner in which they came varied with geography and circumstance. In all cases, it was hard travelin'.

A wooden ship across the North Sea, "with sugarloaf waves, so the boat would rock, where you just crawled into bunks," to Liverpool, the *Lucania,* and on to America. Another: from Italy, by way of Marseilles, "all by myself," on the *Sardinia,* hence to El Dorado, which turned out to be a Massachusetts textile mill. A third: from an Eastern European *shtetl,* "ten of us," by wagon to Warsaw, by train to Hamburg, by train to Liverpool, and five weeks on a freighter to the land of milk and honey. For most, it was *mal de mer* most of the way. For all, it was *kuume* all the way.

When in 1903—or was it '04?—my mother and father came to the United States from the Old Country, their dream was not unique. Steady work and schooling for the boys, who were born during the following decade. He was a tailor, a quiet man. She was a seamstress, nimble of finger and mind. He was easy, seeking no more than his due. She was feverish, seeking something more. Though skilled in her craft, her spirit was the entrepreneur's. Out there, somewhere, was the brass ring. This was, after all, America.

When my father became ill and was unable to work, she made the big move. Out west, to Chicago. She had a tip: a men's hotel up for sale. 1921. It was hard work, but she toughed it out. She was an *hôtelière,* in business for herself. She was May Robson, Apple Annie, making it. These were no apples she was selling; she was a woman of property. They were pretty good years, the twenties. But something went wrong in '29, something she hadn't counted on. The men she admired, the strong, the powerful ones, the tycoons (she envisioned herself as a small-time Hetty Green), goofed up somewhere. Kerplunk went her American Dream.

Most of her tight-fisted savings were lost with the collapse of Samuel Insull's empire. It was a particularly bitter blow for her. He was the industrialist she had most admired, her Chicago titan. She had previously out-jousted a neighborhood banker. R. L. Chisholm insisted on the soundness of his institution, named, by some ironic God, The Reliance State Bank. Despite his oath on his mother's grave and his expressed admiration for *my* mother's thrift, she withdrew her several thousand. His bank closed the following day. Yet the utilities magnate took her, a fact for which she forgave neither him nor herself.*

The visit to R. L. Chisholm on that day of reckoning was a memorable one. At my mother's insistence, I accompanied her to the bank. Often, I had strolled there to the deposit window. Now came the time of the big withdrawal. The banker, a dead ringer for Edward Arnold, was astonished and deeply hurt. He had been, after all, her friend, her advisor, the keeper of her flame. Didn't she trust him? Of course she did; her reservations, though, outweighed her trust. It was an epiphanic moment for me as I, embarrassedly, observed the two. The conversation, which had begun with firm handshakes all around, easy talk, a joke or two, and a semblance of graciousness, ended on a somewhat less friendly note. Both, the banker and my mother, were diminished. Something beyond the reach of either one had defeated both. Neither had the power over his own life worth a damn.

My mother's gods had failed her; and she, who had always believed in making it, secretly felt that she, too, had failed. Though the following years didn't treat her too unkindly, her fires were banked. Her dreams darkened. She died a bitter, cantankerous old woman, who almost, though never quite, caught the brass ring.

---

* *Hard Times: An Oral History of the Great Depression* (New York: Pantheon Books, 1970).

Failure was as unforgivable then as it is now. Perhaps that's why so many of the young were never told about the depression; were, as one indignant girl put it, "denied our own history."

The young mechanic, driving me through the bluegrass country to eastern Kentucky, lets it out, the family skeleton. His father, a fast-talking salesman, was Willy Loman. "I always identified with Willy's son Biff. My father's staying with me and my wife. My brothers' wives don't want him around. They come right out and say so. I think he represents the horror of failure. Both my oldest brothers and my father were steeped one hundred percent in the idea of strength and supremacy, machismo, and success."

During the Christmas bombings of North Vietnam, the St. Louis cabbie, weaving his way through traffic, was offering six-o'clock commentary.

"We gotta do it. We have no choice."

"Why?"

"We can't be a pitiful, helpless giant. We gotta show 'em we're number one."

"Are you number one?"

A pause. "I'm number nothin'." He recounts a litany of personal troubles, grievances, and disasters. His wife left him; his daughter is a roundheel; his boy is hooked on heroin; he loathes his job. For that matter, he's not so crazy about himself. Wearied by this turn of conversation, he addresses the rear-view mirror: "Did you hear Bob Hope last night? He said…"

Forfeiting their own life experience, their native intelligence, their personal pride, they allow more celebrated surrogates, whose imaginations may be no larger than theirs, to think for them, to speak for them, to *be* for them in the name of the greater good. Conditioned toward being "nobody," they look toward "somebody" for the answer. It is not what the American town meeting was all about.

Yet, something's happening, as yet unrecorded on the social seismograph. There are signs, unmistakable, of an astonishing increase in the airing of grievances: of private wrongs and public rights. The heralds are from all sorts of precincts: a family farmer, a blue-collar wife, a whistle-blowing executive. In unexpected quarters, those hitherto quiescent, are finding voice. A long-buried American tradition may be springing back to life. In a society and time with changes so stunning and landscapes so suddenly estranged, the last communiqués are not yet in. The eighties may differ from the seventies by a quantum jump.

The capacity for change is beyond the measure of any statistician or pollster. Among those I've encountered in the making of this book are: an ex-Klan leader who won his state's human relations award; the toughest girl on the block who became an extraordinary social worker; the uneducated Appalachian woman who became the poetic voice of her community; the blue-collar housewife who, after mothering nine, says: "I don't like the word 'dream.' I don't even want to specify it as American. What I'm beginning to understand is there's a human possibility. That's where all the excitement is. If you can be part of that, you're aware and alive. It's not a dream, it's possible. It's everyday stuff."

There are nascent stirrings in the neighborhood and in the field, articulated by non-celebrated people who bespeak the dreams of their fellows. It may be catching. Unfortunately, it is not covered on the six o'clock news.

In *The Uses of the Past,* Herbert Muller writes: "In the incessant din of the mediocre, mean and fraudulent activities of a commercial mass society, we are apt to forget the genuine idealism of democracy, of the long painful struggle for liberty and equality.... The modern world is as revolutionary as everybody says it is. Because the paradoxes of our age are so violent, men have been violently oversimplifying them. If we want to save our world, we might better try to keep and use our heads."

In this book are a hundred American voices, captured by hunch, circumstance, and a rough idea. There is no pretense at statistical "truth," nor consensus. There is, in the manner of a jazz work, an attempt, of theme and improvisation, to recount dreams, lost and found, and a recognition of possibility.

VINE DELORIA

As soon as we began to travel faster in this country, the importance of place got lost. I can get in an airplane in the desert, and in three hours get off in the Great Lakes. I didn't really travel. I wasn't aware of anything happening.

A bleak, rainy morning at O'Hare International Airport, Chicago.

He is a Sioux Indian, en route from Tucson to Washington, D.C. His most celebrated book is Custer Died for Your Sins. *He teaches political science at the University of Arizona. He is forty-five.*

Our conversation is occasionally interrupted by an elderly wait-ress of salty tongue, who constantly refills our coffee cups. She has been casually eavesdropping. "American Dream? Come on, you guys." She recounts, between her self-appointed rounds, a tale of her being cheated of thousands by a crooked lawyer. "American Dream! Are you kiddin'?"

I know a lot of Indian stories about places in America. St. Anthony Falls was once a holy shrine of the Sioux Indians. You go there, and you're filled with wonderment: What did it look like when we had it? What did it really look like before television and fast cars and jet airplanes?

I often think of the Donner party. 1846. Caught in the pass, they ended up as cannibals, eating each other. I remember following the same route, going by it in my Olds 98 on the salt flats. The inter-state highway, from Denver to Cheyenne. I covered those salt flats in about forty-five minutes. In the pioneer days, you had to cross those salt flats in thirty-six hours. If you wasted any more time, you'd arrive at the Sierra Nevadas at a dangerous time of the year. It took the Donners six days. I went past those flats at seventy-five miles an hour, just zap! Knowing all kinds of people died there. You begin to raise questions about the white–Indian conflict.

None of these tribes saw enough whites at any one time to ever regard them as dangerous. If you have a tribe of five hundred sitting on a hillside and a wagon train of two hundred people goes by, that's no threat to you. You hear a lot of stories, traditional ones, that the Indians were afraid of the whites because they thought they were crazy. You read the tremendous sacrifices the pioneers made to get across the Great Plains. You think of your own people who sat on the hillside, who knew every creek and rock for a thousand miles around. They're looking down at these people, who are terrified because they're in tall grass. Neither side understands the other. Perhaps the Donner party might have been saved had they been friends of the Indians, had they not been frightened of these "enemies" who knew the terrain. You have to take a new look at what you thought America was before you can figure out where it's going.

I grew up on the Pine Ridge reservation in South Dakota. It was about thirty-five miles from Wounded Knee. The town was about four blocks long and three blocks wide, off Main Street. It was really only about two blocks of buildings. I remember before they put the pavement in. The roads were just cow pastures. When it rained, you were there for a couple of days. Very few whites lived there.

I went to grade school, half white and half mixed-blooded Indians. They taught us Rudyard Kipling's world view. It was a simplistic theory that societies marched toward industry and that science was doing good for us. We're all Americans and none of us is ever disloyal. The United States has never been on the wrong side of anything. The government has never lied to the people. The FBI is there to help you, and if you see anything suspicious, call them. There was a heavy overtone of the old British colonial attitude. Nothing about the slaves. Minority history just didn't exist. The world somehow is the garden of the white people, and everybody else kind of fits in someplace. And it's not demeaning to fit in, 'cause that's the way God wants it. You're not being put down. Western civilization's finding a place for you.

It was glossed-over history that Americans used to recite on Memorial Day in the twenties and thirties. I remember going as a six-year-old kid to these roundups, where the old cowboys and all the old chiefs would gather. After a big barbecue, some broken down tenor would sing "Old Faithful" and "Wagon Wheels," and everybody would cry. They'd moan about the frontier being closed and they'd beat the drum. It takes you a long time to realize these things aren't real.

My father was an Episcopal missionary on the reservation. His father was too. I suppose our family was one of the first to move from the old ways to the white man's ways. It was a weird situation, schizophrenic. My family had been religious leaders before they'd become Christians. The old Indian religion. I was not just a minister's son. Mine was a long family tradition of medicine men. People came to my father for all sorts of things. He knew all kinds of medicine songs and stories.

He held on to the two cultures without much conflict until the late sixties. The civil rights movement turned him off. The church put tremendous pressure on the Indians to integrate. He said: "We don't have to. We can be what we are without getting into the melting pot." There are thousands of Indian Christians who looked upon Christianity in the old Indian way. The message of Jesus wasn't all that big. But a lot of the Indians were turned off and ended up with no religion. My father just gave up on Christianity.

Maybe my generation is the last one that was affected by Indian values. I'm forty-five. Now I see people, about eight years younger, going to a meeting and starting to dominate things right away.

When I was five and six, older relatives shushed me up at meetings because no one should talk unless the oldest person talks. People of my age still feel these social constraints. If you move eight years down, you find people who've grown up in postwar brashness. The hustler. The further down you move, the worse it gets. The younger people have taken the rat race as the real thing. It's a thing in their heads. In my generation, it was a thing in the heart.

The young Indian as well as the young white has no sense of history whatsoever. I think the Second World War did it. History, for a long time, was dominated by Europe. The United States came out of World War Two as the great power. All of a sudden, we had responsibility. Our history had always been parochial. We were separated by oceans, we didn't know where we were. The anti-Communist paranoia took over: nobody's ever gonna conquer this country, by God. If we're destroyed, it will be self-destruction.

An old Sioux chief, Standing Bear, once said that the white man came to this continent afraid from the very beginning. Afraid of animals and nature and earth. This fear projected itself onto the land and the animals. They became frightened of the whites. When the whites would move in, the animals would move out. I had always thought that was a clever Indian saying until I re-read de Tocqueville last year. He says: You have ten thousand Indians living in an area with animals all around. You get two or three settlers there, and the animals and Indians leave.

You have to ask yourself: What kind of people were these that came here? They must have been absolutely frantic to set down roots. It was more than subduing the land. I mean, that's a hell of a toll to pay for the right to live on a piece of land.

Maybe the American Dream is in the past, understanding who you are instead of looking to the future: What are you going to be? 'Cause we've kind of reached the future. I'm not just talking about nostalgia. I'm talking about finding familiar guideposts. Maybe this is a period of reflection.

Last February, there was a meeting of some medicine men and some Jesuits. One of the medicine men stood up and said the whole problem with America is that everybody tries to be young. He said: "All you guys in the Indian community, you've got to start acting your age. You're all trying to stay young, so there are no wise old men any more. If you're grandfathers, you better start acting like grandfathers. If you're fathers, you better start acting like fathers. Don't act like white men. You can't ever do that."

I think there will emerge a group of people, not a large percentage, who will somehow find a way to live meaningful lives. For the vast majority, it will be increased drudgery, with emotions sapped by institutional confines. A grayness. A lot of people are fighting back.

Somewhere, America stalled in perpetual adolescence. But I don't really despair. You can't despair that you have to grow up.

ANDY JOHNSON

The poorest, the most miserable came here because they had no future over there. To them, the streets of America were paved in gold. They had what the Finns called *kuume,* the American fever.

Aurora, Minnesota, about thirty miles from Eveleth. Population, approximately 2,500. It is iron ore country.

We're at the home of Bill Ojala. His wife, Dorothy, serves us all blueberry pie, homemade. Anton Antilla, ninety-one, who had worked in the mines all his American life, is here too.

Andy Johnson, craggy-faced, appears younger than his years. "I came to the seventy-fifth anniversary of Aurora this summer to see if I could find any of my old pals. I couldn't find a one. The place we lived in, when we came in 1906, it's where that big hole is now in the ground."

I was born in Finland and came here in 1906. My father was the son of a tenant farmer. Rocky soil. He didn't see any future in it. The Russo-Japanese War came along. He was going to be drafted in the army, so he beat it out of there as fast as he could.

My father was a typical Christian and conservative when he came here and for a long time after. In our bedroom, we had a picture of Christ on one wall and Czar Nicholas II on the other. I remember something about the revolution of 1905 in Russia and Finland. The assassination of the governor general of Finland, appointed by the czar. Our neighbors had rifles with fixed bayonets. I didn't understand what it was about, but I could sense a tension. I remember how they were jabbing this bayonet into the ground, trying it out.

We started off on a wooden ship. It was built of rough oak timbers. No paint on 'em, no nothin'. It had a mast in case they ran out of steam. [Laughs.] They had a bull pen, one big room for most of 'em. The women and children had smaller quarters, where you just crawled into bunks. The North Sea is always stormy. You get those sugarloaf-type waves, so the boat would rock. They got sick, all those people in one big room vomiting. Mother took salt fish from home. When we started getting seasick, you'd cut a slice of that fish and eat it.

We went across England by train, then from Liverpool to New York City. It was a Cunard liner, *Lucania*. That was a big boat. When we came to New York harbor, everybody got out on deck to see the Statue of Liberty. My mother picked me up and held me so I could see it. There was a doctor at Ellis Island, and he took a spoon and shoved it in my eye, along with the others, to see if we had any illness. Those that had were returned.

We rode on a train for days on end. We came through some beautiful country. Lotta times, I thought we should stop here, we shouldn't go any further. [Laughs.] We came to New York Mills, Minnesota, a Finnish community. My father was working on the railroad there. He came two years before. We met him, and it was kind of emotional. Coming to America was like being transferred from one century to another. The change was so great.

They bought a bunch of bananas, which I hadn't seen before. I ate too many of 'em and I got sick. I swore off bananas. I didn't eat one for at least ten years. [Laughs.]

I saw the first black man in my life on the platform at the Union Station in Duluth. I couldn't figure out why his face was black. I thought he didn't wash it or something. It didn't dawn on me at that time that people were different. I remember at my grandfather's place reading about Africa and the missionaries. The only literature we had was the Bible and a missionary magazine. In this magazine there was a picture of black people tied together by their hands, one to the other with chains, and there was a big husky white man with a horsewhip. I didn't like the looks of that picture. I asked my aunt: "Why are those people chained?" She said they're slaves, but she didn't explain much further.

As soon as we got settled, my folks bought a Bible. They didn't bring it from the Old Country like a lotta other people did. So I started to read the Bible and learned to read Finnish. I got interested in it, but the stories were so wild and frightening to me.

When I was about thirteen, I got in contact with lumberjacks who had different ideas from my father's. I began to think about things, and my father did the same. He began to read the Finnish paper *Tyomies*. It was left-wing. When somebody first brought it to him, he took a stick from the wood box and carried the paper with that stick and put it in the stove. Soon after World War One started, he was reading it himself, and his views began to change.

Father got a job at the Miller mine. He'd come directly home with his mining clothes. Mother didn't like it at all. She didn't like the surroundings, the strange people. Most of the timber had been cut and everything was a mess. Iron ore on the roads, instead of gravel. When it rained, the stuff would splatter all over.

Father quit his job and got a job at Mohawk mine. I was supposed to start school, but something happened. He either got fired or quit, and he went to Adriatic mine. At the Adriatic, you had Slovenians and Italians and Finns. They all spoke a strange language, they couldn't understand each other. The company liked it that way. Some houses were company-owned, some privately. When we first came here, they were about six feet high, made out of poles stuck in the ground and boxboards nailed to the posts, and tarpaper over that. I don't think they had any floor.

The following summer they built a school, and my sister and I started. Learning English was a little difficult, although when you start playing with other kids, you'd be surprised how fast you learn. I never finished seventh grade because the snow melted too soon. I went to school altogether less than five winters.

There was the booms and the busts, we'd go from one to the other. About 1912, things began to slow down. By 1914, they were pretty bad, until World War One started. We moved out to the country, got a homestead. The government was still giving free land. So we moved out there in the wilderness.

Father got a job in the logging camp as a blacksmith. Mother did some laundry for the bosses. That helped us a lot that winter. When the big logging camps came in, they brought the railroads. My father had been a miner, a carpenter, a farmer, a common laborer. When a person moves so many times from one year, from one job to another, there's reasons for it. He wasn't happy with what he was faced with. When he began reading these papers and talking to people about capitalism and exploitation, he began to see and change his mind.

I didn't pay much attention to politics until I was in the neighborhood of thirty. When things got tough in the thirties, I began to express my views. I had a good job then, working for the county. Every morning, the boss'd pick out certain guys and give 'em a day's work. The guys that didn't get any work would pass under my window, so we got to talking. Well, they started pointing the finger at me.

The county commissioner called me into the office and warned me about talkin' the way I talk. I had my independence, except that it made my livelihood a little more difficult. That's the way it's been up to this day, and I don't think it'll change. When you're once fired for your political views, you're automatically blackballed with the mining companies, even if you never worked for a mining company. The superintendent of the mine was the mayor at one time.

Your American Dream? You got a terrible-looking hole down in the ground where we used to live once. It's filled with water, and the wealth is taken out of the land. I don't know what it's good for. On the other hand, people live in nice houses, they're painted well. There's jobs for those that have jobs, and there are a lot of people on welfare in this county.

I see a wonderful future for humanity, or the end of it.

If we continue this present trend, we're gonna go straight to hell, we're gonna blow ourselves right off this earth, or we'll poison ourselves off. It's up to the people. What bothers me is that they're not concerned. I don't know how to approach 'em. For forty-five years I've written a letter to the newspaper. I've tried to get one every month to at least one paper. That's the only thing I'm able to do.

WALLACE RASMUSSEN

It is 7:00 A.M. A frosty winter morning. The executive offices of Beatrice Foods in Chicago. The long corridors are empty; you walk through as in an Ingmar Bergman dream sequence. You enter a large room; seated at the end of a long table, alone, is the chief executive officer of the corporation. He glances at his pocket watch. There is coffee for himself and his visitor. Big-boned and heavy-set, with calloused hands, he has the appearance of the archetypal elderly workingman in Sunday clothes. He is bluff and genial. He is a winner of the Horatio Alger Award.

I'm just a country boy. Born in Nebraska and came up right through the Great Depression. I'm convinced it will repeat itself when it's time, and probably it'll be good for the country. It will be hard on people who never experienced doing without, but it's amazing what you can get along without. You don't have it, so you begin to spend more time with your family. There's a way in history, a way in nature, of always bringing people back down to earth.

Some people are more aggressive than others. People are always protecting their turf. That's a natural instinct. The bull elk on the mountainside, when he bugles, he doesn't bugle to other bulls. He bugles to them: Stay away from my harem. The male does not fight to be fighting; he fights to protect his territory. You could always tell the survivors because they were always in there punchin'. Takes a lot to get them upset. They would swing with whatever comes along. To me, that's a survivor.

Somebody asked me: Did you ever dream of being in the job you're in? I say no. My only ambition in life was to be just a little bit better off the next day than I was the day before. And to learn a little more than I did the day before. I was always reading. As a child, I read every *Popular Mechanics* magazine I could get ahold of. Even in school, they would bring me things to fix.

In those days, each farmer helped the other farmers. At twelve, I hitched the team and hauled bundles of hay and pitched them into the thrashing machine. I upset a load of bundles by turning too sharply. I went across the ditch. Do you think those farmers would help me? Let's see if he could do it by himself. It was a good lesson because I never upset another one.

I learned the traits of human beings. You can learn from nature why people do what they do. I'm talking about wildlife. I spent my entire life doing some hunting, out of necessity for food on the table. You learn that animals and people have the same habits today that they had two thousand years ago.

I never wanted to be a loser. I always wanted to be the first one off the airplane. I have a theory that when you walk through a crowd in the airport—I don't care how crowded it is—if you look fifty feet ahead, people will separate. Don't look straight at the person, and people will make room for you. Years ago, I took my wife to Tulsa. I was ready to get on the airplane when the fellow said: "Don't you have your wife with you?" I said: "Oh, my gosh, yes." I forgot her. [Laughs.] People would say they saw me on the street and I didn't say hello. I was thinking about something else. It isn't my nature to be friendly.

I think hardship is necessary for life to be good, for you to enjoy it. If you don't know hardship, you don't know when you have it good. Today, the father and mother don't want their children to go through the same hardships. I don't look at it that way. I have two children. One is forty and one is thirty-six. I can still say, "This is what you do," and that's what they do. I'm a firm believer that they had to know things weren't always that easy. There's a price you pay for everything.

People are now so used to being given something for nothing. They think it's for nothing, but there's a price. Loss of their pride, loss of their ability to take care of themselves. It's like caging animals. I don't care how wild the animal was, if you cage him long enough, he forgets how to take care of himself. The same is true about human beings. Like a lion that's forgotten how to take care of himself, they will kill others, the slow ones because they can't catch the fast ones. That's why you have crime today in the element not employed. They don't know how to take care of themselves other than to take away from those that have. A recession or a revolution will bring it back into balance. It's happened throughout history. That's one thing I know out of reading history.

It comes down to—who's gonna be the survivor? It will test the strength of a lot of people. It will be every community for itself. You cannot stand still. You grow or die.

When I left home, I went to California. I had odd jobs delivering handbills. Oh, did I learn a lesson! I couldn't figure out why some of them would deliver a thousand in a couple of hours when it took me all day. I followed one and saw he was putting most of them down the storm drain. I went to the fellow I was working for and asked how come he was allowing him to put them down the storm drain. I put mine all out, I'm wearin' out my shoe leather. For ten cents a day. I could buy a bucket of grapes for ten cents, that was enough to eat. He says: "We expect that." I said: "It's not right." He said: "We're not gonna pay you any more." So I quit the job. You had to be brave to quit jobs that paid ten cents a day. [Laughs.] I think he was rippin' people off. California was then known as the place to do unto others before they do unto you.

I worked three months on an alfalfa ranch at ten dollars a month, room and board. All you'd get was black-eyed peas for breakfast, for dinner, and for supper. The milk was always sour. They gave me a letter that they owed me twenty dollars to take to the owner of the ranch, and he'd pay me. Dumb me, I gave him the letter and I never got my twenty dollars. That was a lesson to me. Trust everybody with reservations.

I came back to Nebraska and helped shuck corn. We sold it at ten cents a bushel and burned the rest of it. Then I got a job putting cedar chests together. I never told anybody I couldn't do anything. The company failed, so I got a job cutting out jigsaw puzzles. I got ten cents for each one.

I was reading about people who were successful and how they did it. How they got ahead. That was basically all my reading. I made up my mind that if I ever got with a big company, I'd never leave. My mother's brother was an engineer at Beatrice in Lincoln. I got a job there. I was nineteen. I started pulling ice out of a tank.

You pull up 400-pound cans with an electric hoist. There was always a challenge: How much could I pull? The maximum was a hundred tons. I always wanted to go over that. The engineer would come in and say: "Slow down." [Laughs.]

I kept all the equipment up myself. I didn't want anybody fooling with it. The chief engineer recognized I had mechanical ability. He said: "Do you think you could handle maintenance in the creamery?" I said: "Sure." [Laughs.] I knew what a creamery looked like. I'd walked through it a couple of times, but that's all. I'd never seen any pasteurizing equipment in my life. But it didn't take me long to learn. I never doubted that anything I intended to do, I could do.

In six months I went to the chief engineer and said: "I don't have enough to do." He said the other man worked at it full-time. I said: "I don't care. You gotta get me something else to do." I wanted to keep busy. So I went to the dairy side, where they bottle milk. I learned a lot from the fellow there, a fine machinist and refrigeration man. Anybody who had information, I would soak it up like a sponge.

It got so, I took care of all the maintenance in the dairy and creamery. I went to him again and said: "I'm running out of something to do." He said: "Why don't you go over to the ice cream plant?" Soon I was taking care of all three. It wasn't enough of a challenge, so I got a job at night, taking care of the air conditioning of a hotel. I also did home wiring. I would require only two, three hours of sleep.

Beatrice offered me the job as chief engineer of the plant in Vincennes, Indiana. It was the largest milk plant in the country. I was twenty-two. The people who were working there were in their forties and fifties, some of them in their sixties. I thought maybe there might be some resentment because of my age. I tried to be tolerant of people's weaknesses, knowing I'd get the maximum amount of work out of them if I treated them with respect.

The man whose place I was supposed to take wasn't capable of handling the job. He was a genius with equipment, but a tinkerer. Say you had a body on the table and it's bleeding to death. The doctor would say: "What kind of car accident was he in?" This fellow would always make an analysis. Consequently, he had four or five people standing around doing nothing. My theory was: Let's get it fixed, then we'll analyze why it broke down.

I finally told the management he's gotta go. That was the first time I knowingly practiced brinkmanship. I needed that job like you need shoes in cold weather. I knew they needed me worse than I needed them. I stayed in my room for two weeks. They called me and said: "He's gone, come on back." From then on, we got the plant in shape.

I worked out of the Chicago office drawing layouts. I had no experience in this. I bought books, started reading, and got the equipment. I told the engineers we have today that I could tear a piece of refrigeration equipment down with a suit on and never get greasy. They don't ever tear them down themselves. If you're going to direct people, you must have knowledge of the job. If somebody comes in and says this is so, I know immediately whether that person is telling me a fact. Facts in your hands before you make the decision, that's part of the survivor.

Another lesson I pass on: Whenever you're going to work for somebody, make sure that you make him successful. Otherwise, you must jump over him. Now, I've had to jump over…[He trails off.]

I always considered that as part of life. This is *our* world. If we're going to keep it a strong society, you have to have strong leaders. You can't have what we have in Washington today.

He refers, wryly, to a profile of himself in Forbes *magazine. "The only thing they said unfair is this last sentence: 'That is a tough and determined man. Even though he's pushing sixty-five, he doesn't allow anybody to do to Wallace Rasmussen what he has done to others.' "*

It can appear to be ruthless at the time that you do it. When someone is not producing in a corporation, or even in a family, and he doesn't recognize he's holding up the works, someone has to make that decision for him. If you're going to be successful, you can't let any person stand in the way. The company is a hundred thousand people and fifty thousand shareholders. We have a moral responsibility to at least a hundred fifty thousand individuals. Multiply a hundred fifty by three and a half, which is the population of the average family, and you got half a million people. We have a responsibility to those who trust us.

You are respected by a hundred thousand employees. Are you feared, too?

[A long, long pause.] You'd rather not say that it was fear, but you have it. You can't help it. Some of it may be awe. Ninety-nine percent of it has to be respect. You have all three. I make it a habit of talking to the most junior person in the office. I find out more from him than I do from the senior officers. [Laughs.] Senior officers try to cover up their mistakes. Poor little junior down here doesn't know he's making mistakes, so I find out more.

When the company was 4.3 billion dollars, I wasn't chairman, I wasn't president, I wasn't executive vice-president. I was a senior vice-president and I had three-fourths of the company as my load. This goes back to '68, '67.

I became president and chief executive officer on July 1, 1976. In those two years, we have grown from 5.2 billion to 7.4 billion. No, no, you absolutely cannot stop your growth. You must increase enough to keep people interested in investing in your company.

There's many people asking: When are you going to retire? I made a comment when I took the job. I would go out when I had eight billion. Now I say I'll go when it's ten.

POSTSCRIPT

He was retired in 1975 as chief executive officer of Beatrice Foods.
The company had reached 7.8 billion dollars.

VERNON JARRETT

He is a columnist for the Chicago Tribune.

I grew up in Paris, Tennessee. People in small towns considered
nowhere identified with somewhere. So we were thirty miles from
Murray, Kentucky, sixty miles from Paducah, a hundred ten miles
from Nashville, forty miles from Clarksville. We were on the L & N
Railroad.

Louisville and Nashville used to come down from Chicago.
It would be about two city blocks from my house. We were always
train-conscious. We used to listen for the train, set your clock by it.
You'd say: "Panama's late today. Number 619 is late." The engineer
would blow his whistle, the people would listen, the dogs would howl.

Country people used to go walking on Sunday afternoons. They
go down to the depot to see who's comin' in and who's leavin'. Or
just to see the train comin' in. The trains always symbolized mobility. Somebody goin' somewhere, somebody leavin'. We were always
aware there was another place outside of this. Somewhere. That
you *could* go somewhere.

When I was a little kid, we used to play a game called swinging,
with a car tire and a tree. One would push and one would be the
conductor. You'd call off the cities: Paducah. St. Louis. Evansville.
Somebody'd say: "I think I'm gonna get off here." And somebody'd
say: 'Naw, I'm gonna wait." And then everybody would say:
"Chicago! Forty-seventh Street!" Listen to a lot of the old blues

songs: "How Long, Baby, Has That Evenin' Train Been Gone?" "Going to Chicago." "Trouble in Mind."

Some of the pictures stand out in my mind right now. People chopping cotton. I used to wander around in the woods, workin' on a sweet-potato patch. When they'd hear the train coming, you'd see 'em standing there, with their hoes or their forks. Like, we'd pay our respects now, the train is comin' by. You'd see that look on their faces, that longing look. You might see folks in bandanas, overalls, older women, young people. They'd all stop in the middle of what they were doin' and they'd wave at the train, waving at anonymous people and maybe anonymous dreams.

In some parts of Mississippi it was a little rough because you had to sneak away. I learned from people who lived on the plantations, where you still had peonage, there was always that train. If push came to shove, you could go. If you lived in those little delta towns, the train was the symbol of where you could go to reclaim yourself as a man or become a woman.

We called ourselves a part of that Illinois Central. The tracks that began somewhere in Louisiana went all the way to Chicago. Chicago even has a different pronunciation. *Chi*cago. These trains were always gonna take you somewhere. They used to have excursions, too. Where you could at least say you'd been there, to the Promised Land. Weekend excursions even to St. Louis. St. Louis was one of those places we black folks called Negro Heavens. There was a movie made once that we stood in line to see when I was a kid in grammar school called *Harlem Heaven*. Bill Bojangles Robinson, the first time I ever saw him. They played it in our high school. It was farmed out and sold to schools and churches. You got to see Harlem. You'd even settle for Detroit. People in Alabama went to "Detroit City." They heard about those jobs with Henry Ford. Of course, for us in Mississippi, Alabama, parts of Georgia, Arkansas, Chicago was our heaven. Understand?

The *Chicago Defender* was our newspaper. You'd grab your newspaperman to see what was going on, black life in big cities. You were always there even if you never moved. Believe it or not, Cairo, Illinois, was one of those places they would brag about. [Laughs.]

We're talkin' about the thirties. We had a world of dreamers. Black people were some of the most creative people in the world, because you had to substitute dreams of what you thought might be the real world of one day. "In the Sweet Bye and Bye" was one of the favorite church songs. "I'm Gonna Lay My Burden Down" and "When the Saints Come Marchin' In." There was a mobility. What kind of crown you gonna wear? My grandmother, an ex-slave, used to talk about the number of stars that are gonna be in her crown when she went to the Promised Land.

I knew many ex-slaves who lived there. My grandmother used to sit around and tell us these stories. She'd mix fiction in with 'em, but some of 'em were true. About her life as a little slave girl. She remembers when General Grant came down to La Grange, Tennessee, and set up the army of the Tennessee. She heard the cannons. She used to tell us stories about how they used to trick Old Marsey. She was what they called a house nigger.

My grandfather on my dad's side was what you'd call a field nigger. These two old-timers used to meet in our home in the winter months, when our parents thought they were too old to live alone on the farm. They used to sit there and tell these stories over and over. She used to tell the ones about when they heard how the Union army was coming down to free the slaves. They would put on this big act. They would go in and tell Old Marsey how sorry they were and that if the Yankees came in, they weren't gonna give them their hams and this and that. And they'd go in the backyard and crack up laughing.

She was a little girl when slavery was ended. Dad's father was a runaway slave. He couldn't read and write. He heard that the Union army was freein' people and he cut out. He didn't even know what state he came from.

Some Sundays in church when they started singin' those old hymns, those people would start laughing and answering each other from across the room. We kids couldn't understand what on earth they were laughing about. I remember one of us got up enough guts to ask what was so funny. They'd say: "We're not really laughin', you youngsters would never understand it." They were really laughing about the fact that they had survived: Here we are sitting up here, free. These are our kids here with us. I've got a home, and my daughter is a schoolteacher. That's what I used to hear my grandmother say.

The thing I remember about these folks was the immense dignity and pride in the way they walked. They walked like straight sticks. They made us stand like that. This always slays me, that all of us had to stand erect. They would go around asking you: "Boy, aren't you gonna be somebody when you grow up?" They'd always say: "I'm never gonna live to see it."

Let me tell you about the day my brother got his master's degree from Fisk University. My dad didn't like any fooling around in church or when one of the great black speakers came to town. There were circuits of people who went around just to inspire you, to tell you about Africa, the sleeping giant. He didn't like anybody talking while somebody was making a speech. Or laughing or snickering. I think of all the kids my dad used to whip for talking when he was principal of the school. In the Fisk University chapel, he was talking to me all through the graduation speech by Dr. Alain Locke, one of the great black scholars.

My mother kept shushing my father. He just kept talking. She said: "Stop talking, people will think we're country and don't know better." He kept talking. I looked up, and tears were running down his face. He told me that in 1893, when he ran away from home "to make somethin' of himself," he helped construct that building where my brother was getting his degree. He leaned over to me and said: "These seats look like the same old iron seats I helped screw into this floor. I used to sneak back in here after the other workers had gone and sleep at night. I never thought I'd live to see the day my son would get a master's degree in this building." You know the funny thing? He was almost laughing, as I used to see the ex-slaves do. It was a celebration of that fact that "I am here, I exist, and there's still some hope." This is one of the real miracles of these people.

My dad used to tell me, when he was close to seventy-nine, that he didn't think any white man ever called him "mister" over four or five times in his whole life. My mother had been called "girl" and "nigger" and "auntie." She was a strikingly good-looking woman.

My dad didn't want to come to Chicago. He figured his thing was in the South. My parents were schoolteachers. My mother and dad put together a hundred and ten years in classroom teaching. They were old-time crusading schoolteachers, mother and father. My dad was known as a school builder.

The school was the size of an average city apartment. They had about two or three other teachers. They were making about twenty-five dollars a month. The kids, believe it or not, learned advanced mathematics. [Laughs.] This is crazy, isn't it? I learned Chaucer's *Canterbury Tales* when I was in the ninth grade. I can almost do it now, in Old English. We had oratorical contests all the time. There was a premium being able to speak well, enunciate clearly. I've lost some of that in the city.

That school to me was one of the most fascinating things I'd ever seen. A frame building. We had outhouses and no running water. They had a hydrant out in the backyard.

I was five years old. I was playing like I was Robert S. Abbott. He was the publisher of the *Chicago Defender*. There were some little towns where it wasn't permitted to land. It was considered inflammatory, encouraging black people to go north. The dream centered around the North.

In 1879 was a great exodus. It was two years after the Tilden-

Hayes Compromise. People were leaving the South en masse. They were called the exodusters. Some of 'em were kidnapped and brought back to Mississippi and Alabama.

I came to Chicago when I was at Great Lakes during World War Two. That's why I joined the navy, just to see Chicago. When I came in, the only blacks were mess stewards. But I'd rather be a mess steward and live around Chicago than be in the army around Louisiana.

I heard about Chicago all my life. Some of the stories were fabricated. You'd hear folks say: "I didn't know I was black until I looked in the mirror." You go up there, you wouldn't believe it. They got a congressman named Oscar De Priest, they got blacks in government, black lawyers, black policemen.

It meant a great place where everybody's treated equal. You could be what you wanted to be. You didn't have to have white people abusing you. And they wouldn't call your mother "girl" or your father "boy." The whole works. Where you could become somebody. That's the stuff we were steeped in as little children. During Negro History Week, people would tell us about the Harlem Renaissance. We had to recite Langston Hughes's poems and Claude McKay's. You used to have to stand up and sing "Lift Every Voice." You sing about your day as if it were a reality. I never felt despair.

Some of the poorest people I knew in the South never really felt outright despair. This optimism was based on the fact that some of the older folks, the cooks, the house boys, the chauffeurs, and even some of the field hands, felt that racism was such a ridiculous thing, they just figured it couldn't last. Black people figured that one day God was gonna rise up and do some damage to the white people. God was "gonna mess the white folks up one of these days for the way they treatin' us." You know what was there, too? The feeling that if you just stick this out, don't commit suicide, don't let it get the best of you, you're gonna win.

When there was despair, you took it out in the church. You'd see it in funerals. Black people have really clung to a genuine love for each other. That's why a funeral said so much. You can't let this person die as though it was nothing happening. A great loss had been suffered. I learned to cry at all funerals, and I didn't know who was dead. I had been inculcated with the idea that something very valuable has passed. I was a little boy. I'd sit there and just cry along with the rest of 'em.

Someone has gone. You'd hear people say: He could have been this or she could have been this if she just had a chance. Sometimes one of the older sisters would lean over and kiss her buddy good-bye. When my father died, my mother went to the funeral home. Before they had the casket ready, she just sat there and patted his hands. She said: "These hands have done a whole lot..."

The mortician across the street was a personal friend of ours. I hadn't seen him for years. A lot of folks didn't understand when I hopped on a plane and flew to Paducah just to say good-bye to him. I came back to Chicago just to meet my deadline. But I had to go by there and see old Bob Woodson, eighty-seven years old. And look at him and remember my childhood. This is the man who embalmed my mother and father. There was no such thing as an anonymous person. This is something that's been lost in the big city.

Oh, I was the biggest dreamer. I'd listen to Duke Ellington. They made us turn off the radio at a certain hour, but we'd sneak in there and hear Duke from the Cotton Club in New York. We finally got a radio to hear Joe Louis fight Max Schmeling. We had a prayer meeting that night. That tells you how desperate we were. Joe Louis was the greatest figure in our lives up until Martin Luther King.

When I first came to Chicago in the forties, I rode the el and I read the newspapers. I would check out on what great name was gonna speak here. I'd go out there and if it was free, I would hang around and get a seat. And I'd walk these great streets. I would write back and say: "I went down South Parkway, can you imagine that?" Or "I stood at the corner of Forty-seventh and South Parkway Saturday night." You'd put that in a letter. Or: I saw so and so. They said if you stood on this corner long enough on Saturday night, you'd see somebody from back home. That's where all of us met and paraded.

We always had a feeling we were on the move, that things were happening. Every time the NAACP would win any kind of little victory, it was a great moment.

Up here you could just let your hair down. When I used to listen at night, it was not only to hear Duke Ellington from the Cotton Club. You also heard the man say: "Fatha Hines from the Grand Terrace in Chicago." It seemed as though from the noise in there the people were just free. White people and black people in there together.

What was it? Thirty-five years ago? My dreams have not expired entirely. There are moments when I waver between despair and hopelessness and flashes of inspiration. Years ago, when we were in trouble, we thought we could one day go north. Well, we are north now. We are at that Promised Land. The Promised Land has less hope now than it had when we were not in the Promised Land. We used to say "We're being abused now, but one day we'll have the ballot. One of these days we're not gonna have presidents and governors who abuse us. One of these days the Ku Klux Klan is not gonna be around lynching us." All that has happened. But we didn't realize that there were some basic corrections that haven't yet been made.

How can you get out? My parents could say: "One day my children are gonna have it better if they could just get an education." The catch is I might get a good job, but the community I'm living in is going to be so overwhelmed by other people's poverty that I won't be able to enjoy it. Do you realize I'm enjoying more luxuries now than the white familes for whom I used to work were able to enjoy? Yet I have less hope now for the vast majority of black people than I did when I first came here. I don't see solutions to the problems the way I did then. There simply aren't enough jobs to go around.

I see more antagonism now than I saw a few years ago. In the South it's different. Some remarkable changes have taken place. I'd never hoped to see a crowd in Mississippi cheering a black half-back. But the North is another story.

Whatever is happening to blacks is an extreme version of what's going to happen to whites. Remember when people identified dope only with black kids? Now, in God-fearin' white middle-class communities, they're worried about their children and narcotics. Remember when common-law living was for black people? Now it's in vogue among young whites.

The ghetto used to have something going for it. It had a beat, it had a certain rhythm, and it was all hope. I don't care how rough things were. They used to say: If you can't make it in Chicago, you can't make it anywhere. You may be down today, you're gonna be back up tomorrow.

You had the packing houses going, you had the steel mills going, you had secondary employment to help "get you over." There was the guy spreading hope every day, the policy-wheel man. Policy was considered a part of our culture before the mob took it over. Everybody played policy. You were always hearing about somebody who hit the day. Oh, so and so hit. Somebody you always heard about was hitting or making it big. [Laughs.]

Now it's a drag. There are thousands of people who have written off their lives. They're serving out a sentence as though there were some supreme judge who said: "You are sentenced to life imprisonment on earth and this your cell here." What do you do if you've got a life sentence? You play jailhouse politics. You hustle, you sell cigarettes, you browbeat other people, you abuse the other cell mates, you turn men into weaklings, and girls you overcome.

There are people who don't see themselves making it in this automated society. Not many white people can figure things out either.

You look at television and you see people pushin' buttons sending people to the moon. You say: "Man, these are people so far ahead of me I don't have a chance." You see people using language and reading skills at which you're incompetent. You say: "Hell it's too late. Maybe I coulda learned but I blew it." You write yourself off. Then you don't see jobs even though you may have learned these things.

A few of us are making it pretty good. This is one thing that frightens me. I think there are some people in high places who've decided this problem can't be solved. We're gonna do what we did in World War One: practice triage. We can salvage maybe one third that's making it. Maybe close to another third is capable of being salvaged. The only thing we can do for the other third is contain them. Keep them from inconveniencing us. We'd just keep them where they are. There are not enough jobs for them. We're not going to rearrange our society so that it's possible for them to have some of the benefits we enjoy. In a few years you may have black people who are doing all right, who may lose identity with those who are not doing so well. Racism is keeping all the haves from getting together. [Laughs.] A few years ago, racism was used to keep black and white workers from getting together. Now it's keeping the upper strata from getting together.

When I got married, some years ago, there were no apartments available. My wife and I gladly lived in the building right across from the Robert Taylor Homes.* I bought a long rope. In case of fire, we'd climb down those nine flights. We didn't care. We knew everything was gonna be beautiful later on. What about people who say everything is not going to be beautiful because there are three generations of unemployed males in the family?

That's something we didn't experience down south. You could always grub out a living, doing something. Food was cheaper. There were odd jobs for you. You can't make it on odd jobs today.

---

* A public-housing project, all black, on Chicago's South Side. It's the largest in the world.

There are a lot of whites in this situation, too. They don't want to admit it. They want black people to bear the whole burden of the crusade against unemployment. There are twenty-six million Americans living below the poverty level. Only around eight million of these are black.

Would you live opposite the Robert Taylor Homes now?

No, I would be frightened. I don't think I could take it unless there were other people, middle-class like me, and we could get together and form some kind of protective association. I tried. I lived in Englewood. Englewood at the time I lived there was number three or four in crime in the country. I lived where the Blackstone Rangers and Disciples fought each other. Some of the property was middle-class, but it was really tough trying to rear children in that community. My neighbors used to walk their dogs at night and gather in the schoolyard. These were not cute little pets. They were dogs that would bite if you entered their homes. When I first moved there, I used to see black women get off the bus at night and off jitneys as late as two in the morning and walk three blocks home on a summer night. They used to walk with purses and shopping bags in the late forties and early fifties. They can't do that tonight.

In 1950 the black population of Chicago was 49,000. At this moment it's close to 1,500,000. A million more people. Most of them came here seeking employment, got stuck, and couldn't go back home because there was nothing there. Our government set up some rules which made it more profitable for a family to break up in order to get welfare. So the black male living in poverty today can't have the respect that black men had when I was a kid. You know the spiritual "Sometimes I feel Like a Motherless Child"? Today, it's sometimes I feel like a fatherless child. That may be worse.

The other day a black mailman was describing a ghetto scene.

The father was giving his son a lecture about staying away from a vicious street gang, to get him to stop threatening and robbing storekeepers. The kid said: "Who in the fuck do you think you are? You ain't shit. How in the hell are you gonna tell me what to do?" This man has no prestige with his own child.

I remember men in the South who were yard boys, never called mister, who were considered Uncle Toms. But their children looked up to them. At home, they represented somebody trying. The janitor in the school where my father was principal was chairman of the board of trustees of the church my dad attended. This will never happen again in our lifetime.

Old man Van Dyke, who worked the city streets, walked around with great poise. Shack Wilkins, who worked at the L & N Railroad, over at the shops, I remember how he kept his shoes shined. Wow. I still do this on Saturdays. I'm imitating Shack Wilkins. He used to buy expensive shoes, Thom McAns. We called them expensive. Boy! He kept them shining. He used to take us chestnut hunting.

On Sundays, they dressed immaculately. We kept our outhouse clean, as many other people did. You shovel out the fecund and put it in a deep post hole and you put lime over it.

When you come to a city like Chicago, you get lost in the crowd. You're just another name. If a kid uses the word "motherfucker," he can do it with impunity because this old lady walking down the street doesn't know him. She doesn't know his mother or his father. You can hear 'em: "Kiss my ass, motherfucker. Go to hell." All this stuff, when some older people are coming by. Sometimes, out of habit, I say: "Can't you respect the sisters, man?" Then they'll calm down.

I remember I was caught playing the dozens once. It's a game of insults that blacks play, where a bunch of kids get together and hit at what they consider your weakest point: your mother. You don't have much else to lose really. "Motherfucker" is not a sweet little name. It means you're the lowest son of a bitch on earth. Mother was the one thing that was permanent in your life, even in slavery. Today, with these kids, it's no longer a game. It's a way of life.

If I'm feeling good and want to have my morale lowered, all I have to do is drive out Madison Street on a bright, beautiful day and look at the throngs of unemployed youngsters in their weird dress, trying to hang on to some individuality. Can't read or write, looking mean at each other. You see kids hanging around, hating themselves as much as they hate others. This is one thing that's contributed to the ease with which gangs kill each other. Another nigger ain't nothin'.

In Englewood, we had a little bay window. I had formed a cooperative. We tried to fix it up and eventually lost it. But it was a pretty good experiment. We weren't trying to leave the ghetto. We were gonna stay there. We were sitting there, watching TV. We had our windows up. There was a walkway alongside. I heard what appeared to be an explosion. I had one of those Mattel guns. Have you seen these toy guns? They're very realistic. This gun looked like a high-powered rifle. Someone had given it to my sons for Christmas. It gives you an indication of the kind of toys they're selling. [Laughs.] I grabbed this gun because I didn't know if somebody was trying to break in.

Here was an unarmed black kid sauntering in the gangway. He had evidently leaped up, hit a light bulb, and made it explode. I thought when he saw me coming down with a gun drawn—it looked like the real thing—he would have held up his hands and said: "Don't shoot, mister, I was just playing." He didn't do a thing but look at me out of the side of his head and say: "What are you excited about, motherfucker? Go ahead and shoot." He didn't give a damn. This kid went away into anonymity.

We have become anonymous. We got lost. When I was coming up, the so-called ghettos had a stability, would you believe it? People didn't move as much as they do today. Folk had a chance to know who was living down the street, who graduated, who got married.

All the black people went to the same churches. All the college graduates came home for Christmas. You had to get up and make a little talk. Your folks wanted to show you off.

You had an inspiration to go to college. But now your inspiration is to become, maybe, a hell of a basketball player because you heard about Cazzie Russell makin' it with the pros. You might want to become an O.J. Simpson because you see him on television. You might want to become a big-time singer 'cause you know Curtis Mayfield lived near the el tracks. But if you can't cut these things, where is your inspiration coming from? A lot of things have contributed to the death of inspiration, outside of race. You got a lot of white people who can't live without an excess of alcohol to keep 'em going because they feel imprisoned, too.

The city is not heaven any more. It is more of a refuge. It is not a city of hope. The whites are victims, too. They have no power. Being white has not paid off for them, but it's the only thing they've got. We have to work out a strategy to give ordinary people power. We've been bullshitting ourselves. We always were every man for himself, while we talked idealism. There must be a new way of thinking.

C. P. ELLIS

We're in his office in Durham, North Carolina. He is the business manager of the International Union of Operating Engineers. On the wall is a plaque: "Certificate of Service, in recognition to C. P. Ellis, for your faithful service to the city in having served as a member of the Durham Human Relations Council. February 1977."

At one time, he had been president (exalted cyclops) of the Durham chapter of the Ku Klux Klan...

He is fifty-three years old.

My father worked in a textile mill in Durham. He died at forty-eight years old. It was probably from cotton dust. Back then, we never heard of brown lung. I was about seventeen years old and had a mother and sister depending on somebody to make a livin'. It was just barely enough insurance to cover his burial. I had to quit school and go to work. I was about eighth grade when I quit.

My father worked hard but never had enough money to buy decent clothes. When I went to school, I never seemed to have adequate clothes to wear. I always left school late afternoon with a sense of inferiority. The other kids had nice clothes, and I just had what Daddy could buy. I still got some of those inferiority feelin's now that I have to overcome once in a while.

I loved my father. He would go with me to ball games. We'd go fishin' together. I was really ashamed of the way he'd dress. He would take this money and give it to me instead of putting it on himself. I always had the feeling about somebody looking at him and makin' fun of him and makin' fun of me. I think it had to do somethin' with my life.

My father and I were very close, but we didn't talk about too many intimate things. He did have a drinking problem. During the week, he would work every day, but weekend he was ready to get plastered. I can understand when a guy looks at his paycheck and looks at his bills, and he's worried hard all the week, and his bills are larger than his paycheck. He'd done the best he could the entire week, and there seemed to be no hope. It's an illness thing. Finally you just say: "The heck with it. I'll just get drunk and forget it."

My father was out of work during the depression, and I remember going with him to the finance company uptown, and he was turned down. That's something that's always stuck.

My father never seemed to be happy. It was a constant struggle with him just like it was for me. It's very seldom I'd see him laugh. He was just tryin' to figure out what he could do from one day to the next.

After several years pumping gas at a service station, I got married. We had to have children. Four. One child was born blind and retarded, which was a real additional expense to us. He's never spoken a word. He doesn't know me when I go to see him. But I see him, I hug his neck. I talk to him, tell him I love him. I don't know whether he knows me or not, but I know he's well taken care of. All my life, I had work, never a day without work, worked all the overtime I could get and still could not survive financially. I began to say there's somethin' wrong with this country. I worked my butt off and just never seemed to break even.

I had some real great ideas about this great nation. [Laughs.] They say to abide by the law, go to church, do right and live for the Lord, and everything'll work out. But it didn't work out. It just kept gettin' worse and worse.

I was workin' a bread route. The highest I made one week was seventy-five dollars. The rent on our house was about twelve dollars a week. I will never forget: outside of this house was a 265-gallon oil drum, and I never did get enough money to fill up that oil drum. What I would do every night, I would run up to the store and buy five gallons of oil and climb up the ladder and pour it in that 265-gallon drum. I could hear that five gallons when it hits the bottom of that oil drum, splatters, and it sounds like it's nothin' in there. But it would keep the house warm for the night. Next day you'd have to do the same thing.

I left the bread route with fifty dollars in my pocket. I went to the bank and I borrowed four thousand dollars to buy the service station. I worked seven days a week, open and close, and finally had a heart attack. Just about two months before the last payments of that loan. My wife had done the best she could to keep it runnin'. Tryin' to come out of that hole, I just couldn't do it.

I really began to get bitter. I didn't know who to blame. I tried to find somebody. I began to blame it on black people. I had to hate somebody. Hatin' America is hard to do because you can't see it to hate it. You gotta have somethin' to look at to hate. [Laughs.] The natural person for me to hate would be black people, because my father before me was a member of the Klan. As far as he was concerned, it was the savior of the white people. It was the only organization in the world that would take care of the white people. So I began to admire the Klan.

I got active in the Klan while I was at the service station. Every Monday night, a group of men would come by and buy a Coca-Cola, go back to the car, take a few drinks, and come back and stand around talkin'. I couldn't help but wonder: Why are these dudes comin' out every Monday? They said they were with the Klan and have meetings close-by. Would I be interested? Boy, that was an opportunity I really looked forward to! To be part of somethin'. I joined the Klan, went from member to chaplain, from chaplain to vice-president, from vice-president to president. The title is exalted cyclops.

The first night I went with the fellas, they knocked on the door and gave the signal. They sent some robed Klansmen to talk to me and give me some instructions. I was led into a large meeting room, and this was the time of my life. It was thrilling. Here's a guy who's worked all his life and struggled all his life to be something, and here's the moment to be something. I will never forget it. Four robed Klansmen led me into the hall. The lights were dim, and the only thing you could see was an illuminated cross. I knelt before the cross. I had to make certain vows and promises. We promised to uphold the purity of the white race, fight communism, and protect white womanhood.

After I had taken my oath, there was loud applause goin' throughout the buildin', musta been at least four hundred people. For this one little ol' person. It was a thrilling moment for C. P. Ellis.

It disturbs me when people who do not really know what it's all about are so very critical of individual Klansmen. The majority of 'em are low-income whites, people who really don't have a part in something. They have been shut out as well as the blacks. Some are not very well educated either. Just like myself. We had a lot of support from doctors and lawyers and police officers.

Maybe they've had bitter experiences in this life and they had to hate somebody. So the natural person to hate would be the black person. He's beginnin' to come up, he's beginnin' to learn to read and start votin' and run for political office. Here are white people who are supposed to be superior to them, and we're shut out.

I can understand why people join extreme right-wing or left-wing groups. They're in the same boat I was. Shut out. Deep down inside, we want to be part of this great society. Nobody listens, so we join these groups.

At one time, I was state organizer of the National Rights party. I organized a youth group for the Klan. I felt we were getting old and our generation's gonna die. So I contacted certain kids in schools. They were havin' racial problems. On the first night, we had a hundred high school students. When they came in the door, we had "Dixie" playin'. These kids were just thrilled to death. I begin to hold weekly meetin's with 'em, teachin' the principles of the Klan. At that time, I believed Martin Luther King had Communist connections. I began to teach that Andy Young was affiliated with the Communist party.

I had a call one night from one of our kids. He was about twelve. He said: "I just been robbed downtown by two niggers." I'd had a couple of drinks and that really teed me off. I go downtown and couldn't find the kid. I got worried. I saw two young black people. I had the .32 revolver with me. I said: "Nigger, you seen a little young white boy up here? I just got a call from him and was told that some niggers robbed him of fifteen cents." I pulled my pistol out and put it right at his head. I said: "I've always wanted to kill a nigger and I think I'll make you the first one." I nearly scared the kid to death, and he struck off.

This was the time when the civil rights movement was really

beginnin' to peak. The blacks were beginnin' to demonstrate and picket downtown stores. I never will forget some black lady I hated with a purple passion. Ann Atwater. Every time I'd go downtown, she'd be leadin' a boycott. How I hated—pardon the expression, I don't use it much now—how I just hated that black nigger. [Laughs.] Big, fat, heavy woman. She'd pull about eight demonstrations, and first thing you know they had two, three blacks at the checkout counter. Her and I have had some pretty close confrontations.

I felt very big, yeah. [Laughs.] We're more or less a secret organization. We didn't want anybody to know who we were, and I began to do some thinkin'. What am I hidin' for? I've never been convicted of anything in my life. I don't have any court record. What am I, C. P. Ellis, as a citizen and a member of the United Klansmen of America? Why can't I go the city council meeting and say: "This is the way we feel about the matter? We don't want you to purchase mobile units to set in our schoolyards. We don't want niggers in our schools."

We began to come out in the open. We would go to the meetings, and the blacks would be there and we'd be there. It was a confrontation every time. I didn't hold back anything. We began to make some inroads with the city councilmen and county commissioners. They began to call us friend. Call us at night on the telephone: "C. P., glad you came to that meeting last night." They didn't want integration either, but they did it secretively, in order to get elected. They couldn't stand up openly and say it, but they were glad somebody was sayin' it. We visited some of the city leaders in their home and talk to 'em privately. It wasn't long before councilmen would call me up: "The blacks are comin' up tonight and makin' outrageous demands. How about some of you people showin' up and have a little balance?" I'd get on the telephone: "The niggers is comin' to the council meeting tonight. Persons in the city's called me and asked us to be there."

We'd load up our cars and we'd fill up half the council chambers, and the blacks the other half. During these times, I carried weapons to the meetings, outside my belt. We'd go there armed. We would wind up just hollerin' and fussin' at each other. What happened? As a result of our fightin' one another, the city council still had their way. They didn't want to give up control to the blacks nor the Klan. They were usin' us.

I began to realize this later down the road. One day I was walkin' downtown and a certain city council member saw me comin'. I expected him to shake my hand because he was talkin' to me at night on the telephone. I had been in his home and visited with him. He crossed the street. Oh shit, I began to think, somethin's wrong here. Most of 'em are merchants or maybe an attorney, an insurance agent, people like that. As long as they kept low-income whites and low-income blacks fightin', they're gonna maintain control.

I began to get that feeling after I was ignored in public. I thought: Bullshit, you're not gonna use me any more. That's when I began to do some real serious thinkin'.

The same thing is happening in this country today. People are being used by those in control, those who have all the wealth. I'm not espousing communism. We got the greatest system of government in the world. But those who have it simply don't want those who don't have it to have any part of it. Black and white. When it comes to money, the green, the other colors make no difference. [Laughs.]

I spent a lot of sleepless nights. I still didn't like blacks. I didn't want to associate with 'em. Blacks, Jews, or Catholics. My father said: "Don't have anything to do with 'em." I didn't until I met a black person and talked with him, eyeball to eyeball, and met a Jewish person and talked to him, eyeball to eyeball. I found out they're people just like me. They cried, they cussed, they prayed, they had desires. Just like myself. Thank God, I got to the point where I can look past labels. But at that time, my mind was closed.

I remember one Monday night Klan meeting. I said something

was wrong. Our city fathers were using us. And I didn't like to be used. The reactions of the others was not too pleasant: "Let's just keep fightin' them niggers."

I'd go home at night and I'd have to wrestle with myself. I'd look at a black person walkin' down the street, and the guy'd have ragged shoes or his clothes would be worn. That began to do somethin' to me inside. I went through this for about six months. I felt I just had to get out of the Klan. But I wouldn't get out.

Then something happened. The state AFL-CIO received a grant from the Department of HEW, a $78,000 grant: how to solve racial problems in the school system. I got a telephone call from the president of the state AFL-CIO. "We'd like to get some people together from all walks of life." I said: "All walks of life? Who you talkin' about?" He said: "Blacks, whites, liberals, conservatives, Klansmen, NAACP people."

I said: "No way am I comin' with all those niggers. I'm not gonna be associated with those type of people." A White Citizens Council guy said: "Let's go up there and see what's goin' on. It's tax money bein' spent." I walk in the door, and there was a large number of blacks and white liberals. I knew most of 'em by face 'cause I seen 'em demonstratin' around town. Ann Atwater was there. [Laughs.] I just forced myself to go in and sit down.

The meeting was moderated by a great big black guy who was bushy-headed. [Laughs.] That turned me off. He acted very nice. He said: "I want you all to feel free to say anything you want to say." Some of the blacks stand up and say it's white racism. I took all I could take. I asked for the floor and I cut loose. I said: "No sir, it's black racism. If we didn't have niggers in the schools, we wouldn't have the problems we got today."

I will never forget. Howard Clements, a black guy, stood up. He said: "I'm certainly glad C. P. Ellis come because he's the most honest man here tonight." I said: "What's that nigger tryin' to do?" [Laughs.] At the end of that meeting, some blacks tried to come up shake my hand, but I wouldn't do it. I walked off.

Second night, same group was there. I felt a little more easy because I got some things off my chest. The third night, after they elected all the committees, they want to elect a chairman. Howard Clements stood up and said: "I suggest we elect two co-chairpersons." Joe Beckton, executive director of the Human Relations Commission, just as black as he can be, he nominated me. There was a reaction from some blacks. Nooo. And, of all things, they nominated Ann Atwater, that big old fat black gal that I had just hated with a purple passion, as co-chairman. I thought to myself: Hey, ain't no way I can work with that gal. Finally, I agreed to accept it, 'cause at this point, I was tired of fightin', either for survival or against black people or against Jews or against Catholics.

A Klansman and a militant black woman, co-chairmen of the school committee. It was impossible. How could I work with her? But after about two or three days, it was in our hands. We had to make it a success. This give me another sense of belongin', a sense of pride. This helped this inferiority feelin' I had. A man who has stood up publicly and said he despised black people, all of a sudden he was willin' to work with 'em. Here's a chance for a low-income white man to be somethin'. In spite of all my hatred for blacks and Jews and liberals, I accepted the job. Her and I began to reluctantly work together. [Laughs.] She had as many problems workin' with me as I had workin' with her.

One night, I called her: "Ann, you and I should have a lot of differences and we got 'em now. But there's somethin' laid out here before us, and if it's gonna be a success, you and I are gonna have to make it one. Can we lay aside some of these feelin's?" She said: "I'm willing if you are." I said: "Let's do it."

My old friends would call me at night: "C. P., what the hell is wrong with you? You're sellin' out the white race." This begin to make me have guilt feelin's. Am I doin' right? Am I doin' wrong? Here I am all of a sudden makin' an about-face and tryin' to deal with my feelin's, my heart. My mind was beginnin' to open up. I was beginnin' to see what was right and what was wrong. I don't want the kids to fight forever.

We were gonna go ten nights. By this time, I had went to work at Duke University, in maintenance. Makin' very little money. Terry Sanford give me this ten days off with pay. He was president of Duke at the time. He knew I was a Klansman and realized the importance of blacks and whites getting along.

I said: "If we're gonna make this thing a success, I've got to get to my kind of people." The low-income whites. We walked the streets of Durham, and we knocked on doors and invited people. Ann was goin' into the black community. They just wasn't respondin' to us when we made these house calls. Some of 'em were cussin' us out. "You're sellin' us out, Ellis, get out of my door. I don't want to talk to you." Ann was gettin' the same response from blacks: "What are you doin' messin' with that Klansman?"

One day, Ann and I went back to the school and we sat down. We began to talk and just reflect. Ann said: "My daughter came home cryin' every day. She said her teacher was makin' fun of me in front of the other kids." I said: "Boy, the same thing happened to my kid. White liberal teacher was makin' fun of Tim Ellis's father, the Klansman. In front of other peoples. He came home cryin'." At this point—[he pauses, swallows hard, stifles a sob]—I begin to see, here we are, two people from the far ends of the fence, havin' identical problems, except hers bein' black and me bein' white. From that moment on, I tell ya, that gal and I worked together good. I begin to love the girl, really. [He weeps.]

The amazing thing about it, her and I, up to that point, had cussed each other, bawled each other, we hated each other. Up to that point, we didn't know each other. We didn't know we had things in common.

We worked at it, with the people who came to these meetings. They talked about racism, sex education, about teachers not bein' qualified. After seven, eight nights of real intense discussion, these people, who'd never talked to each other before, all of a sudden came up with resolutions. It was really somethin', you had to be there to get the tone and feelin' of it.

At that point, I didn't like integration, but the law says you do this and I've got to do what the law says, okay? We said: "Let's take these resolutions to the school board." The most disheartening thing I've ever faced was the school system refused to implement any one of these resolutions. These were recommendations from the people who pay taxes and pay their salaries. [Laughs.]

I thought they were good answers. Some of 'em I didn't agree with, but I been in this thing from the beginning, and whatever comes of it, I'm gonna support it. Okay, since the school board refused, I decided I'd just run for the school board.

I spent eighty-five dollars on the campaign. The guy runnin' against me spent several thousand. I really had nobody on my side. The Klan turned against me. The low-income whites turned against me. The liberals didn't particularly like me. The blacks were suspicious of me. The blacks wanted to support me, but they couldn't muster up enough to support a Klansman on the school board. [Laughs.] But I made up my mind that what I was doin' was right, and I was gonna do it regardless what anybody said.

It bothered me when people would call and worry my wife. She's always supported me in anything I wanted to do. She was changing, and my boys were too. I got some of my youth corps kids involved. They still followed me.

I was invited to the Democratic women's social hour as a candidate. Didn't have but one suit to my name. Had it six, seven, eight years. I had it cleaned, put on the best shirt I had and a tie. Here were all this high-class wealthy candidates shakin' hands. I walked up to the mayor and stuck out my hand. He give me that hand-shake with that rag type of hand. He said: "C. P., I'm glad to see you." But I could tell by his handshake he was lyin' to me. This was botherin' me. I know I'm a low-income person. I know I'm not wealthy. I know they were sayin': "What's this little ol' dude runnin' for school board?" Yet they had to smile and make like they're glad to see me. I begin to spot some black people in that room. I automatically went to 'em and that was a firm handshake. They said: "I'm glad to see you, C. P." I knew they meant it—you can tell about a handshake.

Every place I appeared, I said I will listen to the voice of the people. I will not make a major decision until I first contacted all the organizations in the city. I got 4,640 votes. The guy beat me by two thousand. Not bad for eighty-five bucks and no constituency.

The whole world was openin' up, and I was learnin' new truths that I had never learned before. I was beginnin' to look at a black person, shake hands with him, and see him as a human bein'. I hadn't got rid of all this stuff. I've still got a little bit of it. But somethin' was happenin' to me.

It was almost like bein' born again. It was a new life. I didn't have these sleepless nights I used to have when I was active in the Klan and slippin' around at night. I could sleep at night and feel good about it. I'd rather live now than at any other time in history. It's a challenge.

Back at Duke, doin' maintenance, I'd pick up my tools, fix the commode, unstop the drains. But this got in my blood. Things weren't right in this country, and what we done in Durham needs to be told. I was so miserable at Duke, I could hardly stand it. I'd go to work every morning just hatin' to go.

My whole life had changed. I got an eighth-grade education, and I wanted to complete high school. Went to high school in the afternoons on a program called PEP—Past Employment Progress. I was about the only white in class, and the oldest. I begin to read about biology. I'd take my books home at night, 'cause I was determined to get through. Sure enough, I graduated. I got the diploma at home.

I come to work one mornin' and some guy says: "We need a union." At this time I wasn't pro-union. My daddy was anti-labor, too. We're not gettin' paid much, we're havin' to work seven days in a row. We're all starvin' to death. The next day, I meet the international representative of the Operating Engineers. He give me authorization cards. "Get these cards out and we'll have an election." There was eighty-eight for the union and seventeen no's. I was elected chief steward for the union.

Shortly after, a union man come down from Charlotte and says we need a full-time rep. We've got only two hundred people at the two plants here. It's just barely enough money comin' in to pay your salary. You'll have to get out and organize more people. I didn't know nothin about organizin' unions, but I knew how to organize people, stir people up. [Laughs.] That's how I got to be business agent for the union.

When I began to organize, I began to see far deeper. I began to see people again bein' used. Blacks against whites. I say this without any hesitancy: management is vicious. There's two things they want to keep: all the money and all the say-so. They don't want these poor workin' folks to have none of that. I begin to see management fightin' me with everything they had. Hire anti-union law firms badmouth unions. The people were makin' a dollar ninety-five an hour, barely able to get through weekends. I worked as a business rep for five years and was seein' all this.

Last year, I ran for business manager of the union. He's elected by the workers. The guy that ran against me was black, and our membership is seventy-five percent black. I thought: Claiborne, there's no way you can beat that black guy. People know your background. Even though you've made tremendous strides, those black people are not gonna vote for you. You know how much I beat him? Four to one. [Laughs.]

The company used my past against me. They put out letters with a picture of a robe and a cap: Would you vote for a Klansman?

They wouldn't deal with the issues. I immediately called for a mass meeting. I met with the ladies at an electric component plant. I said: "Okay, this is Claiborne Ellis. This is where I come from. I want you to know right now, you black ladies here, I was at one time a member of the Klan. I want you to know, because they'll tell you about it."

I invited some of my old black friends. I said: "Brother Joe, Brother Howard, be honest now and tell these people how you feel about me." They done it. [Laughs.] Howard Clements kidded me a little bit. He said: "I don't know what I'm doin' here, supportin' an ex-Klansman." [Laughs.] He said: "I know what C. P. Ellis come from. I knew him when he was. I knew him as he grew, and growed with him. I'm tellin' you now: follow, follow this Klansman." [He pauses, swallows hard.] "Any questions?" "No," the black ladies said. "Let's get on with the meeting, we need Ellis." [He laughs and weeps.] Boy, black people sayin' that about me. I won one thirty-four to forty-one. Four to one.

It makes you feel good to go into a plant and butt heads with professional union busters. You see black people and white people join hands to defeat the racist issues they use against people. They're tryin' the same things with the Klan. It's still happenin' today. Can you imagine a guy who's got an adult high school diploma runnin' into professional college graduates who are union busters? I gotta compete with 'em. I work seven days a week, nights and on Saturday and Sunday. The salary's not that great, and if I didn't care, I'd quit. But I care and I can't quit. I got a taste of it. [Laughs.]

I tell people there's a tremendous possibility in this country to stop wars, the battles, the struggles, the fights between people. People say: "That's an impossible dream. You sound like Martin Luther King." An ex-Klansman who sounds like Martin Luther King. [Laughs.] I don't think it's an impossible dream. It's happened in my life. It's happened in other people's lives in America.

I don't know what's ahead of me. I have no desire to be a big union official. I want to be right out here in the field with the workers. I want to walk through their factory and shake hands with that man whose hands are dirty. I'm gonna do all that one little ol' man can do. I'm fifty-two years old, and I ain't got many years left, but I want to make the best of 'em.

When the news came over the radio that Martin Luther King was assassinated, I got on the telephone and begin to call other Klansmen. We just had a real party at the service station. Really rejoicin' 'cause that son of a bitch was dead. Our troubles are over with. They say the older you get, the harder it is for you to change. That's not necessarily true. Since I changed, I've set down and listened to tapes of Martin Luther King. I listen to it and tears come to my eyes 'cause I know what he's sayin' now. I know what's happenin'.

POSTSCRIPT

The phone rings. A conversation.

"This was a black guy who's director of Operation Breakthrough in Durham. I had called his office. I'm interested in employin' some young black person who's interested in learnin' the labor movement. I want somebody who's never had an opportunity, just like myself. Just so he can read and write, that's all."

LEONEL I. CASTILLO

Former director of the United States Immigration and Naturaliza-
tion Service (INS).

"My father's father came from Mexico to Victoria, Texas, in 1880.
He paid a toston, *a half-dollar. That automatically made him a*
U.S. citizen. In the early years of the century, he was fighting for the
right to bury Mexicans in the same grounds as Anglos. There was no
place to bury Mexicans. He finally got a piece of land from some
German Lutherans. It was deeded to our family and the Mexican
community in perpetuity. My grandfather and his friends cleared
the land for the first funerals. We've kept the records since 1898. We
have many, many people buried there."

New immigrants are trying all over again to integrate themselves
into the system. They have the same hunger. On any given day,
there are about three million throughout the world who are apply-
ing to come to the United States and share the American Dream.
The same battles. I still read old newspaper clips: 1886. Housemaid
wanted. We'll accept any person, any color, any nationality, any religion, except Irish. [Laughs.] Rough ads: No Irish need apply.

Most of the undocumented here without papers, without legal
permission, think they're gonna go back home in six months. Relatively few go back. Some old Italians are going back to *pensionares,*
and some old Eastern Europeans are going back home. But, by and
large, immigrants, old and new, stay. They don't feel they know
anyone in the old village. Their children don't speak Polish or Italian
or Greek. Their children are used to air conditioning, McDonald's.

The Vietnamese boat people express it as well as anyone. They
don't know if they're gonna land, if the boat's gonna sink. They
don't know what's gonna happen to 'em, but they've a hunch they
might make it to the U.S. as the "freedom place."

There is the plain hard fact of hunger. In order to eat, a person will endure tremendous hardship. Mexican people who come here usually are not the most destitute. Someone who's too poor can't afford the trip. You've got to buy *coyotes*. A *coyote* is a smuggler of people. He's also called a *pollero*. *Pollo* is chicken. He's the one who guides chickens through the border.

Sometimes the whole family saves up and gives the bright young man or the bright young woman the family savings. It even goes in hock for a year or two. They pin all their hopes on this one kid, put him on a bus, let him go a thousand miles. He doesn't speak a word of English. He's only seventeen, eighteen years old, but he's gonna save that family. A lot rides on that kid who's a busboy in some hotel.

We've had some as young as eleven who have come a thousand miles. You have this young kid, all his family savings, everything is on him. There are a lot of songs and stories about mother and child, the son leaving who may never return. We end up deporting him. It's heartrending.

He's the bright kid in the family. The slow one might not make it, might get killed. The one who's sickly can't make the trip. He couldn't walk through the desert. He's not gonna be too old, too young, too destitute, or too slow. He's the brightest and the best.

He's gonna be the first hook, the first pioneer coming into an alien society, the United States. He might be here in Chicago. He works as a busboy all night long. They pay him minimum or less, and work him hard. He'll never complain. He might even thank his boss. He'll say as little as possible because he doesn't want anyone to know what his status is. He will often live in his apartment, except for the time he goes to work or to church or to a dance. He will stay in and watch TV. If he makes a hundred a week, he will manage to send back twenty-five. All over the country, if you go to a Western Union office on the weekend, you'll find a lot of people there sending money orders. In a southwest office, like Dallas, Western Union will tell you seventy-five percent of their business is money orders to Mexico.

After the kid learns a bit, because he's healthy and young and energetic, he'll probably get another job as a busboy. He'll work at another place as soon as the shift is over. He'll try to work his way up to be a waiter. He'll work incredible hours. He doesn't care about union scale, he doesn't care about conditions, about humiliations. He accepts all this as his fate.

He's burning underneath with this energy and ambition. He outworks the U.S. busboys and eventually becomes the waiter. Where he can maneuver, he tries to become the owner and gives a lot of competition to the locals. Restaurant owners tell me, if they have a choice, they'll always hire foreign nationals first. They're so eager and grateful. There's a little greed here, too. [Laughs.] They pay 'em so little.

We've got horrible cases of exploitation. In San Diego and in Arizona, we discovered people who live in holes in the ground, live under trees, no sanitation, no housing, nothing. A lot of them live in chicken coops.

They suffer from *coyotes,* too, who exploit them and sometimes beat 'em. *Coyotes* advertise. If the immigrant arrives in San Diego, the word is very quick: where to go and who's looking. He'll even be approached. If he's got a lot of money, the *coyote* will manage to bring him from Tijuana all the way to Chicago and guarantee him a job. He'll get all the papers: Social Security, birth certificate, driver's license. The *coyote* reads the papers and finds which U.S. citizens have died and gets copies of all their vital statistics. In effect, the immigrant carries the identity of a dead person.

Often the employer says he doesn't know anything about it. He plays hands off. He makes his bucks hiring cheap labor. The *coyote* makes his off the workers.

Coyotes come from the border with these pickup trucks full of people. They may put twenty in a truck. They bring 'em in all sorts of bad weather, when they're less likely to be stopped. They might be going twenty, twenty-eight hours, with one or two pit stops.

They don't let the people out. There's no urinal, no bathroom. They sit or they stand there in this little cramped space for the whole trip.

A truck broke down outside Chicago. It was a snowstorm. The driver left. People were frostbitten, lost their toes. In Laredo, the truck was in an accident. Everybody ran off because the police were coming. The truck caught fire. No one remembered the two fellows in the trunk. It was locked and no keys. Of course, they burned to death. The border patrol found thirty-three people dying in the deserts of Arizona. They were saved at the last minute and deported. I'll bet you a dollar every one of them, as soon as they are well enough, will try again.

At least a quarter of a million apprehensions were made last year. If we apprehend them at the border, we turn 'em around and ask them to depart voluntarily. They turn around and go back to Mexico. A few hours later, they try again. In El Paso, we deported one fellow six times in one day. There's a restaurant in Hollywood run by a fellow we deported thirty-seven times. We've deported some people more than a hundred times. They always want to come back. There's a job and there's desperation.

In World War Two, we recruited Mexicans to work here. As soon as the war ended and our young men came back, we deported them. In 1954, the deportation problem was so big that the general in charge of immigration ordered Operation Wetback. That one year, we had a million apprehensions. It was similar to what we did during the depression. We rounded everybody up, put 'em on buses, and sent them back to Mexico. Sometimes they were people who merely looked Mexican. The violations of civil liberties were terrible.

Half the people here without papers are not Mexicans. They're from all over the world. They came legally, with papers, as tourists ten years ago. They're much harder to deal with. We're discussing a program that would allow people to have permanent residence, who have been here seven years or more, have not broken any laws, have paid taxes and not been on welfare. You can't be here and become a public charge. All too often, the public gets the impression that all immigrants are on welfare. It's the exact opposite. Very few go on welfare.

A lot of people who are humanitarian, who believe they should be hospitable toward the stranger, are very restrictive when it comes to their jobs. [Laughs.] We've had protests from *mariachis* and soccer players. The *mariachis* are upset because the Mexicans were coming in and playing for less. The manager of soccer teams would rather hire the foreign nationals because often they're better players.

We get people coming in from Haiti, the poorest country in the western hemisphere. They come over by boat and land in Florida. The Floridians raised hell about this. I've even had Cuban-Americans tell me that Haitians were going to destroy their culture. There's a weird pecking order now.

We make three thousand apprehensions at the border every weekend. It's just a little fourteen-mile stretch. Our border patrol knows this little fellow comin' across is hungry. He just wants to work. They know he's no security threat. They say: "It's my job." Many of them come to have a great deal of respect for the people they're deporting. What do you think of a person you deport three, four times, who just keeps coming back? You would never want to get in the same ring with that person.

I'm torn. I saw it in the Peace Corps, when I was in the Philippines. A mother offered you her infant. You're just a twenty-one-year-old kid and she says: "Take my child, take him with you to the States." When you see this multiplied by thousands, it tears you up.

It's clear to me that the undocumented, even more than the immigrant, is a contributor to our society and to our standard of living. It's one of the few groups that has no parasites. They walk the tightrope and try not to fall off. If you're a citizen and you fall, we have a net that catches you: welfare, food stamps, unemployment, social services. If you're undocumented and fall off that tightrope, you can't go to any of the agencies because you may end up bein' deported. He can't draw welfare, he can't use public services. He's not gonna call a policeman even when he's beat up. If he's in a street fight and somebody whips him bad, assaults him, robs him, rapes her there's no complaint. In Baltimore, an employer raped two girls. The person who complained wouldn't give us the names of the victims because she was afraid we'd deport 'em. We end up in this country with enormous abuse against four million people.

The only thing that helps me is remembering the history of this country. We've always managed, despite our worst, unbelievably nativist actions to rejuvenate ourselves, to bring in new people. Every new group comes in believing more firmly in the American Dream than the one that came a few years before. Every new group is scared of being in the welfare line or in the unemployment office. They go to night school, they learn about America. We'd be lost without them.

The old dream is still dreamt. The old neighborhood Ma-Pa stores are still around. They are not Italian or Jewish or Eastern European anymore. Ma and Pa are now Korean, Vietnamese, Iraqi, Jordanian, Latin American. They live in the store. They work seven days a week. Their kids are doing well in school. They're making it. Sound familiar?

Near our office in Los Angeles is a little café with a sign: KOSHER BURRITOS. [Laughs.] A *burrito* is a Mexican tortilla with meat inside. Most of the customers are black. The owner is Korean. [Laughs.] The banker, I imagine, is WASP. [Laughs.] This is what's happening in the United States today. It is not a melting pot, but in one way or another, there is a melding of cultures.

I see all kinds of new immigrants starting out all over again, trying to work their way into the system. They're going through new battles, yet they're old battles. They want to share in the American Dream. The stream never ends.

Hard Times:
An Oral History of the Great Depression
(1970)

INTRODUCTION: A PERSONAL MEMOIR
(AND PARENTHETICAL COMMENT)

This is a memory book, rather than one of hard fact and precise statistic. In recalling an epoch, some thirty, forty, years ago, my colleagues experienced pain, in some instances; exhilaration, in others. Often it was a fusing of both. A hesitancy, at first, was followed by a flow of memories: long-ago hurts and small triumphs. Honors and humiliations. There was laughter, too.

Are they telling the truth? The question is as academic as the day Pilate asked it, his philosophy not quite washing out his guilt. It's the question Pa Joad asked of Preacher Casy, when the ragged man, in a transient camp, poured out his California agony.

"Pa said, 'S'pose he's tellin' the truth—that fella?' The preacher answered. 'He's tellin' the truth, awright. The truth for him. He wasn't makin' nothin' up.' 'How about us?' Tom demanded. 'Is that the truth for us?' 'I don' know,' said Casy."*

I suspect the preacher spoke for the people in this book, too. In their rememberings are their truths. The precise fact or the precise date is of small consequence. This is not a lawyer's brief nor an annotated sociological treatise. It is simply an attempt to get the story of the holocaust known as The Great Depression from an improvised battalion of survivors.

---

* John Steinbeck, *The Grapes of Wrath* (New York, Viking Press, 1939), p. 261.

That there are some who were untouched or, indeed, did rather well isn't exactly news. This has been true of all disasters. The great many were wounded, in one manner or another. It left upon them an "invisible scar," as Caroline Bird put it.*

There are young people in this book, too. They did not experience the Great Depression. In many instances, they are bewildered, wholly ignorant of it. It is no sign of their immaturity, but of ours. It's time they knew. And it's time we knew, too—what it did to us. And, thus, to them.

I myself don't remember the bleak October day, 1929. Nor do I recall with anything like a camera eye the events that shaped the thirties. Rather, a blur of images comes to mind. Faces, voices and, occasionally, a rueful remembrance or a delightful flash. Or the astonishing innocence of a time past. Yet a feeling persists....

Even now, when on the highway, seeing in faint neon, VACANCY, outside a modest motel, I am reminded of my mother's enterprise, The Wells-Grand. I ask myself, with unreasonable anxiety, perhaps, "Will it survive? Will this place be here next year?"

Fear of losing things, of property, is one legacy of the thirties, as a young colleague pointed out. An elderly civil servant in Washington buys a piece of land as often as she can afford. "If it comes again, I'll have something to live off." She remembers the rotten bananas, near the wharves of New Orleans: her daily fare.

That, thanks to technology, things today can make things, in abundance, is a point psychically difficult for Depression survivors to understand. And thus, in severe cases, they will fight, even kill, to protect their things (read: property). Many of the young fail to diagnose this illness because of their innocence concerning the Great Depression. Its occasional invocation, for scolding purposes, tells them little of its truth.

In the mid-twenties, all fifty rooms of The Wells-Grand were

---

* Caroline Bird, *The Invisible Scar* (New York, David McKay Co., 1965).

occupied. There was often a waiting list. Our guests were men of varied skills and some sense of permanence. The only transients were the wayward couple who couldn't afford a more de luxe rendezvous. Mysteriously, there was always room at the inn, even for sinners. Ours were the winking Gospels.

On Saturdays, most of our guests paid their weekly rent. On those evenings, I walked at a certain pace to the deposit window of the neighborhood bank. All the guests, with the exception of a few retired boomers and an ancient coppersmith (made idle by the Volstead Act), had steady jobs. It was a euphoric time.

The weekly magazines, *Judge* and *Life* (pre-Luce), were exciting with George Jean Nathan and Pare Lorentz critiques and Jefferson Machamer girls. *Liberty* carried sports pieces by Westbrook Pegler—the most memorable, a tribute to Battling Siki, the childlike, noble savage destroyed by civilization. *Literary Digest* was still around and solvent, having not yet forecast Alf Landon's triumph some years later. On the high school debating team, we resolved that the United States should or should not grant independence to the Philippines, should or should not join the World Court, should or should not recognize the Soviet Union. We took either side. It was a casual time.

Perhaps it was the best of times. Or was it the worst? Scott Nearing inveighed against dollar diplomacy. Bob La Follette and George Norris took to the hustings as well as the Senate floor in Horatio-like stands against the Big Money. Yet two faces appear and reappear in my mind's eye: Vice Presidents Charles G. Dawes and Charles Curtis; the first, of the responsible banker's jaw, clamped determinedly to an underslung pipe; the other, a genial ex-jockey, of the Throttlebottom look. There was an innocence, perhaps. But it was not quite Eden's.

As for the Crash itself, there is nothing I personally remember, other than the gradual, at first, hardly noticeable, diminishing in the roster of our guests. It was as though they were carted away, unprotesting and unseen, unlike Edward Albee's grandma. At the entrance, we posted a placard: VACANCY.

The presence of our remaining guests was felt more and more, daily, in the lobby. Hitherto, we had seen them only evenings and on weekends. The decks of cards were wearing out more quickly. The black and red squares of the checkerboard were becoming indistinguishable. Cribbage pegs were being more frequently lost.... Tempers were getting shorter. Sudden fights broke out for seemingly unaccountable reasons.

The suddenly-idle hands blamed themselves, rather than society. True, there were hunger marches and protestations to City Hall and Washington, but the millions experienced a private kind of shame when the pink slip came. No matter that others suffered the same fate, the inner voice whispered, "I'm a failure."

True, there was a sharing among many of the dispossessed, but, at close quarters, frustration became, at times, violence, and violence turned inward. Thus sons and fathers fell away, one from the other. And the mother, seeking work, said nothing. Outside forces, except to the more articulate and political rebels, were in some vague way responsible, but not really. It was a personal guilt.

We were carrying the regulars on the books, but the fate of others was daily debated as my mother, my brother and I scanned the more and more indecipherable ledger. At times, the issue was joined, with a great deal of heat, as my brother and I sought to convince our mother that somehow we and our guests shall overcome. In reply, her finger pointed to the undeniable scrawl: the debts were mounting.

With more frequency, we visited our landlord. (We had signed a long-term lease in happier days.) He was a turn-of-the-century man, who had no telephone and signed all his documents longhand. His was a bold and flowing penmanship. There was no mistaking the terms. His adjustments, in view of this strange turn of events, were eminently fair. A man of absolute certainties, who had voted the straight ticket from McKinley to Hoover, he seemed more at sea than I had imagined possible. I was astonished by his sudden fumbling, his bewilderment.

A highly respected Wall Street financier recalled: "The Street had general confusion. They didn't understand it any more than anybody else. *They thought something would be announced.*" (My emphasis.) In 1930, Andrew Mellon, Secretary of Treasury, predicted, "...during the coming year the country will make steady progress." A speculator remembers, with awe, "Men like Pierpont Morgan and John Rockefeller lost immense amounts of money. Nobody was immune."

Carey McWilliams suggests a study of the Washington hearings dealing with the cause of the Depression: "They make the finest comic reading. The leading industrialists and bankers testified. They hadn't the foggiest notion...."

As for our guests, who now half-occupied the hotel, many proferred relief checks as rent rather than the accustomed cash. It was no longer a high-spirited Saturday night moment.

There was less talk of the girls in the Orleans street cribs and a marked increase in daily drinking. There was, interestingly enough, an upswing in playing the horses: half dollar bets, six bits; a more desperate examination of *The Racing Form. Bert E. Collyer's Eye,* and a scratch sheet, passed from hand to hand. While lost blacks played the numbers, lost whites played the nags.

Of my three years at the University of Chicago Law School, little need be said. I remember hardly anything, other than the presence of one black in my class, an African prince, whose land was a British—or was it a French?—possession. Only one case do I remember: it concerned statutory rape. The fault lay not in the professors, who were good and learned men, but in my studied somnolence. Why, I don't know. Even to this day. Was it a feeling, without my being aware, at the time, of the irrelevance of standard procedure to the circumstances of the day? Or is this a rationalization, ex post facto, of a lazy student? It was a hard case all around.

Yet those years, '31 to '34, at the University, did lead to an education of sorts. On my way from The Wells-Grand to the campus, I traveled through the Black Belt. Was it to escape Torts and Real Property that I sought out the blues? I don't know.

I do know that in those gallimaufry shops I discovered treasures: "race records," they were called by men with dollar signs for eyes. The artists, Big Bill, Memphis Minnie, Tampa Red, Big Maceo, among those I remember, informed me there was more to the stuff of life—and Battling Siki and Senegal, for that matter—than even Westbrook Pegler imagined. Or my professors.

Survival. The marrow of the black man's blues, then and now, has been poverty. Though the articulated theme, the lyric, is often woman, fickle or constant, or the prowess of John the Conqueror, its felt truth is his "lowdown" condition. "The Negro was born in depression," murmurs the elderly black. "If you can tell me the difference between the depression today and the Depression of 1932 for the black man, I'd like to know."

It accounts for the bite of his laughter, as he recalls those "hard times": "Why did these big wheels kill themselves? He couldn't stand bringing home beans to his woman, instead of steak and capon. It was a rarity to hear a Negro kill himself over money. There are so few who had any."

And yet, even during the Great Depression, when the white man was "lowdown," the black was below whatever that was. This hard fact was constantly sung around, about, under, and over in his blues.

> I'm just like Job's turkey,
> I can't do nothing but gobble,
> I'm so poor, baby,
> I have to lean against the fence to gabble.
> Yeah, now, baby, I believe I'll change town,
> Lord, I'm so low down, baby,
> I declare I'm looking up at down.

> The men in the mine, baby,
> They all looking down at me....
> —BIG BILL BROONZY

Here the images blur and time turns somersaults. It is the year of Repeal. A classmate and I appear at suddenly-legal taverns. A ritual, in the spirit of the day, comes into play: the house "pops" for every third beer.* It was so in all the taverns we visited. Today, it is a custom more honored in the breach than in the observance.

None I know was more rewarded by the triumph of the Wets than the coppersmith, old Heinicke. He had been the lobby elder, ill, hard of hearing, grown weary with life. Suddenly, his services were in desperate demand by any number of breweries. The shortage of skilled coppersmiths was in direct ratio to the unslaked thirst for beer.

As a result of the six-day week he was putting in, the unexpected harvest of money and, most significantly, the delight in his skills, he was transformed, Faustlike, into a younger man. His newly purchased, superheterodyne radio set, in a baroque cabinet that occupied half his room, was heard loud and clear in all fifty quarters. Ascribe it to his exhilaration as much as to his deafness.

As for the others, political argument, often bitter, often hilarious, replaced desuetude. Aside from F.D.R.'s fireside chats, on Sundays a new voice dominated the lobby. It was Father Charles E. Coughlin, coming through the box radio, high on a wooden pedestal. There were those who muttered, "Turn the Roman off." But it was Matthew McGraw, our gaunt, bespectacled, fiery-eyed night clerk (his resemblance to Father Coughlin was remarkable) who insisted the voice be heard.

Matt was something of an intellectual. Before the Crash, he had been a master carpenter. He was constantly quoting from books, weeklies, and monthly radical journals. He inveighed against the

---

* It was "on the house."

moneyed interests, against the privileged, against monopoly. He quoted Debs, Darrow, Paine.... Somewhere between October, 1929, and November, 1934 (when the Union for Social Justice was formed), something had happened to Matthew McGraw. A forgotten man, his cup of wormwood had flowed over.

A printer remembers his father swinging from Bob La Follette, Wisconsin's progressive Senator, to Father Coughlin. The hurt, frustrated man, hearing of the powerful, alien East, sought an answer. So did the gentle, soft-spoken salesman, who hardly questioned anything. "He has the right idea," his daughter remembers him saying of the priest from Royal Oak. The salesman had voted for Roosevelt.

It was 1936. Having long abandoned any thoughts of following the law, I joined the Illinois Writers' Project. I was a member of the radio division. We wrote scripts inspired by paintings at the Art Institute. They were broadcast over WGN, the Chicago *Tribune*'s station. Colonel McCormick, the publisher, was quite proud of these contributions to the city's culture. Though the front page of his paper invariably featured a cartoon of a loony, subversive professor in cap and gown, or a WPA boondoggler leaning on his shovel, he saw no inconsistency in programming the Great Artists series, with credits: "...under the auspices of the Works Progress Administration, Harry Hopkins, Director." I am told he listened to them regularly, with a great deal of pleasure.

By chance, I became a gangster in radio soap operas, among them, "Ma Perkins," "Betty and Bob" and "First Nighter." The jobs were fairly frequent, but tenure was lacking. Cause of dismissal: Electrocution, life imprisonment, or being shot to death.

As the fervor of unionism spread, with an assist by the Wagner Act, the American Federation of Radio Artists was formed. There was hardly any dissent among the performers. There were, of course, obstinate executives, who played Canute, but the waves rolled over them. The climate, in this instance, was salubrious.

Not so, with other professional unions. The Newspaper Guild, for example. Perhaps my most vivid single memory—certainly my most traumatic—of the Thirties, with which I bring these impressions to a close, concerns this battle in Chicago. The Hearst morning newspaper, the *Herald-Examiner*, was suffering a long and critical strike. Outside the building, journalists picketed. The Hearst delivery trucks were manned by a hard lot; some I remembered as alumni of my high school; some with syndicate friendships. They were employed in a dual capacity: as delivery men and as terrorists. Whenever the situation presented itself, they'd slug a journalist-picket.

I see a tableau: a pale, bloodied reporter lying on the pavement as colleagues and passersby stare in horror. In the middle of the street stands a squat heavyweight, an auto jack in his grasp. His arms and legs are spread-eagled. He appears to be challenging all comers. Yet, I see, quite unblurred, the terror in his eyes.

The rest is history, which I leave to those whose less-flawed memories and reflections comprise this book.

ED PAULSEN

From 1926 on, when he was fourteen, he knocked around and about the states—"I rode the freights" across the land. "I always went back to my home in South Dakota. My sister and her husband had a little farm. It was a retreat. I played semi-pro baseball up there at one time. You know who I faced? Satchell Paige. He was pitching for Bismarck. I worked punching cattle, $10 a month. I was never satisfied to stay there. I was always taking a pop at L.A. or San Francisco.

"Everybody talks of the Crash of '29. In small towns out West, we didn't know there was a Crash. What did the stock market mean to us? Not a dang thing. If you were in Cut Bank, Montana, who owned

stock? The farmer was a ping-pong ball in a very tough game.

"I finished high school in 1930, and I walked out into this thing...." He picked apples in Washington, "hustled sheets" in Los Angeles, and worked on road gangs all along the coast. "It got tougher. We didn't know how to make out in the city. It was terrifying. There were great queues of guys in soup lines. We didn't know how to join a soup line. We—my two brothers and I—didn't see ourselves that way. We had middle-class ideas without a middle-class income. [Laughs.]

"We ended up in San Francisco in 1931. I tried to get a job on the docks. I was a big husky athlete, but there just wasn't any work. Already by that time, if you were looking for a job at a Standard Oil Service Station, you had to have a college degree. It was that kind of market...."

I'd get up at five in the morning and head for the waterfront. Outside the Spreckles Sugar Refinery, outside the gates, there would be a thousand men. You know dang well there's only three or four jobs. The guy would come out with two little Pinkerton cops: "I need two guys for the bull gang. Two guys to go into the hole." A thousand men would fight like a pack of Alaskan dogs to get through there. Only four of us would get through. I was too young a punk.

So you'd drift up to Skid Row. There'd be thousands of men there. Guys on baskets, making weird speeches, phony theories on economics. About eleven-thirty, the real leaders would take over. They'd say: O.K., we're going to City Hall. The Mayor was Angelo Rossi, a dapper little guy. He wore expensive boots and a tight vest. We'd shout around the steps. Finally, he'd come out and tell us nothing.

I remember the demands: We demand work, we demand shelter for our families, we demand groceries, this kind of thing.... Half the guys up there making the demands were Negroes. Now there wasn't a big black colony in San Francisco in those days. But they were pretty cagey, the leaders—they always kept a mixture of black and white.

I remember as a kid how courageous this seemed to me, the demands, because you knew that society wasn't going to give it to you. They'd demand that they open up unrented houses and give decent shelters for their families.* But you just knew society wasn't yielding. There was nothing coming.

This parade would be four blocks long, curb to curb. Nobody had a dime. There were guys on the corner trying to sell apples to this moneyless wonder. [Laughs.]

The guys'd start to yell and there come some horses. They used to have cops on horseback in those days. Then there'd be some fighting. Finally it got to killing. I think they killed three people there that day, besides the wounded. It really got rough because the guys had brought a bunch of marbles and threw them on the street, and the horses were slipping and sliding around. This made the cops mad and they got rough.

There'd be this kind of futile struggle, because somehow you never expected to win. We had a built-in losing complex. That's the way those crowds felt. A lot of them would drift back into the Sally.† By now it's one o'clock, and everybody's hungry. We were a gentle crowd. These were fathers, eighty percent of them. They had held jobs and didn't want to kick society to pieces. They just wanted to go to work and they just couldn't understand. There was a mysterious thing. You watched the papers, you listened to rumors, you'd get word somebody's gonna build a building.

---

* "Thirteen public aid families squatted in a vacant building...they defied the police to evict them. Most were victims of a recent fire. The others decided to abandon their sub-standard housing in favor of the three-story building...'Man, we're going to stake out those apartments just like the early settlers when they took it away from the Indians,' announced Mrs. Pearl Moore, a Tenants' Union representative." (Chicago *Daily News,* February 21, 1969).
† The Salvation Army.

So the next morning you get up at five o'clock and you dash over there. You got a big tip. There's three thousand men there, carpenters, cement men, guys who knew machinery and everything else. These fellas always had faith that the job was gonna mature, somehow. More and more men were after fewer and fewer jobs. So San Francisco just ground to a halt. Nothing was moving.

We were always trying to get to sea, but I didn't have any ticket. Oh, I made that waterfront a thousand times. There used to be those great old liners that sailed out to Hawaii. You could hear the band play "Aloha Away," and all the guys were standing there with tears in their eyes. As though you had somebody going some place. And you didn't know a damn soul. [Laughs.]

We weren't greatly agitated in terms of society. Ours was a bewilderment, not an anger. Not a sense of being particularly put upon. We weren't talking revolution; we were talking jobs.

We'd grown up in small-town high schools. There wasn't much expression, in the press, of the intelligentsia. It was just a tough world, and you had been born into it. I had no great sense of fervor until I went to L.A. and ran into Upton Sinclair in 1934. If I were picking a time when I began to say, "What the hell's this all about?" it came when I wandered into a meeting one day where Upton Sinclair was talking.* This was the winter of '33, '34. There was this little pink-and-white guy up there speaking, the least likely guy ever to be a radical you ever saw. You automatically think of pince-nez glasses and a shock of white hair. His audience was made up mostly of working stiffs.

He pointed out the great piles of oranges, the piles of lumber laying there idle.... They'd put up a rick of oranges and apples, put gasoline over it and set fire to them. Vegetables were being destroyed and everything. Everybody who cried so much later

---

* He was candidate for Governor of California. EPIC was his symbol and credo: End Poverty In California.

about federal programs destroying little pigs ... they should have seen what industry was doing at this time. To keep the price up.

Sinclair's idea was to relate the unemployed to the resources not being used. This appealed to me tremendously. It made sense to have this food eaten up by hungry people. I got a job singing with the quartet that was campaigning with him.

If I had to pick one constant enemy during this time, it was the American Legion. They were made up of home guard types. They were the most vicious enemies of this drifting, reckless, hungry crowd of people. Every place I went, Hoovervilles—they were raided. This bunch of Legionnaires with those damn caps on. Guys with baseball bats, driving them out of the jungles around the railroad grounds. Even in the little towns I lived in. I had a war with those guys by the time I was in high school. They were always the bane of my existence.

They were the Main Streeters. They were doing all right. Merchants, storekeepers, landowners. They had a fix that was just awful to live with. They were hard on the little candidate for Governor. They'd come to his meetings with baseball bats and clubs and break it up. Once, when we sang in the Valley, they attacked us and beat the hell out of us. We barely got out of there.

During the Sinclair campaign, I was going to the library, picking up books I'd never read before, books that never crossed my track. You'd go down to look for work in the morning, and then you'd give up at eleven o'clock and drift into that library. I got my education there, really.

By this time, Roosevelt was President. There was the NRA...mystical things were going on we didn't understand at all. People were talking price-fixing and what have you. Very, very weird world. It didn't mean a damn to us. There were three brothers of us, we got a freight and went down to Portland. They'd started to work on the Bonneville Dam. Beautiful sight down that river. On a decent day, if you set on top of a box car, it was beautiful....

We drifted down to the jungle. We go into a beanery, 'cause there was no train out till eleven that night. In comes a Mexican whore and a colored whore. They order a hamburger. The proprietor says, "I don't serve niggers. Get that dame out of here." The Mexican girl comes back and orders two hamburgers. The guy grumbles, fries up a couple. The colored girl walks in. This guy goes under the counter and comes up with a sap.* He lashes out at the girl's head, bong! Jeez, I think he's killed her. She groans and staggers back off this stool. He cuts around the corner in a wild rage. I put my foot out and trip him. He just went ass over Tecumseh. The girls get out in time. He'd a killed that girl, I believe. We lam out of there, too. We grab the midnight freight and get off at Phoenix. It's a hostile town, so we beat it.

We make an orange freight. We rode in the reefer.† Clear to Kansas City. It goes like a bat out of hell, a rough ride. We broke through the wire netting and ate the oranges. We got vitamins like mad. [Laughs.] But your mouth gets burnt by that acid juice and your teeth get so damn sore from that ride. By the time we got off at K.C., I could hardly close my mouth.

We catch a train into Kansas City, Kansas, that night. At the stops, colored people were gettin' on the trains and throwin' off coal. You could see people gatherin' the coal. You could see the railroad dicks were gettin' tough.

Hal and I are ridin' on the top of the boxcar, it's a fairly nice night. All of a sudden, there's a railroad dick with a flashlight that reaches a thousand miles. Bam! Bam! He starts shooting. We hear the bullets hitting the cars, bam! like that. I throw my hands up and start walking towards that light. Hal's behind me. The guy says, "Get off." I said. "Christ, I can't." This things rollin' fifty miles an hour or more. He says. "Jump." I says, "I can't." He says,

---

* A blackjack.
† The refrigerator car.

"Turn around and march ahead." He marches us over the top. There's a gondola, about eight feet down. He says. "Jump." So I jumped and landed in wet sand, up to my knees.

We come to a little town in Nebraska. Beatrice. It's morning. I'm chilled to the bone. We crawl into a railroad sandbox, almost frozen to death. We dry out, get warmed up, and make the train again. We pull into Omaha. It's night. All of a sudden, the train is surrounded by deputies, with pistols. The guy says. "Get in those trucks." I said, "What for? We haven't done anything." He said, "You're not going to jail. You're going to the Transient Camp."

They drive us up to an old army warehouse. They check you in, take off your clothes, run them through a de-louser, and you take a bath. It's midnight. We come out, and here's a spread with scrambled eggs, bacon, bread, coffee and toast. We ate a great meal. It was wonderful. We go upstairs to bed. Here's a double-decker, sheets, toothbrush, towels, everything. I sat down on this damn bed, I can't tell you, full of wonderment. We thought we'd gone to heaven. Hal's a young punk, he's seventeen. He said, "What the hell kind of a place is this?" I said, "I don't know, but it's sure somethin' different."

The next morning, they called us up to a social worker. By this time, there's a thousand guys in there. They're playing baseball, some guys are washing down walls—bums, bindlestiffs, cynical rough guys who've been on the road for years. It's kind of like a playhouse. It's unbelievable.

Through a social worker, he is assigned to a job with the National Youth Administration, at "a little cold-water college" in Aberdeen, South Dakota. "And then the good life began for me."

"Before Roosevelt, the Federal Government hardly touched your life. Outside of the postmaster, there was little local representation. Now people you knew were appointed to government jobs. Joe Blow or some guy from the corner.

"It came right down to Main Street. Half of them loved it, half of them hated it. There was the immediacy of its effect on you. In Aberdeen, Main Street was against it. But then they were delighted to have those green relief checks cashed in their cash registers. They'd have been out of business had it not been for them. It was a split thing. They were cursing Roosevelt for the intrusion into their lives. At the same time, they were living off it. Main Street still has this fix."

The NYA was my salvation. I could just as easily have been in Sing Sing as with the UN.* Just every bit a chance. Hell, yes. Everybody was a criminal. You stole, you cheated through. You were getting by, survival. Stole clothes off lines, stole milk off back porches, you stole bread. I remember going through Tucumcari, New Mexico, on a freight. We made a brief stop. There was a grocery store, a supermarket kind of thing for those days. I beat it off the train and came back with rolls and crackers. This guy is standing in the window shaking his fist at you.

It wasn't a big thing, but it created a coyote mentality. You were a predator. You had to be. The coyote is crafty. He can be fantastically courageous and a coward at the same time. He'll run, but when he's cornered, he'll fight. I grew up where they were hated, 'cause they'd kill sheep. They'll kill a calf, get in the chicken pen. They're mean. But how else does a coyote stay alive? He's not as powerful as a wolf. He has a small body. He's in such bad condition, a dog can run him down. He's not like a fox. A coyote is nature's victim as well as man's. We were coyotes in the thirties, the jobless.

No, I don't see the Depression as an ennobling experience. Survivors are still ridin' with the ghost—the ghost of those days when things came hard.

---

* He has an administrative job with UNICEF.

ARTHUR A. ROBERTSON

*His offices are on an upper floor of a New York skyscraper. On the
walls are paintings and photographs. A portrait of President Johnson is inscribed "To my friend, a patriot who serves his country."
Another, of Hubert Humphrey—"To my friend, Arthur Robertson,
with all my good wishes." Also, a photograph of Dwight Eisenhower:
"To my friend, Arthur Robertson." There are other mementoes of
appreciation from Americans in high places.*

*He recounts his early days as a war correspondent, advertising
man, and engineer. "We built a section of the Sixth Avenue subway.
I've had a peculiar kind of career. I'm an industrialist. I had been in
Germany where I picked up a number of porcelain enamel plants. I
had a hog's hair concession from the Russian government. I used to
sell them to the outdoor advertising plants for brushes. With several
associates, I bought a company nineteen years ago for $1,600,000.
We're on the New York Stock Exchange now and recently turned
down $200 million for it. I'm chairman of the board. I control the
company. I built it.*

*"I thought seriously of retiring in 1928 when I was thirty. I had
seven figures by the time I was twenty-four."*

In 1929, it was strictly a gambling casino with loaded dice. The few
sharks taking advantage of the multitude of suckers. It was
exchanging expensive dogs for expensive cats. There had been a
recession in 1921. We came out of it about 1924. Then began the
climb, the spurt, with no limit stakes. Frenzied finance that made
Ponzi* look like an amateur. I saw shoeshine boys buying $50,000
worth of stock with $500 down. Everything was bought on hope.

---

* A Boston financier of the twenties. His "empire" crashed, many people were
   ruined. He went to prison.

Today, if you want to buy $100 worth of stock, you have to put up $80 and the broker will put up $20. In those days, you could put up $8 or $10. That was really responsible for the collapse. The slightest shake-up caused calamity because people didn't have the money required to cover the other $90 or so. There were not the controls you have today. They just sold you out: an unwilling seller to an unwilling buyer.

A cigar stock at the time was selling for $115 a share. The market collapsed. I got a call from the company president. Could I loan him $200 million? I refused, because at the time I had to protect my own fences, including those of my closest friends. His $115 stock dropped to $2 and he jumped out of the window of his Wall Street office.

There was a man who headed a company that had $17 million in cash. He was one of the leaders of his industry and controlled three or four situations that are today household words. When his stock began to drop, he began to protect it. When he came out of the second drop, the man was completely wiped out. He owed three banks a million dollars each.

The banks were in the same position he was, except that the government came to their aid and saved them. Suddenly they became holier than thou, and took over the businesses of the companies that owed them money. They discharged the experts, who had built the businesses, and put in their own men. I bought one of these companies from the banks. They sold it to me in order to stop their losses.

The worst day-to-day operators of businesses are bankers. They are great when it comes to scrutinizing a balance sheet. By training they're conservative, because they're loaning you other people's money. Consequently, they do not take the calculated risks operating businesses requires. They were losing so much money that they were tickled to get it off their backs. I recently sold it for $2 million. I bought it in 1933 for $33,000.

In the early thirties, I was known as a scavenger. I used to buy broken-down businesses that banks took over. That was one of my best eras of prosperity. The whole period was characterized by men who were legends. When you talked about $1 million you were talking about loose change. Three or four of these men would get together, run up a stock to ridiculous prices and unload it on the unsuspecting public. The minute you heard of a man like Durant or Jesse Livermore buying stock, everybody followed. They knew it was going to go up. The only problem was to get out before they dumped it.

Durant owned General Motors twice and lost it twice…was worth way in excess of a billion dollars on paper, by present standards, four or five billion. He started his own automobile company, and it went under. When the Crash came, he caved in, like the rest of 'em. The last I heard of him I was told he ended up running a bowling alley. It was all on paper. Everybody in those days expected the sun to shine forever.

October 29, 1929, yeah. A frenzy. I must have gotten calls from a dozen and a half friends who were desperate. In each case, there was no sense in loaning them the money that they would give the broker. Tomorrow they'd be worse off than yesterday. Suicides, left and right, made a terrific impression on me, of course. People I knew. It was heartbreaking. One day you saw the prices at a hundred, the next day at $20, at $15.

On Wall Street, the people walked around like zombies. It was like *Death Takes A Holiday*. It was very dark. You saw people who yesterday rode around in Cadillacs lucky now to have carfare.

One of my friends said to me, "If things keep on as they are, we'll all have to go begging." I asked, "Who from?"

Many brokers did not lose money. They made fortunes on commissions while their customers went broke. The only brokers that got hurt badly were those that gambled on their own—or failed to sell out in time customers' accounts that were underwater. Of course, the brokerage business fell off badly, and practically all pulled in their belts, closed down offices, and threw people out of work.

Banks used to get eighteen percent for call money—money with which to buy stock that paid perhaps one or two-percent dividends. They figured the price would continue to rise. Everybody was banking on it. I used to receive as much as twenty-two percent from brokers who borrowed from me. Twenty-two percent for money!

Men who built empires in utilities, would buy a small utility, add a big profit to it for themselves and sell it back to their own public company. That's how some like Samuel Insull became immensely wealthy. The thing that caused the Insull crash is the same that caused all these frenzied financiers to go broke. No matter how much they had, they'd pyramid it for more.

I had a great friend, John Hertz. At one time he owned ninety percent of the Yellow Cab stock. John also owned the Checker Cab. He also owned the Surface Line buses of Chicago. He was reputed to be worth $400 to $500 million. He asked me one day to join him on a yacht. There I met two men of such stature that I was in awe: Durant and Jesse Livermore.

We talked of all their holdings. Livermore said: "I own what I believe to be the controlling stock of IBM and Philip Morris." So I asked, "Why do you bother with anything else?" He answered, "I only understand stock. I can't bother with businesses." So I asked, "Do men of your kind put away $10 million where nobody can ever touch it?" He looked at me and answered. "Young man, what's the use of having ten million if you can't have big money?"

In 1934—after he went through two bankruptcies in succession—my accountant asked if I'd back Livermore. He was broke and wanted to make a comeback in the market. He always made a comeback and paid everybody off with interest. I agreed to do it. I put up $400,000. By 1939, we made enough money so that each of us could have $1,300,000 profit after taxes. Jesse was by this time in the late sixties, having gone through two bankruptcies.

"Wouldn't it be wise to cash in?" I asked him. In those days, you could live like a king for $50,000 a year. He said he could just never get along on a pittance.

So I sold out, took my profits, and left Jesse on his own. He kept telling me he was going to make the killing of the century. Ben Smith, known as "Sell 'Em Short Ben," was in Europe and told him there was not going to be a war. Believing in Smith, Livermore went short on grain.* For every dollar he owned, plus everything he could pyramid.

When I arrived in Argentina, I learned that Germany invaded Poland. Poor Jesse was on the phone. "Art, you have to save me." I refused to do anything, being so far away. I knew it would be throwing good money after bad.

A couple of months later, I was back in New York, with Jesse waiting for me in my office. The poor fellow had lost everything he could lay his hands on. He asked for a $5,000 loan, which, of course, I gave him. Three days later, Jesse had gone to eat breakfast in the Sherry-Netherlands, went to the lavatory and shot himself. They found a note made out to me for $5,000. This was the man who said, "What's the use having ten million if you can't have big money?" Jesse was one of the most brilliant minds in the trading world. He knew the crops of every area where grain grew. He was a great student, but always over-optimistic.

Did you sense the Crash coming in 1929?

---

* "Selling short is selling something you don't have and buying it back in order to cover it. You think a stock is not worth what it's selling for, say its listed as $100. You sell a hundred shares of it, though you haven't got the stock. If you are right, and it goes down to $85, you buy it at that price, and deliver it to the fellow to whom you sold it for $100. You sell what you don't have." Obviously, if the stock rises in value, selling short is ruinous.... Ben Smith sold short during the Crash and made "a fortune."

I recognized it in May and saved myself a lot of money. I sold a good deal of my stocks in May. It was a case of becoming frightened. But, of course, I did not sell out completely, and finished with a very substantial loss.

In 1927 when I read Lindbergh was planning his memorable flight, I bought Wright Aeronautic stock. He was going to fly in a plane I heard was made by Wright. I lived in Milwaukee then. My office was about a mile from my home. When I left my house, I checked with my broker. By the time I reached my office, I had made sixty-five points. The idea of everything moving so fast was frightening. Everything you bought just seemed to have no ceiling.

People say we're getting a repetition of 1929. I don't see how it is possible. Today with SEC* controls and bank insurance, people know their savings are safe. If everybody believes, it's like believing in counterfeit money. Until it's caught, it serves its purpose.

In 1932 I came to New York to open an office in the Flatiron Building. Macfadden, the health faddist, created penny restaurants. There was a Negro chap I took a liking to that I had to deal with. He agreed to line up seventy-five people who needed to be fed. At six o'clock I would leave my office, I'd march seventy-five of 'em into the Macfadden restaurant and I'd feed em for seven cents apiece. I did this every day. It was just unbelievable, the bread lines. The only thing I could compare it with was Germany in 1922. It looked like there was no tomorrow.

I remember the Bank Holiday. I was one of the lucky ones. I had a smart brother-in-law, an attorney. One day he said to me, "I don't feel comfortable about the bank situation. I think we ought to have a lot of cash." About eight weeks before the bank closings, we decided to take every dollar out of the banks. We must have taken out close to a million dollars. In Clyde, Ohio, where I had a porcelain enamel plant, they used my signature for money. I used to

---

* Securities and Exchange Commission.

come in every Saturday and Sunday and deliver the cash. I would go around the department stores that I knew in Milwaukee and give them thirty-day IOU's of $1.05 for a dollar if they would give me cash.

In 1933, the night Jake Factor, "The Barber," was kidnapped, an associate of mine, his wife, and a niece from Wyoming were dancing in a night club. Each of us had $25,000 cash in our socks. We were leaving the following morning for Clyde, and I was supposed to bring in $100,000 to meet bills and the payroll. We were all dancing on $25,000 apiece. In the very place where Jake Factor was kidnaped for $100,000. The damn fools, they could have grabbed us and had the cash.

CLIFFORD BURKE

The Negro was born in depression. It didn't mean too much to him, The Great American Depression, as you call it. There was no such thing. The best he could be is a janitor or a porter or shoeshine boy. It only became official when it hit the white man. If you can tell me the difference between the depression today and the Depression of 1932 for a black man, I'd like to know it. Now, it's worse, because of the prices. Know the rents they're payin' out here? I hate to tell ya.

He is a pensioner. Most of his days are spent as a volunteer with a community organization in the black ghetto on the West Side of the city.

We had one big advantage. Our wives, they could go to the store and get a bag of beans or a sack of flour and a piece of fat meat, and they could cook this. And we could eat it. Steak? A steak would kick in my stomach like a mule in a tin stable. Now you take the white fella, he couldn't do this. His wife would tell him: Look, if you can't do any better than this, I'm gonna leave you. I seen it happen. He couldn't stand bringing home beans instead of steak and capon. And he couldn't stand the idea of going on relief like a Negro.

You take a fella had a job paying him $60, and here I am making $25. If I go home taking beans to me wife, we'll eat it. It isn't exactly what we want, but we'll eat it. The white man that's been making big money, he's taking beans home, his wife'll say: Get out. [Laughs.]

Why did these big wheels kill themselves? They weren't able to live up to the standards they were accustomed to, and they got ashamed in front of their women. You see, you can tell anybody a lie, and he'll agree with you. But you start layin' down the facts of real life, he won't accept it. The American white man has been superior so long, he can't figure out why he should come down.

I remember a friend of mine, he didn't know he was a Negro. I mean he acted like he never knew it. He got tied downtown with some stock. He blew about twenty thousand. He came home and drank a bottle of poison. A bottle of iodine or something like that. It was a rarity to hear a Negro killing himself over a financial situation. He might have killed himself over some woman. Or getting in a fight. But when it came to the financial end of it, there were so few who had anything. [Laughs.]

I made out during that...*Great* Depression. [Laughs.] Worked as a teamster for a lumber yard. Forty cents an hour. Monday we'd have a little work. They'd say come back Friday. There wasn't no need to look for another job. The few people working, most all of them were white.

So I had another little hustle. I used to play pool pretty good. And I'd ride from poolroom to poolroom on this bicycle. I used to beat these guys, gamble what we had. I'd leave home with a dollar. First couple of games I could beat this guy, I'd put that money in my pocket. I'd take the rest of what I beat him out of and hustle the day on that. Sometimes I'd come home with a dollar and a half extra. That was a whole lot of money. Everybody was out trying to beat the other guy, so he could make it. It was pathetic.

I never applied for PWA or WPA, 'cause as long as I could hustle, there was no point in beating the other fellow out of a job, cuttin' some other guy out....

DOC GRAHAM

A mutual acquaintance, Kid Pharaoh, insisted that we meet. Doc Graham had obviously seen better days.

"My introduction to Chicago was when a guy got his head blowed off right across from where I went to stay. In that neighborhood where I gravitated, there was every kind of character that was ever invented. Con men, heist men, burglars, peet men: you name it, they had it.

"These are highly sophisticated endeavors. To be proficient at it— well, my God, you spent a lifetime. And then you might fall, through not being sophisticated enough. You may have committed a common error, leaving fingerprints...."

I was a caged panther. It was a jungle. Survival was the law of the land. I watched so many of my partners fall along the way. I decided the modus operandi was bad. Unavailing, non-productive. After spending ten Saturdays in jail, one right after another, I changed my modus operandi.

What were you in jail for?

Various allegations. All alleged. I been a con man, a heist man— you name it.

How does a heist man differ from a con man?

One is by force and the other is by guile. Very few people have encompassed both. I was very daring. When I came to the city and seen groceries on the sidewalk, I swore I'd never be hungry again. My family was extremely poor. My father was an unsuccessful gambler, and my mother was a missionary. Not much money was connected with either profession.

A family conflict...?

Yes, slightly. He threw the Bible in the fire. He was right, incidentally. [Laughs.] My mother didn't see it that way.

I'm sixty-one, and I have never held a Social Security card. I'm not knocking it. I have been what society generally refers to as a parasite. But I don't think I'd be a nicer fellow if I held two jobs.

My teacher was Count Victor Lustig. He was perhaps the greatest con man the United States has ever known. Lustig's outstanding achievement was getting put in jail and paying a Texas sheriff off with $30,000 counterfeit. And the sheriff made the penitentiary also. He got to be a believer. And he went into the counterfeit profession.

Another teacher was Titanic Thompson. He was the greatest card mechanic that ever arrived on the scene. Nick the Greek* wouldn't make him a butler. A footman. He couldn't open the door for him. Ace played the crimp. A crimp is putting a weave in a card that you'd need a microscope to see it. I know the techniques, but having had my arm half removed, I had to switch left-handed, deal left-handed. I'm ambidexterous.

An accident...?

With a colored North American. The twenties and early thirties

---

* Another renowned gambler of the time.

was a jungle, where only the strong survived and the weak fell by the wayside. In Chicago, at the time, the unsophisticated either belonged to the Bugs Moran mob or the Capone mob. The fellas with talent didn't bother with either one. And went around and robbed both of 'em.

We were extremely independent. Since I'm Irish, I had a working affiliate with Bugs Moran's outfit. In case muscle was needed beyond what I had, I called on Moran for help. On the other hand, Moran might use me to help him in one of his operations.

The nature of one operation was: if you had a load of whiskey hijacked, we went over and reloaded it on a truck, while several surrounded the place with machine guns, sawed-off shotguns, et cetera.

Did you find yourself in ticklish situations on occasion…?

Many of them. You see this fellow liquidated, that fellow disposed of. Red McLaughlin had the reputation of being the toughest guy in Chicago. But when you seen Red run out of the drainage canal, you realized Red's modus operandi was unavailing. His associates was Clifford and Adams. They were set in Al's doorway in his hotel in Cicero. That was unavailing. Red and his partners once stole the Checker Cab Company. They took machine guns and went up and had an election, and just went and took it over. I assisted in that operation.

What role did the forces of law and order play?

With a $10 bill, you wasn't bothered. If you had a speaking acquaintance with Mayor Thompson,* you could do no wrong. [Laughs.] Al spoke loud to him.

There was a long period during the Depression where the police

---

* William Hale Thompson, three-term mayor of Chicago.

were taking scrip. Cash had a language all of its own. One night in particular, I didn't have my pistol with me, and the lady of the evening pointed out a large score to me. [Laughs.] A squad car came by, which I was familiar with. A Cadillac, with a bell on it. I knew all the officers. I borrowed one of their pistols and took the score. Then I had to strip and be searched by the policemen, keeping honest in the end, as we divided the score. They wanted the right count. They thought I might be holding out on 'em. They even went into my shoes, even.

Oh, many policemen in that era were thieves. Legal thieves. I accepted it as such and performed accordingly. We didn't have no problems. It was an era where there was no bread on the table. So what was the difference whether I put the bread on the table by my endeavor or they put the bread? I performed with a hundred policemen in my time. I can't say nothin' for 'em, nothin' against 'em. I would say they were opportunists. I would say that they were merely persons that didn't perhaps have the courage to go on and do what I did. Nevertheless, they were willing to be a part of it. A minor part, that is.

The era of the times led into criminality, because of the old precept and concepts were destroyed against everyday reality. So when a policeman or a fireman was not being paid, how in the name of God could you expect him to enforce what he knew as the concept of law and order, when you see the beer barons changing hundred-dollar bills, and the pimp and the whorehouse guy had hundred-dollar bills, and the guy digging the sewers couldn't pay his bills? So how could you equate these things?

A good example is Clyde Barrow and Bonnie Parker. They were a product of the era. Dillinger—it wasn't that he was really a tough. No, he was just a product of survival. Actually, Dillinger was a country bumpkin. He realized the odds were stacked against him and performed accordingly. I knew Dillinger. Yeah, I met him on the North Side. And Dillinger was nothing like people wrote about him.

The times produced Dillinger. Pretty Boy Floyd. Baby Face Nelson.

They were dedicated heist men and in the end were killed, to achieve their purpose. By themselves, they didn't need an army.

Al Capone sublet the matter. Capone quickly removed himself from the danger zone, aside from murdering Anselmi and Scalisi with a baseball bat. Bugs Moran to the end—he died for a bank heist in Ohio. They were from two different bolts of cloth. One was a dedicated thief. And one was an intriguing Mediterranean product of guile, et cetera. So you'd have to say that Moran was dedicated while Capone was an opportunist.

How did you get along during those hard times?

By every way known to the human brain. All my brothers were in the penitentiary. I had one brother in Jefferson City, another one in San Quentin, another one in Leavenworth, another one in Louisiana. At that time, I am a fighter. I started boxing in 1925. Fourteen years till 1939. And it's a bloodthirsty thing.

How'd you become a boxer?

Gravitation. Being on the road simulated that fate, trying to grab a buck and so forth. Five different years, *Ring* Magazine rated me the most devastating puncher in the profession, pound for pound.

What was it like, being a boxer in those days...?

Survival. If it worked out that you were on top, you made a living. And if you were three or four shades below the top, you scuffled for a buck. Fighters were very, very hungry.

I made some pretty big scores. But I spent it practically all on getting my brothers out of penitentiaries around the country. At that time, the one in San Quentin stood me thirty thousand, the one in Jefferson City stood me twenty-five thousand. Those were big give-ups in those days.

I lived from the bottom to the top. I lived as good as you could live. I run the gamut of having a butler and a chauffeur to a flop joint, into an open car over night.

He describes the boxing "combination" of those days; the fix; the refusal of his manager and himself to "play ball"; the boxer as an investment, cut up "like a watermelon."

I had many injuries in between. My hands, you can see. [He holds out his gnarled, broken knuckles.] In the meantime, I had to step out and make a dollar otherwise. It was never within the law.

I've switched craps, I've run up the cards, I do the complete bit. Every way known to the human brain. I'm probably a rare species that's left.

Was muscle always involved?

Muscle if you hope to leave with the money. Muscle everywhere, yes. Because for some unknown reason, muscle has been going on since the Roman Army conquered the field with a way of life.

When you enter an endeavor unsuccessfully, then the planning was incorrect. The risk was above the gains, and you stumble along the way. And the windup is a rude awakening with numbers strung out over your back. Unsuccessful in your modus operandi. Sagacity, ingenuity, planning...it involves much weighing, odds against failure, odds against gain—if you care to be in a free society.

I spent much time in jail. That's why I'm a student of the matter.

(At this point, Kid Pharaoh and he conducted a vigorous and somewhat arcane debate concerning the relative dishonesty of Hoover and Roosevelt. The Kid insisted it was Hoover who, by clout, was saved

from "the bucket." Doc was equally certain it was F.D.R. who should
have had "numbers strung out over his shoulders.")

Do you recall your biggest haul during the thirties?

It was alleged—

Who alleged...?

The newspaper report came out as $75,000. We took eight and
were happy about the whole thing.

What was your role during Prohibition?

I was a cheater. After studying under Count Lustig and Titanic
Thompson, I considered it beneath my dignity delivering a barrel
of beer. Although I drink beer. I hustled with crap mobs, on the
crimp, the weave, the holdout—the reason I didn't do the rum running is you can hire a mooch with muscle. But can you hire brains?
Big firms have not succeeded in doing this.

I have met only several proficient men in my time. One of them
was Jack Freed. [Cups hand over mouth, whispers.] D–e–a–d. He
worked right up to the edge of his demise. This is in the evening,
when you are not at home. He was dedicated to his labor. He spent
half his lifetime in the penitentiaries. One of my closest friends. I,
of course, assisted him, from time to time. He accused me of rat-
tling my coat one night, making entrance. I, who have endeavored
in every participation known to the human brain, where art, subterfuge and guile is involved.

I take it you were caught a few times—

Incarcerated. Nothing proven substantially. I was a victim of circumstances. What they were, I didn't say. Yes, I spent a year in Salinas, California, amongst other places. The highlight was when I was nineteen. If I get convicted, I'm going out to join my brother in San Quentin. My brother was doing twenty years there. If I'm not convicted, I'm going up to visit him. I'm going to San Quentin, one way or the other.

And you did?

I did. As a free man. I was fortunate enough in having one of the greatest criminal lawyers of all time defending me.

For someone engaging in your varied skills, do you sense a difference between the thirties and today?

It's so different today, it's unfathomable. You can't conjure what the difference is. Today everything is a robot. Today everything is mechanical. There is very little ingenuity. Everything today is no-personal, there is no personality whatsoever. Everything today is *ipso facto, fait accompli.* In my era they had to prove their point. Today, you don't have to prove your point.

Back then Titanic Thompson steered Arnold Rothstein,* with Nigger Nate Raymond, into one of maybe the biggest card games was ever involved. I was a small feature of it in the Park Central Hotel in New York. Titanic changed the weave [Laughs.], and when Rothstein wound up a half-a-million loser, he said he was cheated. Rothstein became jaded after he lost the half a million, no longer had any interest. No interest in life. After the card game broke up, he said he was no longer interested in this, that or the other. He refused to pay off. So Nigger Nate Raymond held court with him. And that was the end of that.

---

* A gambler and fixer of reknown. He was involved in the Black Sox scandal of 1919.

Held court...?

The S & W people* had the implements that they held court with. That's all. Rothstein didn't have to pay off. You understand what I mean? I know, because I assisted in the operation with Titanic. But let that be as it may. It was unfortunate, yes. But that was his demise.

Were the S & W people popular those days?

Naturally, it was part of your wearing apparel.

Aren't some of the survivors in legitimate enterprises today?

One of the fellows who was a pimp in Chicago is the boss of one of the grandest hotels in Las Vegas. I assisted him in a few small matters. But true to all pimping, he forgot me entirely as he advanced into the autumn of life.

After Prohibition, what did the guys do?

The ones that were adroit enough branched into other fields. If they didn't have any knowledge, they fell by the wayside. I achieved some small success in race tracks. Machine Gun Jack McGurn † couldn't stand the traffic. He got his brains blowed out, branching into other fields.

    The night Prohibition was repealed, everybody got drunk. It was the only decent thing Roosevelt ever did in his Administration. I was not one of his admirers. I tried to fire him on four different

---

* Smith & Wesson, revolver manufacturers.

† It was alleged that he was one of Capone's executioners in the St. Valentine's Day Massacre. He was killed in a bowling alley in 1936, on the eve of St. Valentine's Day.

occasions. If I ever had a person work for me that displeased me, it was Roosevelt. I voted against him four times.

What was it about him you didn't like?

Him being a con man, taking advantage of poor, misguided, gibbering idiots who believed in his fairy tales. The New Deal, the various gimmicks, the NRA...the complete subterfuge, artifice, and guile....

Some say Roosevelt saved our society....

I dare say it would have been saved if Roosevelt's mother and father had never met.

Many people were on relief...on WPA....

I didn't have a thing to do with that, because I was above that. Nevertheless, the people that were involved in it did it merely to get some meat on the plates, some food in the kitchen. It was no more, no less. Survival. None of the connotations of social dissent that has crept in since then. Merely an abstract way of eating....

What do you think would happen if there were a big Depression today?

Very simple. They'd commit suicide today. I don't think they're conditioned to stand it. We were a hardier race then. We'd win wars. We didn't procrastinate. We'd win them or lose them. Today we're a new race of people. They'll quit on a draw—if they see any feasible way to see their way out to quit with any dignity, they'll quit. Back then, you had a different breed of people. You got $21 a month going into the army or the navy. So them guys, they went to win the war. There's been an emancipated woman since the beginning of the war, also.

KID PHARAOH *interjects. "The American woman during the Depression was domesticated. Today, as we move into the late sixties, if you go into any high school, you don't see any classes of cooking any more. You don't see any classes at all in sewing. None of them can boil water. They're all today in business in competition to the male animal. Why should a Playboy bunny make $200 a week? If a veteran goes to war, puts his life up…can't raise a family."*

DOC: *"…a lot of country bumpkins in the city wanting to look at poor, misguided, gibbering idiot waitresses. That they've stripped down like a prostitute, but hasn't sense enough to know that it's on her alleged sex allure that the poor misguided chump is in the place. In the end it amounts to absolutely nothing. A hypothesis of silly nothingness…undressed broads serving hootch, that cannot fulfill…."*

KID PHARAOH: *"…his dick directs him, like radar, to the Playboy Club. In a high moral society—in Russia—guys like Hugh Hefner would be working in the library."*

During the Depression…if a guy had a few drinks with a girl…?

If she had two drinks with him, and she didn't lay her frame down, she was in a serious matter. She could have one, and explain she made a mistake by marrying some sucker that she was trying to fulfill her marriage commitment. But in the thirties, if you had a second drink and she didn't make the commitment where she's going to lay her frame down for you, the entire matter was resolved quickly to the point and could end in mayhem. She was in a serious matter.

In the thirties, then, the individual con man, the heist man, had an easier time with it—all around?

Oh yes, it was much easier then. The Federal Government now has you on practically anything you do. They make a conspiracy whether you accomplish the matter or not. Today, it's fraught with much peril, any type of endeavor you engage in. A nefarious matter. It constantly comes under the heading of a federal statute. The Federal Government then collected taxes, and just a few interstate things, as white slavery, and that was about it.

Today, the Federal Government has expanded into every field. If you use a telephone, as an example, and you put slugs in it, that's a penitentiary offense. Strange as that may seem. So that will give you an idea how far the Federal Government has encroached on a citizen's prerogative.

You think Roosevelt had a role to play in this?

Definitely. He was perhaps the lowest human being that ever held public office. He, unfortunately, was a despot. I mean, you get an old con man at a point in high office, he begins to believe the platitudes that are expounded by the stupid populace about him.

What about the young people, during the Depression...?

The young people in the Depression respected what laws there were. If they'd steal, they tried to do it with dignity. And what not. They respected the policeman. They looked at him with forebearance, that he was a necessary part of society. But, nevertheless, he didn't impede the mere fact of gain.

No, he didn't stop 'em.

The young today are feminized, embryo homosexuals. Stool pigeons.

What about the young dissenters?

If you gave 'em a push, they'd turn into a homosexual. When the German hordes fifty years ago surrounded Paris, Marshall Pétain brought out the pimps, whores, thieves, underground operators, he says: Our playground is jeopardized by the German Hun. Well, all Paris, every thief, burglar, pimp, he come out and picked up a musket. Stopped the German hordes.

Today you don't see any kind of patriotism like that. They're trying to tear down the courthouse, they try to throw paint on Johnson's car. How can you compare that era, coming into this? Those were men, and today you've got to question whether they're homosexual or whether they're not.

Since the Depression, manhood has been lost—the manhood that I knew. Where four or five guys went on an endeavor, they died trying to take the endeavor off. It was no big deal if they did die. If it didn't come off right, there was no recrimination. Everybody put skin off what they set on.

Today, the foible of our civilization is to attack the policeman with a rotten egg, throwing it at him. Or walking around with a placard, that they're against whatever the present society advocates as civilized. Those people today—the Fall of Rome could be compared with it. Because they were the strongest nation on earth, and they disinterrogated into nothing. Through debauchery, through moral decay.

They need a narcotic to do anything, they can't do it on their own. They need a drug. Back in my era, we could cold-bloodedly do it.

OSCAR HELINE

For all his seventy-eight years, he has lived on this Iowa farm, which his father had cultivated almost a century ago. It is in the northwestern part of the state, near the South Dakota border. Marcus has a population of 1,263.

On this drizzly October Sunday afternoon, the main street is deserted. Not a window is open, nor a sound heard. Suddenly, rock music shatters the silence. From what appeared to be a years-long vacant store, two girls and a boy emerge. They are about thirteen, fourteen.

I ask directions. They are friendly, though somewhat bewildered. "An old man?" They are eager to help. One points north; another, south; the third, west. Each is certain "an old man" lives somewhere in the vicinity.

Along the gravel road, with a stop at each of three farmhouses; no sign, no knowledge of "an old man," nor awareness of his name. At each is a tree bearing the identical sticker: "Beware The Dog." One trots forth, pauses warily and eyes the stranger in the manner of Bull Connor and a black militant. The young farmers are friendly enough, but innocent of Oscar Heline's existence.

At the fourth farm, an elderly woman, taken away from the telecast of of the Tigers–Cardinals World Series game, knows.... Several gravel roads back I find him.

The struggles people had to go through are almost unbelievable. A man lived all his life on a given farm, it was taken away from him. One after the other. After the foreclosure, they got a deficiency judgment. Not only did he lose the farm, but it was impossible for him to get out of debt.

He recounts the first farm depression of the twenties: "We give the

*land back to the mortgage holder and then we're sued for the remain-
der—the deficiency judgment—which we have to pay." After the
land boom of the early twenties, the values declined constantly, until
the last years of the decade. "In '28, '29, when it looked like we could
see a little blue sky again, we're just getting caught up with the back
interest, the thirties Depression hit…."*

The farmers became desperate. It got so a neighbor wouldn't buy
from a neighbor, because the farmer didn't get any of it. It went to
the creditors. And it wasn't enough to satisfy them. What's the use
of having a farm sale? Why do we permit them to go on? It doesn't
cover the debts, it doesn't liquidate the obligation. He's out of business, and it's still hung over him. First, they'd take your farm, then
they took your livestock, then your farm machinery. Even your
household goods. And they'd move you off. The farmers were
almost united. We had penny auction sales. Some neighbor would
bid a penny and give it back to the owner.

Grain was being burned. It was cheaper than coal. Corn was
being burned. A county just east of here, they burned corn in their
courthouse all winter. '32, '33. You couldn't hardly buy groceries
for corn. It couldn't pay the transportation. In South Dakota, the
county elevator listed corn as minus three cents. *Minus* three cents
a bushel. If you wanted to sell 'em a bushel of corn, you had to
bring in three cents. They couldn't afford to handle it. Just think
what happens when you can't get out from under….

We had lots of trouble on the highway. People were determined to
withhold produce from the market—livestock, cream, butter, eggs,
what not. If they would dump the produce, they would force the
market to a higher level. The farmers would man the highways,
and cream cans were emptied in ditches and eggs dumped out.
They burned the trestle bridge, so the trains wouldn't be able to
haul grain. Conservatives don't like this kind of rebel attitude and
aren't very sympathetic. But something had to be done.

I spent most of my time in Des Moines as a lobbyist for the state cooperatives. Trying to get some legislation. I wasn't out on the highway fighting this battle. Some of the farmers probably didn't think I was friendly to their cause. They were so desperate. If you weren't out there with them, you weren't a friend, you must be a foe. I didn't know from day to day whether somebody might come along and cause harm to my family. When you have bridges burned, accidents, violence, there may have been killings, I don't know.

There were some pretty conservative ones, wouldn't join this group. I didn't want to particularly, because it wasn't the answer. It took that kind of action, but what I mean is it took more than that to solve it. You had to do constructive things at the same time. But I never spoke harshly about those who were on the highway.

Some of the farmers with teams of horses, sometimes in trucks, tried to get through. He was trying to feed his family, trying to trade a few dozen eggs and a few pounds of cream for some groceries to feed his babies. He was desperate, too. One group tried to sell so they could live and the other group tried to keep you from selling so they could live.

The farmer is a pretty independent individual. He wants to be a conservative individual. He wants to be an honorable individual. He wants to pay his debts. But it was hard. The rank-and-file people of this state—who were brought up as conservatives, which most of us were—would never act like this. Except in desperation.

There were a few who had a little more credit than the others. They were willing to go on as usual. They were mostly the ones who tried to break the picket lines. They were the ones who gained at the expense of the poor. They had the money to buy when things were cheap. There are always a few who make money out of other people's poverty. This was a struggle between the haves and the have-nots.

The original bankers who came to this state, for instance. When my father would borrow $100, he'd get $80. And when it was due, he'd pay back the $100 and a premium besides that. Most of his early borrowings were on this basis. That's where we made some wealthy families in this country.

We did pass some legislation. The first thing we did was stop the power of the judges to issue deficiency judgments. The theory was: the property would come back to you someday.

The next law we passed provided for committees in every county: adjudication committees. They'd get the person's debts all together and sit down with his creditors. They gave people a chance. People got time. The land banks and insurance companies started out hard-boiled. They got the farm, they got the judgment and then found out it didn't do them any good. They had to have somebody to run it. So they'd turn around and rent it to the fella who lost it. He wasn't a good renter. The poor fella lost all his capacity for fairness, because he couldn't be fair. He had to live. All the renters would go in cahoots. So the banks and companies got smart and stopped foreclosing.

Through a federal program we got a farm loan. A committee of twenty-five of us drafted the first farm legislation of this kind thirty-five years ago. We drew it up with Henry Wallace. New money was put in the farmers' hands. The Federal Government changed the whole marketing program from burning 10-cent corn to 45-cent corn. People could now see daylight and hope. It was a whole trans-formation of attitude. You can just imagine…(He weeps.)

It was Wallace who saved us, put us back on our feet. He under-stood our problems. When we went to visit him, after he was appointed Secretary, he made it clear to us he didn't want to write the law. He wanted the farmers themselves to write it. "I will work with you," he said, "but you're the people who are suffering. It must be your program." He would always give his counsel, but he never directed us. The program came from the farmers them-selves, you betcha.

Another thing happened: we had twice too many hogs because

corn'd been so cheap. And we set up what people called Wallace's Folly: killing the little pigs. Another farmer and I helped develop this. We couldn't afford to feed 45-cents corn to a $3 hog. So we had to figure a way of getting rid of the surplus pigs. We went out and bought 'em and killed 'em. This is how desperate it was. It was the only way to raise the price of pigs. Most of 'em were dumped down the river.

The hard times put farmers' families closer together. My wife was working for the county Farm Bureau. We had lessons in home economics, how to make underwear out of gunny sacks, out of flour sacks. It was cooperative labor. So some good things came out of this. Sympathy toward one another was manifest. There were personal values as well as terrible hardships.

Mrs. Heline interjects: "They even took seat covers out of automobiles and re-used them for clothing or old chairs. We taught them how to make mattresses from surplus cotton. We had our freedom gardens and did much canning. We canned our own meat or cured it in some way. There was work to do and busy people are happy people."

The real boost came when we got into the Second World War. Everybody was paying on old debts and mortgages, but the land values were going down. It's gone up now more than ever in the history of the country. The war.... [A long pause.]

It does something to your country. It's what's making employment. It does something to the individual. I had a neighbor just as the war was beginning. We had a boy ready to go to service. This neighbor one day told me what we needed was a damn good war, and we'd solve our agricultural problems. And I said, "Yes, but I'd hate to pay with the price of my son." Which we did. [He weeps.] It's too much of a price to pay....

In '28 I was chairman of the farm delegation which met with Hoover. My family had always been Republican, and I supported him. To my disappointment. I don't think the Depression was all his fault. He tried. But all his plans failed, because he didn't have the Government involved. He depended on individual organizations.

It's a strange thing. This is only thirty-five years ago—Roosevelt, Wallace. We have a new generation in business today. Successful. It's surprising how quickly they forget the assistance their fathers got from the Government. The Farm Bureau, which I helped organize in this state, didn't help us in '35. They take the same position today: we don't need the Government. I'm just as sure as I'm sitting here, we can't do it ourselves. Individuals have too many different interests. Who baled out the land banks when they were busted in the thirties? It was the Federal Government.

What I remember most of those times is that poverty creates desperation, and desperation creates violence. In Plymouth County—Le Mars—just west of us, a group met one morning and decided they were going to stop the judge from issuing any more deficiency judgments. This judge had a habit of very quickly O.K.'ing foreclosure sales. These farmers couldn't stand it any more. They'd see their neighbors sold out.

There were a few judges who would refuse to take the cases. They'd postpone it or turn it over to somebody else. But this one was pretty gruff and arrogant: "You do this, you do that, it's my court." When a bunch of farmers are going broke every day and the judge sits there very proudly and says: "This is my court..."; they say: "Who the hell are you?" He was just a fellow human being, same as they were.

These farmers gathered this one particular day. I suppose some of 'em decided to have a little drink, and so they developed a little courage. They decided: we'll go down and teach that judge a lesson. They marched into the courtroom, hats on, demanded to visit with him. *He* decided he would teach *them* a lesson. So he says: "Gentlemen, this is my court. Remove your hats and address the court properly."

They just laughed at him. They said, "We're not concerned whose court this is. We came here to get redress from your actions. The things you're doing, we can't stand to have done to us any more." The argument kept on, and got rougher. He wouldn't listen. He threatened them. So they drug him from his chair, pulled him down the steps of the courthouse, and shook a rope in front of his face. Then, tarred and feathered him.

The Governor called out the National Guard. And put these farmers behind barbed wire. Just imagine...[he weeps]...in this state. You don't forget these things.

JANE YODER

A house in Evanston. The green grass grows all around. "We're middle middle class. Not upper and not lower, either." Her husband is a junior executive in a large corporation. They have two sons: the elder, a lieutenant in the air force; the other, soon to be married, a graduate of Notre Dame.

"I love the trees. This house represents his struggle and mine. We bought this house on a shoestring. I'm terribly afraid of debt. If I have one fear, it's the rich get richer when you buy on time. All these things that are hidden costs—like with this house, we had to buy it up quickly through a friend of my husband's father. So it was bought without the real estate commission.

"We've always paid our bills along the way. I have a real fear of being trapped into more than I need. I just turn away from it. Security to me is not what we have, but what we can do without. I don't want anything so badly that I can't wait for it. I think a second television set in our bedroom might be kind of nice. But I can dismiss it. We have one. How many can you watch?

"We got married in July of 1940. This cocktail table is an early

decision in those days. And that end table. So my brothers come in, and they say, 'It's amazing. Same stuff is here, and you've added to it. By God, how did you do it?' "

Her father was a blacksmith in a small central Illinois mining town. There were seven children. The mines closed "early, about '28 or '30." The men, among them her father, went to other towns, seeking jobs.

During the Depression, my father took a great deal of psychological abuse. Oh, tremendous. This brother-in-law that was superintendent of the mine…I look at these two men…. I really think my father had a marvelous mind. I wonder what he had the potential to become….

He's like something out of Dostoyevsky. My father was, I think, terribly intelligent. He learned to speak English, a couple of languages, and prided himself on not being like the rest in our neighborhood. He was constantly giving us things from either the paper or some fiction and being dramatic about it…"down with these people that didn't want to think." Just as proud of his kids…but he was schizophrenic. He could look at himself a little bit, and then just run like hell. Because what he saw was painful.

We were struggling, just desperate to be warm. No blankets, no coats. At this time I was in fourth grade. Katie* went to Chicago and bought an Indian blanket coat. I remember this incident of that Indian blanket coat. [Gasps.] Oh, because Katie came home with it and had it in her clothes closet for quite a while. And I didn't have a coat. I can remember putting on that coat in Sue Pond's house. I thought, oh, this is marvelous, gee. I took that coat home, and I waited till Sunday and wore it to church. And then everybody laughed. I looked horrid. Here was this black-haired kid, with a tendency to be overweight. My God, when I think of that…. But I

* Her older sister.

wore that coat, laugh or not. And I can remember thinking: the hell with it. I don't care what…it doesn't mean a thing. Laugh hard, you'll get it out of your system. I was warm.

Before that I had one coat. It must have been a terrible light-weight coat or what, but I can remember being cold, just shivering. And came home, and nothing to do but go to bed, because if you went to bed, then you put the coat on the bed and you got warm.

The cold that I've known. I never had boots. I think when I got married, I had my first set of boots. In rainy weather, you just ran for it, you ran between the raindrops or whatever. This was luxuriating to have boots. You simply wore your old shoes if it was raining. Save the others. You always polished them and put shoe trees in them. You didn't have unlimited shoe trees, either. When the shoes are worn out, they're used around the house. And of the high heels, you cut the heels down and they're more comfortable.

We tell our boys: you have a black sweater, a white sweater, and a blue sweater. You can't wear ten sweaters at once, you can only wear one. What is this thing?…some of the people that I know have thirty blouses. Oh, my God, I have no desire to think where I'd hang them. For what? I can't even grasp it.

If we had a cold or we threw up, nobody ever took your temperature. We had no thermometer. But if you threw up and you were hot, my mother felt your head. She somehow felt that by bringing you oranges and bananas and these things you never had—there's nothing wrong with you, this is what she'd always say in Croatian; you'll be all right. Then she gave you all these good things. Oh, gee, you almost looked forward to the day you could throw up. I could remember dreaming about oranges and bananas, dreaming about them.

My oldest brother, terribly bright, wanted to go on to school to help pay those grocery bills that were back there. But my youngest brother, Frankie, didn't know. Oh, it just overwhelms me some-times when I think of those two younger brothers, who would want to get some food and maybe go to the store. But they would see this $900 grocery bill, and they just couldn't do it.

We all laugh now, because Frankie is now down in New Mexico, and superintendent of two mines. And we all say, "Remember, Frankie?" Frankie's *"To košta puno?"* That's "Did it cost a lot?" Everything that came into the house, he'd say, *"To košta puno?"*

Did it cost much? No matter what you brought in: bread and eggs and Karo syrup. Oh, Karo syrup was such a treat. I don't remember so much *my* going to the store and buying food. I must have been terribly proud and felt: I can't do it. How early we all stayed away from going to the store, because we sensed my father didn't have the money. So we stayed hungry. And we talked about it.

I can think of the WPA…my father immediately got employed in this WPA. This was a godsend. This was the greatest thing. It meant food, you know. Survival, just survival.

How stark it was for me to come into nurses' training and have the girls—one of them, Susan Stewart, lived across the hall from me, her father was a doctor—their impressions of the WPA. How it struck me. Before I could ever say that my father was employed in the WPA, discussions in the bull sessions in our rooms immediately was: these lazy people, the shovel leaners. I'd just sit there and listen to them. I'd look around and realize: sure, Susan Stewart was talking this way, but her father was a doctor, and her mother was a nurse. Well, how nice. They had respectable employment. In my family, there was no respectable employment. I thought, you don't know what it's like.

How can I defend him? I was never a person who could control this. It just had to come out or I think I'd just blow up. So I would say, "I wonder how much we know until we go through it. Just like the patients we take care of. None of them are in that hospital by choice." I would relate it in abstractions. I think it saved me from just blowing up.

I would come back after that and I'd just say: Gee, these are just two separate, separate worlds.

TOM YODER, JANE'S SON

He had entered the room during my conversation with his mother, Jane. His fiancée accompanied him.

It seems just absolutely—it's almost in a black humorous sense—funny to me. To realize that a hundred miles from Chicago, about forty years ago, my mother's brothers, whom I know well now, were out with little rifles, hunting for food to live on. And if they didn't find it, there were truly some empty stomachs. I mean, this is just too much. I don't think my generation can really comprehend what all this means. I've never gone to bed hungry—I wish I had. I haven't, and I probably never will.

Whenever I've griped about my home life, Mother's always said, "I hope you always have it so good." And I'm the kind of person that will say, "Look, what do you mean you hope I always have it so good? I intend when I'm forty to be making $25,000." But I understand what she means. I am grateful for what I have. But it's only human nature that we all want to go on and find something better.

JEROME ZERBE

"They're doing eight pages in color of this apartment in the fall issue of Architectural Digest. *So anybody who cares can see it."*

In the apartment on Sutton Place are all sorts of objets d'art: *jades, prints, photographs, original portraits of friends and acquain-*

tances, statues... "*two Venetian ones I admired in Venice. Hedda Hopper gave them to me. She was my long-time and greatest friend. Everything was given to me. You see, being a poor boy...*" [*Laughs.*]

The thirties? My own poverty. My father allowed me an allowance of $300 a month. On that I went to Paris and started painting. Suddenly he wrote and said: no more money. And what does a painter do in the Depression without money? I came back to America and was offered a job in Cleveland. Doing the menial task—but at the time I was grateful—of art-directing a magazine called *Parade*. $35 a week. It was 1931.

I thought, to goose up the magazine, I would take photographs of people at my own home. In those days, you didn't have strobe lights and all that sort of thing. We had our little Kodak cameras, and would hold up a flash and would open up the flash...but I got photographs of Leslie Howard, Ethel Barrymore, these people. Billy Haines was a great star in those days.

We published them in *Parade*. It was the first time that what we call candid social photography was founded. I had known I'd start something. *Town and Country* asked me to go over various estates and I went over and photographed people I knew. They were all horrified at the thought and couldn't wait for the pictures. [Laughs.]

After my father died, and no money, I sold my library books to the Cleveland Museum and the Cleveland Art Library. With that money, I came to New York and started out. *Town and Country* had guaranteed me $150, which seemed a lot. This is '33.

One day, a gal from Chicago called me up and asked if I would have lunch with John Roy and herself at the Rainbow Room. So we lunched, and he said: "Jerome, it's extraordinary how many people you know in New York. Would you like to come to the Rainbow Room? I'll pay you $75 a week, if you'll come, take photographs, and send them to the papers, and you will have no expenses." The

Rainbow Room, here at the Rockefeller Center. This is 1935. The famous room at the top.

So twice a week, I would give a party and photograph my guests, all of whom were delighted to be photographed. The first night of this, I was so pleased, because I had been so poor. I still had my beautifully tailored clothes from London. I still had the accoutrements of money, but I had no money. You know? It was cardboard for my shirt and my shoes when they got old.

So I went to the El Morocco to celebrate this new job. John Perona said, "I'll take you on the other three nights." That made $150 a week. Then he said, "Jerry, cut out this Rainbow Room racket. They're getting more publicity than I am. I will pay the same amount, if you leave your camera here. You won't have taxi fares, you won't have problems."

So I went to work for John Perona. From 1935 to 1939, I worked at the El Morocco. He's a legend. He's dead now. He was a fabulous guy, just fabulous. He and I fought all the time. And I was always quitting. I adored him.

I invented this thing that became a pain in the neck to most people. I took photographs of the fashionable people, and sent them to the papers. Maury Paul of the *Journal-American,* at least four times a week, would use a large photograph on his society page of important people.

The social set did not go to the Rainbow Room or the El Morocco, until I invented this funny, silly thing: taking photographs of people. The minute the photographs appeared, they came.

They became celebrities at that moment...?

That's right. I would send the photographs not only to New York papers. I sent them to the London *Bystander,* to an Australian paper, to one in Rio...I sent them all over the world. So people would come in to the El Morocco and I would get a note saying:

"The Duchess of Sutherland has arrived and would love to have her photograph taken." [Laughs.] You know?

They were the top, top social. These were the people whose houses, one knew, were filled with treasures. These were the women who dressed the best. These were the women who had the most beautiful of all jewels. These were the dream people that we all looked up to, and hoped that we or our friends could sometimes know and be like.

Do you recall the Crash?

No, because it didn't hit the family. My father had coal mines, and it didn't hit the coal mines until '31. He still gave me $300 a month, and I went to Paris and lived it up.

My father was president of the Ohio and Pennsylvania Coal Company. It was on the West Virginia border—Cadiz, Ohio. Where Clark Gable was born. I went down there, because at the time he offered me the presidency at $12,000 a year. It was an incredibly large amount of money. I'm talking about 1932 or 1933. I went down there and spent two weeks in the town. The mine was 897 feet, the shaft, underground, and the working surface was three and a half miles. I spent two weeks down there and came back and said: "Mother, forgive me, to hell with it."

The men loathed their slovenly wives, and every night they go and play pool or whatever it was. The houses were drab beyond belief. You'd think a woman would at least put up a plant—a flower or something. And suddenly I flew into town with two or three friends for several weekends. We disrupted the place like nobody's business. [Laughs.] We'd go to the bars, and these guys would say: "Jesus, where did you get your shirts?" Where did you get this or that? and I'd say: "Why don't you go to your houses and make them more attractive?" And they said: "Our wives are so goddam slovenly. We don't even want to go to bed with them." I'm talking about the miners. They came out at five o'clock at night absolutely filthy. I've got a photograph of myself, I can show you, as a miner. I can show you how filthy I was.

And they all went through this common shower, got clean. Would they go home? Hah! For food, yes. And their squawling brats. And take right off to a bar. They loathed their life. The manager once said to me, "I never knew what it was to have fun with people until I heard your laughter..."

We all had such fun, of course, and he joined in the fun. And this brings up another story.... At the time I photographed King Paul of Greece, he became a great friend. He said, "Mr. Zerbe, you and I have many friends in common. Do you realize in our position we are never allowed to laugh? Everybody treats us with such respect. And I hear you have outrageous stories."

When you went to this mining town—the year...

1933. Of course, to me it was a horror. That stinking little hotel. The lousy food and the worst service. And I was spoiled. When I was a kid, Mother always said to me: "Jerome, I think it's much easier for you to have your breakfast served in bed." So I always had my breakfast in bed. And I always had the fire lit in my fireplace. I was a very spoiled brat, and I loved that.

Did your friends ever talk much about Roosevelt?

Listen, dear boy, Franklin Roosevelt in those days we didn't even talk about. John Roosevelt and the young Franklin were great friends of mine. I photographed them in my apartment. We never did discuss the old man, ever. Well, I never liked politics. I think all politicians are shits. Franklin—I admired him very much. I thought the American public was so frightfully gullible to allow this man, he was a dying man, to be elected for that last term. Oh, that voice!

"My dear friends...." You know, it became such an irritation. It was so patronizing. It was so the great man talking down to us common little herd.

Was his name ever discussed at El Morocco?

Well, no, actually. I have a great respect for the family. I'm sorry the boys haven't done better. And they haven't. What President's sons have? What happened to the Hoover boys?

Did his name ever come up with some of the people you pho-tographed?

Yes, but always with a rather hatred. They didn't like him. Eleanor was a great woman, who was a real, real schlemiel. You know, making the most of everything she could out of a bad everything. But there was always admiration for her.

Did the people you knew in the thirties ever talk about what hap-pened outside? You know...those on relief...?

I don't think we ever mentioned them. They did in private at the breakfast table or the tea table or at cocktail time. But never socially. Because I've always had a theory: when you're out with friends, out socially, everything must be charming, and you don't allow the ugly.

We don't even discuss the Negro question. Let's forget they're only one-tenth of this country, and what they're putting on, this act—someday they're going to be stepped on like vermin. There's too much. I'm starting a thing: equal rights for whites. I think they've allowed themselves, with their necklaces and their long hair and nonsense, to go too far.

Now I've had the same manservant, who's Negro, for thirty-three years, which is quite a record. I suppose he's my closest friend in the world. He's a great guy, Joseph.

But aren't beads and necklaces worn by some of the beautiful people today, too?

I was thinking tonight…I have to go out to dinner, but I don't have my Malta Cross, which had blue enamel and diamonds, which is really very good. Because I loaned it to somebody. I'll have to wear what I really love, which is my Zuñi Indian. This is authentic and good, and people all accept that.

Do you remember ever seeing apple sellers in the city?

No, there were none of those. Not in New York. Never, never. There were a few beggars. You came to recognize them because they'd be on one block one day and one block the next. And finally one day, I saw this pathetic beggar, whom I'd always felt sorry for. This Cadillac drove up. I'd just given him a quarter. And it picked him up. There was a woman driving it. And I thought: well, if they can drive a Cadillac, they don't need my quarter. His wife had a Cadillac.

You don't recall bread lines or stuff like that?

I never saw one. Never in New York. If they were, they were in Harlem or down in the Village. They were never in this section of town. There was never any sign of poverty.

What does the phrase "New Deal" mean to you?

It meant absolutely nothing except higher taxation. And that he did. He obviously didn't help the poverty situation in the country, although, I suppose…I don't know—New Deal! God! Look at the crap he brought into our country, Jesus!

Do you sense a different feeling toward people on welfare today than there was in the thirties?

Oh listen, we had no little bastards dressed as they are today, putting on acts these days. The children were slapped down by their parents. I think they're encouraged by their parents today. I think our country is in a very dangerous and precarious position, and I would predict, if I dared, that within twenty or thirty years, we're gonna have a complete revolution here in America. Probably a dictatorship.

I feel the signs. The portents are going that way. Look what happened at Columbia. Why, they should have turned the fire hoses on those little bastards and get them out right away. Instead of tolerating them.

Any final thoughts…?

The thirties was a glamorous, glittering moment.

PEGGY TERRY AND HER MOTHER, MARY OWSLEY

It is a crowded apartment in Uptown.* Young people from the neighborhood wander in and out, casually. The flow of visitors is constant; occasionally, a small, raggedy-clothed boy shuffles in, stares, vanishes. Peggy Terry is known in these parts as a spokesman for the

---

* A Chicago area in which many of the southern white émigrés live; furnished flats in most instances.

poor southern whites.... "Hillbillies are up here for a few years and they get their guts kicked out and they realize their white skin doesn't mean what they always thought it meant."

Mrs. Owsley is the first to tell her story.

Kentucky-born she married an Oklahoma boy "when he came back from World War I. He was so restless and disturbed from the war, we just drifted back and forth." It was a constant shifting from Oklahoma to Kentucky and back again; three, four times the route. "He saw the tragedies of war so vividly that he was discontented everywhere." From 1929 to 1936, they lived in Oklahoma.

There was thousands of people out of work in Oklahoma City. They set up a soup line, and the food was clean and it was delicious. Many, many people, colored and white, I didn't see any difference, 'cause there was just as many white people out of work than were colored. Lost everything they had accumulated from their young days. And these are facts. I remember several families had to leave in covered wagons. To Californy, I guess.

See, the oil boom come in '29. People come from every direction in there. A couple years later, they was livin' in everything from pup tents, houses built out of cardboard boxes and old pieces of metal that they'd pick up—anything that they could find to put somethin' together to put a wall around 'em to protect 'em from the public.

I knew one family there in Oklahoma City, a man and a woman and seven children lived in a hole in the ground. You'd be surprised how nice it was, how nice they kept it. They had chairs and tables and beds back in that hole. And they had the dirt all braced up there, just like a cave.

Oh, the dust storms, they were terrible. You could wash and hang clothes on a line, and if you happened to be away from the house and couldn't get those clothes in before that storm got there, you'd never wash that out. Oil was in that sand. It'd color them the most awful color you ever saw. It just ruined them. They was just never fit to use, actually. I had to use 'em, understand, but they wasn't very presentable. Before my husband was laid off, we lived in a good home. It wasn't a brick house, but it wouldn't have made any difference. These storms, when they would hit, you had to clean house from the attic to ground. Everything was covered in sand. Red sand, just full of oil.

The majority of people were hit and hit hard. They were mentally disturbed you're bound to know, 'cause they didn't know when the end of all this was comin'. There was a lot of suicides that I know of. From nothin' else but just they couldn't see any hope for a better tomorrow. I absolutely know some who did. Part of 'em were farmers and part of 'em were businessmen, even. They went flat broke and they committed suicide on the strength of it, nothing else.

A lot of times one family would have some food. They would divide. And everyone would share. Even the people that were quite well to do, they was ashamed. 'Cause they was eatin', and other people wasn't.

My husband was very bitter. That's just puttin' it mild. He was an intelligent man. He couldn't see why as wealthy a country as this is, that there was any sense in so many people starving to death, when so much of it, wheat and everything else, was being poured into the ocean. There's many excuses, but he looked for a reason. And he found one.

My husband went to Washington. To march with that group that went to Washington…the bonus boys.

He was a machine gunner in the war. He'd say them damn Germans gassed him in Germany. And he come home and his own Government stooges gassed him and run him off the country up there with the water hose, half drownded him. Oh, yes *sir*, yes sir, he was a hell-raiser [laughs—a sudden sigh]. I think I've run my race.

PEGGY TERRY'S STORY:

I first noticed the difference when we'd come home from school in the evening. My mother'd send us to the soup line. And we were never allowed to cuss. If you happened to be one of the first ones in line, you didn't get anything but water that was on top. So we'd ask the guy that was ladling out the soup into the buckets—everybody had to bring their own bucket to get the soup—he'd dip the greasy, watery stuff off the top. So we'd ask him to please dip down to get some meat and potatoes from the bottom of the kettle. But he wouldn't do it. So we learned to cuss. We'd say: "Dip down, God damn it."

Then we'd go across the street. One place had bread, large loaves of bread. Down the road just a little piece was a big shed, and they gave milk. My sister and me would take two buckets each. And that's what we lived off for the longest time.

I can remember one time, the only thing in the house to eat was mustard. My sister and I put so much mustard on biscuits that we got sick. And we can't stand mustard till today.

There was only one family around that ate good. Mr. Barr worked at the ice plant. Whenever Mrs. Barr could, she'd feed the kids. But she couldn't feed 'em *all*. They had a big tree that had fruit on it. She'd let us pick those. Sometimes we'd pick and eat 'em until we were sick.

Her two daughters got to go to Norman for their college. When they'd talk about all the good things they had at the college, she'd kind of hush 'em up because there was always poor kids that didn't have anything to eat. I remember she always felt bad because people in the neighborhood were hungry. But there was a feeling of together....

When they had food to give to people, you'd get a notice and you'd go down. So Daddy went down that day and he took my sister and me. They were giving away potatoes and things like that. But they had a truck of oranges parked in the alley. Somebody asked them who the oranges were for, and they wouldn't tell 'em. So they said, well, we're gonna take those oranges. And they did. My dad was one of the ones that got up on the truck. They called the police, and the police chased us all away. But we got the oranges.

It's different today. People are made to feel ashamed now if they don't have anything. Back then, I'm not sure how the rich felt. I think the rich were as contemptuous of the poor then as they are now. But among the people that I knew, we all had an understanding that it wasn't our fault. It was something that had happened to the machinery. Most people blamed Hoover, and they cussed him up one side and down the other—it was all his fault. I'm not saying he's blameless, but I'm not saying either it was all his fault. Our system doesn't run by just one man, and it doesn't fall by just one man, either.

You don't recall at any time feeling a sense of shame?

I remember it was fun. It was fun going to the soup line. 'Cause we all went down the road, and we laughed and we played. The only thing we felt is that we were hungry and we were going to get food. Nobody made us feel ashamed. There just wasn't any of that.

Today you're made to feel that it's your own fault. If you're poor, it's only because you're lazy and you're ignorant, and you don't try to help yourself. You're made to feel that if you get a check from Welfare that the bank at Fort Knox is gonna go broke.

Even after the soup line, there wasn't anything. The WPA came, and I married. My husband worked on the WPA. This was back in Paducah, Kentucky. We were just kids. I was fifteen, and he was sixteen. My husband was digging ditches. They were putting in a water main. Parts of the city, even at that late date, 1937, didn't have city water.

My husband and me just started traveling around, for about three years. It was a very nice time, because when you're poor and you stay in one spot, trouble just seems to catch up with you. But when you're moving from town to town, you don't stay there long enough for trouble to catch up with you. It's really a good life, if you're poor and you can manage to move around.

I was pregnant when we first started hitchhiking, and people were really very nice to us. Sometimes they would feed us. I remember one time we slept in a haystack, and the lady of the house came out and found us and she said. "This is really very bad for you because you're going to have a baby. You need a lot of milk." So she took us up to the house.

She had a lot of rugs hanging on the clothesline because she was doing her house cleaning. We told her we'd beat the rugs for her giving us the food. She said, no, she didn't expect that. She just wanted to feed us. We said, no, we couldn't take it unless we worked for it. And she let us beat her rugs. I think she had a million rugs, and we cleaned them. Then we went in and she had a beautiful table, full of all kind of food and milk. When we left, she filled a gallon bucket full of milk and we took it with us.

You don't find that now. I think maybe if you did that now, you'd get arrested. Somebody'd call the police. The atmosphere since the end of the Second War—it seems like the minute the war ended, the propaganda started. In making people hate each other.

I remember one night, we walked for a long time, and we were so tired and hungry, and a wagon came along. There was a Negro family going into town. Of course, they're not allowed to stop and eat in restaurants, so they'd cook their own food and brought it with 'em. They had the back of the wagon filled with hay. We asked them if we could lay down and sleep in the wagon, and they said yes. We woke up, and it was morning, and she invited us to eat with 'em. She had this box, and she had chicken and biscuits and sweet potatoes and everything in there. It was just really wonderful.

I didn't like black people. In fact, I hated 'em. If they just shipped 'em all out, I don't think it woulda bothered me.

She recalls her feelings of white superiority, her discoveries. "If I really knew what changed me...I don't know. I've thought about it and thought about it. You don't go anywhere, because you always see yourself as something you're not. As long as you can say I'm better than they are, then there's somebody below you can kick. But once you get over that, you see that you're not any better off than they are. In fact, you're worse off 'cause you're believin' a lie. And it was right there, in front of us. In the cotton field, chopping cotton, and right over in the next field, there's these black people—Alabama, Texas, Kentucky. Never once did it occur to me that we had anything in common.

"After I was up here for a while and I saw how poor white people were treated, poor white southerners, they were treated just as badly as black people are. I think maybe that just crystallized the whole thing."

I didn't feel any identification with the Mexicans, either. My husband and me were migrant workers. We went down in the valley of Texas, which is very beautiful. We picked oranges and lemons and grapefruits, limes in the Rio Grande Valley.

We got a nickel a bushel for citrus fruits. On the grapefruits you had to ring them. You hold a ring in your hand that's about like that [she draws a circle with her hands], and it has a little thing that slips down over your thumb. You climb the tree and you put that ring around the grapefruit. If the grapefruit slips through, you can't pick it. And any grapefruit that's in your box—you can work real hard, especially if you want to make enough to buy food that day—you'll pick some that aren't big enough. Then when you carry your box up and they check it, they throw out all the ones that go through the ring.

I remember this one little boy in particular. He was really a beautiful child. Every day when we'd start our lunch, we'd sit under the trees and eat. And these peppers grew wild. I saw him sitting there, and every once in a while he'd reach over and get a pepper and pop it in his mouth. With his food, whatever he was eating. I thought they looked pretty good. So I reached over and popped it in my mouth, and, oh, it was like liquid fire. He was rolling in the grass laughing. He thought it was so funny—that white people couldn't eat peppers like they could. And he was tearing open grapefruits for me to suck the juice, because my mouth was all cooked from the pepper. He used to run and ask if he could help me. Sometimes he'd help me fill my boxes of grapefruits, 'cause he felt sorry for me, 'cause I got burned on the peppers. [Laughs.]

But that was a little boy. I felt all right toward him. But the men and the women, they were just spics and they should be sent back to Mexico.

I remember I was very irritated because there were very few gringos in this little Texas town, where we lived. Hardly anybody spoke English. When you tried to talk to the Mexicans, they couldn't understand English. It never occurred to us that we should learn to speak Spanish. It's really hard to talk about a time like that, 'cause it seems like a different person. When I remember those times, it's like looking into a world where another person is doing those things.

This may sound impossible, but if there's one thing that started me thinking, it was President Roosevelt's cuff links. I read in the paper how many pairs of cuff links he had. It told that some of them were rubies and precious stones—these were his cuff links. And I'll never forget, I was setting on an old tire out in the front yard and we were poor and hungry. I was sitting out there in the hot sun, there weren't any trees. And I was wondering why it is that one man could have all those cuff links when we couldn't even have enough to eat. When we lived on gravy and biscuits. That's the first time I remember ever wondering why.

And when my father finally got his bonus, he bought a secondhand car for us to come back to Kentucky in. My dad said to us kids: "All of you get in the car. I want to take you and show you something." On the way over there, he'd talk about how life had been rough for us, and he said: "If you think it's been rough for us, I want you to see people that really had it rough." This was in Oklahoma City, and he took us to one of the Hoovervilles, and that was the most incredible thing.

Here were all these people living in old, rusted-out car bodies. I mean that was their home. There were people living in shacks made of orange crates. One family with a whole lot of kids were living in a piano box. This wasn't just a little section, this was maybe ten-miles wide and ten-miles long. People living in whatever they could junk together.

And when I read *Grapes of Wrath*—she bought that for me [indicates young girl seated across the room]—that was like reliving my life. Particularly the part where they lived in this Government camp. Because when we were picking fruit in Texas, we lived in a Government place like that. They came around, and they helped the women make mattresses. See, we didn't have anything. And they showed us how to sew and make dresses. And every Saturday night, we'd have a dance. And when I was reading *Grapes of Wrath* this was just like my life. I was never so proud of poor people before, as I was after I read that book.

I think that's the worst thing that our system does to people, is to take away their pride. It prevents them from being a human being. And wondering why the Harlem and why the Detroit. They're talking about troops and law and order. You get law and order in this country when people are allowed to be decent human beings. Every time I hear another building's on fire, I say: oh, boy, baby, hit 'em again. [Laughs.]

I don't think people were put on earth to suffer. I think that's a lot of nonsense. I think we are the highest development on the earth, and I think we were put here to live and be happy and to enjoy everything that's here. I don't think it's right for a handful of people to get ahold of all the things that make living a joy instead of a sorrow. You wake up in the morning, and it consciously hits you—it's just like a big hand that takes your heart and squeezes it—because you don't know what that day is going to bring: hunger or you don't know.

POSTSCRIPT

(A sudden flash of memory by Peggy Terry, as I was about to leave.)
"It was the Christmas of '35, just before my dad got his bonus. We didn't get anything for Christmas. I mean nothing. Not an orange, not an apple—nothing. I just felt so bad. I went to the church, to the children's program and I stole a Christmas package. It was this pretty box and it had a big red ribbon on it. I stole it off the piano, and I took it home with me. I told my mother my Sunday school teacher had given me a Christmas present. When I opened it, it was a beautiful long scarf made out of velvet—a cover for a piano. My mother knew my Sunday school teacher didn't give me that. 'Cause we were living in one room, in a little shack in what they called Gander Flat. [Laughs.] For a child—I mean, they teach you about Santa Claus and they teach you all that stuff—and then for a child to have to go to church and steal a present…and then it turned out to be something so fantastic, a piano scarf. Children shouldn't have to go around stealing. There's enough to give all of them everything they want, any time they want it. I say that's what we're gonna have."

We Still See Their Faces

AN INTRODUCTION TO THE
50TH ANNIVERSARY EDITION OF
THE GRAPES OF WRATH *

It is 1988. We see the face on the six o'clock news. It could be a Walker Evans or Dorothea Lange shot, but that's fifty years off. It is a face of despair, of an Iowa farmer, fourth generation, facing fore-closure. I've seen this face before. It is the face of Pa Joad, Muley Graves, and all their lost neighbors, tractored out by the cats.

In the eyes of Carroll Nearmyer, the farmer, is more than despair; there is a hardly concealed wrath: as there was in the eyes of his Okie antecedents.

> Sure, cried the tenant farmers, but it's our land. We were born on it, and got killed on it, and we died on it. Even if it's no good, it's still ours. That's what makes it ours—being born on it, working on it, dying on it. That makes ownership, not a paper with numbers on it.
> (*The Grapes of Wrath,* Chapter Five)

Listen to Carroll Nearmyer. I had visited his farm, twenty-four miles southeast of Des Moines. It was a soft, easy twilight in May 1987: "There was several times I had the gun to my head and she didn't know it. And then I got damn mad. I got to thinkin' about it and I got madder. These people don't have the right to do this to me! I have worked, I have sweated, and I have bled. I have tried out there to keep this place goin'. And then they tried to take it away from me!"

---

* Studs Terkel, "Introduction: We Still See Their Faces," from *The Grapes of Wrath* (1989).

During a trip in 1987 through Iowa and Minnesota, I saw too many small towns with too many deserted streets that evoked too many images of too many rural hamlets of the Great Depression. I could not escape the furrowed faces and stooped frames of John Steinbeck's people. It was a classic case of life recapitulating art. The work of art, in this instance, caught more than people; it was their "super-essence" [Steinbeck's word].

It was a flash forward fifty years. The boarded-up stores and houses. The abandoned jalopies. The stray dog. The pervasive silence. "It's both a silence of protest and a silence of acceptance," observed my companion, who was doing the driving.

> The men were silent and they did not move often. And the women came out of their houses to stand beside their men—to feel whether this time the men would break. The women studied the men's faces secretly, because the corn could go, as long as something else remained.
>
> (*The Grapes of Wrath,* Chapter One)

What was that something else? It had something to do with respect for Self; sought from those dear to him and at least a semblance of it demanded from the Others. It was something he had to husband and preserve by himself, alone. Therein lay the fatal flaw; a fault he had to discover the hard way.

A half century later, Carolyn Nearmyer, Carroll's wife, recognized it. "The women are apt to talk to other farm wives about their problems, rather than sit down with their husbands. If I was to come up with a suggestion, he'd get very upset. It was not that I did not know as much as he did. It was just he was keeping it inside himself."

Ma Joad knew it, too. Though in her good-bye to Tom, she says, "I don' un'erstan', I don' really know," she does know. Her generous heart gives the lie to her words. In Tom's reply, Preacher Casy's transcendental vision comes shining through:

Maybe like Casy says, a fella ain't got a soul of his own, but on'y a piece of a big one—and then…. Then I'll be all around in the dark. I'll be everywhere—wherever you look. Wherever they's a fight so hungry people can eat, I'll be there. Wherever there's a cop beatin' up on a guy, I'll be there. Why, I'll be in the way guys yell when they're mad an'—I'll be in the way kids laugh when they're hungry an' they know supper's ready. An' when our folks eat the stuff they raise an' live in the houses they build—why, I'll be there.

(The Grapes of Wrath, Chapter Twenty-eight)

There are constant variations on this theme throughout *The Grapes of Wrath,* as in a symphony. The novel is constructed more like a piece of music rather than mere prose. It is not unlike Frank Lloyd Wright's approach to architecture. As Bach and Beethoven were ever with the architect as he conceived buildings, as he reflected on the vision of his *lieber meister,* Louis Sullivan, so as we learn from the journal he kept during the book's composition, John Steinbeck was listening to the lushness of Tchaikovsky and the dissonance of Stravinsky, while he traveled with the Joads and their fellow tribesmen.

And when there was a pause in the recorded music, there was still a sort of rhythm: the incessant bup-bup-bup of the washing machine. Always, there was the beat, as though it were the beat of a throbbing heart, caught and held by these uprooted people whom he had come to know so well. "I grew to love and admire the people who are so much stronger and braver and purer than I am."*

In the musical architecture of the book are point and counterpoint. Each chapter, recounting the adventures of the individual family, the Joads, is followed by a brief contrapuntal sequence: the tribe, the thousands of Okie families on the move. The one, the many, all heading in the same direction. The singular flows into the plural, the "I" into the "We." It is an organic whole.

---

* Robert J. DeMott, *Working Days: The Grapes of Wrath Journal* (New York: Viking, 1989).

Organic was Wright's favorite word. The work had to flow naturally, whether it were a building or a book. Everything was of one piece, as the fingers on a hand, the limbs on a tree. It was not accidental that Wright's Imperial Hotel withstood the Tokyo earthquake of 1924. It was not accidental that *The Grapes of Wrath* has withstood another earthquake.

Preacher Casy's vision, as revealed to Tom Joad, was presaged by earlier variations on the theme. During the journey to California, twenty or so Okie families rested at a campsite, near a spring:

> In the evening a strange thing happened; the twenty families became one family, the children were the children of all. The loss of a home became one loss, and the golden time in the West was one dream. And it might be that a sick child threw despair into the hearts of twenty families, of a hundred people; that a birth there in a tent kept a hundred people quiet and awestruck through the night and filled a hundred people with the birth-joy in the morning.
>
> (*The Grapes of Wrath,* Chapter Seventeen)

And, finally, at saga's end, comes the breath-stopping incident in the barn. Outside, are the torrential rains and floods. Inside, Rose of Sharon, having lost her baby, offers her mother's milk to the starving stranger. It is much like an olden Child ballad—the stunning last verse. And yet so natural.

There were doubts expressed by friends who had read the manuscript. Why a stranger? Steinbeck knew why intuitively. The impulse was right, organically so. It fit like—well, the fingers on a hand, the limbs on a tree.

This book is more than a novel about an epic journey in an overcrowded, heavy-laden old Dodge jalopy across Highway 66, across hot desert sands, on toward Canaanland, the land of milk and honey; and further on toward disillusion and revelation. It is an anthem in praise of human community. And thus survival. It is astonishingly contemporary.

During a Minnesota farmland trip in 1987, my companion

points toward a barren field that appears endless. There are vast spaces that offer the odd appearance of crowds of baldheads. The color—the pallor—is a sickly, sandy gray.

"All those acres," she says, "not a tree, not a blade of grass. Nothin' to stop the wind from blowin' across. When you lose the farm, they bulldoze the grove down. Our land is very vulnerable. It's now dry and wide open to Mother Nature to do with as she pleases. There's six inches of topsoil left. It used to be six feet. Multiply this—these white tops—by hundreds of thousands of acres, all of a sudden, with a dry spell and drought and a wind, you've got a dust storm. Will it happen again? People are beginning to talk about it." Simultaneously, we mumble: *"The Grapes of Wrath."* The drought of 1988 has underscored our mutual apprehension of the year before and the aching relevance of Steinbeck's book.

When asked, "What is the best novel you read in 1988?" the reply comes easy: *The Grapes of Wrath*. The third time around merely adds to its dimension. Dorothy Parker, at the time of its publication in 1939, called it "the greatest American novel I have ever read." She'll get no argument in these quarters.

The eighties, we have been informed, are distinguished by a mean-spiritness that has trickled down from high places, by an ethic of every man for himself, by a disdain for those up against it. It reveals itself even in our idiomatic language: Victims are defined as "losers." The word, with its new meaning, has become as common—and as popular—as "bottom line." Since there is obviously no room for "losers" at the top, there is no bottom for them either. The Joads would indubitably have fallen into that dark recess; as millions of our dispossessed fall today.

It isn't that the thirties lacked for meanness spirit. God knows, the Joads and their uprooted fellows encountered it all the way. And then some. Aside from the clubs of the vigilantes, the maledictions of the big growers, and the stony cold of the banks, there were people like Joe Davis's boy.

As the caterpillar tractors rolled on and smashed down the homely shacks of the tenant farmers, they were driven by the sons of neighbors.

> The man sitting in the iron seat did not look like a man; gloved, goggled, rubber dust mask over nose and mouth, he was part of the monster, a robot in the seat....
>
> After a while, the tenant who could not leave the place came out and squatted in the shade beside the tractor.
>
> "Why, you're Joe Davis's boy!"
>
> "Sure."
>
> "Well, what you doing this kind of work for—against your own people?"
>
> "Three dollars a day.... I got a wife and kids. We got to eat. Three dollars a day, and it comes every day."
>
> "That's right", the tenant said. "But for your three dollars a day, fifteen or twenty families can't eat at all. Nearly a hundred people have to go out and wander on the roads for your three dollars a day. Is that right?"
>
> And the driver said, "Can't think of that. Got to think of my own kids.... Times are changing, mister, don't you know?"
>
> (*The Grapes of Wrath*, Chapter Five)

Fifty years later, the wife of the Iowa farmer tells this story. It had happened to her a month or so before our encounter: "When the deputy came out to take our stuff away from us, I asked him, 'How can you go home and face your family?' I happen to know he has an eight-year-old girl too. 'How can you sleep tonight knowing that someday this could be you?' He said, 'If I didn't do it, somebody else would be here. To me, it's just a job.' To me, that's heartless people. I wouldn't do that to somebody just because I needed the money."

Joe Davis's boy has always been around. From his point of view, it's quite understandable. It's every man for himself, buddy. In the eighties, there is considerably less onus attached to his job. Who wants to be a "loser"?

Yet, the Joads, for all their trials, found something else en route to California; and even before the trek began. We first meet Tom, just paroled from MacAlester pen.

> The hitch-hiker, stood up and looked across through the windows. "Could ya give me a lift, mister?"
>
> The driver looked quickly back at the restaurant for a second. "Didn' you see the *No Riders* sticker on the win'shield?"
>
> "Sure—I seen it. But sometimes a guy'll be a good guy even if some rich bastard makes him carry a sticker."
>
> The driver, getting slowly into the truck, considered the parts of this answer. If he refused now, not only was he not a good guy, but he was forced to carry a sticker, was not allowed to have company. If he took in the hitchhiker, he was automatically a good guy and also he was not one whom any rich bastard could kick around. He knew he was trapped, but he couldn't see a way out. And he wanted to be a good guy.
>
> (*The Grapes of Wrath,* Chapter Two)

I ran into Sam Talbert, a trucker out of West Virginia, a few months before writing this introduction. "It scares me sometimes thinkin' people are never goin' to learn. I sometimes get to thinkin' people's gettin' too hard-hearted. There's no trust in anybody. Used to be, hitchhiking, you'd get a ride. Now they're afraid they'll be robbed, but people has always been robbed all their life. So it's hard for me to pass up a hitchhiker."

Sam may be on to something. It's not so much not learning as it is tribal memory that's lost. A past, a history has been erased as effortlessly as chalk on a blackboard is erased. It's easy to decry the young clod who says, "A Depression to me is when I can't sit down on my chaise lounge and have a beer and this boob tube in my face." Too easy, perhaps.

The young Atlanta woman bites closer to the core of the apple. "Depression tales were almost like fairy tales to me. The things they teach you about the Depression in school are quite different from how it was. You were told people worked hard and somehow things got better. You never hear about the rough times. I feel angry, as though I were protected from my own history."

When World War Two ended the Great Depression and postwar prosperity, as well as God, blessed America, millions who had all their lives lived on the razor's edge suddenly experienced a security they had never before enjoyed. It was much easier then to suffer amnesia than to remember the dark times of the thirties.

It was so even for the sons and daughters of Okies.

The exquisite irony has not been lost on Jessie De La Cruz. Her family of farm workers has been at it since the thirties. Her hunger has always been Okie hunger. "We worked the land all our lives, so if we ever owned a piece of land, we felt we could make it." Perhaps that's why Muley Graves, stubbornly, mulishly stayed on even though nothing remained but dusty old dust.

Perhaps that's why Jessie was so stunned by the forgettery of those who may have shared her experience, or whose mothers and fathers certainly did. "There's a radio announcer here in Fresno. He always points out, 'I was an Okie. I came out here and I made it. Why can't these Chicanos make it?' " The man at the mike could be little Winfield, the ten-year-old kid of Ma and Pa Joad, Tom's baby brother.

An elderly seamstress, who has seen hard times all her life, thinks this may be more than wild conjecture. "People fergits. I've know'd people lost someone in the war, they gits a little money an' they fergits. I've know'd Depression people, they fergits so easy."

It wasn't by chance that organizers of Cesar Chavez's farm workers union, during the Delano grape strike of the sixties, often cited *The Grapes of Wrath* to "revive old passions for a new battle."*

"Finished this day—and I hope to God it's good." That's how John Steinbeck ended his day's work on October 26, 1938. The longhand manuscript was in the hands of others now. He had begun this job some five months before; but with constant inter-

---

* Jackson J. Benson, *The True Adventures of John Steinbeck, Writer: A Biography* (New York: Viking, 1984).

ruptions—guests, all sorts of noise, pleas from hard-up strangers, urgings to help the abused farm workers—he had put in no more than a hundred working days.

There is no evidence of any written outline; it was all in his head. In his mind's eye, he envisioned the novel *in toto,* even to the final startling scene. Incongruous though it seems, a couple of other creative artists worked in this manner: Mozart and Fats Waller.

Though he was already a success, self-doubt had him on the hip. *Of Mice and Men* had been acclaimed as a novel and was on its way to becoming a smash hit as a play. If anything, this added to his burden. His doing so well in the midst of so much misery and injustice was the hound gnashing at Steinbeck's social conscience. He had been in the fields, he had worked them in preparation for this book; he had seen their faces. "The success will ruin me sure as hell." Guilt was his unrelenting companion during those hundred feverish days.

His diary is replete with self-denigration. "Funny how mean and little books become in face of such tragedies." "I've reached a point of weariness where it seems lousy to me." "I'm not a writer. I wish I were." Yet an almost messianic urgency drove him on.

Self-doubt be damned, he was part of that caravan; he was as much a pilgrim on the Joad hegira as Preacher Casy or Uncle John. Consider this entry in his journal, July 15, 1938: "It is the 35th day. In sixteen more days, I'll be half through. I must get my people to California before then." And there's that damn desert ahead. "Get it done, by God, and they still aren't across." My people.

There is nothing Pirandellian about this writing, nothing detached and ironic. His characters were not on the loose, searching out the author. They were on the loose, of course, but the author was their constant companion. He had become a member of their tribe.

John Steinbeck had witnessed vigilantes and the town's respectables bust a grape strike in the town of Delano in 1936. And bust more than a few heads. It was his home turf. He had seen the pinched features of the five thousand migrant families flooded out of Visalia. He knew, first hand, what was happening all along Imperial Valley. He was on his way to becoming an expert witness: working the fields, doing stoop labor. It was a job he sought.

Fortunately, there was an administration in Washington that understood. President Franklin Roosevelt was surrounded by a circle of men who had something of a sense of history, something the blacks call a "feeling tone." They knew that ways, yet untried, had to be found to meet the need: the restoration of a people's shattered faith in themselves. They called on the skills of creative people to reveal the landscape, to touch the hearts and challenge the minds of America. Government agencies, new to the American experience, came into being.

The Farm Security Administration (FSA) was one. Some of the most indelibly remembered photographs of the thirties were the work of artists, commissioned by the FSA: among them, Walker Evans, Margaret Bourke-White, Dorothea Lange, and Ben Shahn. The durable documentaries, *The Plow That Broke the Plains* and *The River* were produced by the FSA. The writer-director was the gifted film maker, Pare Lorentz, a friend and colleague of John Steinbeck.

It was in fact one of these New Deal agencies, the Resettlement Administration (RA), that collaborated with the author in the work that subsequently became *The Grapes of Wrath*.

Let C. B. (Beanie) Baldwin tell it. He was deputy director of the Resettlement Administration: "I got a call from John Steinbeck. He wanted some help. He was planning to write this book on migrant workers. Will Alexander and I were delighted.* He said,

---

* Alexander had succeeded the maligned Rexford Tugwell as director of the Resettlement Administration. It was Tugwell, a member of Roosevelt's Brains Trust, who had conceived the idea of migratory labor camps, run by the migrants themselves: a lesson in participatory democracy.

'I'm writing about people and I have to live as they live.' He planned to go to work for seven, eight weeks as a pea picker or whatever. He asked us to assign someone to go along with him, a migrant worker. We chose a little guy named Collins, out of Virginia.

"I paid Collins' salary, which was perhaps illegal. He and Steinbeck worked in the fields together. Steinbeck did a very nice thing. He insisted Collins be technical director of the film [of *The Grapes of Wrath*], this little migrant worker. And he got screen credit."

John Ford's classic film is remarkably faithful to Steinbeck's vision. Aside from Nunnally Johnson's superb adaptation, it may have been the presence of Tom Collins on the set that assured such detailed accuracy. Woody Guthrie's *Dustbowl Ballads,* a collection of eight memorable songs, were inspired not only by his own hard traveling but by the film, which he had seen before he read the book.

Tom Collins became Steinbeck's valued guide and companion, during all those workdays. It was he who offered folk wisdom; the inside and outside of the ways, customs, and reflections of these people. "Detail, detail, detail," Steinbeck writes in his journal, "looks, clothes, gestures. I need this stuff. It is exact and just the stuff that will be used against me if I am wrong. Tom is so good." Collins became the model for Jim Rawley, the migrant camp director in the book. He had himself managed one such camp. The second half of the book's dedication is "To Tom, who lived it."

The hard truth captured in *The Grapes of Wrath* was corroborated several months later with the publication of *Factories in the Field: The Story of Migratory Labor in California.* It was the work of Carey McWilliams, the state's Commissioner of Immigration and Housing: a rare public servant.

Steinbeck *had* to have it just right; there was to be not even the slightest error. He knew that the powerful growers, represented by the Associated Farmers, would be infuriated by the book. They were. "The Associated Farmers have begun an hysterical personal attack on me both in the papers and a whispering campaign. I'm a Jew, a pervert, a drunk, a dope fiend."

In his journal, he tells of a friendly sheriff warning him against staying in hotel rooms alone. "The boys got a rape case set for you. A dame will come in, tear off her clothes, scratch her face and scream and you try to talk yourself out of that one. They won't touch your book but there's easier ways."

They did touch his book. They did more than that. On a couple of occasions, they burned it in his home town. Today, Salinas has named a library after him and the Chamber of Commerce takes pride in being "Steinbeck Country."

The battle is not quite over. Today, *The Grapes of Wrath,* the master work of a Nobel Laureate, is the second most banned book in our school and public libraries.

It isn't the language. The colloquial profanities are mild indeed, certainly by today's standards. It must be something else. What? Perhaps the author has offered the reason: "I am completely partisan on the idea of working people to the end that they may eat what they raise, wear what they weave, use what they produce, and share in the work of their hands and heads." Tom Joad's vision was John Steinbeck's vision; a subversive impulse in some quarters.

If you were to choose the one episode that most disturbed the powerful, it may be the one that appears in the government camp sequence. After the Joads had left the wretched Hooverville, about to be burned down by the vigilantes, they came upon this place. As Tom checks in for the family, he is informed:

> "Folks here elect their own cops.... There's five sanitary units. Each one elects a Central Committeeman. Now that committee makes the laws. What they say goes."
> "S'pose they get tough," Tom said.
> "Well, you can vote 'em out jus' as quick as you vote 'em in."
> "...Then there's the ladies. They keep care of the kids an' look after the sanitary units. If your ma isn't working, she'll look after the kids

for the ones that are working, an' when she gets a job—why, there'll be others...."

"Well, for Christ's sake! Why ain't there more places like this?"

"You'll have to find that out for yourself."

(*The Grapes of Wrath,* Chapter Twenty-one)

That Steinbeck captured the "feeling tone," as well as the literal truth, of a resettlement camp has since been underscored by the testimony of John Beecher, the southern poet. He himself managed such a camp for black sharecroppers in the Florida Everglades:

"When the day came to open, we just opened the gate and let anybody in that wanted to come in. No references or anything like that. It was enough for us that a family wanted to live there. We didn't hire guards either and nobody carried a club or a pistol in all that camp that held a thousand people.

"We just got them altogether and told them it was their camp. And there wouldn't be any laws, except the ones they made for themselves through their elected Council. The Council said a man couldn't beat his wife up in camp. And when a man came in drunk, he was out by morning. They had to pay their rent and out of it came money for the nursery school. And they started a co-op, without a dollar in it that the people didn't put up.

"Some of the men and women on that Council couldn't so much as write their names. Remember these were just country people off sharecrop farms in Georgia and Alabama. Just ordinary cotton pickers, the kind planters say would ruin the country if they had the vote. All I know is: My eyes have seen democracy work."

Let that serve as a brief resumé of Chapter Twenty-one of *The Grapes of Wrath.*

No wonder the Associated Farmers and their friends in Congress were so furious. (For the record: Of all the New Deal agencies, the Resettlement Administration, responsible for these camps, was the most bitterly attacked in Congress and in the press.) No wonder Peggy Terry felt otherwise.

She remembers the day somebody handed her a well-thumbed paperback. "...And when I read *Grapes of Wrath,* that was like reliving my whole life. I was never so proud of poor people before as I was after I read this book."

I imagine John Steinbeck would have valued that critique as much as the Nobel Prize for Literature he won in 1962.

Robert J. DeMott has said all that needs to be said. He writes in his introduction to *Working Days* "...of a man whose fiercely concentrated will and driven imagination enriched the literature of his time and redeemed the tag end of a terrifying decade.... of his willingness to risk everything to write the best he could with what gifts he had, and in doing so to reveal, unblinking, the harsh shape of paradise."

"The Good War":
An Oral History of World War Two
(1984)

INTRODUCTION

"I was in combat for six weeks, forty-two days. I remember every hour, every minute, every incident of the whole forty-two days. What was it—forty years ago?" As he remembers aloud, the graying businessman is transformed into a nineteen-year-old rifleman. Much too tall for a rifleman, his mother cried.

This is a memory book, rather than one of hard fact and precise stastic. In recalling an epoch, some forty years ago, my colleagues experienced pain, in some instances; exhilaration, in others. Often it was a fusing of both. A hesitancy, at first, was followed by a flow of memories: long-ago hurts and small triumphs. Honors and humiliations. There was laughter, too.

In 1982, a woman of thirty, doing just fine in Washington, D.C., let me know how things are in her precincts: "I can't relate to World War Two. It's in schoolbook texts, that's all. Battles that were won, battles that were lost. Or costume dramas you see on TV. It's just a story in the past. It's so distant, so abstract. I don't get myself up in a bunch about it."

It appears that the disremembrance of World War Two is as disturbingly profound as the forgettery of the Great Depression: World War Two, an event that changed the psyche as well as the face of the United States and of the world.

The memory of the rifleman is what this book is about; and of his sudden comrades, thrown, hugger-mugger, together; and of those men, women, and children on the home front who knew or did not know what the shouting was all about; and of occasional actors from other worlds, accidentally encountered; and of lives lost and bucks found. And of a moment in history, as recalled by an ex-corporal, "when buddies felt they were more important, were better men who amounted to more than they do now. It's a precious memory."

On a September day in 1982, Hans Göbeler and James Sanders are toasting one another in Chicago. Mr. Göbeler had been the mate on a German submarine, U-505. Mr. Sanders had been the junior flight officer on the U.S.S. *Guadalcanal*. Thirty-eight years before, one tried his damndest, as a loyal member of his crew, to sink the other's craft about two hundred miles off the coast of West Africa. Now they reminisce, wistfully.

"Every man, especially the youth, can be manipulated," says Mr. Göbeler. "The more you say to him that's the American way of life, the German way of life, they believe it. Without being more bad than the other is. There's a great danger all the time." Mr. Sanders nods. "It could happen. People could be fooled. Memory is short."

For me, it was forty-odd years ago. I was in the air force, 1942–1943. I never saw a plane; if I did, I wouldn't have had the foggiest idea what to do with it. Mine was limited service. Perforated eardrum. It was stateside all the way, safe and uneventful. Yet I remember, in surprising detail, the uneventful events; and all those boy-faces, pimply, acned, baby-smooth. And bewildered.

From Jefferson Barracks, Missouri, to Fort Logan, Colorado, to Basic Training Center 10, North Carolina, my peregrinations were noncombative in nature. How I became a sergeant may have had something to do with my age. I was ten years older than the normal GI and, willy-nilly, became the avuncular one to the manchildren. Special Services, they called it.

The other barracks elder was a crooked ex-bailiff from New

Orleans. He was forty. Propinquity, the uniform, and the adventure made us buddies. Even now, I remember those wide-eyed wonders, our nightly audience, as Mike and I held forth. Who knows? Perhaps we were doing the state some service in giving these homesick kids a laugh or two. In any event, they were learning something about civics hardly taught in school, especially from Mike.

When he and I, on occasion, goofed off and, puffing five-cent Red Dot cigars, observed from the warm quarters of the PX toilet our young comrades doing morning calisthenics in the biting Rocky Mountain air, it was without any sense of shame. On the contrary. Mike, blowing smoke rings, indicated the scene outside and, in the manner of General MacArthur, proclaimed, "Aintchu proud of our boys?" I solemnly nodded. The fact is we were proud of them; and they, perversely, of us. Memento mores.

Seated across the celebratory table from Hans Göbeler and Jim Sanders, I think of the nineteen-year-old rifleman. "It was sunshine and quiet. We were passing the Germans we killed. Looking at the individual German dead, each took on a personality. These were no longer an abstraction. They were no longer the Germans of the brutish faces and the helmets we saw in the newsreels. They were exactly our age. These were boys like us."

"Boys" was the word invariably used by the combat-protagonists of this book. The references were to enemy soldiers as well as our own. The SS were, of course, another matter. Even the most gentle and forgiving of our GIs found few redeeming attributes there. So, too, with the professional warrior of Imperial Japan. As for the Japanese citizen-soldier, let a near-sighted, bespectacled American corporal (now a distinguished near-sighted, bespectacled economist) tell it: "In Guam, I saw my first dead Japanese. He looked pitiful, with his thick glasses. He had a sheaf of letters in his pocket. He looked like an awkward kid who'd been taken right out of his home to this miserable place."

Paul Douglas, the liberal Illinoisan, volunteered for the marines at fifty "to get myself a Jap." True, it did no harm to his subsequent campaign for the United States Senate. There was nothing unusual in Mr. Douglas's pronouncement. "Jap" was a common word in our daily vocabulary. He was a decent, highly enlightened man caught up in war fever as much as fervor. It was the doyen of American journalists, Walter Lippmann, who strongly urged internment for Niseis and their fathers and mothers.

For the typical American soldier, despite the perverted film sermons, it wasn't "getting another Jap" or "getting another Nazi" that impelled him up front. "The reason you storm the beaches is not patriotism or bravery," reflects the tall rifleman. "It's that sense of not wanting to fail your buddies. There's sort of a special sense of kinship."

An explanation is offered by an old-time folk singer who'd been with an anti-aircraft battery of the Sixty-second Artillery: "You had fifteen guys who for the first time in their lives were not living in a competitive society. We were in a tribal sort of situation, where we could help each other without fear. I realized it was the absence of phony standards that created the thing I loved about the army."

There was another first in the lives of the GIs. Young kids, who had never wandered beyond the precinct of their native city or their small hometown or their father's farm, ran into exotic places and exotic people, as well as into one another, whom they found equally exotic.

"The first time I ever heard a New England accent," recalls the Midwesterner, "was at Fort Benning. The southerner was an exotic creature to me. People from the farms. The New York street-smarts." [Author's note: The native New Yorker was probably the most parochial, most set in his ways, and most gullible.]

One of the most satisfying moments during my brief turn as a "military man" came at a crap game. It was in Jefferson Barracks. A

couple of hotshots from New York and Philadelphia had things seem-
ingly going their way. I and several others lost our pokes in short
order. Along came this freckled, skinny kid off an Arkansas farm, his
Adam's apple bobbing wildly. It appeared that the easterners had
another pigeon. An hour or so later, the street-smart boys were thor-
oughly cleaned out by the rube. It was lovely. City boys and country
boys were, for the first time in their lives, getting acquainted.

In tough circumstances, as a war prisoner or under siege or waiting for Godot, what was most on the soldier's mind was not women
nor politics nor family nor, for that matter, God. It was food. "In
camp," a prisoner of the Japanese recalls, "first thing you talked
about is what you wanted in your stomach. Guys would tell about
how their mother made this. Men would sit and listen very atten-
tively. This was the big topic all the time. I remember vividly this
old Polack. One guy always wanted him to talk about how his
mother made the cabbage rolls, the *golabki.* He had a knack of
telling so you could almost smell 'em. You'd see some of the fellas
just lickin' their lips. Tasting it. You know?"

Food. Fear. Comradeship. And confusion. In battle, the order of
the day was often disorder. Again and again survivors, gray, bald,
potbellied, or cadaverous, remember chaos.

The big redhead of the 106th Infantry Division can't forget his
trauma. "So here I am wandering around with a whole German
army shooting at me, and all I've got is a .45 automatic. There
were ample opportunities, however, because every place you went
there were bodies and soldiers laying around. Mostly Americans.
At one time or another, I think I had in my hands every weapon the
United States Army manufactured. You'd run out of ammunition
with that one, you'd throw it away and try to find something else."

The lieutenant recalls an experience some five days after D-Day.
"We were in dug-in foxholes, in a very checkered position. There
were Germans ahead of us and Germans in the back of us. Ameri-

cans over there ahead of these Germans. There was no straight front line. It was a mess."

A mess among the living, perhaps. There was order, of a sort, among the dead. At least for the Germans. A Stalingrad veteran is haunted by the memory of the moment. "I was sleeping on the bodies of killed German soldiers. The Germans were very orderly people. When they found they didn't have time to bury these bodies, they laid them next to each other in a very neat and orderly way. I saw straight rows, like pieces of cordwood. Exact."

A woman, born in 1943, cannot forget the camp photographs in *Life*. She had been casually leafing through some old issues in a Pennsylvania school library. She was twelve at the time. "In those grainy photos, you first think it's cords of wood piled up. You look again, it shows you human beings. You never get the picture out of your eye: the interchangeability of the stacks of human bodies and the stacks of cords of wood. There is something curious about the fascination with horror that isn't exhausted anywhere. Prior to finding these pictures, there were merely hints of something to a sheltered girl, nothing she could put together."

Between the winter of 1941 and the summer of 1945, Willie and Joe, dogfaces, and their assorted buddies grew up in a hurry. It wasn't only the bullet they bit. It was the apple. Some lost innocence, abroad. "I went there a skinny, gaunt mama's boy, full of wonderment," says the rifleman. "I came back much more circumspect in my judgment of people. And of governments."

Others were not quite so touched. "I got one eye. My feet hangs down. I got a joint mashed in my back. I got a shoulder been broke. Feel that knot right there." The Kentucky guardsman offers a litany of war wounds, but is undaunted. "I'd go fight for my country right today. You're darn right. I'd go right now, boy."

They all came back home. All but 400,000.

At home, the fourteen-year-old Victory girl grew up in a hurry, too. "What I feel most about the war, it disrupted my family. That really chokes me up, makes me feel very sad that I lost that. On December 6, 1941, I was playing with paper dolls: Deanna Durbin, Sonja Henie. I had a Shirley Temple doll that I cherished. After Pearl Harbor, I never played with dolls again."

After the epochal victory over fascism, the boys came back to resume their normal lives. Yet it was a different country from the one they had left.

> In 1945, the United States inherited the earth.... at the end of World War II, what was left of Western civilization passed into the American account. The war had also prompted the country to invent a miraculous economic machine that seemed to grant as many wishes as were asked of it. The continental United States had escaped the plague of war, and so it was easy enough for the heirs to believe that they had been anointed by God.*

We had hardly considered ourselves God's anointed in the thirties. The Great Depression was our most devastating experience since the Civil War. Somewhere along the line, our money machine had stripped its gears.

The sixteen million Americans out in the cold reached for abandoned newspapers on park benches and—would you believe?—skipped over the sports section and flipped feverishly to Help Wanted. A hard-traveling survivor recalls an ad being answered at the Spreckels sugar refinery in San Francisco: "A thousand men would fight like a pack of Alaskan dogs to get through. You know dang well, there's only three or four jobs."

With the German invasion of Poland in 1939, it all changed. The farewell to a dismal decade was more than ceremonial: 1939 was the end and the beginning. Hard Times, as though by some twentieth-century alchemy, were transmuted into Good Times. War was our Paracelsus.

True, the New Deal had created jobs and restored self-esteem

---

* Lewis H. Lapham, "America's Foreign Policy: A Rake's Progress," *Harper's,* March 1979.

for millions of Americans. Still, there were ten, eleven million walking the streets, riding the rods, up against it, despairing. All this changed under the lowering sky of World War Two. What had been a country psychically as well as geographically isolated had become, with the suddenness of a blitzkrieg, engaged with distant troubles. And close-at-hand triumphs.

Our huge industrial machine shifted gears. In a case of Scripture turned upside down, plowshares were beaten into swords (or their twentieth-century equivalents: tanks, mortars, planes, bombs). In the words of President Franklin D. Roosevelt, Dr. New Deal was replaced by Dr. Win The War.

Thomas (Tommy the Cork) Corcoran, one of FDR's wonder boys, remembers being called into the Oval Office: " 'Tommy, cut out this New Deal stuff. It's tough to win a war.' He'd heard from the people who could produce the tanks and other war stuff. As a payoff, they required an end to what they called New Deal nonsense."

James Rowe, who had been a young White House adviser, recalls: "It upset the New Dealers. We had a big PWA building program. Roosevelt took a big chunk of that money and gave it to the navy to build ships. I was shocked. A large number of businessmen came down as dollar-a-year men. Roosevelt was taking help anyplace he could get it. There was a quick change into a war economy."

And prosperity came. Boom had a double meaning.

For the old Iowa farmer, it was something else. Oh yes, he remembered the Depression and what it did to the farmers: foreclosures the norm; grain burned; corn at *minus* three cents a bushel; rural despair. Oh Yes, it changed with the war. "That's when the real boost came. The war—" There is a catch in his voice. He slumps in his rocker. His wife stares at the wallpaper. It is a long silence, save for the *tick-tock* of the grandfather's clock. "—it does something to your country. It does something to the individual. I had a neighbor just as the war was beginning. We had a boy ready to go to service. This neighbor told me what we needed was a damn good war, and we'd solve our agricultural problems. And I said, 'Yes, but I'd hate to pay with the price of my son.' Which we did." He weeps. "It's too much of a price to pay."

The retired Red Cross worker wastes no words: "The war was fun for America. I'm not talking about the poor souls who lost sons and daughters. But for the rest of us, the war was a hell of a good time. Farmers in South Dakota that I administered relief to and gave 'em bully beef and four dollars a week to feed their families, when I came home were worth a quarter-million dollars, right? It's forgotten now."

It had, indeed, become another country. "World War Two changed everything," says the retired admiral. "Our military runs our foreign policy. The State Department has become the lackey of the Pentagon. Before World War Two, this never happened. Only if there was a war did they step up front. The ultimate control was civilian. World War Two changed all this."

It is exquisite irony that military work liberated women from the private world of *Küche, Kinde, Kirche.* "I remember going to Sunday dinner one of the older women invited me to," the ex-school-teacher remembers. "She and her sister at the dinner table were talking about the best way to keep their drill sharp in the factory. I never heard anything like this in my life. It was just marvelous. But even here we were sold a bill of goods. They were hammering away that the woman who went to work did it to help her man, and when he came back, she cheerfully leaped back to the home."

Though at war's end these newborn working women were urged, as their patriotic duty Over Here, to go back home where they "naturally belonged" and give their jobs back to the boys who did their patriotic duty Over There, the taste for independence was never really lost. Like that of Wrigley's chewing gum, found in the pack of every GI, its flavor was longer-lasting. No matter what the official edict, for millions of American women home would never again be a Doll's House.

War's harsh necessity affected another people as well: the blacks. Not much had happened to change things in the years between the two world wars. Big Bill Broonzy, the blues singer, commemorated his doughboy life in World War One:

> When Uncle Sam called me, I knew I would be called the real McCoy.
> But when I got in the army, they called me soldier boy.
> I wonder when will I be called a man?

As in 1917, black servicemen were almost exclusively in labor battalions: loading ships, cleaning up, kitchen work, digging one thing or another. They were domestics abroad as well as at home. Mythology had long been standard operating procedure: blacks were not to be trusted in combat. To this, Coleman Young offered a wry touch of history: "The black Tenth Cavalry was with Teddy Roosevelt at San Juan Hill. They saved his ass." As the war dragged on, and casualties mounted alarmingly, black soldiers were sent up front. Grudgingly, they were allowed to risk their lives in combat. Lieutenant Charles A. Gates tells of the 761st Tank Battalion. All black. "We were very well disciplined and trained. The German army was confused. They couldn't see how we could be in so many places at the same time." There was astonishment on the part of our generals as well as theirs. It took thirty-five years for the 761st to get a Presidential Unit Citation.

These were rare adventures for black GIs in World War Two. A schoolteacher recalls his days as a sergeant with the Quartermaster Corps: "That's where most of us were put. We serviced the service. We handled food, clothing, equipage. We loaded ammunition, too. We were really stevedores and servants."

At home, things were somewhat different. Like women, blacks were called upon. Their muscles and skills, usually bypassed, were needed in defense plants. The perverse imperatives of war brought about relatively well-paying jobs for black men and women who would otherwise have been regarded with less than benign neglect.

Even this might not have come about had it not been for the constant pressure from the black community.

"I got a call from my boss. 'Get your ass over here, we got a problem.' " Joseph Rauh, working in Washington, remembers June of 1941. " 'Some guy named Randolph is going to march on Washington unless we put out a fair employment practices order.* The President says you gotta stop Randolph from marching. We got defense plants goin' all over this goddamn country, but no blacks are bein' hired. Go down to the Budget Bureau and work something out.' "

It was not noblesse oblige that brought forth Executive Order 8802, establishing the Fair Employment Practice Committee.

Wartime prosperity had extended into an exhilarating period of postwar prosperity. The United States had become the most powerful industrial as well as military power in the world. Its exports were now as truly worldwide as its politics. For the returning GI, it was a wholly new society. And a new beginning.

"I had matured in those three years away," says the middle manager of a large corporation. He had come from a family of blue-collar workers in a blue-collar town. I wanted to better myself more than, say, hitting the local factory. Fortunately, I was educated on the GI Bill. It was a blessing. The war changed our whole idea of how we wanted to live when we came back. We set our sights pretty high. All of us wanted better levels of living. I am now what you'd call middle class."

The suburb, until now, had been the exclusive domain of the "upper class." It was where the rich lived. The rest of us were neighborhood folk. At war's end, a new kind of suburb came into being. GI Joe, with his persevering wife/sweetheart and baby, moved into the little home so often celebrated in popular song.

---

* A. Philip Randolph, president of the Brotherhood of Sleeping Car Porters. He and other black leaders were planning a march urging the administration to pass a fair employment practices act.

Molly and me and baby makes three. It was not My Blue Heaven, perhaps, but it was something only dreamed of before. Thanks to the GI Bill, two new names were added to American folksay: Levittown and Park Forest.

A new middle class had emerged. Until now, the great many, even before the Depression, had had to scuffle from one payday to the next. "When you went to the doctor's," remembers the California woman, "it may have been ten dollars, but that was maybe a third of my father's salary as a milkman."

"The American myth was alive," reminisces a Sioux Falls native. "Remember the '49 cars in the *National Geographic?* Postwar cars. New design, new body style. In the colored Sunday funnies there'd be ads for the new cars. We'd been driving Grandpa Herman's old prewar Chrysler. It was the only car on the block. Now everybody was getting a car. Oh, it was exciting."

It was, indeed, a different world to which Telford Taylor returned from Germany. He had been the chief American prosecutor during twelve of the thirteen Nuremberg trials. "When I came back home in 1949, I was already in my early forties. I'd been away from home seven years and was out of touch with things politically. I thought that Washington was still the way I'd left it in 1942. By 1949, it was a very different place. I had left Washington at a time when it was still Roosevelt, liberalism, social action, all these things. When I came back in the late forties, the Dies Committee...the cold war. I was a babe in the woods. I didn't know what hit me."

The cold war. Another legacy of World War Two.

The year Telford Taylor returned to the States, Archibald MacLeish wrote a singularly prescient essay:

Never in the history of the world was one people as completely dominated, intellectually and morally, by another as the people of the United States by the people of Russia in the four years from 1946 through 1949. American foreign policy was a mirror image of Russian foreign policy: whatever the Russians did, we did in reverse. American domestic politics were conducted under a kind of upside-

down Russian veto: no man could be elected to public office unless
he was on record as detesting the Russians, and no proposal could
be enacted, from a peace plan at one end to a military budget at the
other, unless it could be demonstrated that the Russians wouldn't
like it. American political controversy was controversy sung to the
Russian tune; left-wing movements attacked right-wing movements
not on American issues but on Russian issues, and right-wing movements replied with the same arguments turned round about....

All this...took place not in a time of national weakness or decay
but precisely at the moment when the United States, having engi-
neered a tremendous triumph and fought its way to a brilliant victory in the greatest of all wars, had reached the highest point of
world power ever achieved by a single state.*

The ex-admiral says it his way: "World War Two has warped our
view of how we look at things today. We see things in terms of that
war, which in a sense was a good war. But the twisted memory of it
encourages the men of my generation to be willing, almost eager, to
use military force anywhere in the world."

In a small midwestern rural town, a grandmother, soft and
gentle, is certain she speaks for most of the townsfolk. "People here
feel that we should have gone into Vietnam and finished it instead
of backing off as we did. I suppose it's a feeling that carried over
from World War Two when we finished Hitler. I know the older men
who fought in that war feel that way."

Big Bill Broonzy put it another way. It happened quite inadver-
tently one night in a Chicago nightclub. He had been singing a
country blues about a sharecropper whose mule had died. It was his
own story. During the performance, four young hipsters made a
scene of walking out on him. I, working as MC that night, was furious. Big Bill laughed. He always laughed at such moments.
Laughin' to keep from cryin', perhaps. "What do these kids know
'bout a mule? They never seen a mule. How do you expect somebody
to feel 'bout somethin' he don't know? When I was in Europe, all

---

* MacLeish's piece of 1949, "The Conquest of America," was reprinted in the
Atlantic Monthly, March 1980.

those places, Milano, Hamburg, London, I seen cities bombed out. People tellin' me 'bout bombins. What do I know 'bout a bomb? The only bomb I ever did see was in the pictures. People scared, cryin'. Losin' their homes. What do I know 'bout that? I never had no bomb fall on me. Same thing with these kids. They never had no mule die on 'em. They don't even know what the hell I'm talkin' 'bout."

Big Bill, at that moment, set off the most pertinent and impertinent of challenges: Must a society experience horror in order to understand horror? Ours was the only country among the combatants in World War Two that was neither invaded nor bombed. Ours were the only cities not blasted into rubble. Our Willie and Joe were up front; the rest of us were safe, surrounded by two big oceans. As for our allies and enemies, civilian as well as military were, at one time or another, up front: the British, the French, the Russians (twenty million dead; perhaps thirty million, says Harrison Salisbury), as well as the Germans, the Italians, the Japanese. Let alone the Slavs of smaller spheres. And, of course, the European Jews. And the Gypsies. And all kinds of *Untermenschen*.

True, an inconsolable grief possessed the families of those Americans lost and maimed in the Allied triumph. Parks, squares, streets, and bridges have been named after these young heroes, sung and unsung. Yet it is the casual walkout of the four young hipsters in that Chicago nightclub that may be the rude, fearsome metaphor we must decipher.

The elderly Japanese *hibakisha* (survivor of the atom bomb), contemplates the day it fell on Hiroshima. He had been a nineteen-year-old soldier passing through town. "The children were screaming, 'Please take these maggots off our bodies.' It was impossible for me, one soldier, to try to help so many people. The doctor said, 'We can't do anything. Sterilize their wounds with salt water.' We took a broom, dipped it into the salt water and painted over the bodies. The children leaped up: 'I'm gonna run, I must run.' " The interpreter corrects him: "In the local dialect, it means 'thank you.' "

The tall young rifleman understands the horror. He was being retrained, after his European near-misses, for the invasion of Japan when the first atom bomb was dropped. "We ended halfway across the Pacific. How many of us would have been killed on the mainland if there were no bomb? Someone like me has this specter." So does his quondam buddy: "We're sitting on the pier in Seattle, sharpening our bayonets, when Harry dropped that beautiful bomb. The greatest thing ever happened. Anybody sitting at the pier at that time would have to agree." The black combat correspondent sees it somewhat differently: "Do you realize that most blacks don't believe the atom bomb would have been dropped on Hiroshima had it been a white city?" Witnesses to the fire bombings of Dresden may dispute the point.

The crowning irony lay in World War Two itself. It had been a different kind of war. "It was not like your other wars," a radio disk jockey reflected aloud. In his banality lay a wild kind of crazy truth. It was not fratricidal. It was not, most of us profoundly believed, "imperialistic." Our enemy was, patently, obscene: the Holocaust maker. It was one war that many who would have resisted "your other wars" supported enthusiastically. It was a "just war," if there is any such animal. In a time of nuclear weaponry, it is the language of a lunatic. But World War Two...

It ended on a note of hope without historic precedent. *On a Note of Triumph* is what Norman Corwin called his eloquent radio program heard coast-to-coast on V-E Day, May 8, 1945.

> Lord God of test-tube and blueprint
> Who jointed molecules of dust and shook them till
>   their name was Adam,
> Who taught worms and stars how they could live together,
> Appear now among the parliaments of conquerors and
>   give instruction to their schemes:
> Measure out new liberties so none shall suffer for his
>   father's color or the credo of his choice....

The day of that broadcast is remembered for a number of reasons by a West Coast woman. "V-E Day. Oh, such a joyous thing! And San Francisco was chosen for the first session of the UN. I was ecstatic. Stalin, Churchill, and Roosevelt met, and somehow war never again would happen." She was an usher at the War Memorial Opera House, where the UN first met in June of '45. "I was still in my little Miss Burke School uniform. Little middy and skirt. I was part of it. And so deeply proud. When the Holocaust survivors came out, I felt we were liberating them. When the GIs and Russian soldiers met, they were all knights in shining armor, saving humanity." She laughs softly. "It's not that simple. World War Two was just an innocent time in America. I was innocent. My parents were innocent. The country was innocent. Since World War Two, I think I have a more objective view of what this country really is."

The Red Cross worker thinks of then and now. "To many people, it brought about a realization that there ain't no hidin' place down here. That the world is unified in pain as well as opportunity. We had twenty, twenty-five years of greatness in our country, when we reached out to the rest of the world with help. Some of it was foolish, some of it was misspent, some was in error. Many follies. But we had a great reaching out. It was an act of such faith." He tries to stifle an angry sob. "Now, we're being pinched back into the meanness of the soul. World War Two? It's a war I still would go to."

The ex-captain, watching a Dow-Jones ticker, shakes his head. "I don't have as much trust in my fellow man as I once did. I have no trust in my peers. They're burnt-out cases. In the war, I was trying to do something useful with my life…"

A thousand miles away, the once and forever tall young rifleman, though gray and patriarchal, stares out the window at the Chicago skyline, the Lake, and beyond. "World War Two has affected me in many ways ever since. In a short period of time I had the most tremendous experiences of all of life: of fear, of jubilance, of misery, of hope, of comradeship, and of endless excitement. I honestly feel grateful for having been a witness to an event as monumental as anything in history and, in a very small way, a participant."

ROBERT RASMUS

I've lived about thirty-eight years after the war and about twenty years before. For me it's B.W. and A.W.—before the war and after the war. I suspect there are a lot of people like me. In business, there'll be times when I say, This really worries the heck out of me, but it's really minor compared to having to do a river crossing under fire. [Laughs.]

He is six feet four or five, graying. He is a business executive, working out of Chicago. Obviously he's kept himself in pretty good shape. His manner is gentle, easy, unruffled.

I get this strange feeling of living through a world drama. In September of '39 when the Germans invaded Poland, I was fourteen years old. I remember my mother saying, "Bob, you'll be in it." I was hoping she'd be right. At that age, you look forward to the glamour and have no idea of the horrors.

Sure enough, I was not only in the army but in the infantry. Step by logistic step, our division was in combat. You're finally down to one squad, out ahead of the whole thing. You're the point man. What am I doing out here—in this world-cataclysmic drama—out in front of the whole thing? [Laughs.]

You saw those things in the movies, you saw the newsreels. But you were of an age when your country wasn't even in the war. It seemed unreal. All of a sudden, there you were right in the thick of it and people were dying and you were scared out of your wits that you'd have your head blown off. [Laughs.]

I was acutely aware, being a rifleman, the odds were high that I would be killed. At one level, animal fear. I didn't like that at all. On the other hand, I had this great sense of adventure. My gosh, going across the ocean, seeing the armies, the excitement of it. I was there.

This wouldn't have been true of most, but I was a skinny, gaunt kind of mama's boy. I was going to gain my manhood then. I would forever be liberated from the sense of inferiority that I wasn't rugged. I would prove that I had the guts and the manhood to stand up to these things. There were all these things, from being a member of the Western world to Bobby Rasmus, the skinny nineteen year old who's gonna prove that he can measure up. [Laughs.]

I remember my mother during my thirty-day furlough. Continuous weeping. She said, "Bob, you've got to tell your captain you're too tall to be a rifleman." [Laughs.] The only way I could get her off that was to say, "I'll tell him, Ma." Of course, I didn't.

I was in training at Fort Benning, Georgia. If you got sick and fell back more than a week, you were removed from your battalion. I got the flu and was laid back for eight days. I was removed from my outfit where all my buddies were. I was heartbroken.

My original group went to the 106th Division and ended up being overwhelmed in the Battle of the Bulge. I remember letters I sent my buddies that came back: Missing in action. Killed in action. These were the eighteen year olds. It was only because I got the flu that I wasn't among them.

When I went in the army, I'd never been outside the states of Wisconsin, Indiana, and Michigan. So when I woke up the first morning on the troop train in Fulton, Kentucky, I thought I was in Timbuktu. Of course, I was absolutely bowled over by Europe, the castles, the cathedrals, the Alps. It was wonderment. I was preoccupied with staying alive and doing my job, but it seemed, out of the corner of my eye, I was constantly fascinated with the beauty of the German forests and medieval bell towers. At nineteen, you're seeing life with fresh eyes.

The first time I ever heard a New England accent was at Fort Benning. The southerner was an exotic creature to me. People from the farms. The New York street-smarts. You had an incredible mixture of every stratum of society. And you're of that age when your need for friendship is greatest. I still see a number of these people. There's sort of a special sense of kinship.

The reason you storm the beaches is not patriotism or bravery. It's that sense of not wanting to fail your buddies. Having to leave that group when I had the flu may have saved my life. Yet to me, that kid, it was a disaster.

Kurt Vonnegut, in *Slaughterhouse Five,* writes of the fire bombing of Dresden and the prisoner-of-war train in Germany. A lot of my buddies who were captured were on that train. I didn't know that until three days ago when a middle-aged guy with white hair like mine stopped me on the street and said, "Hey, aren't you Bob Rasmus?" I said, "Aren't you Red Prendergast?" He'd been in the original training group, gone to the 106th Division, taken to Germany, was on the troop train that got strafed. I knew him for about five months, thirty-nine years ago, and had never set eyes on him since. I was only in combat for six weeks, but I could remember every hour, every minute of the whole forty-two days.

In Boston Harbor, we actually saw the first visible sign of the war: an Australian cruiser tied up next to the troop ship. There was a huge, jagged hole in the bow. The shape of things to come. There was a lot of bravado, kidding.

Our impression of France, those of us who grew up in the thirties, was French maids, French poodles, a frivolous type of people. So it was striking to see these stolid peasants walking behind horse-drawn plows. The area we were in had not yet been hit by the war. I was struck by the sheer beauty of the countryside, the little villages, the churches. This sort of thing the impressionists did.

Going to the front, I can remember the cities in Belgium: Liège, Namur. We were going through towns and villages. We were hanging out of the cars of the trains and on the roofs. We had all this extra candy from our K rations and would just throw them out to the kids. There was a sense of victory in the air. They had already been liberated. They were elated.

All of a sudden, the tone changes. You get off the train on the border in that little corner of Holland and Germany. We're near Aachen, which had been absolutely leveled by Allied bombings. Rubble, nothing but rubble. Here was the ancient city of Aix-la-Chapelle, just a sea of rubble. We've had forty-eight hours enjoying being part of the victorious army. Now the party's over. You're within a few miles of the front. You're off the train into trucks. You hear gunfire in the distance.

Everybody sobered up very rapidly. We drove on for a few miles and there was a second city, Düren, totally wiped out. It was one of the most bombed-out cities in Germany. Now we're moving forward on foot.

They moved us into what they called a quiet front. Our division occupied a frontage on the Rhine, south of Cologne. We simply relieved another division that had been there, the Eighth. We moved into the same foxholes. You know it's getting close. It's still sort of exciting. Nobody's gotten killed yet. To me, it was interesting because of the architecture. From the distance I could see the Cologne cathedral, with the twin towers.

We stayed in bombed-out buildings. It was almost surreal. Here's a cross-section of a four-story, where every room is open to the atmosphere on one side and there's another room that is still intact. This was true all the way through Europe.

The very first night, our squad was in comfortable quarters. Our one side was completely open, but on the other side were beds and kitchens and what-not. It was almost theatrical. Since the Germans were the enemy and evil, we never had any sense of guilt that we were in somebody's apartment. Any abuse of the apartment, like throwing dishes out the window, was what they deserved.

Whatever was there in the way of food and drink, we would make use of.

One of the things we had was this old music box. It could play whole melodies. We had two disks. One was "Silent Night" and the other was "We Gather Together to Ask the Lord's Blessing." I had a typical Lutheran churchgoing background. Here am I hearing a Christmas carol and a hymn that I'd sung many times in church.

I was sort of schizophrenic all through this period. I was a participant, scared out of my wits. But I was also acutely aware of how really theatrical and surreal it was.

Three days later we pulled out, crossed the Rhine, and cut off a German pocket. As we were moving out of this area of sheared-off buildings, there were courtyards with fruit trees in blossom. And there were our heavy mortars blasting away across the river. I had been seeing shadowy figures moving around. Were they infiltrators or just a bush that I was imagining? And there in sight was the Cologne cathedral amidst all this wreckage.

We've seen a little of the war now. We've seen planes dropping bombs over on the other side. We've sent out patrols, have captured prisoners. But we really hadn't been in it ourselves. It was still fun and dramatics. When the truck took us from Cologne south through Bonn, for me it was, Hey, Beethoven's birthplace! But when we crossed a pontoon bridge and I saw a balloon of fire, I knew the real combat was going to begin. I had the feeling now that we were gonna be under direct fire, some of us were gonna be killed. But I was also enormously affected by the beauty of the countryside. We were in rolling hills and great forests. It stretched out for mile after mile. I could almost hear this Wagnerian music. I was pulled in two directions: Gee, I don't wanna get killed. And, Boy, this is gorgeous country.

Our uniforms were still clean. We were still young kids who hadn't seen anything. You could see these veteran troops. Their uniforms were dirty, they were bearded, there was a look in their eyes that said they'd been through a lot. A sort of expression on their faces—You're gonna find out now. A mixture of pity and contempt for the greenhorns.

We started seeing our first dead, Germans. You drew the obvious inference: if Germans were dead, the Americans were getting killed farther up the line. Night fell, we were up within a couple of miles of where the action would begin. We were passing through our artillery emplacements. Incessant firing. It was reassuring to see how much artillery we had, but disturbing to see all these German dead. I had never seen a dead body before, except in a funeral home.

We were told that the next morning we would be on the attack. I remember the miserable cold. By this time, I had taken up cigarette smoking, wondering what my mother would think when I came back. [Laughs.] I felt sickish, I was cold, I was scared. And I couldn't even get one last cigarette.

We were awakened before dawn. I honestly don't know whether I dreamed it or whether it really happened. I've asked buddies I've seen since the war: Can you remember these ambulances and army surgeons getting their gear out? I have such an absolute recollection of it, but nobody else remembers it. It had a dreamlike quality: just seeing surgeons ready to work. Here we were still healthy, still an hour or two away from actual combat. It added to the inevitability that really bad, bad things were going to happen.

Our platoon of thirty men was to take a small town. At the time, I was a bazooka man. I'll never forget that sense of unreality as we were moving through the woods to this village, which we could just see a few hundred yards away. There were sheep grazing in the fields. By now there's gunfire: machine guns, rifle fire, mortar shells.

You'd lost your sense of direction. This was not a continuous front. These were piercing, probing actions. You'd take a town, then to the next river, then across the river and then the next one.

This was the first. Now I can see actual mortar shells landing in this meadow. German 88s. They were hitting the tile roofs of these houses and barns. My initial reaction: they're not hurting anything. Oh, a few tiles being knocked loose, but it's still a beautiful sunny day. The meadow is lovely. Here we are in a medieval village. This reaction lasted three seconds. These sheep started getting hit. You were seeing blood. Immediately you say, Soon it's gonna be us torn up like these animals. You sense all these stages you've gone through. And now (laughs), the curtain has gone up and you're really in it.

We captured that town without any casualties. I think the German troops had moved out. My confidence is coming back a little. Gee, we captured a town and didn't even see a German. Later that afternoon, we were moving up to take another town. We have a sense that things aren't going too well. We seem out of radio contact with the other rifle companies. I sense an apprehension by our officers.

All of a sudden, we spotted a group of German soldiers down by the slope of this hill, perhaps fifty. We were strung out, a couple of platoons. We would be on the ground, get up on command, and start firing right into this group of Germans. We did catch them by surprise. They responded quickly, firing back, machine guns and rifles. We had them well outnumbered, our company, about 240. We did the march-and-fire. It was a new maneuver we'd never done in training. We learned. I noticed that some of our guys were getting hit. It was all in a few minutes. We killed most of the Germans. A few might have gotten away, but we wiped them out. Our guys were getting killed, too. Irony again, the first one killed was our platoon sergeant.

You have to understand the culture of our company. Most of our privates were college types. They had been dumped en masse into these infantry divisions. The cadre of noncommissioned officers were old-timers. They were mostly uneducated country types, many of them from the South. There was a rather healthy mutual contempt between the noncoms and the privates. This sergeant was the most hated man. One of the nineteen-year-olds, during maneuvers, was at the point of tears in his hatred of this man who was so unreasonable and so miserable. He'd say, "If we ever get into combat, I'm gonna kill 'im. First thing I'll do." Who's the first one killed? This sergeant. I'm sure it was enemy fire. I would bet my life on it. I'm sure the guys who said they would kill him were horrified that their wish came true.

"I'm gonna kill 'im" is said a million times.

I'm sure our company was typical. We had x percent of self-inflicted wounds. There's no question that a guy would blow his toe off to get out of combat. People would get lost. These combat situations are so confused that it's very easy to go in the other direction. Say you get lost, get sick, get hurt. By the time you get back to your outfit, a couple of days have gone by.

We remember examples of Caspar Milquetoast: ordinary people showing incredible heroism. But you have to accept the fact that in a cross section of people—in civilian life, too—you've got cowards and quitters. Our radio man shot up his radio: he thought we were going to be captured. Panic. I became a bazooka man because our bazooka man threw his weapon away and I picked it up. He ran off.

Our captain said, "Pick up the bodies. We don't leave our dead to the enemy." We're now cut off and have to join the rest of our battalion. We had to improvise stretchers. I took off my field jacket and turned the arms inside out. We poked rifles through the arms and fashioned a stretcher. We got the sergeant on ours and, jeez, half his head was blown off and the brains were coming out on my hands and on my uniform. Here's the mama's boy, Sunday school, and now I'm really in it.

I remember lying in that slit trench that night. It was a nightmare. I'd now seen what dead people look like, the color out of their face. I think each person in my squad went through this dream of mine. Daylight came and we moved out into another town. This is twenty-four hours of experience.

Those who really went through combat, the Normandy landings, the heavy stuff, might laugh at this little action we'd been in, but for me…We were passing people who were taking over from us, another company. We had one day of this. Our uniforms were now dirty and bloody and our faces looked like we'd been in there for weeks. Now *we* had the feeling: You poor innocents.

We weren't able to bring those bodies back with us. The mortar fire became too much. The next morning, our squad was assigned to go back and recover the bodies. It was sunshine and quiet. We were passing the Germans we killed. Looking at the individual German dead, each took on a personality. These were no longer an abstraction. These were no longer the Germans of the brutish faces and the helmets we saw in the newsreels. They were exactly our age. These were boys like us.

I remember one, particularly. A redhead. To this day, I see the image of this young German soldier sitting against a tree. This group was probably resting, trying to make their escape. The whole thing might have been avoided had we been more experienced and called down in German for them to surrender. They probably would have been only too glad. Instead, out of fear, there was this needless slaughter. It has the flavor of murder, doesn't it?

What I remember of that day is not so much the sense of loss at our two dead but a realization of how you've been conditioned. At that stage, we didn't hate the Germans just for evil the country represented, their militarism, but right down to each individual German. Once the helmet is off, you're looking at a teen-ager, another kid. Obviously you have to go on. There are many, many more engagements.

A few days, later, we're in Lüdenscheid. It's near the Ruhr pocket. Two Allied armies had crossed the Rhine fifteen miles apart. It's a pincer movement, closing in a pocket of 350,000 Germans. Under Field Marshal Model, I believe. They just don't surrender overnight. They're gonna fight it out. Our job, all the way through Germany, was to move as fast as you could on trucks, on tanks, until you came up against resistance. Some towns fell without a battle. Others, quite a bit of resistance. You'd assume the worst.

You were constantly behind the lines and then moved up. You'd pass through your artillery and you knew you were getting closer. Pretty soon things would thin out. Just an hour earlier there were an awful lot of GIs around. As you got closer to action, it was only your platoon, and then it was your squad ahead of the other two. You were the point man for the squad.

I thought, This is incredible. We've got these great masses of troops, of quartermasters and truckers and tanks and support troops, and then all of a sudden it's so lonely. [Laughs.] You're out ahead of the whole thing.

In Lüdenscheid, we were in the hills looking down. It was dead silence in the town, except that you became aware of German ambulances with the big red crosses on the roofs. We didn't know whether it was a trick. There was something mysterious about that sight. The bells started tolling in the city. You didn't know what to make of it. Was this the opening of a major battle? Were they going away? There was very little resistance and we took the town.

Now I began to get an inkling of some other evil abroad. We were very much aware that the Germans had mobilized the Poles, the French, the captive countries, into workers on farms and in factories. As each town was captured, you were liberating Slavs, Poles, French, whatever. It was often highly emotional. The idea of those death camps still hadn't reached us at all. I marvel as I think back on it. When we took Lüdenscheid, our platoon stayed overnight in what was a combination beer hall, theater, festival-type thing, with a stage and a big dance floor. There in the middle of the floor was this mountain of clothing. I realize now that was probably the clothing they'd taken from the people that went to Dachau or another camp. It really didn't register with us what that might have been. You knew this wasn't just a Salvation Army collecting clothes. I remember it because that was the day Roosevelt died.

Every town had a certain number of slave laborers. It might range from handfuls to hundreds, depending on whether there was industry in that town. The final one we captured in the Ruhr was Letmathe. There was a large number of Italian laborers who worked in a factory. There were quite a few Russians. The military government hadn't yet moved in. I remember the Russians taking the horses and running them up and down the street to get their circulation up and then kill them for food. A Russian was going to kill the horse with a hatchet. I wasn't up to shooting the horse myself, but I let him use my pistol. We were aware of the starvation and the desperate measures they would take.

You had these spontaneous uprisings where the slave laborers and war prisoners the Germans had in these towns would just take over. It was very chaotic.

I remember where a Russian was in the process of strangling a German in the cellar of our building. This was a moment of truth for me. I was still nurturing the notion that every individual German was evil and the Russians were our allies. Somehow I got the picture that the Russian was carrying out vengeance. He claimed this German had killed his buddy. In that confused situation you couldn't tell whether it was true or whether it was a grudge carried out or what. It didn't take much deliberation to stop it. The Russian broke out in tears when I wouldn't let him kill the German. He just sobbed. Reflecting on it later, I had reason to believe his story was true. But I wasn't up to letting it happen.

We were aware that the Russians had taken enormous losses on the eastern front, that they really had broken the back of the German army. We would have been in for infinitely worse casualties and misery had it not been for them. We were well disposed toward them. I remember saying if we happen to link up with 'em, I wouldn't hesitate to kiss 'em.

I didn't hear any anti-Russian talk. I think we were realistic enough to know that if we were going to fight them, we would come out second best. We hadn't even heard of the atomic bomb yet. We'd just have to assume that it would be masses of armies, and their willingness to sacrifice millions of troops. We were aware that our leaders were sparing our lives. Even though somebody would have to do the dirty work in the infantry, our leaders would try to pummel the enemy with artillery and tanks and overpower them before sending the infantry in. If that was possible.

I've reflected on why people my age and with my experience don't have that spontaneous willingness to be part of the nuclear freeze. It's the sense that the Germans were willing to lose millions of men. And they did. Every German house we went to, there would be black-bordered pictures of sons and relatives. You could tell that most of them died on the eastern front. And the Russians lost twenty million.

Later, we were back in the States being retrained for the Japanese invasion. The first atom bomb was dropped. We ended halfway across the Pacific. How many of us would have been killed on the mainland if there were no bomb? Someone like me has this specter.

In the final campaign down through Bavaria, we were in Patton's army. Patton said we ought to keep going. To me, that was an unthinkable idea. The Russians would have slaughtered us, because of their willingness to give up so many lives. I don't think the rank of the GIs had any stomach for fighting the Russians. We were informed enough through press and newsreels to know about Stalingrad. I saw the actual evidence in those black-bordered pictures in every German household I visited. Black border, eastern front, nine out of ten.

I have more disapproval of communism today than ever. I think our government did try to stimulate a feeling about good Uncle Joe. The convoys to Murmansk. We had this mixed feeling: Gee, we're glad they did the lion's share, the overwhelming bulk of the dying, the breaking the back of the German armies. And individually, they can't be all that bad. In any case, we don't want to fight 'em. [Laughs.]

The thing that turned me against the Vietnam War was an issue of *Life* magazine in '68. It had a cover picture of the hundred men that died in Vietnam that week. I said, Enough. I don't want to stand here as a veteran of World War Two saying that we somehow took a stand that was admirable. We are bad as the rest if we don't think independently and make up our own minds. We were willing to go along as long as it seemed an easy victory. When it really got tough, we started re-examining.

World War Two was utterly different. It has affected me in many ways ever since. I think my judgment of people is more circumspect. I know it's made me less ready to fall into the trap of judging people by their style or appearance. In a short period of time, I had the most tremendous experiences of all of life: of fear, of jubilance, of misery, of hope, of comradeship, and of the endless excitement, the theatrics of it. I honestly feel grateful for having been a witness to an event as monumental as anything in history and, in a very small way, a participant.

PEGGY TERRY

She is a mountain woman who has lived in Chicago for the past twenty years. Paducah, Kentucky, is her hometown. She visits it as often as her meager purse allows.

The first work I had after the Depression was at a shell-loading plant in Viola, Kentucky. It is between Paducah and Mayfield. They were large shells: anti-aircraft, incendiaries, and tracers. We painted red on the tips of the tracers. My mother, my sister, and myself worked there. Each of us worked a different shift because we had little ones at home. We made the fabulous sum of thirty-two dollars a week. [Laughs.] To us it was just an absolute miracle. Before that, we made nothing.

You won't believe how incredibly ignorant I was. I knew vaguely that a war had started, but I had no idea what it meant.

Didn't you have a radio?

Gosh, no. That was an absolute luxury. We were just moving around, working wherever we could find work. I was eighteen. My husband was nineteen. We were living day to day. When you are involved in stayin' alive, you don't think about big things like a war. It didn't occur to us that we were making these shells to kill people. It never entered my head.

There were no women foremen where we worked. We were just a bunch of hillbilly women laughin' and talkin'. It was like a social. Now we'd have money to buy shoes and a dress and pay rent and get some food on the table. We were just happy to have work.

I worked in building number 11. I pulled a lot of gadgets on a machine. The shell slid under and powder went into it. Another lever you pulled tamped it down. Then it moved on a conveyer belt to another building where the detonator was dropped in. You did this over and over.

Tetryl was one of the ingredients and it turned us orange. Just as orange as an orange. Our hair was streaked orange. Our hands, our face, our neck just turned orange, even our eyeballs. We never questioned. None of us ever asked, What is this? Is this harmful? We simply didn't think about it. That was just one of the conditions of the job. The only thing we worried about was other women thinking we had dyed our hair. Back then it was a disgrace if you dyed your hair. We worried what people would say.

We used to laugh about it on the bus. It eventually wore off. But I seem to remember some of the women had breathing problems. The shells were painted a dark gray. When the paint didn't come out smooth, we had to take rags wet with some kind of remover and wash that paint off. The fumes from these rags—it was like breathing cleaning fluid. It burned the nose and throat. Oh, it was difficult to breathe. I remember that.

Nothing ever blew up, but I remember the building where they dropped in the detonator. These detonators are little black things about the size of a thumb. This terrible thunderstorm came and all the lights went out. Somebody knocked a box of detonators off on the floor. Here we were in the pitch dark. Somebody was screaming, "Don't move, anybody!" They were afraid you'd step on the detonator. We were down on our hands and knees crawling out of that building in the storm. [Laughs.] We were in slow motion. If we'd stepped on one…

Mamma was what they call terminated—fired. Mamma's mother took sick and died and Mamma asked for time off and they told her no. Mamma said, "Well, I'm gonna be with my mamma. If I have to give up my job, I will just have to." So they terminated Mamma. That's when I started gettin' nasty. I didn't take as much baloney and pushing around as I had taken. I told 'em I was gonna quit, and they told me if I quit they would blacklist me wherever I would go. They had my fingerprints and all that. I guess it was just bluff, because I did get other work.

I think of how little we knew of human rights, union rights. We knew Daddy had been a hell-raiser in the mine workers' union, but at that point it hadn't rubbed off on any of us women. Coca-Cola and Dr. Pepper were allowed in every building, but not a drop of water. You could only get a drink of water if you went to the cafeteria, which was about two city blocks away. Of course you couldn't leave your machine long enough to go get a drink. I drank Coke and Dr. Pepper and I hated 'em. I hate 'em today. We had to buy it, of course. We couldn't leave to go to the bathroom, 'cause it was way the heck over there.

We were awarded the navy E for excellence. We were just so proud of that E. It was like we were a big family, and we hugged and kissed each other. They had the navy band out there celebrating us. We were so proud of ourselves.

First time my mother ever worked at anything except in the fields—first real job Mamma ever had. It was a big break in everybody's life. Once, Mamma woke up in the middle of the night to go to the bathroom and she saw the bus going down. She said, "Oh my goodness, I've overslept." She jerked her clothes on, throwed her lunch in the bag, and was out on the corner, ready to go, when Boy Blue, our driver, said, "Honey, this is the wrong shift." Mamma wasn't supposed to be there until six in the morning. She never lived that down. She would have enjoyed telling you that.

My world was really very small. When we came from Oklahoma to Paducah, that was like a journey to the center of the earth. It was during the Depression and you did good having bus fare to get across town. The war just widened my world. Especially after I came up to Michigan.

My grandfather went up to Jackson, Michigan, after he retired from the railroad. He wrote back and told us we could make twice as much in the war plants in Jackson. We did. We made ninety dollars a week. We did some kind of testing for airplane radios.

Ohh, I met all those wonderful Polacks. They were the first people I'd ever known that were any different from me. A whole new world just opened up. I learned to drink beer like crazy with 'em. They were all very union-conscious. I learned a lot of things that I didn't even know existed.

We were very patriotic and we understood that the Nazis were someone who would have to be stopped. We didn't know about concentration camps. I don't think anybody I knew did. With the Japanese, that was a whole different thing. We were just ready to wipe them out. They sure as heck didn't look like us. They were yellow little creatures that smiled when they bombed our boys. I remember someone in Paducah got up this idea of burning everything they had that was Japanese. I had this little ceramic cat and I said, "I don't care, I am not burning it." They had this big bonfire and people came and brought what they had that was made in Japan. Threw it on the bonfire. I hid my cat. It's on the shelf in my bathroom right now. [Laughs.]

In all the movies we saw, the Germans were always tall and handsome. There'd be one meanie, a little short dumpy bad Nazi. But the main characters were good-lookin' and they looked like us. The Japanese were all evil. If you can go half your life and not recognize how you're being manipulated, that is sad and kinda scary.

I do remember a nice movie, *The White Cliffs of Dover.* We all sat there with tears pouring down our face. All my life, I hated England, 'cause all my family all my life had wanted England out of Ireland. During the war, all those ill feelings just seemed to go away. It took a war.

I believe the war was the beginning of my seeing things. You just can't stay uninvolved and not knowing when such a momentous thing is happening. It's just little things that start happening and you put one piece with another. Suddenly, a puzzle begins to take shape.

My husband was a paratrooper in the war, in the 101st Airborne Division. He made twenty-six drops in France, North Africa, and Germany. I look back at the war with sadness. I wasn't smart enough to think too deeply then. We had a lotta good times and we had money and we had food on the table and the rent was paid. Which had never happened to us before. But when I look back and think of him...

Until the war he never drank. He never even smoked. When he came back he was an absolute drunkard. And he used to have the most awful nightmares. He'd get up in the middle of the night and start screaming. I'd just sit for hours and hold him while he just shook. We'd go to the movies, and if they'd have films with a lot of shooting in it, he'd just start to shake and have to get up and leave. He started slapping me around and slapped the kids around. He became a brute.

One of the things that bothered him most was his memory of this town he was in. He saw something move by a building and he shot. It was a woman. He never got over that. It seems so obvious to say—wars brutalize people. It brutalized him.

The war gave a lot of people jobs. It led them to expect more than they had before. People's expectations, financially, spiritually, were raised. There was such a beautiful dream. We were gonna reach the end of the rainbow. When the war ended, the rainbow vanished. Almost immediately we went into Korea. There was no peace, which we were promised.

I remember a woman saying on the bus that she hoped the war didn't end until she got her refrigerator paid for. An old man hit her over the head with an umbrella. He said, "How dare you!" [Laughs.]

Ohh, the beautiful celebrations when the war ended. They were selling cigarettes in Paducah. Up until that hour, you couldn'ta bought a pack of cigarettes for love or money. Kirchoff's Bakery was giving away free loaves of bread. Everybody was downtown in the pouring rain and we were dancing. We took off our shoes and put 'em in our purse. We were so happy.

The night my husband came home, we went out with a gang of friends and got drunk. All of us had a tattoo put on. I had a tattoo put up my leg where it wouldn't show. A heart with an arrow through it: Bill and Peggy. When I went to the hospital to have my baby—I got pregnant almost as soon as he came home—I was ashamed of the tattoo. So I put two Band-Aids across it. So the nurse just pulls 'em off, looks at the tattoo, and she says, "Oh, that's exactly in the same spot I got mine." She pulled her uniform up and showed me her tattoo. [Laughs.]

I knew the bomb dropped on Hiroshima was a big terrible thing, but I didn't know it was the horror it was. It was on working people. It wasn't anywhere near the big shots of Japan who started the war in the first place. We didn't drop it on them. Hirohito and his white horse, it never touched him. It was dropped on women and children who had nothing to say about whether their country went to war or not.

I was happy my husband would get to come home and wouldn't be sent there from Germany. Every day when the paper came out, there'd be somebody I knew with their picture. An awful lot of kids I knew, went to school and church with, were killed.

No bombs were ever dropped on us. I can't help but believe the cold war started because we were untouched. Except for our boys that went out of the country and were killed, we came out of that war in good shape. People with more money than they'd had in years.

No, I don't think we'd have been satisfied to go back to what we had during the Depression. To be deprived of things we got used to. Materially, we're a thousand times better off. But the war turned me against religion. I was raised in the fundamentalist faith. I was taught that I was nothing. My feeling is if God created me, if God sent his only begotten son to give his life for me, then I am something. My mother died thinking she was nothing. I don't know how chaplains can call themselves men of God and prepare boys to go into battle. If the Bible says, Thou shalt not kill, it doesn't say, Except in time of war. They'll send a man to the electric chair who in a temper killed somebody. But they pin medals on our men. The more people they kill, the more medals they pin on 'em.

I was just so glad when it was over, because I wanted my husband home. I didn't understand any of the implications except that the killing was over and that's a pretty good thing to think about whether you're political or not. [Laughs.] The killing be over forever.

E. B. (SLEDGEHAMMER) SLEDGE

Half-hidden in the hilly greenery, toward the end of a winding country road, is the house he himself helped build. It is on the campus of the University of Montevallo, a forty-five-minute drive from Birmingham, Alabama.

On the wall near the fireplace—comforting on this unseasonably cool day—is a plaque with the familiar Guadalcanal patch: "Presented to Eugene B. Sledge. We, the men of K Co., 3rd Bn., 5th Reg., 1st Marine Div., do hereby proudly bestow this testimonial in expression of our great admiration and heartfelt appreciation to one extraordinary marine, who had honored his comrades in arms by unveiling to the world its exploits and heroism in his authorship of WITH THE OLD BREED AT PELELIU AND OKINAWA. *God love you, Sledgehammer. 1982." It is his remarkable memoir that led me to him.**

Small-boned, slim, gentle in demeanor, he is a professor of biology at the university. "My main interest is ornithology. I've been a birdwatcher since I was a kid in Mobile. Do you see irony in that? Interested in birds, nature, a combat marine in the front lines? People think of bird-watchers as not macho."

There was nothing macho about the war at all. We were a bunch of scared kids who had to do a job. People tell me I don't act like an ex-marine. How is an ex-marine supposed to act? They have some Hollywood stereoptype in mind. No, I don't look like John Wayne.

---

* Novato, Calif.: Presidio Press, 1981.

We were in it to get it over with, so we could go back home and do what we wanted to do with our lives.

I was nineteen, a replacement in June of 1944. Eighty percent of the division in the Guadalcanal campaign was less than twenty-one years of age. We were much younger than the general army units.

To me, there were two different wars. There was the war of the guy on the front lines. You don't come off until you are wounded or killed. Or, if lucky, relieved. Then there was the support personnel. In the Pacific, for every rifleman on the front lines there were nineteen people in the back. Their view of the war was different than mine. The man up front puts his life on the line day after day after day to the point of utter hopelessness.

The only thing that kept you going was your faith in your buddies. It wasn't just a case of friendship. I never heard of self-inflicted wounds out there. Fellows from other services said they saw this in Europe. Oh, there were plenty of times when I wished I had a million-dollar wound. [Laughs softly.] Like maybe shootin' a toe off. What was worse than death was the indignation of your buddies. You couldn't let 'em down. It was stronger than flag and country.

With the Japanese, the battle was all night long. Infiltratin' the lines, slippin' up and throwin' in grenades. Or runnin' in with a bayonet or saber. They were active all night. Your buddy would try to get a little catnap and you'd stay on watch. Then you'd switch off. It went on, day in and day out. A matter of simple survival. The only way you could get it over with was to kill them off before they killed you. The war I knew was totally savage.

The Japanese fought by a code they thought was right: *bushido.* The code of the warrior: no surrender. You don't really comprehend it until you get out there and fight people who are faced with an absolutely hopeless situation and will not give up. If you tried to help one of the Japanese, he'd usually detonate a grenade and kill himself as well as you. To be captured was a disgrace. To us, it was impossible, too, because we knew what happened in Bataan.

→ 197 ←

Toward the end of the Okinawa campaign, we found this emaciatated Japanese in the bunk of what may have been a field hospital. We were on a patrol. There had been torrential rains for two weeks. The foxholes were filled with water. This Jap didn't have but a G-string on him. About ninety pounds. Pitiful. This buddy of mine picked him up and carried him out. Laid him out in the mud. There was no other place to put him.

We were sittin' on our helmets waitin' for the medical corpsman to check him out. He was very docile. We figured he couldn't get up. Suddenly he pulled a Japanese grenade out of his G-string. He jerked the pin out and hit it on his fist to pop open the cap. He was gonna make hamburger of me and my buddy and himself. I yelled, "Look out!" So my buddy said, "You son of a bitch. if that's how you feel about it—" He pulled out his .45 and shot him right between the eyes.

This is what we were up against. I don't like violence, but there are times when you can't help it. I don't like to watch television shows with violence in them. I hate to see anything afraid. But I was afraid so much, day after day, that I got tired of being scared. I've seen guys go through three campaigns and get killed on Okinawa on the last day. You knew all you had was that particular moment you were living.

I got so tired of seein' guys get hit and banged up, the more I felt like takin' it out on the Japanese. The feeling grew and grew, and you became more callous. Have you ever read the poem by Wilfred Owen? The World War One poet? "Insensibility." [He shuts his eyes as he recalls snatches of the poem and interpolates] "Happy are the men who yet before they are killed/Can let their veins run cold.... And some cease feeling/Even themselves or for themselves. Dullness best solves/The tease and doubt of shelling." You see, the man who can go through combat and not be bothered by the deaths of others and escape what Owen calls Chance's strange arithmetic—he's the fortunate one. He doesn't suffer as much as the one who is sensitive to the deaths of his comrades. Owen says you can't compare this man to the old man at home, who is just callous and hardened to everything and has no compassion. The young man on the front line develops this insensitivity because it is the only way he can cope.

You developed an attitude of no mercy because they had no mercy on us. It was a no-quarter, savage kind of thing. At Peleliu, it was the first time I was close enough to see one of their faces. This Jap had been hit. One of my buddies was field-stripping him for souvenirs. I must admit it really bothered me, the guys dragging him around like a carcass. I was just horrified. This guy had been a human being. It didn't take me long to overcome that feeling. A lot of my buddies hit, the fatigue, the stress. After a while, the veneer of civilization wore pretty thin.

This hatred toward the Japanese was just a natural feeling that developed elementally. Our attitude toward the Japanese was different than the one we had toward the Germans. My brother who was with the Second Infantry Division in the Battle of the Bulge, wounded three times, said when things were hopeless for the Germans, they surrendered. I have heard many guys who fought in Europe who said the Germans were damn good soldiers. We hated the hell of having to fight 'em. When they surrendered, they were guys just like us. With the Japanese, it was not that way. At Peleliu, my company took two prisoners. At Okinawa, we took about five. We had orders not to kill the wounded, to try to take prisoners. If they surrendered, they'd give you information. But the feeling was strong…Some guys you meet say they didn't kill any wounded. They weren't up there living like animals, savages.

Our drill instructor at boot camp would tell us, "You're not going to Europe, you're going to the Pacific. Don't hesitate to fight the Japs dirty. Most Americans, from the time they're kids, are taught not to hit below the belt. It's not sportsmanlike. Well, nobody has taught the Japs that, and war ain't sport. Kick him in the balls before he kicks you in yours."

I've seen guys shoot Japanese wounded when it really was not necessary and knock gold teeth out of their mouths. Most of them had gold teeth. I remember one time at Peleliu, I thought I'd collect gold teeth. One of my buddies carried a bunch of 'em in a sock. What you did is you took your K-bar [he displays a seven-inch knife], a fighting knife. We all had one because they'd creep into your foxhole at night. We were on Half Moon Hill in Okinawa about ten days. It happened every night.

The way you extracted gold teeth was by putting the tip of the blade on the tooth of the dead Japanese—I've seen guys do it to wounded ones and hit the hilt of the knife to knock the tooth loose. How could American boys do this? If you're reduced to savagery by a situation, anything's possible. When Lindbergh made a trip to the Philippines, he was horrified at the way American GIs talked about the Japanese. It was so savage. We *were* savages.

When I leaned to make the extraction, as the troops used to say, this navy medic, Doc Castle, God bless his soul, said, "Sledgehammer, what are you doing?" I says, "Doc, I'm gonna get me some gold teeth." He said [very softly], "You don't want to do that." I said, "All the other guys are doin' it." He says, "What would your folks think?" I said, "Gosh, my dad is a medical doctor back in Mobile, he might think it's interesting." He said, "Well, you might get germs." I said, "I hadn't thought of that, doc." In retrospect, I realized Ken Castle wasn't worried about germs. He just didn't want me to take another step toward abandoning all concepts of decency.

I saw this Jap machine-gunner squattin' on the ground. One of our Browning automatic riflemen had killed him. Took the top of his skull off. It rained all that night. This Jap gunner didn't fall over for some reason. He was just sitting upright in front of the machine gun. His arms were down at his sides. His eyes were wide open. It had rained all night and the rain had collected inside of his skull. We were just sittin' around on our helmets, waiting to be relieved. I noticed this buddy of mine just flippin' chunks of coral into the skull about three feet away. Every time he'd get one in there, it'd splash. It reminded me of a child throwin' pebbles into a puddle. It was just so unreal. There was nothing malicious in his action. This was just a mild-mannered kid who was now a twenti-eth-century savage.

Once on another patrol, on Okinawa, I saw Mac take great pains to position himself and his carbine near a Japanese corpse. After getting just the right angle, Mac took careful aim and squeezed off a couple of rounds. The dead Japanese lay on his back with his trousers pulled down to his knees. Mac was trying very carefully to blast off the head of the corpse's penis. He succeeded. As he exulted over his aim, I turned away in disgust. Mac was a decent, clean-cut man.

We had broken through the Japanese lines at Okinawa. I had a Thompson submachine gun and went in to check this little grass-thatched hut. An old woman was sitting just inside the door. She held out her hands. There was an hourglass figure tattooed on it to show she was Okinawan. She said, "No Nipponese." She opened her kimono and pointed to this terrible wound in her lower abdomen. You could see gangrene had set in. She didn't have a chance to survive and was obviously in great pain. She probably had caught it in an exchange of artillery fire or an air strike.

She very gently reached around, got the muzzle of my tommy gun, and moved it around to her forehead. She motioned with her other hand for me to pull the trigger. I jerked it away and called the medical corpsman: "There's an old gook woman, got a bad wound." This is what we called the natives in the Pacific. "Hey, doc, can you do anything?"

He put a dressing on it and called someone in the rear to evacu-ate the old woman. We started moving out when we heard a rifle shot ring out. The corpsman and I went into a crouch. That was an

M-1, wasn't it? We knew it was an American rifle. We looked back toward the hut and thought maybe there was a sniper in there and the old woman was acting as a front for him. Well, here comes one of the guys in the company, walking out, checking the safety on his rifle. I said, "Was there a Nip in that hut?" He said, "Naw, it was just an old gook woman. She wanted to be put out of her misery and join her ancestors, I guess. So I obliged her."

I just blew my top: "You son of bitch. They didn't send us out here to kill old women." He started all these excuses. By that time, a sergeant came over and we told him. We moved on. I don't know what was ever done about it. He was a nice guy, like the boy next door. He wasn't just a hot-headed crazy kid. He wanted to join the best. Why one individual would act differently from another, I'll never know.

We had all become hardened. We were out there, human beings, the most highly developed form of life on earth, fighting each other like wild animals. We were under constant mortar fire. Our wounded had to be carried two miles through the mud. The dead couldn't be removed. Dead Japs all around. We'd throw mud over 'em and shells would come, blow it off, and blow them apart. The maggots were in the mud like in some corruption or compost pile.

Did you ever get to know a Japanese soldier?

One of the few we captured at Okinawa was a Yale graduate. He spoke perfect English, but we never said anything to him. I must be perfectly honest with you, I still have a great deal of feeling about them. The way they fought. The Germans are constantly getting thrown in their face the horrors of nazism. But who reminds the Japanese of what they did to China or what they did to the Filipinos? Periodically, we remember Bataan.

It always struck me as ironic, the Japanese code of behavior. Flower arranging, music, striving for perfection. And the art of the warrior. Very often, we'd get a photograph off a dead Japanese. Here would be this soldier, sitting in a studio, with a screen behind and a table with a little flower on it. Often he'd be holding a rifle, yet there was always that little vase of flowers.

We all had different kinds of mania. To me, the most horrible thing was to be under shellfire. You're absolutely helpless. The damn thing comes in like a freight train and there's a terrific crash. The ground shakes and all this shrapnel rippin' through the air.

I remember one afternoon on Half Moon Hill. The foxhole next to me had two boys in it. The next one to that had three. It was fairly quiet. We heard the shell come screeching over. They were firing it at us like a rifle. The shell passed no more than a foot over my head. Two foxholes down, a guy was sitting on his helmet drinking C-ration hot chocolate. It exploded in his foxhole. I saw this guy, Bill Leyden, go straight up in the air. The other two kids fell over backwards. Dead, of course. The two in the hole next to me were killed instantly.

Leyden was the only one who survived. Would you believe he gets only partial disability for shrapnel wounds? His record says nothing about concussion. He has seizures regularly. He was blown up in the air! If you don't call that concussion…The medics were too busy saving lives to fill out records.

Another kid got his leg blown off. He had been a lumberjack, about twenty-one. He was always telling me how good spruce Christmas trees smelled. He said, "Sledgehammer, you think I'm gonna lose my leg?" If you don't think that just tore my guts out…My God, there was his field shoe on the stretcher with this stump of his ankle stickin' out. The stretcher bearers just looked at each other and covered him with his poncho. He was dead.

It was raining like hell. We were knee-deep in mud. And I thought, What in the hell are we doin' on this nasty, stinkin' muddy ridge? What is this all about? You know what I mean? Wasted lives on a muddy slope.

People talk about Iwo Jima as the most glorious amphibious operation in history. I've had Iwo veterans tell me it was more similar to Peleliu than any other battle they read about. What in the hell was glorious about it?

POSTSCRIPT

During the next day's drive to the airport, he reflected further: "My parents taught me the value of history. Both my grandfathers were in the Confederate Army. They didn't talk about the glory of war. They talked about how terrible it was.

"During my third day overseas, I thought I should write all this down for my family. In all my reading about the Civil War, I never read about how the troops felt and what it was like from day to day. We knew how the generals felt and what they ate.

"We were told diaries were forbidden, because if we were killed or captured, any diary might give the Japanese information. So I kept little notes, which I slipped into the pages of my Gideon's New Testament. I kept it in a rubber bag I got off a dead Jap. I committed the casualties to memory. We had more than a hundred percent in Okinawa and almost that many at Peleliu.

"Any time we made an attack, I recited the Twenty-third Psalm. Snafu Shelton says, 'I don't know what it is that got us through. I was doin' a hell of a lot of cussin' and Sledgehammer was doin' a hell of a lot of prayin'. One of those might have done it.' Some of the survivors never knew I was keepin' notes: 'We just thought you were awfully pious.' Some of the guys were very religious. But some of 'em, after a while, got so fatalistic they figured it was nothing but dumb chance anyway."

PETER OTA

I think back to what happened—and sometimes I wonder: Where do I come from?

He is a fifty-seven-year-old Nisei. His father had come from Oki-
nawa in 1904, his mother from Japan. He's an accountant. His
father had worked on farms and in the coal mines of Mexico. After
thirty-seven years building a fruit and vegetable business, he had
become a successful and respected merchant in the community. He
was a leader in the Japanese Chamber of Commerce of Los Angeles.

On the evening of December 7, 1941, my father was at a wedding. He was dressed in a tuxedo. When the reception was over, the FBI agents were waiting. They rounded up at least a dozen wedding guests and took 'em to county jail.

For a few days we didn't know what happened. We heard nothing. When we found out, my mother, my sister, and myself went to jail. I can still remember waiting in the lobby. When my father walked through the door, my mother was so humiliated. She didn't say anything. She cried. He was in prisoner's clothing, with a denim jacket and a number on the back.

The shame and humiliation just broke her down. She was into Japanese culture. She was a flower arranger and used to play the *biwa,* a Japanese stringed instrument. Shame in her culture is worse than death. Right after that day she got very ill and contracted tuberculosis. She had to be sent to a sanitarium. She stayed behind when we were evacuated. She was too ill to be moved. She was there till she passed away.

My father was transferred to Missoula, Montana. We got letters from him—censored, of course—telling us he was all right. It was just my sister and myself. I was fifteen, she was twelve. In April 1942, we were evacuated to Santa Anita. At the time we didn't know where we were going, how long we'd be gone. We didn't know what to take. A toothbrush, toilet supplies, some clothes. Only what you could carry. We left with a caravan.

Santa Anita is a race track. The horse stables were converted into living quarters. My sister and I were fortunate enough to stay in a barracks. The people in the stables had to live with the stench. Everything was communal. We had absolutely no privacy. When you went to the toilet, it was communal. It was very embarrassing for women especially. The parent actually lost control of the child. I had no parents, so I did as I pleased. When I think back what happened to the Japanese family...

We had orders to leave Santa Anita in September of 1942. We had no idea where we were going. Just before we left, my father joined us. He was brought into camp on the back of an army state truck, he and several others who were released from Missoula. I can still picture it to this day: to come in like cattle or sheep being herded in the back of a pickup truck bed. We were near the gate and saw him come in. He saw us. It was a sad, happy moment, because we'd been separated for a year.

He never really expressed what his true inner feelings were. It just amazes me. He was never vindictive about it, never showed any anger. I can't understand that. A man who had worked so hard for what he had and lost it overnight. There is a very strong word in Japanese, *gaman*. It means to persevere. Old people instilled this into the second generation: You persevere. Take what's coming, don't react.

He had been a very outgoing person. Enthusiastic. I was very, very impressed with how he ran things and worked with people. When I saw him at Santa Anita, he was a different person.

We were put on a train, three of us and many trains of others. It was crowded. The shades were drawn. During the ride we were wondering, what are they going to do to us? We Niseis had enough confidence in our government that it wouldn't do anything drastic. My father had put all his faith in this country. This was his land.

Oh, it took days. We arrived in Amache, Colorado. That was an experience in itself. We were right near the Kansas border. It's a desolate, flat, barren area. The barracks was all there was. There were no trees, no kind of landscaping. It was like a prison camp. Coming from our environment, it was just devastating.

School in camp was a joke. Let's say it was loose. If you wanted to study, fine. If you didn't, who cared? There were some teachers who were conscientious and a lot who were not. One of our basic subjects was American history. They talked about freedom all the time. [Laughs.]

After a year, I was sent out to Utah on jobs. I worked on sugar beet farms. You had to have a contract or a job in order to leave camp. The pay was nominal. We would have a labor boss, the farmer would pay us through him. It was piecework. Maybe fifteen of us would work during the harvest season. When it was over, we went back to camp.

If you had a job waiting, you could relocate to a city that was not in the Western Defense Command. I had one in Chicago, as a stock boy in a candy factory. It paid seventy-five cents an hour. I was only in camp for a year. My sister was in until they were dismantled, about three and a half years. My father was in various camps for four years.

I went from job to job for a year. I had turned draft age, so I had to register. It's ironic. Here I am being drafted into the army, and my father and sister are in a concentration camp waiting for the war to end.

I was in the reserve, not yet inducted, in the middle of 1944, when I received a wire from my father saying that my mother was very ill. I immediately left Chicago for Amache, Colorado, to get my clearance from the Western Defense Command. It took several days. While I was waiting, my mother passed away.

Since we wanted her funeral to be at the camp where my father and sister were, I decided to go on to California and pick up her remains. At Needles, California, I was met at the train by an FBI agent. He was assigned to me. He was with me at all times during my stay there. Whether I went to sleep at night or whether I went to the bathroom, he was by my side.

As soon as we stepped off the train at the Union Station in Los Angeles, there was a shore patrol and a military police who met me. They escorted me through the station. It was one of the most...[He finds it difficult to talk.] I don't even know how to describe it. Any day now, I'd be serving in the same uniform as these people who were guarding me. The train stations at that time were always filled. When they marched me through, the people recognized me as being Oriental. They knew I was either an escaped prisoner or a spy. Oh, they called out names. I heard "dirty Jap" very distinctly.

After we got to the hotel, the FBI agent convinced the military that it wasn't necessary for them to stay with me. But he had to. He was disgusted with the whole situation. He knew I was in the reserve, that I was an American citizen. He could see no reason for him to be with me. But he was on assignment. We spoke personal things. His wife was having a baby, he couldn't be with her. He thought it was ridiculous.

I was in the armored division at Fort Knox. We were sent to Fort Mead for embarkation when the European war ended. They didn't know what to do with us Japanese Americans. We were in our own units. Should they send us to the Pacific side? They might not be able to tell who was the enemy and who was not. [Laughs.]

The war ended while I was at Fort McDowell on San Francisco Bay. That was the receiving point for Japanese prisoners captured in the war. I went back with a boatload of them. I didn't know how they'd react to me. I was very surprised. The professional soldiers who were captured during the early days of the war in Guadalcanal, Saipan, never believed the war ended. They would always say, when the subject came up, it was propaganda. The civilian soldiers were very different. We could get along with them. They were very young—*boheitai,* boy soldiers. We could relate to them as to children. They were scared. They had nothing to go back to. Okinawa was devastated. A lot of them lost their families.

My furloughs were spent in camp, visiting my father and sister. Going to camp was like going home for me, to see my family. We made the best of what we had. We celebrated Christmas in the American fashion. We tried to make our lives go easy.

We came back to Los Angeles at the end of the war, believing that there was no other way but to be American. We were discouraged with our Japanese culture. My feeling at the time was, I had to prove myself. I don't know why I had to prove myself. Here I am, an ex-GI, born and raised here. Why do I have to prove myself? We all had this feeling. We had to prove that we were Americans, okay?

My mother and father sent me to a Japanese school teaching the culture. My wife and I did nothing with our children in that respect. We moved to a white community near Los Angeles. It was typical American suburb living. We became more American than Americans, very conservative. My wife and I, we talk about this. We thought this was the thing we had to do: to blend into the community and become part of white America.

My children were denied a lot of the history of what happened. If you think of all those forty years of silence, I think this stems from another Japanese characteristic: when shame is put on you, you try to hide it. We were put into camp, we became victims, it was our fault. We hide it.

My oldest daughter, Cathy, in her senior year at college, wanted to write a thesis about the camp experience. She asked if we knew people she might interview. Strange thing is, many people, even now, didn't want to talk about it. Some of the people she did talk to broke down. Because this was the first time they had told this story. This is the same thing I did. When I first went into detail, it just broke me up. When it came out, I personally felt good about it. It was some-thin' that was inside of me that I've wanted to say for a long time.

How do the Sansei feel about it—your daughter's generation?

Very angry. They keep saying, "Why did you go? Why didn't you fight back?" They couldn't understand it. They weren't raised in our culture. Today, I would definitely resist. It was a different situation at that time. This is what we tried to explain to our daughter. Today if this happened, I think a majority of the Japanese would resist.*

When I think back to my mother and my father, what they went through quietly, it's hard to explain. [Cries.] I think of my father without ever coming up with an angry word. After all those years, having worked his whole life to build a dream—an American dream, mind you—having it all taken away, and not one vindictive word. His business was worth more than a hundred thousand. He sold it for five. When he came out of camp, with what little money he had he put a down payment on an apartment building. It was right in the middle of skid row, an old rooming house. He felt he could survive by taking in a little rent and living there. My sister worked for a family as a domestic. He was afraid for her in this area. He died a very broken man.

My wife and I, we're up on cloud nine right now. Our daughter just passed the California bar. Guess what she's doing? She works for the redress and reparations group in San Diego.† How's that?

---

* Jun Kurose, a Nisei internee from Seattle: "When we were told to evacuate, the American Friends Service Committee said: 'Don't go, we will help you.'…Some of the Japanese were saying: 'Stay out of this, you're making it rougher for us.' If we'd listened to the Friends, we might have been able to avert much suffering. We went willingly, we really did." (From *American Dreams: Lost and Found* [New York: Pantheon Books, 1980], p. 168.)

† A movement for redress of grievances has come into being on behalf of Japanese Americans who were interned during the war years.

BETTY BASYE HUTCHINSON

On first meeting her, you sense that she had once upon a time been a beauty queen. She is sixty.

I was in the class of '41, the last high school class. You see? By that winter Leslie Bidwell would be dead at Pearl Harbor. My class would be dying.

Oroville was a little mining town eighty miles above Sacramento. My stepfather was a tenant farmer and owned just a little bit of land. He had just got electricity three years before. We lived in the kitchen because that's where it was warm. My stepfather kept things to himself. He would read the papers, but he never shared. My mother was busy feeding all her kids. I was the first one of nine children to graduate from high school.

I was dancing at Fresno State, at a big ball, when I first realized Pearl Harbor had happened. It was a whole week later. I was a hayseed Basye.

Immediately, I was going to become a nurse. That was the fastest thing I could do to help our boys. Here I was only one semester at Fresno State, and by February 5, I was out at the hospital as a registered nurse.

It was expensive for me. You had to pay something like twenty dollars a month to live at the nurses' home. I didn't have any money. Fortunately, the Cadet Nurse Corps came into existence. The government paid for us to become nurses. That really saved me.

I remember February 5, '42. Our superintendent called us all together. Two little Japanese girls, sitting in front, who had come into class like me—why in the world are we saying goodbye to them? I couldn't understand what had happened. They were gone and I never, never saw them again. It must have been okay if President Roosevelt said it was okay. But I knew those girls should have been nurses.

I wanted to really have something to do with the war. It meant my kid brother on a tanker in the Mediterranean, delivering oil to Africa, to Italy. It meant losing several more Oroville schoolmates. It meant my boyfriend, whom I'd been engaged to ever since we left high school. He'd joined the marines and was gone. It meant just an end to all that life I had known just a few months before.

"He was president of the student body. I was an athlete, a drum majorette, everything. In February of '42, I was all-American drum majorette. I was offered a movie contract. I was going to be a star in this thing, this movie called Twirl Girl. *[Laughs.] I was in nurse's training when the call came in. I just said, 'Thank you, but I have to go back to duty.'*

"It was that picture in all the national papers. Cheesecake. I don't think the word 'cheesecake' had been invented yet. I had a baton under my arm and I was standing on a pedestal. Posed, with one leg up. Really short skirt and little velvet boots on. [Laughs.] My hair was full and long and red.

"It was one of the first available pinup pictures. Suddenly the fan mail started coming in. I still have clippings, letters from all over the world. 'Cause I was busy at the hospital, they would come to my aunt. The poor postman would carry boxes of this mail. The college began to send these pictures out to the boys who would write from different places and ask for a picture. Servicemen.

"I have one in French I've never translated. One from Argentina. One of them said, 'As soon as the war is over, we'll get together and we'll have a wonderful time. Would you please wait? You are the most beautiful person I've ever seen, but you look wholesome.' It was just that kind of time."

All the regular nurses began to drop out and join the army. Many of my instructors left. We were down to just a skeleton crew at the county hospital. In Fresno. The student nurses were running the whole hospital.

You were supposed to stay in for three years as a student nurse, but the army took us out six months early. We went down to our first military assignment at Hoff General Hospital in Santa Barbara. We were given uniforms with a nice little cocky beret. It was basic training really, because most of us were gonna go into the service. About six months later, we went back to Fresno to graduate, get our pins, and say goodbye. The day President Roosevelt died, I was an official army nurse. I felt even more committed to go ahead.

I was on an orthopedic ward. Quite a few wounded paratroopers. I remember rubbing the backs of these people who had casts from head to foot. You could hardly find their backs through all these bandages and pulleys. It's not like plastic surgery where the really deformed people are. I was struck by the horror of it, but it wasn't as bad as what was to come.

Now I go to Dibble General Hospital in Menlo Park. In six weeks, we became so skilled in plastic surgery that they wouldn't let us go. Six-week wonders. It was coming to the end of the war and now they needed plastic surgery. Blind young men. Eyes gone, legs gone. Parts of the face. Burns—you'd land with a fire bomb and be up in flames. It was a burn-and-blind center.

I spent a year and a half in the plastic-surgery dressing room. All day long you would change these dressings. When you were through with those who were mobile, who would come by wheelchair or crutches, you would take this little cart loaded with canisters of wet saline bandages. Go up and down the wards to those fellas who couldn't get out of bed. It was almost like a surgical procedure. They didn't anesthetize the boys and it was terribly painful. We had to keep the skin wet with these moist saline packs. We would wind yards and yards of this wet pack around these people. That's what war really is.

I'll never forget my first day on duty. First Lieutenant Molly Birch introduced me to the whole floor of patients: "This is Lieutenant Basye." They'd say, What? Hayseed? Oh, Basie. Oh, Countess. So I got the name Countess.

I was so overwhelmed by the time I got to the third bed: this whole side of a face being gone. I wouldn't know how to focus on the eye that peeked through these bandages. Should I pretend I didn't notice it? Shall we talk about it? Molly led me down to the next bed: The Nose, she called him. He had lost his nose. Later on, I got used to it, all this kidding about their condition. He would pretend to laugh. He would say, "Ah yes, I'm getting my nose." He didn't have any eyebrows, a complete white mass of scars. The pedicle was hanging off his neck. He had no ears—they had been burned off. They were going to be reconstructed. But the nose was the important thing. Everyone nicknamed him The Nose. He didn't mind—well, I don't know that. Molly was right. She was giving them a chance to talk about what happened. At the time, I couldn't stand it.

As soon as we got back to the nurse's station behind glass, I went to the bathroom and threw up. Then she knew. She didn't introduce me to the patients who were in the private room that day, 'cause they were far the worst. They couldn't get up and couldn't joke so much. The next day she took me to them, one at a time. I was beginning to anesthetize myself.

I remember this one lieutenant. Just a mass of white bandages, with a little slit where I knew his eyes were. This one hand reaching out and saying, "Hi, Red." There were many, many, many more with stumps, you couldn't tell if there was a foot there or not, an eye, an arm, the multiple wounds. It wasn't just the one little thing I was used to in nurse's training. This is what got to me.

Oh, there were breakups. The wife of The Nose was going to divorce him. What can we do to make her understand? That was the talk all over. The doctor wanted her to understand it'll take time, he'll get his face back. But they broke up. She couldn't stand it. That was pretty common.

Sitting at the bedside of this young flyer who went down over Leyte. He got his own fire bomb. Next to his bed is a picture of this handsome pilot beside his P-38. He wants to be sure I see it: "Hi, Red, look. This is me." He was never gonna leave that bed until he got his face back. That handsome photograph he insisted be there, so that's the person you'll see.

He was very hard to manage because he would scream when they changed his dressing. He was insistent that he never was gonna leave that room until they brought him back to where he was before. The staff couldn't quite figure this out. Why isn't he quiet? Why can't he be brave when they're changing his dressing? What does he think we are, miracle makers? This mystique builds up that Bill can't handle it as well as the others. Be brave, be brave.

I can't say I ever really became used to it. But I became more effective as a nurse and adopted a kind of jocularity. I began to be able to tell jokes, banter back and forth. When I'd come in pushing the cart, there'd always be hooting and yelling: Hey, Red, Hayseed, Countess, come in, I got a cookie for you. There was a lot of alluding to sexuality. One said to me, "Why do you always walk that way?" I didn't know how I walked, but I had a walk. I said, "I don't know." And they all howled.

Having pretty young nurses around was very important to them. You were not supposed to date enlisted men, but you could date officers. I escorted Bill, the pilot, for the first outing out of his room. I talked him into escorting me to the officers' club. He still had a bandage on his one eye, terrible scars, one side of his face gone, and these pedicles of flesh. You look absolutely grotesque and you know. We had a drink at the club. He looked around and saw other cases there. So he began to get used to it.

One of the nurses in charge fell in love with an enlisted man. She carried on a very quiet love affair with him. We never alluded to it. After about a year, they were married. It was always a secret in those days. It was discouraged. I've always had the theory that they made us officers to keep the army nurses for the officers. We were just technicians. I was just a twenty-two-year-old kid who knew how to do bedpans. Why was I an officer? I feel it was a way to keep us away from the hordes and keep us for the officers. Oh, there was a terrible class feeling.

The doctors were the givers of gifts to these men. They were gods on a pedestal. The elusive, mobile god, who moves in and out and doesn't stay there very long, under a terrible amount of pressure. The nurses were counsel when marriages broke up. The doctors were busy someplace else.

V-J Day occurred while I was still at the hospital. Oh, wow! Just total chaos. Our superintendent of nurses led a conga line up and down the hospital, serpentine, up past every bed. This took hours, because it was ward after ward. [Laughs.] Everybody joined in. Absolute bedlam.

The hospital closed and they sent the patients out to other places. Plastic surgery was going to go on for years on these people. I went down to Pasadena. This is '46. We took over the whole hotel, one of the big, nice old hotels right there on the gorge. All my friends were still there, undergoing surgery. Especially Bill. I would walk him in downtown Pasadena—I'll never forget this. Half his face completely gone, right?

Downtown Pasadena after the war was a very elite community. Nicely dressed women, absolutely staring, just standing there staring. He was aware of this terrible stare. People just looking right at you and wondering: What is this? I was going to cuss her out, but I moved him away. It's like the war hadn't come to Pasadena until we came there.

Oh, it had a big impact on the community. In the Pasadena paper came some letters to the editor: Why can't they be kept on their own grounds and off the streets? The furor, the awful indignation: the end of the war and we're still here. The patients themselves showed me these letters: Isn't it better for them if they're kept off the streets? What awful things for us to have to look at. The patients kidded about that. Wow, we're in Pasadena.

This was my slow introduction to peacetime, through the eyes of that woman when she looked at my friend Bill. It's only the glamour of war that appeals to people. They don't know real war. Well, those wars are gone forever. We've got a nuclear bomb and we'll destroy ourselves and everybody else.

I swallowed all this for years and never talked about it. 'Cause I got busy after the war, getting married and having my four children. That's what you were supposed to do. And getting your house in suburbia. You couldn't get anybody to really talk about the war. Oh, the men would say, When I was in Leyte—buddy-buddy talk. Well, their buddies got killed, too. They never talked of the horrors.

My husband had been in the South Pacific. You could never get the father of my four children to talk about the war. It was like we put blinders on the past. When we won, we believed it. It was the end. That's the way we lived in suburbia, raising our children, not telling them about war. I don't think it was just me. It was everybody. You wouldn't fill your children full of these horror stories, would you?

When I think of the kind of person I was, a little hayseed from Oroville, with all this altruism in me and all this patriotism that sent me into the war! Oh, the war marked me, but I put it behind me. I didn't do much except march against Vietnam. And my oldest son, I'm happy to say, was a conscientious objector.

It's just this terrible anger I have. What is this story I want to tell? I even wrote short stories for myself. I started an autobiography, and always the war came up. This disappointment. We did it for what? Korea? Vietnam? We're still at war. Looking back, it didn't work.

In 1946, my house burned with all my mementoes. The only thing that was saved, inside a hope chest, was this scrapbook of burned-edged pictures. Of me, when I was in the service.

Today, we're going through the *romance* of war. Did you see *The Winds of War?* It was nothing, worse than nothing. It didn't tell us what's wrong with war or the reality of war. They showed that picture of Pearl Harbor, that pretty place, all bombed up. Wasn't he on the hill, looking down, the hero? I was trying to find some saving grace. But it wasn't like you were there. Somebody should have said, See, underneath this water is Leslie Bidwell. He died, you see?

Part II

The City

Division Street:
America
(1967)

INTRODUCTION

On undertaking this assignment, I immediately called Dr. Philip Hauser, former chairman of the University of Chicago's Sociology Department, one of the country's best informed demographers. Is there a street in Chicago today where all manner of ethnic, racial, and income groups live? His reply—though a blow—was not unexpected. There is none. The nomadic, transient nature of contemporary life has made diffusion the order—or disorder—of the city. The bulldozer and the wrecking ball have played their roles.

I was on the prowl for a cross-section of urban thought, using no one method or technique. I was aware it would take me to suburbs, upper, lower, and middle income, as well as to the inner city itself and its outlying sections. (I was about to say "neighborhoods," but this word has lost its meaning.)

I guess I was seeking some balance in the wildlife of the city as Rachel Carson sought it in nature. In unbalanced times, balance is as difficult to come by as Parsifal's Grail.

In no instance did I deliberately seek out the bizarre in people. It would serve as much purpose as visiting a Topless A-Go-Go (as drearily unrevealing). And yet: the part-time Syndicate tiger is as indigenous to our city—any large American city, I suspect—as the social lioness. Each has pertinent comments to make on urban life in the twentieth century.

So, too, with the window washer newly arrived to the middle class and the two ad-agency men, one of whom loves his job as much as the other loathes it; the tortured house painter–home-owner, who seeks respectability in his restricted neighborhood, and the wife of the ex-Wall Street lawyer, who risks respectability to integrate hers; the ADC mother seeking beauty, and the affluent steelworker for whom life's beauty has fled; the cabdriver finding his lost manhood in the John Birch Society, and the schoolteacher celebrating her humanhood; the Appalachian couple scoring in the big city, and the auto-body shop foreman who refuses to score; the blind woman who sees, and the sighted girl who doesn't; some going with the grain, others against.

Accident and improvisation played as much part in the making of this book as any plan. More. I had an idea of the kind of people I wanted to see: homeowners, homemakers, landladies, project dwellers, old settlers, new arrivals, skilled hands, unskilled, the retired, the young, the *haut monde*, the demimonde, and the solid middle *monde*—like Margaret Fuller, I was out to swallow the world. My world was my city. What with the scattering of the species, it had to be in the nature of guerilla journalism.

A tip from an acquaintance. A friend of a friend telling me of a friend or nonfriend. A nursed drink at a tavern where a high-rolling bartender held forth. A chance encounter with a bright-eyed boy-hood companion grown into an unquietly desperate man. An indignant phone call from a radio listener. A face, vaguely familiar, on the morning bus. A stentorian voice, outside City Hall, calling out my name. A wintry night in an Appalachian area, a hailed cab, the driver talking of a film, its impact on him, the meaning of courage; an appointment the following morning, a nearby bar. My seat companion on a bus, a Negro grandmother, bitter and strangely gleeful. The housewife next door, prototype of TV commercial heroines. An accidental shove on a crowded Loop corner, while awaiting the change in traffic lights; an apology; a phrase that holds my attention; we go for coffee; a life unfolded at the restaurant table. All these urban phenomena were factors in the making of this book.

An unexpected obstacle, in some few instances, was my identity. I had appeared on television and radio programs in the city and thus was a "celebrity." Possibly there would be a tendency in the other to say things he thought I wanted to hear. The encounter would, in this event, be wholly worthless. This was not so in most cases, though at such times I was impelled to use self-deprecatory profanity to clear the air. To many, my name and face meant nothing; that was a valuable timesaver.

I realized quite early in this adventure that interviews, conventionally conducted, were meaningless. Conditioned clichés were certain to come. The question-and-answer technique may be of value in determining favored detergents, toothpaste, and deodorants, but not in the discovery of men and women. It was simply a case of making conversation. And listening. Talk of childhood invariably opened the sluice-gates of dammed-up hurts and dreams. From then on, there were occasional questions dependent on the other's flow.

There were, of course, key questions, asked idiomatically rather than academically, that would occur and recur. I had to be sure, though, that my companion was ready. It was in sharp contrast to conversations I had conducted on my radio programs with celebrated figures, who were ever-ready. (This is in no way a reflection on the latter group. The themes were their professional as well as human concern. They were accustomed to talk as well as write about them.) It should be made clear, however, that a number of people in this book are highly literate; they're merely noncelebrated, that's all. As for articulateness, each person found it in his own way and in his own good time.

Often my companion introduced the themes himself: civil rights and Vietnam were two notable examples. Passions ran deep in these matters, even among the more diffident. Time itself and the flow of words brought them to the surface. Neither was much prompting needed for reflections on automation; here, too, strong feelings were quickly surfaced. The Bomb was something else again. In almost all cases, I introduced the question. The thought of it was simply too overwhelming for them to willingly put into words.

Surprisingly, God was an also-ran in their thoughts (again, with several exceptions). Like a stage mother, I had to push Him forward. Once He was introduced into the conversation, He was immediately and effusively acknowledged. (And in a few cases, rebuffed.) Whether God is dead or merely sleeping or really is a has-been is for theologians to have a high old time with. It is not the subject of this book. It is merely an observation. You will notice, too, that His son fares in a rather astonishing manner.

We come now to the role played by the tape recorder. On occasion, it might have become an inhibiting factor, making for self-consciousness, were it not for my clowning. I'd kick it, not too hard, in the manner of W. C. Fields with a baby or a recalcitrant picket fence. With him, it was a state of war; with me, it was merely a matter of proving my ally's neutrality. Since the tape recorder did not retaliate, its nonviolent nature was made clear to my companion. With most, its presence had no effect one way or the other.

When the recorder went wrong (this happened a number of times), I swore at it. During each of these instances, my companion laughed and seemed to feel more relaxed. (This may provide its own commentary on man's true feeling about technological advance.) I soon became aware that my playing Jacques Tati's Mr. Hulot helped break whatever tensions might have existed. (It came naturally to me, since I have never been able to drive a car, ride a bicycle, roller-skate, swim, dance, or engage in any such form of coordinative activity.) Yet, paradoxically, without my abused mechanical ally, this book would not have been possible. There is such a thing as base ingratitude—even to a machine.

The locales of these encounters were varied. Frequently it was the home of the subject, or his place of work, or a quiet corner of the radio studio, or my house, or a booth in the restaurant, or the front seat of a car. On occasion, there was coffee or a can of beer or a shot of whiskey, or in the case of a gracious elderly lady, a memorable meal. ("Even cooking takes love," she said.)

Most of the guests in my mother's hotel were single men. Many were skilled craftsmen: tool-and-diemakers, coppersmiths, chefs, master carpenters. They were a proud and stiff-necked lot. There were occasions when, for no likely reason, a fight would break out, a furious one—a pinochle game, a dispute over a nickel. The men earned what was good money in those days. Why, then, the fist and the blow over a lousy buffalo nickel? I didn't understand.

Now I understand. It wasn't the nickel. It was the harsh word, the challenging word, in the presence of peers: "Liar!" The nickel was not the matter, nor the dollar. Humiliation was the matter. Unless strong measures were taken. "Let's sit down and reason together" had no meaning while one had lost face.

Though there may be fewer such craftsmen today than there were then, face is still the matter.

Another recurring theme, to put it harshly and, perhaps, cruelly: the cop-out. "What can I do? Nothing." This plea of individual impotence had ironic overtones. It was voiced more frequently by those who called for a national show of potency and, indeed, violence than by the fewer others. Each of the subjects may have come to his belief or lack of it in his own ornery way; yet evidence seems overwhelming that mass media, with their daily litany of tribute to things rather than men, played their wondrous role.

Each of the subjects is, I feel, uniquely himself. Whether he is an archetypal American figure, reflecting thought and condition over and beyond himself, is for the reader to judge, calling upon his own experience, observations, and an occasional look in the mirror.

Although there is a Division Street in Chicago, the title of this book was metaphorical.

FLORENCE SCALA

I was born in Chicago, and I've always loved the city. I'm not sure any more. I love it and I hate it every day. What I hate is that so much of it is ugly, you see? And you really can't do very much about it. I hate the fact that so much of it is inhuman in the way we don't pay attention to each other. And we can do very little about making it human ourselves.

What I love is the excitement of the city. There are things happening in the city every day that make you feel dependent on your neighbor. But there's detachment, too. You don't really feel part of Chicago today, 1965. Any more. I don't feel any.

I grew up around Hull House, one of the oldest sections of the city. In those early days I wore blinders. I wasn't hurt by anything very much. When you become involved, you begin to feel the hurt, the anger. You begin to think of people like Jane Addams and Jessie Binford* and you realize why they were able to live on. They understood how weak we really are and how we could strive for something better if we understood the way.

My father was a tailor, and we were just getting along in a very poor neighborhood. He never had money to send us to school; but we were not impoverished. When one of the teachers suggested that our mother send us to Hull House, life began to open up. At the time, the neighborhood was dominated by gangsters and hoodlums. They were men from the old country, who lorded it over the people in the area. It was the day of moonshine. The influence of Hull House saved the neighborhood. It never really purified it, you know what I mean? I don't think Hull House intended to do that.

---

* Jessie Binford, a colleague of Jane Addams, had lived at Hull House from 1906 until the day of its demolition in 1965. For many years she was director of the Juvenile Protective Association, which she helped found.

But it gave us…well, for the first time my mother left that darn old shop to attend Mother's Club once a week. She was very shy, I remember. Hull House gave you a little insight into another world. There was something else to life besides sewing and pressing.

Sometimes as a kid I used to feel ashamed of where I came from because at Hull House I met young girls from another background. Even the kinds of food we ate sometimes…you know, we didn't eat roast beef, we had macaroni. I always remember the neighborhood as a place that was alive. I wouldn't want to see it back again, but I'd like to retain the being together that we felt in those days.

There were Negroes living in the neighborhood even then, but there was not the tension. I've read about those riots in Chicago in the twenties—the race riots. But in our neighborhood it never did come to any kind of crisis. We used to treat each other as neighbors then. Now we look at each other differently. I think it's good and bad in a way. What we're doing is not understanding, some of us, what it was like then. I think that the American-born—the first generation, the second generation—has not hung on to what his mother and father had. Accepting someone naturally as a man. We don't do that today.

I think that the man who came over from Europe, the southern European especially, who was poor, could understand and see the same kind of struggle and have immediate sympathy for it. He accepted the Negro in the community as a man who is just trying to make a way for himself, to make a living. He didn't look upon him as a threat. I think it was the understanding that both were striving. Not out of some great cause, but just in a human way.

I'm convinced that the first- and second-generation hasn't any concern about the other person's situation. I think money and position are hard to come by today and mean an awful lot, and now they see the Negro as a threat. Though they may say he's inferior, they know darn well he's not. He's as clever as we are and does many things better than we can. The American-born won't accept this, the first and second generation family, especially among the Italians and Poles, and the Irish, too. Remember Trumbull Park?*

Through my teens I had been a volunteer at Hull House. After the War, Eri Hulbert, Jane Addams' nephew, told me of a dream he had. The Near West Side, our area, could become the kind of place people would *want* to live in, close to the city. Did I think this was possible? I said no, people didn't care enough about the neighborhood to rebuild it. But he introduced me to the idea of city planning. He felt the only hope for big cities, in these communities that were in danger of being bulldozed, was to sit down and look and say we have a responsibility here. He convinced me that you could have a tree on the West Side, see?

That's where my life changed. I became involved with a real idea and talking to people like the banker, the social worker, and the Board of Trustees at Hull House. But I suddenly realized my inadequacy. I simply couldn't understand their language, you know? I had to go back to school.

This is where I began to lose the feeling of idolatry you have about people. I think that's bad. I idolized the people that were involved in Hull House. I thought they could never make a mistake. I was later to find out they were the ones who could hurt me the most. I feel that people have to be prepared always for imperfections in everyone, and we have to feel equal, really, to everyone. This is one of the things lots of slum kids, people who came out of poor areas, don't have. Not to be afraid to say something even though it may be way off base. I did this many times and I'd be embarrassed, realizing I had said something that had nothing to do with what they were talking about. But Eri Hulbert kept saying it makes no difference. Just keep at it. You're as good as they are.

---

* Several years ago, a Negro family, having bought a home in Trumbull Park, was stoned out of the neighborhood.

Miss Binford and Jane Addams resented being treated as special persons. This was the kind of thing they had to cut through all the time. Yet we insisted on treating them as special people, in an uncomfortable kind of way. These feelings of confidence, you know, ego, so necessary—most of us in the neighborhood didn't have it. Most of us hung back, see.

In those days it was a new idea. You had to fight the politician who saw clearance and change as a threat to his power, his clout.* He likes the kind of situation now around Maxwell Street,† full of policy and hot goods being sold on the market and this kind of stuff that could go on and on without too much interference from authority because it's so oppressed. The rotten housing and no enforcement of codes and all that business. We had a tough time selling the Catholic Church, too. From '47 to '56 were rough years. It was tough selling people on the idea that they could do it for themselves, that it was the only way it could be done. Their immediate reaction was: You're crazy, you know? Do you really think this neighborhood is worth saving?

All the meetings we had were so much frustration. Eri Hulbert was trying to lead us in a democratic way of doing something about our city. The misunderstandings never came from the neighborhood people. It arose out of the Hull House Board's unwillingness to understand. He couldn't get his point across.

Eri Hulbert committed suicide before our plan was accepted by the city. His death, more than anything else, opened a door which I never dreamed could open. You know, there's a real kind of ugliness among nice people. You know, the dirty stuff that you think only hoodlums pull off. They can really destroy you, the nice people. I think this is what happened to Eri, the way he was deserted by his own. I think it really broke his heart. What disturbs

---

* Clout: a Chicago idiom for "drag," "pull," "political power."
† Chicago's celebrated open market area.

me is that I was a grown woman, close to thirty, before I could see. Sometimes I want to defend the rotten politicians in my neighborhood. I sometimes want to defend even gangsters. They don't pretend to be anything but what they are. You can see what they are. They're not fooling anybody, see? But nice people fool you.

I'm talking about the Board of Trustees, the people who control the money. Downtown bankers, factory owners, architects, people in the stock market. The jet set, too. The young people, grandchildren of old-timers on the Board, who were not really like their elders, if you know what I mean. They were not with us. There were also some very good people, those from the old days. But they didn't count so much any more. This new crowd, this new tough kind of board members, who didn't mind being on such a board for the prestige it gave them, dominated. These were the people closely aligned to the city government, in real estate and planning. And some very fine families, old Chicago families. [Laughs.] The nicest people in Chicago.

Except for one or two of the older people, they made you feel that you had to know your place. You always felt this. That's the big argument about the poverty program today. You cannot have the nice rich people at the top passing on a program for the poor, because they simply *don't* understand, they *can't* understand. These people meet in board meetings once a month. They come by the main street into the building and out they go. They've never had anybody swear at them or cry or ask for help or complain the kind of way people do in our neighborhood. They just don't know.

In the early sixties, the city realized it had to have a campus, a Chicago branch of the University of Illinois. (There was a makeshift one at the pier out on the lake.) There were several excellent areas to choose from, where people were not living: a railroad site, an industrial island near the river, an airport used by businessmen, a park, a golf course. But there was no give. The mayor looked for advice. One of his advisors suggested our neighborhood as the ideal site for the campus. We were dispensable. He was a member of the Hull House Board. It was a strange thing, a very strange thing. Our alderman, he's not what I'd call a good man—even he tried to convince the Mayor this was wrong. But the Mayor was hearing other voices. The nice people.

The alderman alerted us to the danger. Nobody believed it. The priest himself didn't believe it. They had just opened the parish, a new church, a new school. Late in the summer of 1960, the community could have been touched off. But the people were in the dark. When the announcement came in 1961, it was a bombshell. What shocked us was the amount of land they decided to take. They were out to demolish the entire community.

I didn't react in any belligerent way until little kids came knocking at the door, asking me to attend a meeting. That's where the thing got off the ground. It was exciting to see that meeting, the way people felt and the way they talked and the way—they hurt—to hear our Italian priest, who had just become an American. This was in February, we had just celebrated Lincoln's birthday. He had just become a citizen, he couldn't understand.

Though we called the Mayor our enemy, we didn't know he was serving others. It was a faceless thing. I think he'd just as soon have had the University elsewhere. But the pressures were on. We felt it as soon as our protests began.

A member of the Hull House Board took me to lunch a couple of times at the University Club. The University Club—lunch—me! My husband said, go, go, have a free lunch and see what it is she wants. What she wanted to do, really, was to dissuade me from protesting. There was no hope, no chance, she said. I had had a high regard for her. I've been thinking she's probably one of those on the Board who would have fought the people's end. But she was elected to convince me not to go on. The first time I went, I thought this was a friend through whom we could work. But I could see, you know, that she allowed me to be just so friendly, and there was a place beyond which I couldn't go. There was a difference now. I stayed in my place, but I said what I wanted to say. There was a place beyond which she couldn't go, either. See? I was glad to experience it anyway.

I think I understand her. She had strong ties with old Hull House and she was really a good person who ought not have allowed this to happen and she knew it. When the lunches failed to bring anything off, I had no more contact with any of them on that level. We reached the letter-writing stage. We no longer used the phone.

I shall never forget one board meeting. It hurt Miss Binford more than all the others. That afternoon, we came with a committee, five of us, and with a plea. We reminded them of the past, what we meant to each other. From the moment we entered the room to the time we left, not one board member said a word to us. No one got up to greet Miss Binford nor to speak to her. No one asked her a question. The chairman came forward, he was a gentleman, and showed us where to sit.

Miss Binford was in her late eighties, you know. Small, birdlike in appearance. She sat there listening to our plea and then she reminded them of what Hull House meant. She went back and talked, not in a sentimental way, about principles that must never waver. No one answered her. Or acknowledged her. Or in any way showed any recognition of what she was talking about. It's as though we were talking to a stone wall, a mountain.

It was pouring rain and we walked out of the room the way people walk out who feel defeat. I mean we walked out trying to appear secure, but we didn't have much to say to each other. Miss Binford could hardly speak at all. The shock of not being able to have any conversation with the board members never really left her. She felt completely rejected. She knew then there would be no help anywhere. In the past, whenever there was a serious problem in the juvenile courts, she could walk into the Mayor's office and have a talk with him, whoever he was. Kelly, for instance, or Kennelly, or Cermak. And never fail to get a commitment from him. Never. But she knew after this meeting, she'd never find that kind of response again. And sure enough, to test herself, she made the rounds. Of all the people who had any influence in town, with whom she had real contact, not one responded. They expressed sympathy, but it was hands off. Something was crushed inside her. The Chicago she knew had died.

I don't think we realized the stakes involved in this whole urban renewal system. The money it brings in, the clout necessary to condemn land…a new Catholic Church was demolished, too. It had opened in '59, built near Hull House with the city's approval. The Church was encouraged to go ahead and build, so as to form the nucleus for the new environment, see? It cost the people of the area a half million dollars. The Archdiocese lends the parish money, but the parish has to repay. It's a real business arrangement.

Now the people of the area have learned a good deal, but it was a bitter education. The politicians' actions didn't bother us as much. We hated it, we argued about it, we screamed about it out loud. Daley gave the orders and the alderman followed it. This kind of thing we could understand. But we could never understand the silence of the others. A group wanted to picket the Archdiocese, but I felt it was wrong, because we were put into a position of fighting education, the University being built, you know.

Here we were in a big Roman Catholic city, we'd be looked upon as a bunch of fanatics. As I think back on it now, the instinctive responses of the people, who are thought of as being uneducated, were better than my own. I was very anxious we should not be looked upon as people from the slums, many of us Italians and Mexicans. We had to proceed in an orderly manner. We overdid that. We should have picketed the Archdiocese. We should have been tough with Hull House. We should have spoken the truth from the beginning.

Most of the people who left the area were deeply embittered.

They said never again will they ever become involved about anything in their city. They'd had it. This was a natural kind of thing because it was a pretty brutal two and a half years. But I don't know now. This is a big question to ask: whether that experience gave any meaning to their lives? If they turn their backs on it, it's been a failure as far as I'm concerned. There's a danger of their becoming extremists in the self-indulgent sense. They'll be concerned with themselves and their own safety and nothing else. It has happened with some of them.

I don't believe so much any more. I don't believe so much in people as I used to. I believe in *some* people but not in all people any more. I feel I have to be careful about this business of believing in all people. That's the number one change, I think. And I've found there are certain kinds of liberals who'll sell you out, who make life miserable for great numbers of people when they will not see beyond their narrow views. I'm thinking of Urban Renewal, and the huge Negro ghettos that have sprung up and have your heart break at the kind of overcrowding and rotten environment that's developed. It's an evil thing the liberal community does: it wants to see the slums cleared but doesn't fight to see housing for lower-income groups built first. It reinforces all the terrible things we're talking about in the big cities. Segregates the poor people, particularly the Negro people, and this goes on and on.

In an area like ours, the uprooting is of another kind. I lived on the same block for over forty-five years; my father was there before me. It takes away a kind of stability big cities need. Lots of the people have moved into housing no better than the kind they lived in. Some have moved into public housing. The old people have really had it worse. Some have moved into "nicer" neighborhoods, but they're terribly unhappy, those I've spoken with. Here, downtown in the Loop, everything is clearing and building and going up. And the social workers in this town, boy! I can hardly look at them with respect any more. The way they've knuckled down to the system themselves, because everybody wants a Federal grant or something. They don't want to be counted out. I'm sick of the whole mess and I don't know which way to go.

There are the little blessings that come out of struggle. I never knew Jessie Binford as a kid at Hull House. I used to see her walking through the rooms. She had such dignity, she just strode through the rooms and we were all kind of scared of her. In the past four or five years, we became close friends. I really knew the woman. It meant something to her, too. She began to know the people in the way she knew them when she first came to Hull House as a young girl. It really gave her life, this fight. It made clear to her that all the things she really believed in, she believed in all the more. Honor among people and honor between government and people. All that the teacher tells the kids in school. And beauty.

There was a Japanese elm in the courtyard that came up to Miss Binford's window. It used to blossom in the springtime. They were destroying that tree, the wrecking crew. We saw it together. She asked the man whether it could be saved. No, he had a job to do and was doing it. I screamed and cried out. The old janitor, Joe, was standing out there crying to himself. Those trees were beautiful trees that had shaded the courtyard and sheltered the birds. At night the sparrows used to roost in those trees and it was something to hear, the singing of those sparrows. All that was soft and beautiful was destroyed. You saw no meaning in anything any more. There's a college campus on the site now. It will perform a needed function in our life. Yet there is nothing quite beautiful about the thing. They'll plant trees there, sure, but it's walled off from the community. You can't get in. The kids, the students, will have to make a big effort to leave the campus and walk down the streets of the area. Another kind of walling off...

To keep us out. To keep the kids out who might be vandals. I don't see that as such a problem, you know. It wasn't the way Jane Addams saw it, either. She believed in a neighborhood with all kinds of people, who lived together with some little hostility, sure, but nevertheless lived together. In peace. She wondered if this couldn't be extended to the world. Either Jane Addams brought something to Chicago and the world or she didn't.

POSTSCRIPT

In 1964, Florence Scala ran as an Independent for Alderman of the First Ward against a candidate who had the support of both major parties. She received 3,600 votes against her opponent's 8,600. As she recalls: "There were people from all over Chicago campaigning for me, some people I never saw before nor have I seen since. A small number from the community had the courage to come out. And it took guts in a neighborhood like that, where clout is so important. But really it was...students, older people, the Independent Voters of Illinois...just a lot of people from all over, expressing their indignation not only about happenings in the First Ward but about the city as a whole. I think they were expressing support of what seemed to be an individual yelling out, you know, and they wanted to help. They weren't always people I see eye to eye with. There were some far to the right and I couldn't understand what it was in me they wanted to support. But there was something. I have a kind of sympathy for whatever it was that was frustrating them. I really do, because they felt themselves unable to count somewhere. And there were people way over on the left. But I feel most of them were moderates, who were responding to this thing."

DENNIS HART

"Did you see Lord Jim?*" he asked. He's a cabdriver, working the night shift. He has an insect-exterminator business on the side. He has a wife and two children. He identified himself with Conrad's*

hero because it was about "*a man finding courage. The most impor-tant thing in life.*"

He had known abject poverty in Chicago, where he was born, and on an Arkansas farm, where his family had spent several years. "*I found an old potato in the back yard, I ate it like an animal. There was just nothing else.*" Poverty was crushing his spirit: "*I lost face. I lost com-posure.*" His teeth are bad because of the Milky Way and Snickers bar dinners he had so often as a newsboy in the city. When the family had returned to Chicago, the slight southern accent he had picked up led to ridicule by his classmates and to fights: "*It was a matter of saving face. I lost more fights than I won, but you couldn't back down.*"

His father, whom he greatly admires, had left home at twelve, lived in hobo jungles, came up the hard way: "*He didn't look rugged. He had that young determined look about him, about to gain a piece of life, a place for himself.*" What he finds most admirable in his father is his courage: he had worked as an FBI informer. "*I was never very close to him. I don't think I ever panned out to be what he wanted.*" His two younger brothers were Golden Gloves fighters; he wasn't as good. "*But I know he's proud of me today.*"

"*I don't think you can ever stop proving yourself to your father. More than that, you have to prove to yourself what you really are inside you: whether you're willing to die for what you believe. If the cause is great enough, you'd be willing to die.*"

In the last five years, I've become a Republican precinct captain. I also went on to become chairman of the Goldwater campaign in my ward. It was because I was trying to be somebody. I had these doubts about myself as to whether I had any courage in me at all or was I just gonna be a plant instead of a man.

If I die, I don't want to die a natural death that most people suc-cumb, say at sixty years old. If I could die on some battlefield some-place, doing something good, I feel my life would be worthwhile. I want my death to be worth something. If the time comes, I want to die with some pride. I want to die like a man, not like an animal.

When I read Goldwater's book, I identified with my own experiences in life. Because he spoke of the hardship of the individual, things he endured. He himself didn't, he's more of an aristocratic family, but he seemed to understand me. An individual should stand for more than a handout. This is the way America is. You fight for what you get, and once you get it, you hold on to it: your pride, your bread and butter, and what not.

If they dropped the Bomb today, the man who would succeed most is not the man with the brawn but the man with the brains. I feel if this was a wilderness, I could make out quite amply—if I knew a little bit about everything. I'm not worried about them dropping the Bomb. I've lived in a wilderness all my life. Atheists are those most fearful of the Bomb. A man who is truly religious and believes in God doesn't run around worrying about these things. He knows there's a Hereafter.

Freedom is the most important thing in your life. We're facing an enemy today that's gonna annihilate us unless we retaliate in one way or another. We have to face up to it, Bomb or no Bomb. Otherwise, we're a bunch of cowards.

I am now a member of the John Birch Society. It is a great society, one I believe in and one I would fight for. The more it was criticized, it made me all the more want to become a John Bircher. I was hoping somebody would invite me to a meeting and sure enough it took place. I've never been prouder to join an organization in my whole life.

It was an image I saw in these people. When they speak, they speak sense. My grandfather never had much of an education, but he was strong enough to know right from wrong. These people are putting their cards on the table and calling an ace an ace and a king a king and saying exactly what they think. They're saying the whole problem is very simple. Life is complicated enough without saying it's more complicated than it is. The sooner we try to uncomplicate our lives…if you complicate things, you are only asking for trouble. But if you try to simplify things, you find solutions will come much easier.

Has this helped you overcome your self-doubts, your fears?

A man has to find himself. What caused my fears was the fact that we moved around so much. I never seemed to have found a home—until now. I used to be very scared. I've been saved three times. I fell into a dam once, when I was going to a Y camp. I was scared and I was saved. One time, out here on Lake Michigan, the undertow got me. And I had to be saved that time. At school, I was swimming, we were taking a test, and all of a sudden I tightened up. I got scared. I'm a three-time loser and I came through this. I can't fail again.

For the last five years, I had to take my family to the beach and go swimming. Every Sunday I had to lick this fear. I think I have. Boxing has given me a little bit of composure. I've been over to the Joe Louis Gym, I've been over at CYO. I've boxed a lot with my brothers. Boxing to me is the greatest thing in the world for composure—to lick one's fear and to go right to it. A lot of people think the important thing is knocking the other guy down. The important thing is to keep yourself from getting hurt.

You've been hurt a good deal?

Definitely. I got to the point when I found I was becoming very cold and this bothered me. I was afraid to see others be hurt around me and I was becoming very calloused to their feelings, to their wants, to their needs. More than anything else, beside my fear, this bothered me. I'd seen people cry and I felt no feeling for them. I didn't know what was going wrong with me.

I guess maybe it's growing old and realizing you're gonna meet your Maker sooner or later. You have to feel something for other people. There was a time in my early twenties, I'd see people bleed, I'd see people cry. I didn't feel anything. I began to hate myself. Now I feel I've conquered this also. Crying with this man when he's hit, I feel the punch. It keeps you young. Old people become calloused. A conservative feels pain for other people because a conservative is closer to God.

I think really what changed me was working as a guard in the County Jail. So many of the things are so unnecessary. You hear the train whistle coming through at three in the morning. Why are these guys here? They're so young. One fella said, "What time is it?" And I said, "Why? Are you gonna catch a plane or something?" After I said it, after I made the punch on the clock, I realized I made a damn fool of myself. I went back and I actually apologized to this guy in a roundabout way. A guard is not supposed to give in in any way whatsoever. You're supposed to stay above these guys. But I felt like a damn jackass. I think it was the human thing to do.

As I sat down, I had to think of a way to apologize. I didn't come out and say to this man, "I'm sorry for what I said." But I went back and paid a little more attention to him and he understood that I was sorry and I felt I was forgiven.

Do you ever cry?

Yes. I feel better any time I cry. I saw my grandfather cry, he was the most kindhearted and warm person I ever knew. He would rock me for hours on a rocking chair. I felt if crying is good enough for him, it's good enough for me. I don't feel one cries in the open, unless you're around friends, unless it's death or sickness in the family. Recently my grandmother was taken to the hospital and I cried like a baby in front of the nurses and everything. In order to be a man, I have to have a heart also. This is part of his composure. Every time I cry, I feel more like a man later on.

I have seen Negroes cry. Around Christmas, this one, his wife ran out on him, took the bankbook and everything. I remember he took me in like a brother. He ran a tavern. A young fella, very good-looking. I remember the tears in his eyes. I know they have feelings. I know that they love just as deeply as we love, if not more so.

I personally felt his grief more than if it was a white man crying. It's a rare incident to see a white man cry. I've known white people who make it a habit to cry to gain whatever they want to get. But I've yet to see a Negro cry for his own personal gain. If a Negro cries, he cries because he's truly hurt.

I feel the Negro will fight with us when the time comes. I think someday he's gonna make a great American. I have many Negro friends. One of my best friends, he says he'd kill for me. I don't believe in the demonstrations. I think this causes chaos. The Negro's goal is to join our society in a productive way. He will go out of his way to purchase things, and purchasing things, he contributes to the wealth of our great society. He wants to become part of it. The fastest way for a white man to be friends with a Negro is not to give him a dollar—and this is where I sympathize with Barry Goldwater—but to teach him something you know yourself. I've had Negroes working for me in my business. He wants to learn from the white man.

Why do you think they voted so overwhelmingly against Goldwater?

Because they didn't take time out to read his book. And also the strong feeling toward Kennedy. This is why the conservatives didn't have a true test. People, myself included, sat in front of the television set and saw a great man defeated and they cried. If they didn't cry openly, they cried inwardly.

I look at the white people and it irritates me. Every white man wants to make a million dollars. His goal in life is a summer yacht out on Lake Michigan here, a yacht and soaking up the sun out here. He has no goal. The Negro definitely has a goal in life. The white people have to find themselves, they have to keep looking and find out what it is, because if they don't, the communists can take over this country without a shot being fired.

How do your conservative friends and your John Birch colleagues feel about you and your Negro friends?

Nothing was ever said in front of me. They knew how I felt. Maybe they made an exception in my case because I deal with them in my business. Even if this wasn't, they'd have found it in their heart to accept it. I really think there's good in all people.

Do you feel your fellow John Birch members have joined for the same reason you have—to overcome fear?

I don't think so. Maybe they just don't show their fear. This one fellow I know very well, he's a member of the Knights of Columbus. He's done very well for himself. He's not yet thirty, he's well-to-do. Most of these are middle-income people, who have found their place in the sun and who want to grasp on to it, they see an enemy and they feel there's a need to destroy him. Not destroy him physically. If they knew a communist on the street, a John Birch would be the last one to throw a stone. The average individual, if he saw a communist on the street, he would pick up a stone and throw it at him. A John Birch member would identify him and he might try to bring him back over to capitalism. Communists only know what they're taught. If they knew what it was, they'd probably come over because this is a very fruitful life in America. They would want a piece of it, instead of trying to chop the cherry tree.

People just like myself, hard-working people, seem to have more of a goal than the average white person today. They have a goal, they know what's mapped out before them. Martin Luther King scares me because he's done destructive things in peaceful ways.

I've talked to many white people who despise him. In the white race, he stirs up resentment. They feel he's going too far, upsetting our society as we know it. And I think nuns and priests who've been demonstrating are being taken in. The type of peace they're advocating is going to cause havoc and destruction and this is what the Commies want.

What kind of leader would you like?

To me, the ultimate would be General MacArthur. I wrote a biography about him when I was in school. He was what every young boy wanted to be when he grew up. He was debonair. He had pride in what he was doing. He loved his people, though he never showed emotion, though it came out in his voice. I feel he got a rotten, dirty deal from some of our own people in this country. He was a man that could not be bought out. He didn't care what the majority of people wanted in a democracy. He knew what was right and he did it.

Didn't you work on behalf of Florence Scala?

Yes. There was a warm person here. She was the greatest personality I've ever known among women. She made you feel you were fighting for more than just one cause. I convinced many of my young friends and my young brothers to come out with me on this. We expected trouble. We faced the Syndicate. They're tough and they throw their weight around.

We came into the polling place. The policeman was fifteen minutes late. It was his duty to be fifteen minutes late, that's how he got his job. So the dirty work would take place before he showed up. They started to fight with us. It looked like it would be a free-for-all, there was even guns. We didn't back down. Toward the end of the day, we received compliments from our opposition. It was the greatest experience of my life, in courage. Not only was I going to try to prove to myself that I was going to be a man, but I was doing it for a great person and a great cause.

LUCY JEFFERSON

When I first came from Mississippi, I was so young and ignorant. But I was freer, you know? I think I had a little bit more room to move around in than I have now. Because I think the white man wasn't so afraid then. There wasn't enough of us. There's too many of us now, I think that's what frightened him. Nobody noticed you then. You were there but nobody bothered about seeing you.

She lives in the low-rise Robert Brooks Housing Project on the Near West Side. Hers is described as a row house. It was neatly furnished; some pies were in the oven; there were books all over.

My supervisor once said to me, "Now Lucy, you sit out here at this desk and answer the phone. And I think you should tell me what's going on because people here say things to you that they wouldn't dare say to me. And because, after all, you're just part of the furniture." Oh boy, did I give a chuckle. Yeah. I laughed to myself and I said, now here's a chance for all the hate in the world. But you know what really happened? I felt so sorry for the poor thing. Some Negro went out to the steel mill and he shot up a lot of people, and after that—Oh, I tell ya, I'm very wicked—after that I'd take her arm and say, "Miss Pruner, I want to talk to you about somethin'." And I slammed the door and she'd freeze. I wasn't going to do anything to her, but she...[Prolonged laughter.] I am just telling you how wicked I am. I'm an awful louse. [Soft chuckle.]

I walk down the street, I smoke a cigarette. Well, ladies aren't supposed to do that. But I'm no lady. [Laughs.] I just have the best old time. Sometimes, it amuses, you know. When I get blue and disgusted, I go get me some beer and get cockeyed drunk, stay at home. I don't go out. I don't believe in taverns. Then you say, why the hell do you drink beer? Because I like it. There's a lot of things that I don't like.

I just don't like doles. I wouldn't accept one dime from anybody. I'm not gonna raise my children on Aid. Why should I? There's enough money in America for me to raise my children. Now one is seventeen, one is twenty-one. And I absolutely refused to accept these handouts from anybody. How am I gonna teach these children of mine what a pleasure it is in accomplishment? Do you realize what it means if I'm gonna sit here and accept this check? We can't go to the zoo because there's carfare. Everything has to be pinpointed.

We took the little money that we made, brought it home, and we said, "Okay, Melvin would count it maybe one day, Corrine would count it the next payday." And they'd say, "Okay, what are you going to do this time, mom? Does the rent have to be paid?" And I'd say, "No, not this time." "Well, then, we can go to the show?" and I'd say, "Yes, we can go to the show this time. Meet me downtown when I get off from work." I'd go to the ten-cent store when I got off from work and buy a pound of candy, mixed. I'd meet 'em at the show. We'd go in. Now this means, this is about five dollars and some cents out of this paycheck. We don't go but about every two-three months. Or maybe less. I always had a picnic basket and picnic jugs and all this junk. Because these things are essential wherein they could get around and see what is happening.

I worked at Wesley Hospital for about eleven years. As an aid in physical therapy. I worked part time and went to school part time, as a practical nurse. There was this woman that was very kind to me. She used to tell me, "Lucy, why don't you get on Public Aid until you can finish school. Don't let your pride stop you." Maybe I didn't realize exactly what she meant by pride. But I just—gave it

up. With all the stuff attached to it, maybe that's why...the publicity, the degradation, see?

Everybody's screaming now: Oh, these women on ADC. Why
hasn't somebody told these people that they're on ADC because
you gave all this money to keep from hirin' 'em? Years and years
ago. This didn't just start, you know. You don't keep people in a
certain category for hundreds of years and expect them to come out
and do all these things. For generations and generations they've
been just barely making it. Now what do you expect? Plums?

Hell, we're as poor as Joseph's goat, as far as that goes. We
pinch pennies every day, but truly we don't think anything about it.
When I get paid we know exactly what we're gonna eat for two
weeks. I buy whatever sale is on, that's what we eat. I go to Hill-
man's or George's or something, whatever's on sale. Say, for
instance, we're gonna make spareribs today. That's okay. We might
have spareribs and sauerkraut. If the steak's cheap enough, we
might even have steak once in a while. But for two long weeks we
know exactly what kind of meat we're gonna have. So what we do,
we wrap it around, we got potatoes in the house, we got rice in the
house, we got frozen vegetables in the house, so we build a meal
around this thing. So far as being poor is concerned, boy I bet I got
a monopoly on that. [Laughs.]

It's a very fashionable hospital, Wesley. The clientele there are
usually people that's got money. To me they were fascinating. All
those beautiful clothes. You know, I could dream and see myself in
this role. Then naturally I continued to read, self-educated almost.
This man came in one day and he suffers from a backache. He usually gets a heat and massage to the low back. He knew me and of
course all the clientele called me by my first name, which I
resented. But it turned out to be an asset. So he came in and said,
"Lucy, what are you reading?" And I said, *The Status Seekers*. And
he said, "Don't read that junk." And I said, "By the way, you're in
the advertising business." I had loads of fun, loads of fun.

They call you by the first name, the students, everybody. You see, this was the policy to keep the Negro in his place. But I happened to be the kind of Negro that became controversial, because I read such things as *The American Dilemma* and I walk around with the book in my hand, see? I defied them in so many ways. I almost terrified 'em.

You know, it got so every time I got on an elevator—"What are you reading? What are you reading? What are you reading?" [Laughs.] And I'd begin to enjoy this thing, you know. I was having the best old time. I was absolutely terrifying 'em. Everybody was yelling: "Lucy, Lucy!" Maybe that's why I say, the first name, it came in very handy. Because if they hadda just said, "Jefferson," nobody probably'd ever knowed it was me. But by making this so commonplace, here's this Negro woman, every time you see her she's reading a different book. You know what I'd do? I'd go to the library and get these books, and I'd just dash back home and read these. And truly it became a game with me. I don't think I ever had more fun in my life than I had working right there.

I guess I was darn near fifty then. That's the reason why I say I was havin' a ball. I'm carrying the book by Faulkner, paperback, in my pocket, you know. But this particular time I didn't realize that the heading of the book was sticking out just a little above. The students, doctors, interns got on…"Faulkner!!" [Prolonged laughter.]

What is it they're afraid of?

This is what—you are just breaking down this stereo thing that all Negroes are ignorant, they won't read, they won't do this, they won't help themselves. Once they see you're trying to do it…You see what? They're not really worrying so much about the Negro, they're worried about themselves. When I really want to fight them, you know what I do, I glare at 'em. They cringe. [Laughter.]

I have learned that a Negro woman can do anything she wants to do if she's got enough nerve. So can a white man. But a white woman and a Negro man are slaves until this day. I'll tell you why. The white man has set his woman up on a pedestal. He's trying to prove to her how superior he is. Truly he's not superior, he's just another little boy. She has to stay there if she wants to be anybody. But if she ever learns anything and she strays, she's an outcast. Me, you know what I can do? I can do any cotton-pickin' thing I feel like doin'.

The white woman is more a slave than you?

Oh, by all standards. The black woman has to have nerve, though. She has to have experience. And she needs a little education to go along with it. You know this is such a strange thing. I don't know why people like mystery. Love is so beautiful. It can be beautiful, with any group of people...Florence Scala and I can sit here...

We talk about all facets of our lives, things we wouldn't dare say to anybody else in public. And somebody else, even a Negro, walks in my back door, we shut up. Because it's taboo. They might say it was Uncle Tomming, or they could make it look ugly. These things are hard to understand. Two human beings could have so much in common that they can really sit down and talk about their own lives, their own failures, their own misgivings, and truly speaking tell you about some of my absolute traits that I don't like. Two women, we're just two women. So here is this cloak of mystery. Everybody, even the neighbors, gawking. When she comes in, you know. The curtains are moving, or they come boldly to the door and watch, as though, well, here is the enemy.

Florence, with Florence what I tried to teach in this particular neighborhood, here's a woman everybody says, oh well, she's Italian, she doesn't have the interest. Damn that, this is a woman that you *need* to talk to. She doesn't live on Lake Shore Drive. I tried to show them the little, simple, down-to-earth qualities about this particular woman. But, my God, this Petrillo,* whoever the hell he is, what are you going to tell him? The man has no interest in white or black. If you're poor, see? He's living in another world altogether.

This is the Berlin Wall right over here. You see, we don't even have a ten-cent store. Woolworth doesn't find it profitable. We don't have a bank. After all, everybody here is on Welfare. So if you want to get your check cashed, I go downtown to the bank. I usually go to Sears or Wards or somewhere where I've got a charge account. This is where you get a check cashed, unless you want to go to the currency exchange and pay somebody to get your check cashed. Well, I don't make that kind of money to give somebody money to cash my check. We don't have any facilities here that poor folks need. On Michigan Avenue, where people can get along without it, you got your ten-cent stores. I did all my shopping in a ten-cent store when I worked at Wesley.

Here again, it's the white man's standards. You know, I laugh sometimes. Just like these books we have in our schools. Dick and Jane, here's this pretty rosy-cheeked white woman and she's got on a pretty dress and a lovely little apron and she's standing out on this lawn and here's this big huge driveway, goes to two, three acres. All this stuff, and she's waving goodbye to her son. He's off on his way to school, you know. And this is what they teach the children in projects. [Laughter.] Boy, this is really something.

I was trying to live by white man's standards myself. I didn't realize it. One day the school sent for me. I'm kind of a stickler for not laying off the job, so I sent my mother. The principal told her Melvin was a problem child. He must have been about seven then. When I got off from work at five o'clock, I chased myself home to fix supper. I couldn't see the forest from the trees. I was so busy trying to get home, trying to get dinner, trying to help with home-

---

* Donald Parillo: Florence Scala's victorious machine-backed opponent in the aldermanic election of '64. The two women met during this campaign.

work, trying to get him to bed, so he'd get enough sleep. Do you realize what a vicious cycle this is? I didn't realize what I was doing to my children. Because I was rushing them to death. I was rushing myself to death.

I asked for help. I realized that all the voices Melvin heard were female voices. My voice, his sister's voice, his grandmother's voice, his teacher's voice. I began to get frightened. I went down to the I.S.U. something, I talked with them. They decided I was the one needed the psychoanalyzing. They had me in a conference and there were about twelve psychiatrists, all around. Somebody was taking notes and what have you. Nobody said one word about tomorrow. I explained to the people that my child, he's wandering away and I'm afraid he needs male companionship. I'm not asking you to give him anything, just a few minutes of your time. Till this day I didn't get it.

This is what would happen at work. Instead of sending a card: Mrs. Jefferson, come to school to see about your son...they'd call up. When the phone would ring, honest to God, you know what? My blood pressure would rise, because now I was so afraid. "Lucy!" Whenever a call came in, I knew something was wrong. And when this truant officer would phone, one of the girls would answer.

Boy, oh boy, here I go. I didn't like this, see? I was furious, because I thought this was invading my private life. The way I raise my children was my own private business. Let's say I was ashamed. This would be a better word. I wouldn't have admitted it then, but I can admit it now. Because, you see, the stigma of all Negro children are lazy, they don't do this, they don't do that, you know. See, I didn't want anybody to think my children wasn't up to par, or wasn't up to the white man's standards. Well, I blowed that long ago. [Laughs.]

I couldn't afford to go to the PTA meetings. They don't do a damn thing but drink coffee anyway. I like coffee and I like to drink it in the morning, but I have to go to work, and they had PTA meetings at one o'clock in the day. I couldn't lay off my job to go down there to chitchat with them. I think they had PTA meetings twice in the last ten years at night. They're no damn good anyway.

Melvin was doing very poorly and I was getting letters. You know, they send you all these little items. Come to see me, come to school, because your child is not working up to his capacity. I don't know why they just don't tell you the truth about it, instead of using all these vague, false phrases. I thought he was just being lazy, but the child couldn't read. He couldn't spell. He was at Crane High, out there in the ghetto. I laid off from work the next day. I got up, cocked my hat up Miss Johnny Aside…I wanted to let him know I was plenty mad then. Oh yeah, I visited Crane. Melvin was having three study periods in a row. Gee, this is kind of crazy, studying what? I went to see this study hall. And this is the auditorium. It has a false ceiling, and there's very few lights, and there's children everywhere, male and female, and about the only thing they can do there is make love. Most of the kids can't read anyway, but if they could, they wouldn't be able to see. So I went to the counselor and he said, "It costs $10,000 to put up this business of putting lights in and the school system doesn't have the money" and blah, blah, blah. I said, "But in the meantime, what are you going to do about all these children in there, these boys and girls, these young men and women?" I said, "Maybe they can't read but they can do other things in there, such as getting babies." He said, "Well, well…we don't have anywhere else to put 'em."

You're talking about teachers. I bet he never had the same teacher twice in two weeks in two years. It's a disgrace to keep on calling these places schools. I think the best thing we can say about them, these are meeting places where people get up every morning, give their children a dollar, seventy-five cents, or whatever the heck they give 'em, and these kids go off. Schools you learn in. They could take a store front on Roosevelt Road or anywhere and clean it up, put some seats in there, and put some books in. But see, you can't learn anything where there is no books. Melvin went a whole half year at Crane, didn't have a book. If I woke up in a house that didn't have a book in, I'd just burn it down, it wouldn't be any good. To me, they're my life blood. Types of caps, gowns, all that crap, it don't mean nothing.

Oh, what am I *really* looking for? For my daughter to have her baby. This is her first. Her marriage turned out bad. I would like for her to finish her college education. She's gonna need it to help her child, to rear her child. The only thrill left for me is to see my grandchild come and see what I can do about him. Won't that be fun? You know, I'll be able to afford things that would give him incentive to paint, music, literature, all these things that would free his little soul. Other than that, no bother. Melvin? Am I going to give him a chance to be a man or not? I took that chance when I let him go to Selma. I was scared to death. And I was very proud. I was afraid he was too young, because he was only sixteen, to know what was really happening. But I couldn't afford to tell him. I wouldn't have given him a chance to be a man. This was his chance. And I didn't want to steal it.

Let's face it. What counts is knowledge. And feeling. You see, there's such a thing as a feeling tone. One is friendly and one is hostile. And if you don't have this, baby, you've had it. You're dead.

KID PHARAOH

He was standing outside his hot-dog shop, somewhere on the North Side of the city. He was observing the sky. "Think it'll rain?" I asked. "I'm looking at them high rises," he replied. "Wish they were mine." During the conversation, I was rewarded with three fifty-cent cigars.

Guys like me are the nucleus of the street. All the newcomers are the real Johnny-come-latelies, are not familiar with the location, of what it stands for, of what it is. I been in Chicago all my life, was born and raised here. My dad was a speculator on the market, sometimes successful, most of his life not. I'm an ex-prize fighter by profession.

I never graduated high school, and I missed absolutely nothing. You learn nothing in school, nothing. The truth of the matter is you learn it on the outside. A guy goes to school, what does he want to be? A doctor? A lawyer? These are the two biggest thieves in our society. One steals legitimate, the other kills legitimate. Charge you what they want. They never pay the Uncle what he's entitled to. Guys like me they want to put in jail. Because I'm dedicated to one principle: taking money away from unqualified dilettantes who earn it through nepotism. I work at this and I'm good at my trade. I don't labor. Outside of being a prize fighter, I took an oath to God I would never again labor. But there's a million people on the street that want to be taken and should be taken, and they're gonna be taken.

Me and my brothers have the same philosophy. We set a snare, we trap these guys who come in. They're all either biologically or physically insecure. They believe what they read in the papers and everyone reads fiction and they're all scared. We sell two things: we sell the item of fear and we give them the security they never had in their life. And whatever they have, we take from them. They're more than willing to give it.

How did they get it? Did they earn it? Did they inherit it? Did they marry the boss's daughter? What's their qualifications? Half of one percent of America is qualified. You walk into any department store, for example, and you want to change a hat. He says, wait a minute, we'll send you to so-and-so. So-and-so sends you to the second floor, he's not qualified. By the time it's through, the whole afternoon is shot. Who's an authority? Who's really an authority that you know today? You can't name one.

During the Depression when I was a little boy, and I was hustling, selling newspapers or shining shoes or setting pins, or stealing ginger ale bottles off the Lake Shore Drive area, someone was the boss. Today there's no such thing as the boss. He's not really qualified.

My dad worked as a WPA man. We were on relief. I could see me and my kid brother going down to the Fair Store to get shoes on government stamps. I can see myself hustling food, luggin' oranges home and potatoes home. And this is the greatest thing that ever happened to guys like me. I mean, I loved it. This is what the system calls for, this is where you pick yourself up and go. Without money, you're a bum on the park, you're nothing. Who are you? You can't get yourself in an icebox. You can't get your hand out of one. You can't get your hand in one. What's the measuring stick of our system? He's a money guy, respect 'im. What do you do with a bum? Extend the evening felicitations. Is it a woman? She'll offer you a biological reward. If you've got currency, you'll offer her some luxury. The other mooch who got everything from his dad, the hell with him. Take it away from him. Hook, crook, slingshot, canoe, we must shaft this guy, got to take it away from him. But don't hurt him.

Now how do I survive? I live at the Belden Stratford, I manage a new car every year, I take my steam baths three times a week, I take a manicure, a pedicure. Now how do I get it? I don't break the law. If you steal it, you go to jail. You're in a trick bag. Now there are people on the street that have money, they don't know what to do with it. How do I take this money away from these guys? I play the Freudian theory, long may Freud live.

It's amazing, my reputation. People telling how qualified you are as Tom the Tough Guy and Pistol Pete. I got some good publicity as a prize fighter in the newspapers and I've gotten some bad publicity. People believe what they read. So then leave them think that way. My brother was in trouble recently. All the papers had him on the front page. He was on television. He was scared. I said, "Fool, you'll go out and raise all the money in the world." He came back in a week, he says, "You know, I made fourteen thousand?" "Double it. People want to help people, especially tough guys. They *need* you. They believe what they read. We know you're innocent, but let's take it from 'em." And we did. He was a celebrity. They worship celebrities. Tom the Tough Guy and Pistol Pete. This is the giant of their society. Who else is a giant? Some faggot movie star that puts powder on his face? What qualifies him? The entire country today moves on physiogomy. If you're attractive, it'll open the door. I can't get in. What's my best shot? The arm. I use it.

Everybody is really scared because they watch all this nonsense on television. No such thing as a tough guy, they're all dead. Now these people come in, say in the Old Town section where I bum in the late hours after I close this shop. We have a reputation of being some tough guys, but we're really not. We're very gracious gentlemen, we extend the utmost courtesies to everyone. But we don't tip our hand. As long as they believe it, leave them believe it. 'Cause their currency, we want to take it away from them, not by heisting them, but by encouraging them to do what they want. This boy who killed himself in Arizona, this MacDonald boy of Zenith. Now why couldn't I grab someone like him. We've often discussed it. He was insecure. Psychiatrists couldn't cure him, but we woulda cured him. We'd put a dent in him a little. Given him courage he never had. He had a Freudian complex of rejection. It was a broken-up family. And we'd of explained to him what to do with this type of money.

Why shouldn't we take it from them? Legally, with the semi-muscle. It can get you killed, but if you work it right, the greatest thing in the world is the semi-muscle. You put that fear in 'em that'll help them. I work on contracts, like in business. It's an oral contract. Now if they give me a contract, they come to me with some trouble. If called upon to perform, I perform. If not, I subcontract. Example. They're usually in debt. Or someone owes them money. Or they're extremely fond of women. Someone's cutting in on their girl. Their wife is an infidelist. There's all kinds of conditions. They're afraid, everybody's scared. I give them security. If their wife is an infidelist, I muscle the guy she's makin' love with. I run him off. If somebody owes him money, somebody's after him, I chase him away. See? Now this guy's in debt to me. The biggest mistake of his life. He should really paid 'em, because I've got him for the rest of his life. I'll always noodge him for some currency or another. I'll always go into him. You just can't imagine how many insecure people we have in this country. Say, in the Cuban crisis, remember? I was getting a manicure that day and my manicurist was so scared she didn't know if she was gonna have a heart attack. And I said, "Look, Louise, don't be afraid, sweetheart. They're gonna turn back the minute they get there, they're gonna make a U-turn." You know what happened? They got no chance with the Uncle. Everybody's scared—of something.

Are you scared of anything?

Absolutely nothing. And this is a dangerous society. People like to hurt people. Why do people go to Indianapolis Speed Race, two, three hundred thousand? To see the little guys run around in a car? Hell, no. They go to see people killed. If a man's brains can put a plane in the sky, why can't a man's brain kill ya? He does, he can use it, he's on the streets right now. Killers are stalking all day long, faggots are on the streets, peeking Toms are on the streets, teenagers are on the streets, you gotta use a baseball bat on 'em, guys like myself from the 43rd Ward, here in the Metropolitan area of Chicago. We don't believe in contaminating the morals. We run these guys off.

We don't want 'em around. If they come in a restaurant where we bum, or some faggot starts congregatin' around, they assemble— we run 'em off. We don't like 'em. I certainly have to protect my nieces and nephews. The law isn't qualified. The law protects these dilettantes and degenerates.

If I was a dictator, I would exercise genocide for all degenerates. I would slay them. Take most of these educated guys. Think they know what to do? You put them in Lincoln Park for three-quarters of an hour, and you'd have to take one of our little boy scouts who have to go in and take them out again. They wouldn't know how to get out. How does a man survive in a capitalistic system? Say you work twenty years on a job, you've lost it. What would you do now? My element can survive. Heaven forbid, we should live with a bomb, a fire, a flood, we'll survive.

How?

The mongrel and the pedigree. The pedigree will run across the street, is it not so, he'll get hit by the car? The mongrel will survive. He has the cunning to duck the car.

A dog, a mongrel?

Yeah, put me down as a dog, yeah.... You must be sincere in my element. Like Sam Giancana. Momo.* Now they've got this man in a trick bag, in a penal institution. They've taken his right away. It's unfair. It's not the way the American system works. The aggravation of putting this man away for no reason at all. He's my element. I don't prefer a lot of them because they're prejudiced toward their element of nationality. The same as the rise and fall of the Roman Empire. A one-way street cannot survive. He's fair with his money. He didn't forget people. Everybody who came out of jail he helped them, he made money for them, and he put them in power. He was qualified. Martin Luther King, put him away. What's he good for?

---

* Reputedly a leader of the Syndicate.

The American Negro not only has everything, now he's tampering with our white women. Women today seem to prefer pigmentation. I have two nieces, I'm worried about that. That some colored guy—and I'm the last guy in the world to be prejudiced—this guy comes to the big city and has a comb job on his head. They bust out in these attractive suits and they seem to have some sort of education about them. Most of the girls who prefer pigmentation are not metropolitanites. They're from Ohio, Iowa, Indiana, or some of them buck towns.

Some war veterans who are laying in some basket in a hospital, they'll never go to him to arouse his biological urge or pat him on the back or give him a vote of confidence, a note of thanks, nonsense. What about the American soldier who went off to war? Who came back, who's in trouble with automation over his vocation? He's entitled to nothing, he's a mooch. What about the average layman who has labored hard and long in this country without an education, raised a family, sent boys off to war? He's in his vintage years. All of a sudden his building is worth thirty-five thousand dollars and he goes to bed feeling secure. In the morning, a Negro moves next door and his building is worth seventeen thousand. They've destroyed everything they've ever moved in. There's a revolt in the making, let me suggest it to you. When it will come, I don't know. How it will come, I don't know. Who will organize this revolt...but it'll come.

The best people for communities are the Japanese. They're never above a whisper. Their homes are immaculate. Show me a Japanese on the street after ten o'clock. Show me one, I'll offer a universal challenge to all. Did you ever see one arrested? Did you ever see one under the influence of an intoxicated beverage? Did you ever see 'em pregnant, Japanese girls who are not married? Of course not, there's love in the home. Say for the Negroes, they're animals. There's no love in the home. Not only wants to move the white man over, he wants to be there with him. They have a long-range plan of dissolving this pigmentation through intermarriage.

I thought you admired aggressiveness?

Yeah, but you ain't gonna muscle me. I'm a capitalist and they're gonna have to fight me and I ain't gonna lose. There's a lot of legit-imate people like myself. My system may be outdated. I might have been a success at the turn of the century. Today with all the laws and Supreme Court rulings, I haven't even got a chance. If I was born forty years ago, I believe I would have been a multimillionaire. I shoot the same shot that Rockefeller shot while somebody was tapping an oil well that was competitive to him. He put guys in trick bags. Got 'em in jail. There's a history written about these guys. John Astor, with his trapping, with his furs. Hitting guys. This is the way the system works. What else is there? These new laws are holding them back, destroying incentive. Our enemies are calling us capitalistic. We're not.

Capitalism ideally is for any bum in the park to come with an idea or be aggressive enough to find a place in the sun for himself, can go as high as he wants and as long as he wants.

Even if he has to step on others?

He must, he must. In our society, you must do it. It doesn't work any other way. People will hurt you, kill you.

To me the most important thing is helping someone who is in need. Financially, if I have the currency or any way shape or form, I can help people. And I do. Taking an oath before a high court and before God, we, we do it.

You believe in God?

I really don't. I'm a dedicated agnostic. Who was Jesus Christ? He was an excellent, I would say a con man. He learned hypnotism in India. When He lammed out of Israel, they wanted to shaft Him because He was causing all this nonsense and riots, He said He was the Son of God. Today they wouldn't kill Him. They would have offered Him psychiatric supervision, because the dear boy was in need of this. When He fed the multitude the fish, He hypnotized a half a dozen. They carried on the word. Who did He feed? He fed nobody. Who did He cure of leprosy? He hypnotized the people. They got up and they walked. He got Himself killed at thirty-two years of age. He couldn't keep His big bazoo shut. Did you know that Pontius Pilate offered to give this man a number? He said, "Now look, Jesus, you're a marvelous boy. Why don't you go off in the wilderness and cut this nonsense out, and go about your business. Quit causing all these riots." This man wanted to be killed. And he told Him, "If you want to be killed, I gotta hang up two criminals. So be it." Hit his hand on the table and they strung Him up. He was a rabble rouser.

Same thing with Martin Luther King. They asked the opinion of our great President, Harry Truman, and he said this guy was strictly a troublemaker, period. I thought Truman was marvelous. Because he was a guy that come up in the capitalistic system of politics from nothing to a giant. And this is the way our system works. From Daley here, from Kelly before him, from Nash before him...from the two Irishmen, Hinky Dink and Bathhouse John.* Boss Tweed in New York and what's his name in Boston—Curley. These were the giants that built the cities. These are the guys that built our country. They elect presidents. All these guys came up the hard way...shoeshine guys and bust-out crapshooters...shoot a

---

* "Bathhouse John" Coughlan and Michael "Hinky Dink" Kenna ruled Chicago's First Ward from 1892 for almost fifty years. This was the city's most celebrated vice district. The annual First Ward Ball was the social event of the season, attended by pimps, prostitutes, madams, political and social leaders—all the celebrities of the era. Tribute, material as well as spiritual, was paid to Bathhouse John and Hinky Dink on this occasion. There was reciprocity, of course: a wide-open area the year round.

shot against blackjack. These are the guys we need in our country. Who needs educated mooches?

The greatest man in the twentieth century in my opinion—and I hope I don't offend anybody—is Mau Too Sung. He did something the world could never do. He feeds the multitudes. It's amazing about Peking. Like myself, the average-layman in business for himself in a hot-dog business, I'm always in trouble with flies. An ordinary fly who's a pest. Now Mau Too Sung has come up with a chemical. They've come up with somethin' which even us, the capitalistic system, does not have. There are no flies in Peking. He's a guy who's come up so hard.

You admire Harry Truman and Mao Tse-Tung and Momo Giancana.

And Daley. He's the greatest mayor Chicago ever had. Here's a man dedicated to civilizing the city. He takes his paycheck and sits home trying to think how to do something for the city. He was smart enough and I believe intelligent enough and he fell into I must say luck, though qualified when called upon. Most of his competitors died off and he knew when to seize power. I'm for him a hundred percent. When my mother died eight years ago, I got a condolence telegram from the mayor. It was humble of him to do that, very humble indeed. For the mayor of the second largest city of the world's greatest country to send such a telegram to an ex-prize fighter without a high-school diploma with the element that I'm in, my God, I should say yes.

Was he acquainted with you or your mother?

Of course not. My friend, Terry Boyle,* probably encouraged him.

---

* Terence Ignatus Boyle. He appears in the complete edition of *Division Street: America.*

I'm a Democrat at heart anyway. I take the less of the two evils. Look at Chicago. There's all the sky rises and new roads and so forth. Qualified authorities tell me that a group of real-estate men control this urban renewal. I believe in slum clearance but this isn't the way to do it. All the benefits, no matter if it goes up, down, or sideways, they wind up with all the money. They all cut the pot together. They condemn the property they want to condemn and they throw in the high rises. They do it legally. I wish it was me.

There's a song I love. I never forgot it. "A man with a dream, a mighty man is he. For dreams make the man, the man he wants to be." You can be anything in this world you want to be, if you dream hard enough, long enough.

TOM KEARNEY

An apartment in a high-rise complex on the Near South Side of the city, adjacent to Michael Reese Hospital. A well-thumbed copy of Gunnar Myrdal's An American Dilemma *was on the coffee table.*

I've been a policeman for twenty-three hard years. You have to work odd hours, often long hours. Yesterday I was assigned to the parade, the astronauts, White and McDivitt. We reported for duty at six-thirty in the morning and weren't released until five o'clock in the evening. That was without any time off at all. No lunch period or anything.

I worked as a patrolman and a detective. Then I was promoted to a detective sergeant and from there I went to the traffic division. So I've covered all bases so far.

Sometimes you're disenchanted, you're disillusioned, you're cynical. When people attempt to offer a bribe. I know I've been negligent in my duty because I should have arrested the person. At the same time, that's universal, everywhere. I turn it down. I told him, you know, "No harm trying. But I just don't go that way." [Laughs sadly.] It's a corrupt society.

You think you're a wise guy until you run into situations where you shoulda known better and didn't. The night before I went on my vacation, I was out in the squad car, and you travel alone, you know. The radio signaled for a police officer. They needed help on a 10-1. So over the air came this signal, a couple of blocks from where I was. I got there and found an officer struggling with two young men and they were giving him a pretty good battle. So I joined in. At fifty-three, when you take those blows, you absorb them, you know. You just don't shake them off. I went on my vacation the next day with bruises. Shins all beat up. But there's nothing else I can do, you see?

I was born in Chicago, my father was born in Chicago, and my grandfather was born here. His father came to America to dig the Sag Canal. They were promised they could have farmland where they could grow anything. In the winter, they'd dig the canal. Unfortunately, it was all rocks. So they wound up with a rock farm.

There's something you gotta understand about the Irish Catholics in Chicago. Until recently, being a policeman was a wonderful thing. 'Cause he had a steady job and he knew he was gonna get a pension and they seemed to think it was better than being a truck driver, although a truck driver earns far more than a policeman today.

Someone had to be police, you know? They sacrificed anything. They just knew that so-and-so in the family would be. It was another step out of the mud. You figured at least you'd have some security. They felt they no longer worked with their hands. They weren't laborers any more.

If the Depression hadn't come along, my father would have been able to do more educational-wise for us. He couldn't provide. There was no money for two years. At that time, the firemen and policemen weren't paid. My father was a fireman for forty years. They were the only ones who didn't get their back pay. Whoever could work and earn anything at all…that's what kept us going.

I recall the hunger marches. I remember the police at that time, they had mounted police. I had a job at Madison and Canal, and they were marching, trying to get into the Downtown area, from the west to the east. The police charged them. Whether they were right or wrong, I didn't know then. I was too much concerned with my own self. 'Cause things were rather brutal and you expected that, you know.

I remember at Blue Island and Ashland—there's a lumber company there now—that was a big transient camp. I remember the food lines. I also remember getting off the Elevated and men waiting in line for the newspaper. If you were through reading it, they'd take it. They had a little code among themselves. After you got your newspaper, you moved away from the line. What they used them for was probably to sleep on….

There's no colored there [Bridgeport]. A mixture of white—different ethnic groups: Polish, Slavic, Irish, Italian, anything and everything. A few Jewish families. In the old days, it was all Irish. The streets, the names were Irish. The street my grandmother lived on was named after one of my father's sisters who died very young.

We moved farther south, to Roseland. My father was assigned there. It was a community begun by people who had left Pullman. They had rebelled against the company by moving out. If you worked for him you had to live in one of his Company houses. You bought from the Company store. If profits fell below a certain level, wages were cut. The rents weren't lowered, the rents remained the same. Now, of course, there's nothing much over there.

My father was one of the radicals. Even though he had status, you know, being a fireman and the fact he got a pension, he used to say, "Why should I get a pension when the fellow next door doesn't get one?" He was a good Irish Catholic, so he wasn't a Commie, but at the same time he used to say, "You know, maybe they got something over there that we should know about, because they keep on talking about how bad it is over there."

My family wasn't devout. Certain things my mother, of course, insisted upon. On Good Fridays, you had to sit in a chair in the kitchen. In those days they didn't have any foam rubber seats. It was hard wood. And you had to sit there till about five minutes to twelve. Don't laugh and don't talk. You sat for three hours. She had some of an idea that it helped you spiritually. But I don't think we were deeply religious.

I find myself at odds with the Church at various times. I knew the nuns taught me some things that weren't true. At the same time, I realized they themselves didn't know whether they were true or not. They were simple women, you know. You say you'd rather have your son go to a public school because he's gonna have to get along with those people and he might as well start young. The same as going to school with the colored. You're going to have to get along with them. They're here, so you might as well go to school with them and get along with them.

How do you feel about young nuns and priests taking part in street demonstrations?

They have every right to do so, although not to violate the law. I'm not saying that because I'm a policeman, but simply because having been in parochial school all my life, all I ever heard was: "Don't do anything wrong." Respect for authority.

Today things are changing. If one married outside the religion I remember this: "Oooh, tear out all my hair. I can't face my friends, we gotta move." Oooh, terrible, terrible. And what happened? I have five brothers and one sister. Of the brothers, one is a bachelor. The rest of us married Protestants. My sister married a Protestant. My older brother had two daughters. They raised one a

Catholic and one a Protestant. The girl raised a Catholic married a Protestant and the one raised a Protestant married a Catholic. Today, for convenience's sake, my brother and his wife go to the Catholic Church. She hasn't been converted, but just goes for convenience's sake. It isn't any big deal any more.

It's changing rapidly. Look at the city. Of course, everyone resists change, good or bad. Even if it's good for them, they resist it. Take the color situation today. The whites, they're only fighting a rear-guard action. The walls are coming down, that's all. The tragedy is that the program of the colored is still negative. There's no reason to lead a march or sit in the streets any more, as I see it. Because they've won, there's no question about it. They've got to find a way to have the whites accept them.

Unfortunately, the colored man came to the industrial North just too late. He came after there were so few jobs to begin with. The Caucasian immigrants came with nothing but their hands and they worked in steel mills and maybe they were snapping cinders, which is one of the most difficult jobs and the lowest paid. They watched another fellow do a job and they learned his job and climbed up. Well, the colored man didn't have that opportunity after the wave of migration from the South. There were so few labor jobs that he could start out from and learn how to get up. The machine took care of that. They didn't need him any more. One man can do the work of ten today.

What do you think the objective of the colored is?

The same as mine, the same as mine. Everything best for him and his family that he can possibly have. I can see where they'd want to move away from a completely colored neighborhood and integrate. I can understand that. He also understands that his family is gonna have to live with whites and if he doesn't live with the whites he can't understand them either. The colored man says: "Well, you don't know us." Naturally we don't. They don't know the white either.

I think people are intelligent enough to accept integration. We've done one thing, it's a bad thing, but I can't think of anything better. The quota. It's bad because you have to exclude someone sometimes, but the whites wouldn't have any fear of being overwhelmed. And the colored wouldn't have any fear that the white would run. This high-rise complex I live in now works on a quota. It's highly controlled.

Most of urban renewal is bad in a sense. People were displaced. Yet it had to be done. Where we're sitting now was one of the foulest slums in America. It was worse than Calcutta, believe me. I've been in here as a police officer on many occasions. Right across the street, they had a fence to protect the institution there. It must have been eighteen feet in the air, with barbed wire.

Actually it's not really integrated now because there's no community life here at all. You don't know the fella next door usually. Your wife may meet them or something like that, but you yourself come and go, that's all. There's no way for people to know one another. You at least vote together, you know, at election time. Well, each building is its own precinct. So people just go in and out. There isn't any standing outside like you do normally at an election. There's no church in the immediate vicinity. Most people, they have to go several blocks to an known place. And these complexes have very few children. An adult population, more or less concerned with their own problems. When we first moved in here, I thought I'd go insane, being cooped in and actually nowhere to go, because the neighborhood is sterile. It's not a neighborhood at all.

People don't want to become involved. Most people have had some dealings with court, like traffic courts. People have sat for long periods of time, waiting for their case to be called. In criminal court, they've found themselves returning there and then continuances being granted after continuances. This man, he loses his day's pay from work. If it's a woman, she becomes frightened, that they might retaliate in some way. The fear. Like many cabdrivers that don't report a robbery, 'cause normally they might not have eight or ten dollars when he's held up. He won't report it because he'd lose a day's work if they finally apprehended the offender and the loss is a loss.

This fear of involvement. I wondered why there were so few colored in the crowd greeting the astronauts yesterday. Most of the fellows said, "They don't care if anybody went to the moon. They don't have any feeling about it." I said, I don't think that's true. We were briefed to search for colored people who might be a threat, you know. It was the week of demonstrations. The average colored person is just like you and I. If there was a great crowd some place and there was a threat to all people wearing blue shirts, you certainly wouldn't go down there in a blue shirt.

Do you have any colored friends?

Oh yes. Yes. [Pause.] I *say* colored friends and I *think* colored friends...but actually I really don't know.

You don't know what they think of you?

Not really. I can understand that. Because if I were colored, I'd be bitter, too. I *think* I'd try to control myself, try to be rational about it. I remember one night, a colored schoolteacher I know, we're at a party, an interracial party, very nice. She forgot the potency of martinis and I was sitting talking to her and suddenly she looked at me very hard and said, "You're my Caucasian enemy." Very indignantly. Of course, I realized, you know...I mean, she just didn't realize how potent a martini was. So you really don't know.

Some guys that I know, colored, we talk and discuss the family and how things are going, and how their wives are and things like that, but I don't think I know. [Pause.] I don't think I know.

My son, a twenty-two-year-old boy, who's been going to college, I really don't think I know *him*. I think he knows me better than I know him. That's one thing he really doesn't like. I think he'd like it the other way around. The younger generation doesn't think too highly of us. They think we made a mess of things, which we did. We seem to lead disorganized lives. Most of us dislike the work we're doing. Most of us are anxious to go someplace else, thinking we could leave our troubles behind. They love us, our sons and daughters. But at the same time, they don't think we did things correctly. They're critical of us. They discuss things far more intelligently than we do. They think for themselves.

One day he brought up a charming little blond girl, not overly dressed, but not ragged or beatnik type. She was going down South to teach in one of the Freedom schools. Very much enthused about it. And she seemed to have a good idea why she was doing it. I mean she wasn't looking for publicity or anything like that. She really thought she should be doing this. And then again, he met a colored girl, a beautiful creature, who also had a brilliant mind, you know, straight A student, one of those types. And she had absolutely no interest in civil rights. None. Couldn't mean less to her, although she identifies with the colored people. She makes no attempt to pass, 'cause she could very easily. And then he has a friend whose sister and mother are both active in the civil rights movement. The sister was arrested twice in the last week.

Did you have to arrest her?

No, I...[Laughs.] It woulda really been funny, you know. I asked her, "Now what is this about police brutality?" And she said, the way some policeman talk, you know, and then I suppose holler at them at some degree or another, I mean to keep them in control and get them in the wagon or something. But I said, "What happened to you?" I mean, the voice means nothing, I mean, I holler at people, too, you know—stand back, or something. Well, she said, "When the policeman arrested me, he said, 'Now come along, honey, step up in the wagon.' " [Laughs.] That was police brutality.

…So the difference in them, more freedom. You never say, "Go to your room, I want to talk to your mother." When I was a boy, when they had company, I was always excluded. Today, even when our son was young, he sat in on conversation and he learned to judge and evaluate things. In my home, when my father was there, he got the paper. When he was through with it, you got it. That's all. Sometimes he didn't get through with it until you were in bed. About the only thing that was discarded was the comics on Sunday. They didn't think you were interested in other things.

I was surprised to see what these young people were thinking. Civil rights. Some couldn't care less. Others were militant. Then others like himself approved of what was going on but didn't participate. They had some very good ideas about it. Some of the most controversial things, Vietnam, Cuba.

They began wondering. Of course they have more time. You and I have to make a living. But their level of conversation is much higher than the adults' level today. I think we tend to be more humorous, even if we force it, probably because of age and years of work. I find myself in a group, visiting, where there's very little conversation of any depth. Did you hear the latest Polish joke? or things like that. Or talk about some play or movie. You know, there's no…

But these young people really have a feeling. They trade views. I find they seldom argue in a—in disagreement. They give and take, back and forth, but they don't stand on their points. They want to know the other person. They seem to accept other people more easily than we did.

The only thing is there's a great many pressures on them. The fear of the draft is always there. It's stupid, they feel. It doesn't accomplish a thing, and why do it. They don't seem—outside of this one girl who was arrested twice in one week for sitting in the streets—they don't seem to have any great drive. I mean, it's a problem. Everything is so complex.

They see all our values changing. Just as we see the city changing, with the expressways and with the high-rise living, which I never thought I'd live or could possibly afford.

You're two years away from retirement. Do you look forward to it?

Not particularly. I do in one way. I'd like to take up something else if I can. Be able to enter—this sounds sort of corny—more of a community life, in a smaller community where you participated more, you know. *In doing something.*

I myself haven't done everything a man should do. Some guy once said the four things a man had to do: he had to be in love, he had to get married, he had to have children, and he had to fight a war. So you accomplish these things, and I did. Now there's the Bomb. As far as I'm concerned, I'd hold on as long as I could. I don't think this is as serious with the older generation, this fear, as it is with the young. They believe here's a possibility of working your way out of this intelligently and we don't seem to work toward that end. We're constantly in turmoil. That's the older generation. After you're fifty, it's all the way down, no speed limits. That's it, you've had it. I mean you have nothing left.

A policeman starts out young and very impressionable, and you see people at their worst, naturally. You don't go into the better homes, because they have fewer problems, or they keep them under control. Sure, a man and wife argue, but usually it's on a quiet level. In the poorer classes of homes, frustrations are great, pressures are tremendous. They turn on the TV set and they have these give-away programs and someone's winning thousands of dollars. Or if they're watching a play of some kind, everything's beautiful and lovely. They watch this and they don't have any of it and they can't get any of it. Then when an argument breaks out, the closest one to 'em, he's gonna get it. We were taught, you know, if my mother and father argued, my mother went around shutting down the windows and the doors because they didn't want the neighbors to hear 'em. But they deliberately open the doors and open the windows, screaming and hollering, and it's a release from their emotions. So when they have an argument, it's a good argument and it necessitates the police coming to quiet it down. Naturally, the impression of a young police officer is that they aren't really people, you know, get rid of them.

I've often worked with policemen who became very angry when we'd arrest a narcotic addict, a burglar. And then have to notify the parents. This one police officer, he used to get insane, he'd be so mad. Why couldn't you do something with your son? One day I finally said to him, "What would you do if your son came home and said he was a junkie?" He wouldn't know what to do. He wouldn't know why his son did it. The son would know, but he wouldn't. You understand?

CHESTER KOLAR

A technician at an electronics plant. There were glory days. Once, he had conducted a program over a foreign-language radio station. He was celebrated in his community then.

I'm cold to it, these Vietnam photos. And most of my friends, the technicians, are cold to it. The only thing is their remark: "What to you know about that?" If you're gonna worry about that...and today we got so many people that are so easy to falling in this category of worrying, that actually what makes a lot of people sick.

Some people can't stand this. They shut the TV off. You heard of the guy who kicked the TV tube and took a pistol and shot into the—I mean, he was off his nut. I don't know if you ran across some of these people, they're very nervous-type people. As a matter of fact, if someone shouts, they jump. I'm cold to it.

These people sit around this radio and TV and they listen to all these broadcasts. I think this news we're having is doing us more harm than good. I'm speaking of those that are disinterested and it's being crammed down their throats. Over the radio comes a message. Special bulletin: so many people killed. I mean, what are they trying to fire up? This poor man that's trying to get his eight hours of work done to keep his family going, pay his rent, and buy his food which is so high today, he gets all excited about what's going to happen. What does John Q. Public know what should happen? Let's not stick our nose into something we know nothing about.

Why should he worry about these things? We should know once a month, let's have a review of the news: what will happen and what has happened. These people are worried about something they shouldn't be worried about. They should be worried about painting their rooms and fixing something up where they could become industrious.

GEORGE MALLEY (A.K.A. HENRY LORENZ)

Mid-North, adjacent to the artsy-crafty area, Old Town. A frame house, two and a half stories. It has seen better days; yet the siding salesman's offensive has been hurled back. Outside stairway, wood, steep. The Lorenz apartment is in the process of being painted and refurnished. A White Sox ball game on TV was switched off as the conversation began. "We weren't watching it anyway," said Henry.

A Java bird in a cage; a set of the Book of Knowledge; *a set of* Great Books of the Western World.

His was a hard childhood, one of a family of thirteen. "I was lost in the shuffle somewhere." At twelve, he dropped out of school and became a workingman: a bed company, an iron foundry, the state roads, "swinging a sixteen-pound sledge in the sun for ten hours." He had been a carpenter and is now a house painter.

We've lived in this neighborhood twenty years. First, we had the old German area, people who were here for years and years and years. I'm talking about people who were here thirty to sixty years. Then after the war, we had this terrific influx of folks from Europe. These people were so unaccustomed to the life they found here that the—making a quick dollar became a mania with them. It didn't take them long to become aware of the housing shortage.

I know one family bought the house we lived in for $6,500 and a very, very short time later his asking price was $24,000. I think he got about twenty. A good forty percent of the property in this area in the past twenty years have changed hands four to six times. All of a sudden we started getting this other type of people: professional people, artists, doctors, lawyers, sculptors. You see, we had a period from the lowest to the highest. But the lowest are being priced out.

In this block here, we have something in common. Each one is trying to do something with the house he's living in. Trying to progress as rapidly as he can, and so on and so forth. When you find you have something in common with your neighbor, you take time out to know it. No strangers. I know just about everybody around here. When someone is ready to sell, there are a half a dozen people ready to buy it. We are entering on a threshhold of permanency again. I feel good about it. I'm part of it. I welcome this change.

The city has changed for the good. You know, I'm not sure what good is any more. See? Traditions of the past, there are some that I miss. Chicago was a big city before and yet it was pretty much like a small town. Neighborhood after neighborhood, you know, were like small towns themselves. People integrated, relatives visited, you had more friends, you talked more, you got to know each other. You know what I mean? You miss this. There was more music, home-made music, you understand. You were able to develop yourself to a far greater extent. We knew everybody in the neighborhood.

Families do very little today. Years ago, when you were a kid, on Saturday nights, Sunday, you invariably went to somebody's house or somebody came to your house. You played cards, you picnicked, you maybe talked. All these things. You used to read more. You had no other ways to entertain yourself. You don't find that today.

We generally stay home, watch the television set, for three, four years we were fans, real TV fans. But the television set broke down. I'm telling you, we were literally sick. We didn't know what to do. We became desperate. We yelled at each other. Some of the arguments we had took place at this time. Suddenly there was something gone. It was like, gee, I don't know what. Something died. What are we gonna do? Where can we find a television repair? Will he be able to get here on time? It was a real tragedy.

What did you do before you had a TV set?

Oh, that's easy. She played a guitar. I played a harmonica. We used to play, we used to sing. Instead of going to bed at one or two in the morning, we might go to bed anywhere from nine-thirty to ten-thirty in the evening. We'd lay for three hours and talk, back and forth. We got to know each other pretty well. I haven't talked to her since we got the television set.

The boys have grown up pretty much with it. I don't think it's been detrimental to the kids, oddly enough. They know there's more to the world than what's across the street. You understand?

They see many, many, many things. They witness things we never could. They begin to speak...

I have tried to analyze my boys. I found I did not father any geniuses. This is definite. I've established this. Not only my sons, but neither am I, right, Hazel? So I asked myself where do we go from here? So all right. The door to college is open. It's like I've told both these boys: Shoot for college. If you can't make college, you've made an honest effort in high school. Then get into a trade, one of the trades.

Frankly speaking, if they did this, they'd be far better off themselves and their future families. I think this college bit is overrated by far. Because I know of my own experience. Say, thirty-five to forty years ago, if a boy told you he was a high-school graduate, he stood out in the crowd. Is this correct? He stood out in the crowd. But today...

The man on the bread route not long ago told me there was an opening to drive the truck but a college education was necessary. It's becoming so commonplace. What college actually is doing today, it's becoming the equivalent of what was formerly four years high school, nothing more.

No, I don't long for the past. Much of the past has been a trial, more or less....

The big question in my mind is how long I'll be able to sit comfortably here—in this neighborhood. How long this is going to last. I have an instinctive fear, I don't know why, that it could end at any time. I feel very uncomfortable living in the big city. For some reason or other, I—I dread the thought that me and my family will find ourselves swimming in some kind of blood bath. There's not a question in the world about it. Any thinking man or woman will see this. If they don't, they're deaf, dumb, and blind to the facts of life. In black-white relations. We haven't got a solution and I don't see any solution in sight. Because man is thinking no different than he ever thought.

My feeling about the Negro is this: I never try to think of him in terms of is he equal to me or isn't he equal to me. I don't know and he doesn't know. I admit to this: I am a man and he is a man. I can't say to a Negro, "You are equal to me." Some are, some aren't. The average Negro is not. I am not saying he won't be and that he might not surpass me one day. My father came here when he was seven years old from Europe, couldn't read or write the American—the English—language. He had no relatives here whatsoever, outside of one cousin who was just about in the same boat he was. Yet he made his way. Scholastically, he got nowhere. Insofar as making a lot of money, he didn't get anywhere. But this is one of the lessons I've learned, it is not so much what you make or how you make it as it is what you do with it after you've made it. And here is where the Negro is not very smart. Because the average Negro's mind, when he gets a given amount of money—he could forward his education with it—but the average Negro thinks about how big a car he could buy, how many clothes he could put on his back, and whether or not he could afford a diamond or two.

I fear the Negro today. By and large, the Negro represents violence. I don't think the issue involves civil rights any more. It's gone beyond. Right now in the heart of the average Negro is vengeance. You better believe it. They intend to make me pay for what my great, great, great ancestors did to them. I am completely innocent of this. Even the so-called good Negroes. In their hearts they are too timid in themselves to come forward, so we don't think they feel this way. But you would be amazed, if we could open and bare their hearts, how many of them have this feeling for revenge in their hearts.

We talk about this constantly on our block. In tones of how can we stop it? What can we do to stop it? But there is a feeling of defeatism in everything they say. You detect it. A feeling as if they have been sold out. They feel as though their government has sold them out.

I tried to analyze this in my mind and I see the Negro is going to make great strides by virtue of the fact that he has the force, the militant force of the government behind him. This is the only reason he is going to make these strides. I am going to gain access to your home, but only because there is a man strong enough to break your door down behind me. You fear the man behind me. I haven't gained much in admittance, have I?

Now it's an odd thing, the white people on every hand are screaming about what we owe the Negro, they're telling us the wrongs we have done, the wrongs we have committed against the Negro in the past, and they're doing everything in their power to alleviate this thing, to change it, to make it right. But each damned one of them, you better believe this, each one of them is wondering how much money have I got at my command? Where can I move if he moves next door to me? How far can I get?

Depending on where they fit in the economy, where they fit distance-wise from the Negro, you can tell who is going to speak the loudest and the hardest for the Negro. The farther he is away from him and the more money he has, the more harder he will fight for him. But let the Negro breathe down his neck!

I am afraid that in the future somebody is going to come up. I don't know who, I don't know what. Some kind of a man is going to come up and be a leader. Who knows? I really don't know. Goldwater, if they're lucky. They had their chance to be lucky, and to my way of thinking they were very unlucky. They had their opportunity to be lucky and they rejected Goldwater. *He sounded like me myself.* A Goldwater could be a wonderful thing, but look out, I'm afraid it could be someone more like the John Birch Society. Today it's condemned, tomorrow it's our religion.

The Birch Society, there are many things to be said for it and there are many things against it. They're not all wrong. Just like the murderer like Hitler was, he wasn't all wrong. But he certainly fell short of right, wasn't he?

You'd be surprised how easy it could happen, how easy. You can get people in the right state of emotion, this is all you need. Then reason goes out the window. Because you can't experience the two things at one and the same time, can you?

Maybe this is some form of sin on my part, I don't know.

The average white person, you ask him about integration, is the Negro equal? He wants to scream *NO*. But he thinks back and he's a Christian. Now he knows in his heart that he doesn't believe he's equal, but all this Christian training almost forces him to say yes. He's saying yes to a lie, but he has to come face-to-face with the truth someday. We in our lifetime won't find the answers at all.

I was raised in a Bohemian Catholic family. I remained a Catholic until I was about thirty. And then certain things became untenable. So I grew away from it. Maybe I'll be condemned to a certain kind of damnation, I don't know.

The world should take Christianity and ban it for a certain period of years. Just shelve it for a while, give it a rest. Give Christianity and God a rest and teach man he's living in a world that belongs to him, and he's only going to get out of the world what he puts into it. Teach man that in order to stand he's got to stand on the two feet the good Lord gave him and not use the Lord as a third foot or a third hand: "What I can't do, oh Lord, you will do for me. Or help me to do."

Religion has been holding the Negro back for many, many years. The Negro has been taught to sing the Lord's praises, you understand. And he's been left with an understanding that whatever his shortcomings are, the good Lord will compensate for them. Or the talents he refuses to use. He can't expect God to solve his problems for him.

I tell you for every ounce religion has served, it held man equally back as much. To me the biggest sin has been committed by religion itself. Number one: instilling fear in men. Fear is the biggest killer of all. It doesn't always completely kill, but it can slow a man down. Every time I turn around, they tell you you should do things because in fear of God. It's how wrathful He is, how much He can be, how He can punish an eye for an eye and all these sort of things. And then in the same damn breath they tell me that God is Love. I can't reconcile the two, I can't. You understand what I mean?

They tell me about the omnipotence of God. He is all things, on heaven and earth, He is all things. And then in the same breath, they tell me about the Devil. Now if God is all things, there is nothing that exists outside of God. Where do you place the Devil? Where is he, in God? I can't conceive of the Devil being within God. Does He embody the Devil, too? I don't believe this stuff, I can't...can you?

Man is a creature of habit. He gets something, he grows to like it, he possesses it, he hates to give it up. Sometimes he'll defend a thing to the death rather than give it up and it actually may not be worth anything. You've got to release some of the old ideas. If something's going to live, you've got to let something die, too. I mean, you can't have life without death.

Yesterday was Good Friday. Tomorrow is Easter Sunday. What do you think would happen to Jesus Christ if He returned to earth tomorrow?

If Jesus returned to earth tomorrow and the average person were to see Him on the street, they would look at Him, point a finger and say, "You lousy bum, why don't you go back to Old Town? Why don't you shave? Why don't you take a bath? Why don't you wash the garments you're wearing." You better believe it. I think He'd be crucified, condemned as being some kind of crackpot. This I'm sure of.

* * *

1 9 7 7 *

He has since moved to a new home on the city's northwest side. A blue collar community. "Call it middle-working class. The other neighborhood where I lived for eighteen years was changed by the new bread coming in with their rehabs. These quite clever young people. Intellectuals they were not. [Laughs] Pseudo-intellectuals, yes. We didn't speak the same language. But I still haven't found what I'm looking for.

During the sixties, I used to talk to my boys a lot. At the time, they took issue with me, especially when it came to race. I thought they were trying to turn the world upside down. Now, strangely enough, I see a lot of what they had to say come about. I lived to see the change. Now, they're for law and order at any price. They're for hit 'em over the head if there's no other way.

I guess they've become adults. In our society when you become an adult, you stake you become an adult, you stake your claim. They have property now. They both have homes. They're doing fine. Once my sons called me a bigot, narrow-minded. I said, "Fifteen years from now, you're going to be a different person." I was right, but I am the one that changed most dramatically.

Twelve years ago, I didn't understand things in light of what I see today. I'm surprised at myself. I feel I could live with black people now. Yes, I still worry about violence. But I'm sure the black man has the identical worry, even more so than I have. So we're sharing something in common, see?

I have learned you better not become too attached to anything, so attached that you can't let go. You understand what I mean? My boys have reached the point where they're accumulating things.

---

* From *American Dreams: Lost and Found.* (He died before I began working on *Race: How Blacks and Whites Think and Feel about the American Obsession.*)

The foremost thought in their minds is to protect it. They have to look for someone to protect it from. All right? So God help the first one who gets in their path. And you know what that is? They have become what they once called me. I have gone on to another plateau. I can't explain it, I mean the change in me.

I wish I lived in a world that didn't know what money was. I wish I lived in a world where I didn't guage the worth of a man's life by the color or shade of a man's skin. I wish I could live to see the day where Washington enacted a law that made man, once a month, come to a common meeting place and give him a lesson that forced him to think, to exercise his brain. Just to get a man used to it and find out how delicious it is.

My sons tell me I'm too soft for this world anymore. And I tell 'em, "Thank God."

EVA BARNES

It was dark. There were dim lights and vague television noises in the one-family frame dwellings; off the highway, on the far southwest side of the city, recently incorporated as part of Oak Lawn. Dogs barked along the unpaved roads. Nobody seemed to know where Eva Barnes lived.

At the tavern, a barmaid, a weary forty, mumbled sullenly, "I dunno." A man and a woman, on adjacent stools, vaguely pawed at each other. They were out of focus. In the process, a bottle of Hamms was toppled onto the bar. The other man abandoned the shuffleboard and, after a rough sea journey across the room, found us, at last. Genial, he offered directions: a graceful wave of the arm out toward the scattered dim lights. On the TV set, above and behind the bar, a Western with a high Nielsen rating was on. Nobody watched.

Eventually, we saw her, hugely silhouetted against her doorway.

Yeah, just a few yards away. And they sit. If you go in there and talk, they don't talk nothing but sex. Sex. I won't even go in there. I rent the tavern out. That's mine. I go in there a coupla times, and the kind of people that hang around, I don't have no use for. She probably don't know because she never seen me.

It's a league of nations. But as far as Negro, not in this section here. There is in Oak Lawn, I don't know where. We have truck drivers, I think the majority are truck drivers, drivers for newspaper companies and drivers for big oil companies and building trades. All ages. You can find from newlyweds just married months up to married fifty years, or I guess more.

I don't go in their homes visiting them. But I know them. We meet at the mailbox, say hello. We meet in the store, say hello. I don't go to church, so I won't lie and say I meet 'em in church. Maybe that's one reason, too, that there's a little resentment, because I don't go to church and they know it.

The biggest change I saw? Oh gee, supermarkets. [Laughs.] And it seems like people are more afraid of talking to anything to progress us, you know. If you talk about improvements, your neighborhood or anything, right away they're afraid of being called a communist. That this is the word they're afraid of.

I remember in 1951, when my husband was paralyzed and our septic system got clogged up in the tavern over there…if it wasn't true, it would be funny. I couldn't get anybody for any money to open the tiles up. 'Cause the water was backing up in the tavern. And I was working out there and you know how the tar is out from the sewer, and it clings to your skin. [Laughs.] My poor nine-year-old son was up to his elbows, he was all covered with that black tar. And myself.

I had the tavern closed up that day. Because I couldn't go draw a glass of beer with these dirty hands, run and wait on people. So then my neighbors came in, Mr. Hanson and a couple of other neighbors, walking down the street, saying, "Look at her, working like a communist." I thought to myself, Gee whiz, why do they have to say I'm working like a communist? I'm tryin' to keep this goin' myself. I can't get nobody to work. Why do they brand me like that?

She was born in Riverton, Illinois, near Springfield. Her father was a miner. "We moved like gypsies from one town to another. I would go crazy mentioning all of them." She scores off the names of ten mining towns. She remembers a girl friend who was widowed seven times in mine disasters, as well as losing a father and two brothers; company stores and scrip; five brothers and sisters dead at infancy; babies' nipples out of cheesecloth; hired out for housework at nine; going to seventh grade at school.

I came to Chicago all by myself, two months before I was twelve. And it was wintertime in 1923, and I had sixty-five cents in my pocket. And the next day, girl friends that I had gone to school with, older than me, they come over and they took me to look for a job. So I got one at Omaha Packing, piecework. And I don't think I'd ever got the job, but I was an overgrown girl then and I looked big for my age then.

And I got in line there. I think there was about two hundred and fifty people, Negro and white. Standing on the platform waiting to be picked up for a job. There was no union in those days. And this employment manager comes out and he says, "Hey, you big one over there"—he points his finger at me. "Hey, you big one." I turned around and he said, "Don't turn around, I mean you. Come here." And I says, "Me?" And he said, "Yeah, you. How old are you, about nineteen?" I says, "Mmm-hmm." [Laughs.] I was afraid to open my mouth. I was only twelve years old. They hired me as a nineteen-year-old.

He says, "You know how to sharpen a knife?" Well, back in the coal mines, we used to butcher our own hogs and our own beef, and

I said, "Sure, I know how to sharpen a knife." And he hands over a knife to me and I start sharpening. So he says, "Okay, go to work." So I worked Omaha Packing Company for quite a while, piecework. I was making good money. My first paycheck, I made so good, I don't remember exactly how much it was, but it was an unusually big check. And I got scared. I thought the company made a mistake, so I quit the job.

I done practically everything in the stockyards. I worked till they started organizing the CIO. They took us off piecework and put us on bonus, which we didn't like. Because bonus you had to work harder than you had to work piecework. Nobody represented us. So the men were organized, but we women weren't. So there was a fella, Bob Riley, he come up and he asked me, "Eva, how would you like to organize your women?" By then I was about twenty-one years old.

Oh, in those nine years, I was married and divorced before I was eighteen. And married a second time and I had two children. My first husband was a coal miner and he was an alcoholic...how can you build a home when the man is not responsible?...

My first wedding, I'll never forget as long as I live. Went back, married this coal miner from Bullpit, and we got married in St. Rita's Church, that's just a few miles near where I was born. I was sixteen. Of course, I won't go into the ages of the man. But the wedding we had in those days was more than a week long. The neighbors all pitched in. We went to the farm and bought a whole calf and a whole pig. I think it was 150 chickens and homebrew and homemade wine. Everything was homemade. And we got married in church with everything, bridesmaids and High Mass and everything. The whole works. In fact, even the coal company superintendent, he brought silver for a present for us. And because I danced with him, he gave me thirty-five dollars if I would sell him my wedding shoes. I sold him my wedding shoes, everything was sold. [Laughs.] I was sitting in only my slip, even the dress was sold for me. Just to raise money for the newlyweds in those days.

This was 1925. And of course there's a lot of pictures taken, we were in the *State Register* in Springfield, paper there.

The shivaree, I don't think they do this no more. But we had shivaree every night. Maybe two, three o'clock in the morning, they would be banging cans and making all kinds of noise. The rule was you couldn't sleep at all. And the next morning, you go around and you figure you won't be able to face these people. You know you're ashamed, the wedding is still on. I think there was more fun in the wedding then. Nowadays they go with cars around tooting the horns and everything, but I still think 1925 was natural wedding days.

It was different then. Sure, miners lived poor and the only ones that really had money is the woman that has lotta boarders and women that bootlegs, this is prohibition time. But the woman that didn't bootleg and had boarders, she just lived from hand to mouth, like here in the city from pay to pay. But I remember we'd go out picnics, we'd go out fishing, all families. Everything for the picnic. And then when you went to the picnic, there was no money exchanged, no commercial, everything like one big family. They'd cook a pot of mulligan stew and everybody'd share out of that. That was a picnic. Today you go on a picnic, what is it? It's commercial. You buy your ticket, you buy your popcorn, you buy your beer. If you haven't got a fistful of money, you haven't got no picnic.

Anyway, my wedding was the biggest wedding in Sangamon County in 1925. They said that nobody has a wedding like St. Rita's, the church was dressed up real beautiful. These were the days when I was a very religious woman. And not long after that, when the priest told me to hit my husband with a skillet in the head because he asked for meat on Friday, I thought, well, bad as he is, I still loved him. I didn't think it was right for the priest to tell me to hit my husband in the head with a skillet. [Laughs.] I didn't go for that very much. I thought, what the heck kind of priest is he? So right there, I didn't believe in fighting or hitting. I said, no. So I better don't go to church, I just quit going altogether. But my children were Christian-raised....

I think they put me to work at every job in the stockyards Pork trimmer. I worked in the laundries. I even worked in the offal. It's where all the guts and everything come in there. This is Depression time now, it's in the thirties. This is when they bumped a Negro girl to save me a job, 'cause I had two sons. And I didn't like the idea, but then there was a fella named Dick White, he was cutting the pigs' heads and he says, "Don't worry about it," he says, "we're used to it already." He was colored.

And working on these guts, you know, open, and I had to sterilize and wash them. And the ones that were condemned you couldn't touch it, if you did, you would get a hog itch. And you had to keep your hands in a cold shower on them all the time because to get that hog itch off you. I was sick to my stomach and my children used to say when I got home, "Mommy, we love you but you smell awful." But you get used to it. [Laughs.] You work in it so long, you can't smell nothing no more.

But this I'll never forget, this colored boy—not boy, man—Dick White, I'll never forget his name. I don't know what happened to him but he saved my job. And he says, "You'll get used to this job. Just don't think that that's what it is, pretend it's some flowers or something." [Laughs.] And I got used to it....

And then we started organizing the women in there because the men were organized. And then this Bob Riley said, "Don't organize so fast." I had forty women the first day I went out. I said, "They all want union, they want to get better wages." I said, "We're doing the same kind of work men are doing, trimming meat, sharp'ning our own knives, why don't we get paid the same like the men?" They're only paying us, I think, twenty-eight cents an hour. Identical work. And the men were getting fifty-nine cents an hour. So I told him, I said, "When we get union in, we're gonna get the same wages."

That's Depression time, then Roosevelt came in. And I was carrying the biggest Roosevelt button. I was working for a radio company then. Assembling radios. I go to the job, and didn't know that the company was for the opposition. A big Roosevelt button, they told me to take it off. I said, "No, I'm for Roosevelt." They said, "You're for Roosevelt, you get out, you don't get a job." So I got laid off.

And this is election day, the day Roosevelt's election day, I just got through voting for Roosevelt and I lose my job. I had a job all the way through the Depression, and now the first day Roosevelt gets elected, I lose a job. So this is when I met my second husband. He died.

And both of us were looking for a job. He got a job himself as a beef lugger. A man that carries half a steer or quarter, hind or front, from these hooks that are in the freezers and puts them in the truck. It's heavy work and my husband was a pretty strong guy. But it took him. Later on it come up on him.

And then it was funny again. All the time after we got married, we're looking for a job. He's too old and I'm too fat. I was young enough, but too heavy. So what are we gonna do? So we went into the tavern business.

John Woods, he heard me singing in a Legion club, and he says, "Eva, you're singing for somebody else making money. Why don't you open your own tavern?" I said, "I haven't got the money." He said, "You find a place, I'll back you up." And I said, "Well, I got a place on 31st and Halsted, my old neighborhood, lot of people knew me there."* He said, "Fine, as long as you know the people. Give me two days, I want to look over the place." He says, "Fine, good location."

So we got everything practically. All the beer, all the liquor, everything. New Year's Eve, we want to open, no electric, no gas, we're in the dark. [Laughs.] And I called him up, I says, "John,

---

* The area known as Bridgeport. Mayor Daley has lived there all his life.

they need fifty-dollar deposit for gas and electric and I haven't got it." He says, "Jesus Christ, you woman, you got everything, over a thousand dollars worth of equipment in that place and you forget a measly fifty dollars." So we opened the tavern on candlelight. We had candles all over the place.

Those days, I don't know...today, I don't think I know anybody who would do that, the cooperation of people. And here this big manager of a brewery company helps me out. And then the whiskey houses, they brought in all the whiskey and wine and liquors and everything. And the lady across the street, the tavern lady, she closed her own tavern up. She knew we were new, we didn't know how to mix drinks, we didn't know how to make a highball, we didn't know nothing. [Laughs.] She closes up her tavern, takes her bartender, takes all the glasses, we run out of glasses, she comes across the street, put her bartender behind the bar. Frank from 24th and Halsted, he brings his two bartenders, Steve on Archer Avenue, he's got a tavern there today yet. Steve, Frank, Rudy, the three of them behind the bar, they told us to get out and go with your guests. They took over the bar.

I never heard of anybody today going out helping anybody like that. Right here, say, I lived all these years, and when my husband was paralyzed all these years and sick, he never turned down neighbors of anybody passed away, for a flower piece, a sympathy to the neighbor. And yet when he passed away, nobody came to my door and said they were sorry to see Herman go.

The answer is selfishness and greed and jealousy. My own tenants, six months they don't pay no rent. He can't pay no rent, he's a truck driver and he's behind. Got four kids, I feel sorry for them, but I have to do something. I gotta pay taxes, I can't keep up for nothing. But he says, "Gee, what the heck you bothering me for this rent for. You don't need the money." He said, "You're loaded with money." Now this is the idea, you're always loaded with money. They don't know.

But it's deeper than this, the more I think about it. It's this fear, fear of everything. Fear of the war in Vietnam, fear of communism, fear of atomic bombs. There's a fear there. I am not afraid of nobody or nothing. The only thing I am afraid of is in case there should be an atomic war, if it hits me or anywhere close, I hope it hits me fast. And that's all, there would be nothing of me. Just like striking a match.

Myself, I get confused. The President tells ya that he don't want no war, it's peace. You pick up a paper, they're bombing children. And television, the guys being interviewed, talking about peace, and the picture shown where the women and children are being bombed and slaughtered and murdered. How long if I think that way and I have a bad feeling, how long will other people that their mentality's not strong enough, to separate the cause of it? Fear. What's gonna happen to our kids, our grandchildren?

Lotta them are afraid of their jobs, losing their jobs. Because the government's maybe got some contract with some company. For example, we got one fellow here works with the government, with this here carbonic gas or whatever it is. If he opens his mouth up too much, he can lose his job. And the senators or congressmen, they personally don't take interest in their own country, right here, what's going on.

The colored. We had a tavern on 61st Street and State, three and a half years, Negro neighborhood. I tell you I never was insulted no place by not a Negro person over there. They respected me highly. It took a white fella to come in and insult me because I wouldn't serve him beer, he was too drunk. And if it wasn't for these poor Negro fellas, I'd a probably killed this man. [Laughs.] Because he called me a dirty name.

It just burns me up when they say, Woo! Those Negro people! My kids would go out in the street, my little girl would be out on the street, nobody bothered, nobody touched. One day I'm lookin' for my little girl, and she was only four years old then, and I went to the back yard. They had a quilt spread out on the lawn and had my little girl sittin' in the middle, 'cause she had a white organdy dress on. [Laughs.] Little colored girls and boys all around, so she don't get off and get her dress soiled. They were watching her. [Laughs.] They don't care how dirty the quilt got but just don't get her dress soiled, watching her.

Today I had an argument. I just got mad because I heard them back and forth and they started telling: Those Negroes, they're so filthy. Everything is the Negroes. I said, "Do you ever stop to think that the white trash of the white people do the same thing?"

I know they sit in taverns and booze all night long. That's why we never did make a lot of money in taverns. My husband couldn't stand it. If he knew there was a family man or woman, he'd tell 'em, "Get out and go by your kids. You drink two, three glasses of beer, that's enough. Go home, watch your children." "What's the matter, don't you like our money?" they would say. "We don't have to come here if you're like that." So we never made any money.

In Bridgeport, I know what's going on over there. Old-timers that have homes, and they're afraid that the neighborhood's gonna be run-down. That's what they're afraid of. Because they listen to the reputation of State Street.

I don't know how to explain it. I was never anti-Negro, because I don't remember when I don't know a Negro living next door. When I grew up, there was nothing for my father to bring a couple of Negro fellas that he worked in the mines in the gang with, for supper. Or my dad taking us by the hand Sunday morning after church, and it was nothing at all to spend Sunday morning after church to go by them. The first time I tasted homemade cornbread was by a Negro family.

Just because my skin is white, that doesn't make me better than he is. Or it doesn't make him better if his skin is black. A lot of people think, my skin is white, I don't even have to go to school....

One particular woman in this neighborhood, when her daughter wanted to go to school so bad, she said, "You don't need no high school. What do you need high school for? Get married and raise kids." "Gee whiz," I said, "she'd make a better mother if she has an education. Don't deny her. If she wants to go to school, get an education, give it to her, let her go. If you can't afford it, it's different." But, "Oh, no, she don't need it." Today what is she? She's just a baby factory, that's all she is.

Education is very important. Always, always. I raised my children in the rottenest business a child can grow up in. They grew up and all got education from that tavern business. I could thank Roosevelt for it. If it wasn't for Roosevelt being elected and repealing the Eighteenth Amendment, well, I'd still be bootlegging. [Laughs.] When I was sixteen years old, I knew how to make moonshine and home-brew. [Laughs.]

Oh, I done everything. I was a riveter during the war. I worked even in a rubber factory. In those days, they used insulation rubber around the automobile, around the windows, I was the trimmer on that. And I made steering wheels on a great big bandsaw. I don't know how I didn't get my arms cut off. [Laughs.] Made steering wheels and working in a candy factory. Now listen, just I'm telling you…. I wasn't a bad-looking girl, I mean, I had opportunities….

You're not a bad-looking woman now.

Thank you. When I hear people say, ah, the children are bad, delinquency from broken homes, and girls turn bad because they have nobody…. I had all the opportunities in the world to become bad. All of it. In fact, one case worker, Irma Cline, I'll never forget….

…During the Depression, there was an old couple that needed a stove. And she wouldn't give them the requisition to get the stove to heat their place up. So I went to the relief station and put that Cline against the wall. I got her by the throat and she suggested that I come in for the stove. And she said, "You're not a bad-looking woman. Why don't you get yourself a job and buy a stove yourself?" She thought it was for me. I said, "It's not for me, it's for an old couple." I said, "I'm helping them all I can. I can't help them no more." And that's when she made the suggestion that I am not a bad-looking woman. She said, "Why don't you get married?" I said, "What do you want me to do? Get a mattress on my back and walk up and down 35th Street?" This get married. I had all the opportunities in the world to become bad. I didn't. I worked.

I don't see why people should have to struggle for everything that's important to them. In the Constitution they tell us that under the Constitution.... I found out by being arrested, when you're arrested you have no Constitution.

Why were you arrested?

For to end the war in Vietnam, with the students. I was demonstratin'. I think it's good. It's good exercise for me. [Laughs.] The only way I get my exercise is in these demonstrations. Marches, and for a good cause, I don't mind that.

What made you join it?

Well, I tell you, my first husband, though he was no good, I don't know if it was the First World War or what had to do with it, but he was wounded in the First World War real bad, that he was pensioned. Old Soldiers' Home, all crippled up. Decorated in some kind of medal he got over there, to end all wars. So his sons won't have to fight in the wars. Well, along comes Hitler, so then my oldest son, before the end he was old enough already. Thank God that my first one come home safe.

And my second son, when the Korean War started, he was old enough to get in the Korean War. He had this thick, bushy hair head, when he come back, I think two and a half years, when he come back he was bald-headed. And he's a different boy altogether. I think this Korean business had to do. Well, he isn't...how should I tell you? 'Cause maybe he's a man now. He isn't jolly any more, he isn't...[she has difficulty here]...he's very strict with his own children, it's just like a bully...the army training, the meanness is in you. And left in you. He's not...the meanness is not taken out of you when he comes down to civilian society. But maybe I'm wrong, I don't know.... He was never a bully, now he's a bully. And I guess they train 'em like that.

Now this boy I got, this last one. He's a good boy, he's never given me trouble. He's never missed a day of school. He's never been late to school. He's never harmed anything. I tell you what kind he is, if there's a mosquito, he won't kill the mosquito, he says, "Oh, let him go." [Laughs.] And gets along with everybody. And little kids, they're just crazy for him.

He's a policeman?

Yeah. He always wanted to be a policeman and I...He's a boy, I never let him have a toy gun. I says, "I don't want my children to have guns." I won't buy a gun, I won't allow in my house a gun.

I never did fight, I'm not a fighter, I never fight with policemen even. [Laughs.] I left my husbands to it, but I never fight with them. I'm afraid. I'm too big, I weigh three hundred pounds, my husband weighs 150 pounds. If I hit 'em, I could kill 'em.

I don't want my son to go to Vietnam. All right, he's got a dangerous job, he's a policeman. So I feel different about it. He's got a gun on him, he's doing everything what I'm against. But as long as he knows...he knows I don't believe in police brutality. No way. *No way.* If I ever hear that he's brutal in any way, I don't care—he never got a whipping—but I would beat the shit out of him. I would. You got to defend yourself, but you don't have to provoke it.

Because when I was picked up after that demonstration, there was a lot of them police were there, trying to provoke us on. Even the matrons, they'd come to me and say, "Now, missus, why are you demonstrating with these Commies?" Students. And here's a priest, nuns, marching along, and police calling them Commies. I don't see that. She's got the upper hand, the matron, she takes my purse away, takes my glasses away, then she says you can make one phone call. I said all right. Then they lock me up in a cell, everything's taken away from you. I says, "Can I have a paper cup so I can get a glass of water." This is four o'clock we were picked up. No, I wait till ten o'clock.

But then she takes you again, they just move you from one cell to another cell, and then they fingerprint you and take your picture and all the time, they're talking, they says, "You ought to be ashamed of yourself. Why don't you stay home and mind your own business? Why don't you take care of your family, instead of going mingling with all these bunch of hoodlums and bums?" This is the only time I ever come in a bunch with the intellectuals, the educated students, university students. Here I'm in this neighborhood sitting here, I could become a dummy. And there I learned something. I learned geographical locations, the games we played. That I haven't played since we were kids, you know, in spelling class. [Laughs.] But this was not a spelling class. And all these different freedom songs. But the beauty part of it is they take your glasses away, then they come around and bring Bibles for you to read. And you can't see your hand in front of you, how you gonna read the Bible?

And I said to her, the matron, I says, "You got the upper hand all right, I'm not gonna argue with you." "Shut up." I says, "I'm not saying nothing, I just said you got the upper hand." "Shut up." That's all what they know, just shut up. I could probably buy and sell her if I wanted to.... I pay her taxes, I pay her wages, I pay big tax, I pay $1,200 a year for taxes, how much taxes she's paying?

But I can't talk to her. I have no right to say nothing to her. I've seen people get arrested in southern part of Illinois. My father was arrested for bootlegging. I never seen him treated like that. And here, I'm marching peacefully, and he says, "Are you gonna move or you don't move?" I says, "I'll move."

The cop?

Yeah. So I moved a little bit. He comes back again, he says, "I told you to move." So I moved again. I says, "I'm movin'." He said, "Are you gonna walk to the patrol wagon peacefully or do we carry you?" [Laughs.] And I took a look at him and I says, "Look, I don't want your officers get ruptured," I says, "I'll walk." [Laughs.] And then he recognized me at the HUAC....

At the anti-HUAC, we weren't doing nothing. We were just marching because they were persecuting the doctor.* I don't even know the doctor, I only know his reputation. I don't know him personally, but I know what I read about him, what a good doctor he is, what a humble man he is. And so I said, "Well, I gotta go defend that man. I gotta be one of the people to be counted." I can't set home. The students that were arrested were marching here. They were happy to see me. The police, too....

He said, "Hi, there." He called me by my name, the policeman. I said, "How'd you ever remember my name?" He says, "Aren't you the little lady that didn't want my officers to get ruptured?" I said, "Yeah, gee." Then he smiled. And every one of them officers, they were real nice to me. I thought, you know, maybe they'd get snotty or sarcastic or stuff, but even some of them were singing freedom songs.

But I can't see why they allowed them Nazis, like all right, one of

---

* A distinguished physician conducting research in heart disease for the Chicago Board of Health, who was cited for contempt by the House Committee on Un-American Activities.

the Nazis that were demonstrating against us, here he took his hand and grabbed by his privates and he went and shook his privates at this lady that was behind me, a Negro woman. And I said, "Boy, that's a very intellectual guy doing that." And he says, "To you, too." And the officer was looking at him doing that, and if he was on our side, somebody doing like that, they probably would put him in jail. *They* can do it. So whose side is the law on? We don't know for sure whether Hitler's dead or alive. [Laughs.] We got a lotta them here.

Was that the first time you were ever arrested? When you marched for peace?

First time in my life, and I've done some things that I shoulda been arrested for. [Laughs.] Like I said, I was sixteen years old, I cooked moonshine, and they could smell it. The chief, who lived right across the street, never pinched me. I made home-brew and they never pinched me. And I ran parties all hours of the night, and nobody had me arrested. For peace, they arrest me. I said, "My God," I said, "I wonder if I murdered somebody in Mississippi, would they arrest me?"

You see, how I got arrested.... I had $750 worth of savings bonds in my purse and about $470 cash money. Then I had the title, the deed to the property that I was changing. I went to take them out of one box and closer to home. In the meantime, this demonstration was going on. And these students see my peace button and ask if I could help them make the amount of people look bigger.

In the cell, I hear a banging on that steel wall. And I'm a heavy woman, but tacked onto this steel wall is the other cell. And every time I move, that wall would move and shake. [Laughs.] And some voice from this other cell hollers, "Hey you, quit moving in your bed. Every time you move, you knock me out of my bed." Her bed would bounce up, you know. And she said, "What are you arrested for?" I said, "I'm arrested for peace." I said, "What are you arrested for?" She said, "Me, too. Soliciting." I said, "Without a license?" She says, "Why do you need a license?" I said, "Where you from? You from Chicago? You gotta have a license for everything." She said from Long Island. I said, "When you come to Chicago, you go County Building and you ask for a solicitor's license. Then nobody can arrest." [Laughs.] Then the matron comes, she said, "Will you shut up?" [Laughs.]

Later on, she said, "You was kidding me." And I said, "Yes, I was kidding you, I know what you mean." But I said, "You girls are foolish anyway." I said I had a tavern on 61st and State and I used to see girls get picked up and they picked them up, the police themselves. And these are white policemen, I've seen 'em. And they come in and tell my husband, get that streetwalker out of here. They call her worse names than streetwalker. And my husband would say, "If you know she's such a woman, why don't you put a mark on her, so people could tell? I don't want to get my face slapped, going to tell her, you so-and-so. Listen, she's not doing no harm. She comes in, spends her money, just as good as anybody else's."

I've seen where the policemen picked up these girls and the girls would flip their wallets over the bar and let my husband hold their wallets for them, because the policemen would take their wallets from them, take them a couple of blocks around and drop them off in the alley some place: "Now, next time you better have more money. See?" They'd take the money from 'em, encourage it: go ahead some more. In fact, if you don't have more money, they're gonna give you maybe with a billy club, the beating or something. Yeah, the vice squad. Now this I live with, I seen it. And if it went on then, it's still going on now.*

Maybe some day I will get hurt. I don't distrust nobody when I'm out. I never turn around, like a lot of women, turn around to see

---

* During 1965, two Negro prostitutes were found slain. An accusation was made of police involvement. The case is unsolved.

who's following them. This is a funny thing, the matron, she asked me, she said, "You with all this real-estate property, all these deeds and titles you're carrying, you ought to be ashamed of yourself. How are you not afraid to walk the Chicago streets with all this in your purse?" I said, "Lady, you're a matron and you don't have faith in Chicago?" I walked through State Street, Cottage Grove, and Halsted many times, nobody bothered me. I could tell a person if he's out to hate me or he's friendly. I mean, is he gonna be taking me? When I was in the tavern business, you had to be that way. And yet I lost. Somebody, some I trusted....

Most that disturbs me today is when I talk to some of my neighbors, none of them, they don't like this Vietnam going on, but here's where they say: "What's the use? Who are we? We can't say nothing. We have no word. We got the President. We elected him. We got congressmen in there. They're responsible. Let them worry. Why should I worry about it?" It's already pounded into them, you're just a little guy, you vote and you're through, it won't do no good anyhow.

I think different. I think, like they say, that if I'm a voter, I should have a say-so in this. In everything...But anything good for the people is never given easy. Never given easy.

I saw coal miners come out the coal mines all crushed. I saw in the First World War. My mother had seven young boys come from Europe to stay with us, worked a little while in the coal mines and they were drafted into the American Army. They were young boys, I think, twenty, twenty-one years old and they never came back. My mother had seven stars in her window. Instead of saying they came from Lithuania, they said they came from Ledford, Illinois. So they sent the stars to my mother, and whatever little belongings they had, little chains or something.... Just enough, there is death enough. I don't like to see nobody get killed. I don't like to see nobody get hurt. This world is beautiful to live....

POSTSCRIPT

I asked her about that one phone call she was allowed while in jail: "About two or three o'clock in the morning, the matron come up to me and asked me if I was gonna have that phone call made. I said, 'Yes, make it.' 'Well, who you want us to call?' I said, 'Call my son.' She says, 'You want us to tell that he should come and bail you out?' I said, 'No, I don't want him to come bail me out.' I said, 'Tell him to take the beans off the stove, because they're gonna get spoiled.' It was hot that day."

Working:
People Talk About What They Do All Day and How They Feel About What They Do
(1972)

INTRODUCTION

This book, being about work, is, by its very nature, about violence—
to the spirit as well as to the body. It is about ulcers as well as accidents, about shouting matches as well as fistfights, about nervous
breakdowns as well as kicking the dog around. It is, above all (or
beneath all), about daily humiliations. To survive the day is triumph
enough for the walking wounded among the great many of us.

The scars, psychic as well as physical, brought home to the
supper table and the TV set, may have touched, malignantly, the
soul of our society. More or less. ("More or less," that most
ambiguous of phrases, pervades many of the conversations that
comprise this book, reflecting, perhaps, an ambiguity of attitude
toward The Job. Something more than Orwellian acceptance,
something less than Luddite sabotage. Often the two impulses are
fused in the same person.)

It is about a search, too, for daily meaning as well as daily bread,
for recognition as well as cash, for astonishment rather than
torpor; in short, for a sort of life rather than a Monday through
Friday sort of dying. Perhaps immortality, too, is part of the quest.
To be remembered was the wish, spoken and unspoken, of the
heroes and heroines of this book.

There are, of course, the happy few who find a savor in their
daily job: the Indiana stonemason, who looks upon his work and
sees that it is good; the Chicago piano tuner, who seeks and finds

the sound that delights; the bookbinder, who saves a piece of history; the Brooklyn fireman, who saves a piece of life...But don't these satisfactions, like Jude's hunger for knowledge, tell us more about the person than about his task? Perhaps. Nonetheless, there is a common attribute here: a meaning to their work well over and beyond the reward of the paycheck.

For the many, there is a hardly concealed discontent. The blue-collar blues is no more bitterly sung than the white-collar moan. "I'm a machine," says the spot-welder. "I'm caged," says the bank teller, and echoes the hotel clerk. "I'm a mule," says the steelworker. "A monkey can do what I do," says the receptionist. "I'm less than a farm implement," says the migrant worker. "I'm an object," says the high-fashion model. Blue collar and white call upon the identical phrase: "I'm a robot." *"There is nothing to talk about,"* the young accountant despairingly enunciates. It was some time ago that John Henry sang, "A man ain't nothin' but a man." The hard, unromantic fact is: he died with his hammer in his hand, while the machine pumped on. Nonetheless, he found immortality. He is remembered.

As the automated pace of our daily jobs wipes out name and face—and, in many instances, feeling—there is a sacrilegeous question being asked these days. To earn one's bread by the sweat of one's brow has always been the lot of mankind. At least, ever since Eden's slothful couple was served with an eviction notice. The scriptural precept was never doubted, not out loud. No matter how demeaning the task, no matter how it dulls the senses and breaks the spirit, one *must* work. Or else.

Lately there has been a questioning of this "work ethic," especially by the young. Strangely enough, it has touched off profound grievances in others, hitherto devout, silent, and anonymous. Unexpected precincts are being heard from in a show of discontent. Communiqués from the assembly line are frequent and alarming: absenteeism. On the evening bus, the tense, pinched faces of young file clerks and elderly secretaries tell us more than we care to know. On the expressways, middle management men pose without grace behind their wheels as they flee city and job.

There are other means of showing it, too. Inchoately, sullenly, it appears in slovenly work, in the put-down of craftsmanship. A farm equipment worker in Moline complains that the careless worker who turns out more that is bad is better regarded than the careful craftsman who turns out less that is good. The first is an ally of the Gross National Product. The other is a threat to it, a kook—and the sooner he is penalized the better. Why, in these circumstances, should a man work with care? Pride does indeed precede the fall.

Others, more articulate—at times, visionary—murmur of a hunger for "beauty," "a meaning," "a sense of pride." A veteran car hiker sings out, "I could drive any car like a baby, like a woman changes her baby's diaper. Lots of customers say, 'How you do this?' I'd say, 'Just the way you bake a cake, miss.' When I was younger, I could swing with that car. They called me Lovin' Al the Wizard."

Dolores Dante graphically describes the trials of a waitress in a fashionable restaurant. They are compounded by her refusal to be demeaned. Yet pride in her skills helps her make it through the night. "When I put the plate down, you don't hear a sound. When I pick up a glass, I want it to be just right. When someone says, 'How come you're just a waitress?' I say, 'Don't you think you deserve being served by me?' "

Peggy Terry has her own sense of grace and beauty. Her jobs have varied with geography, climate, and the ever-felt pinch of circumstance. "What I hated worst was being a waitress. The way you're treated. One guy said, 'You don't have to smile; I'm gonna give you a tip anyway.' I said. 'Keep it. I wasn't smiling for a tip.' Tipping should be done away with. It's like throwing a dog a bone. It makes you feel small."

In all instances, there is felt more than a slight ache. In all instances, there dangles the impertinent question: Ought not there be an increment, earned though not yet received, from one's daily work—an acknowledgement of man's *being?*

An American President is fortunate—or, perhaps, unfortunate—that, offering his Labor Day homily, he didn't encounter Maggie Holmes, the domestic, or Phil Stallings, the spot-welder, or Louis Hayward, the washroom attendant. Or especially, Grace Clements, the felter at the luggage factory, whose daily chore reveals to us in a terrible light that Charles Dickens's London is not so far away nor long ago.

Obtuseness in "respectable" quarters is not a new phenomenon. In 1850 Henry Mayhew, digging deep into London's laboring lives and evoking from the invisible people themselves the wretched truth of their lot, astonished and horrified readers of the *Morning Chronicle*. His letters ran six full columns and averaged 10,500 words. It is inconceivable that Thomas Carlyle was unaware of Mayhew's findings. Yet, in his usual acerbic—and, in this instance, unusually mindless—manner, he blimped, "No needlewoman, distressed or other, can be procured in London by any housewife to give, for fair wages, fair help in sewing. Ask any thrifty housemother. No *real* needlewoman, 'distressed' or other, has been found attainable in any of the houses I frequent. Imaginary needlewomen, who demand considerable wages, and have a deepish appetite for beer and viands, I hear of everywhere...."* A familiar ring?

Smug respectability, like the poor, we've had with us always. Today, however, and what few decades remain of the twentieth century, such obtuseness is an indulgence we can no longer afford. The computer, nuclear energy for better or worse, and sudden, simultaneous influences flashed upon everybody's TV screen have raised

---

* E. P. Thompson and Eileen Yeo, *The Unknown Mayhew* (New York: Pantheon Books, 1971).

the ante and the risk considerably. Possibilities of another way, discerned by only a few before, are thought of—if only for a brief moment, in the haze of idle conjecture—by many today.

The drones are no longer invisible nor mute. Nor are they exclusively of one class. Markham's Man with the Hoe may be Ma Bell's girl with the headset. (And can it be safely said, she is "dead to rapture and despair"? Is she really "a thing that grieves not and that never hopes"?) They're in the office as well as the warehouse; at the manager's desk as well as the assembly line; at some estranged company's computer as well as some estranged woman's kitchen floor.

Bob Cratchit may still be hanging on (though his time is fast running out, as did his feather pen long ago), but Scrooge has been replaced by the conglomerate. Hardly a chance for Christmas spirit here. Who knows Bob's name in this outfit—let alone his lame child's? ("The last place I worked for, I was let go,* recalls the bank teller. "One of my friends stopped by and asked where I was at. They said, 'She's no longer with us.' That's all. I vanished.") It's nothing personal, really. Dickens's people have been replaced by Beckett's.

> Many old working class women have an habitual gesture which illuminates the years of their life behind. D. H. Lawrence remarked it in his mother: my grandmother's was a repeated tapping which accompanied an endless working out of something in her head; she had years of making out for a large number on very little. In others, you see a rhythmic smoothing out of the hand down the chair arm, as though to smooth everything out and make it workable; in others, there is a working of the lips or a steady rocking. None of these could be called neurotic gestures, nor are they symptoms of acute fear; they help the constant calculation.†

In my mother's case, I remember the illuminating gesture associated with work or enterprise. She was a small entrepreneur, a Mother Courage fighting her Thirty Years' War, daily. I remember

---

* E. P. Thompson and Eileen Yeo, *The Unknown Mayhew.*

† Richard Hoggart, *The Uses of Literacy* (New York: Oxford University Press, 1957).

her constant feeling of the tablecloth, as though assessing its quality, and her squinting of the eye, as though calculating its worth.

Perhaps it was myopia, but I rarely saw such signs among the people I visited during this adventure. True, in that dark hollow in Eastern Kentucky I did see Susie Haynes, the black lung miner's wife, posed in the doorway of the shack, constantly touching the woodwork, "as though to smooth everything out and make it all workable." It was a rare gesture, what once had been commonplace. Those who did signify—Ned Williams, the old stock chaser, Hobart Foote, the utility man—did so in the manner of the machines to which they were bound. Among the many, though the words and phrases came, some heatedly, others coolly, the hands were at rest, motionless. Their eyes were something else again. As they talked of their jobs, it was as though it had little to do with their felt lives. It was an alien matter. At times I imagined I was on the estate of Dr. Caligari and the guests poured out fantasies.

To maintain a sense of self, these heroes and heroines play occasional games. The middle-aged switchboard operator, when things are dead at night, cheerily responds to the caller, "Marriott Inn," instead of identifying the motel chain she works for. "Just for a lark," she explains bewilderedly. "I really don't know what made me do it." The young gas meter reader startles the young suburban housewife sunning out on the patio in her bikini, loose-bra'd, and sees more things than he would otherwise see. "Just to make the day go faster." The auto worker from the Deep South will "tease one guy 'cause he's real short and his old lady left him." Why? "Oh, just to break the monotony. You want quittin' time so bad."

The waitress, who moves by the tables with the grace of a ballerina, pretends she's forever on stage. "I feel like Carmen. It's like a gypsy holding out a tambourine and they throw the coin." It helps her fight humiliation as well as arthritis. The interstate truckdriver, bearing down the expressway with a load of seventy-three thousand pounds, battling pollution, noise, an ulcer, and kidneys that act up, "fantasizes something tremendous." They all, in some manner, perform astonishingly to survive the day. These are not yet automata.

The time study men of the General Motors Assembly Division made this discomfiting discovery in Lordstown. Gary Bryner, the young union leader, explains it. "Occasionally one of the guys will let a car go by. At that point, he's made a decision 'Aw, fuck it. It's only a car.' It's more important to just stand there and rap. With us, it becomes a human thing. It's the most enjoyable part of my job, that moment. I love it!" John Henry hardly envisioned that way of fighting the machine—which may explain why he died in his prime.

There are cases where the job possesses the man even after quitting time. Aside from occupational ticks of hourly workers and the fitful sleep of salaried ones, there are instances of a man's singular preoccupation with work. It may affect his attitude toward all of life. And art.

Geraldine Page, the actress, recalls the critique of a backstage visitor during her run in *Sweet Bird Of Youth*. He was a dentist. "I was sitting in the front row and looking up. Most of the time I was studying the fillings in your mouth. I'm curious to know who's been doing your dental work." It was not that he loved theater less, but that he loved dentistry more.

At the public unveiling of a celebrated statue in Chicago, a lawyer, after deep study, mused, "I accept Mr. Picasso in good faith. But if you look at the height of the slope on top and the propensity of children who will play on it, I have a feeling that some child may fall and be hurt and the county may be sued...."

In my own case, while putting together this book, I found myself possessed by the mystique of work. During a time out, I saw the film *Last Tango in Paris*. Though Freud said *lieben und arbeiten* are the two moving impulses of man, it was the latter that, at the moment, consumed me. Thus, I saw on the screen a study not of redemption nor of self-discovery nor whatever perceptive critics may have seen.

During that preoccupied moment I saw a study of an actor *at work*. He was performing brilliantly in a darkened theater (apartment), as his audience (the young actress) responded with enthusiasm. I interpreted her moans, cries, and whimpers as bravos, huzzahs, and olés. In short, I saw the film as a source of a possible profile for this book. Such is the impact of work on some people.

A further personal note. I find some delight in my job as a radio broadcaster. I'm able to set my own pace, my own standards, and determine for myself the substance of each program. Some days are more sunny than others, some hours less astonishing than I'd hoped for; my occasional slovenliness infuriates me...but it is, for better or worse, in my hands. I'd like to believe I'm the old-time cobbler, making the whole shoe. Though my weekends go by soon enough, I look toward Monday without a sigh.

The danger of complacency is somewhat tempered by my aware-ness of what might have been. Chance encounters with old school-mates are sobering experiences. Memories are dredged up of three traumatic years at law school. They were vaguely, though pro-foundly, unhappy times for me. I felt more than a slight ache. Were it not for a fortuitous set of circumstances, I might have become a lawyer—a determinedly failed one, I suspect. (I flunked my first bar examination. Ninety percent passed, I was told.)

During the Depression I was a sometime member of the Federal Writers' Project, as well as a sometime actor in radio soap operas. I was usually cast as a gangster and just as usually came to a vio-lent and well-deserved end. It was always sudden. My tenure was as uncertain as that of a radical college professor. It was during these moments—though I was unaware of it at the time—that the surreal nature of my work made itself felt. With script in hand, I read lines of stunning banality. The more such scripts an actor read, the more he was considered a success. Thus the phrase "Show Business" took on an added significance. It was, indeed, a business, a busyness. But what was its meaning?

If Freud is right—"his work at least gives him a secure place in a portion of reality, in the human community"*—was what I did in those studios really work? It certainly wasn't play. The sales charts of Proctor & Gamble and General Mills made that quite clear. It was considered *work*. All my colleagues were serious about it, deadly so. Perhaps my experience in making life difficult for Ma Perkins and Mary Marlin may have provided me with a metaphor for the experiences of the great many, who fail to find in their work their "portion of reality." Let alone, a secure place "in the human community."

Is it any wonder that in such surreal circumstances, status rather than the work itself becomes important? Thus the prevalence of euphemisms in work as well as in war. The janitor is a building engineer; the garbage man, a sanitary engineer; the man at the rendering plant, a factory mechanic; the gravedigger, a caretaker. They are not themselves ashamed of their work, but society, they feel, looks upon them as a lesser species. So they call upon promiscuously used language to match the "respectability" of others, whose jobs may have less social worth than their own.

(The airline stewardess understands this hierarchy of values. "When you first start flying…the men you meet are airport employees: ramp rats, cleaning airplanes and things like that, mechanics…. After a year we get tired of that, so we move into the city to get involved with men that are usually young executives…. They wear their hats and their suits and in the winter their black gloves.")

Not that these young men in white shirts and black gloves are so secure, either. The salesman at the advertising agency is an account executive. "I feel a little downgraded if people think I'm a salesman. Account executive—that describes my job. It has more prestige than just saying, 'I'm a salesman.' " A title, like clothes,

---

* Sigmund Freud, *Civilization and Its Discontents* (New York: W. W. Norton and Co., 1962).

may not make the man or woman, but it helps in the world of peers—and certainly impresses strangers. "We're all vice presidents," laughs the copy chief. "Clients like to deal with vice presidents. Also, it's a cheap thing to give somebody. Vice presidents get fired with great energy and alacrity."

At hospitals, the charming bill collector is called the patients' representative! It's a wonderland that Alice never envisioned. Consider the company spy. With understandable modesty, he refers to himself as an industrial investigator. This last—under the generic name, Security—is among the most promising occupations in our society today. No matter how tight the job market, here is a burgeoning field for young men and women. Watergate, its magic spell is everywhere.

In a further bizarre turn of events (the science of medicine has increased our life expectancy; the science of business frowns upon the elderly), the matter of age is felt in almost all quarters. 'Thirty and out" is the escape hatch for the elderly auto worker to the woods of retirement, some hunting, some fishing.... But thirty has an altogether different connotation at the ad agency, at the bank, at the auditing house, at the gas company. Unless he/she is 'with it" by then, it's out to the woods of the city, some hunting, some fishing of another sort. As the work force becomes increasingly younger, so does Willy Loman.

Dr. John R. Coleman, president of Haverford College, took an unusual sabbatical during the early months of 1973. He worked at menial jobs. In one instance, he was fired as a porter-dishwasher.

> I'd never been fired and I'd never been unemployed. For three days I walked the streets. Though I had a bank account, though my children's tuition was paid, though I had a salary and a job waiting for me back in Haverford, I was demoralized. I had an inkling of how professionals my age feel when they lose their job and their confidence begins to sink.*

---

* *New York Times,* June 10, 1973.

Dr. Coleman is 51.

Perhaps it is this specter that most haunts working men and women: the planned obsolescence of people that is of a piece with the planned obsolescence of the things they make. Or sell. It is perhaps this fear of no longer being needed in a world of needless things that most clearly spells out the unnaturalness, the surreality of much that is called work today.

> Since Dr. Coleman happens to be chairman of the Federal Reserve Bank of Philadelphia, he quit his ditchdigging job to preside over the bank's monthly meeting. When he looked at the other members of the board, he could not keep from feeling that there was something unreal about them all.*

Something unreal. For me, it was a feeling that persisted throughout this adventure. (How else can I describe this undertaking? It was the daily experience of *others,* their private hurts, real and fancied, that I was probing. In lancing an especially obstinate boil, it is not the doctor who experiences the pain.)

I was no more than a wayfaring stranger, taking much and giving little. True, there were dinners, lunches, drinks, some breakfasts, in posh as well as short order places. There were earnest considerations, varying with what I felt was my companion's economic condition. But they were at best token payments. I was the beneficiary of others' generosity. My tape recorder, as ubiquitous as the carpenter's tool chest or the doctor's black satchel, carried away valuables beyond price.

On occasions, overly committed, pressed by circumstance of my own thoughtless making, I found myself neglecting the amenities and graces that offer mutual pleasure to visitor and host. It was the Brooklyn fireman who astonished me into shame. After what I had felt was an overwhelming experience—meeting him—he invited me to stay "for supper. We'll pick something up at the Ital-

---

* Ibid.

ian joint on the corner." I had already unplugged my tape recorder. (We had had a few beers.) "Oh, Jesus," I remember the manner in which I mumbled. "I'm supposed to see this hotel clerk on the other side of town." He said, "You runnin' off like that? Here we been talkin' all afternoon. It won't sound nice. This guy, Studs, comes to the house, gets my life on tape, and says, 'I gotta go'…" It was a memorable supper. And yet, looking back, how could I have been so insensitive?

The camera, the tape recorder…misused, well-used. There are the *paparazzi;* and there is Walker Evans. The portable tape recorder, too, is for better or for worse. It can be, tiny and well-concealed, a means of blackmail, an instrument of the police state or, as is most often the case, a transmitter of the banal. Yet, a tape recorder, with microphone in hand, on the table or the arm of the chair or on the grass, can transform both the visitor and the host. On one occasion, during the play-back, my companion murmured in wonder, "I never realized I felt that way." And I was filled with wonder, too.

It can be used to capture the voice of a celebrity, whose answers are ever ready and flow through all the expected straits. I have yet to be astonished by one. It can be used to capture the thoughts of the non-celebrated—on the steps of a public housing project, in a frame bungalow, in a furnished apartment, in a parked car—and these "statistics" become persons, each one unique. I am constantly astonished.

As with my two previous books, I was aware of paradox in the making of this one. The privacy of strangers is indeed trespassed upon. Yet my experiences tell me the people with buried grievances and dreams unexpressed do want to let go. Let things out. Lance the boil, they say; there is too much pus. The hurts, though private, are, I trust, felt by others too.

Seven years ago, seeking out the feelings of "ordinary" people living out their anonymous lives in a large industrial city, "I was on the prowl for a cross-section of urban thought, using no one method or technique." Three years later, I was on the prowl for the memories of those who survived the Great Depression. In each case, my vantage was that of a guerrilla. I was somewhat familiar with the terrain. In the first instance, it was the city in which I had lived most of my life. It concerned an actual present. In the second, it was an experience I had shared, if only peripherally. It concerned an actual past. But this one—in which the hard substance of the daily job fuses to the haze of the daydream—was alien territory. It concerned not only "what is" but "what I imagine" and "what might be."

Though this was, for me, a more difficult assignment, my approach was pretty much what it had been before. I had a general idea of the kind of people I wanted to see; who, in reflecting on their personal condition, would touch on the circumstances of their fellows. Yet, as I suspected, improvisation and chance played their roles.

Cases come to mind.

While riding the El, I was approached by a singularly tall stranger. Hearing me talking to myself (as I have a habit of doing), he recognized my voice as "the man he listens to on the radio." He told me of his work and of his father's work. He told me of two of his students: a young hospital aide and a young black man who works in a bank. They, too, are in this book.

There was a trip to eastern Kentucky to see the remarkable Joe Begley, who is worth a book by himself, though none of his reflections are found in this one. It was his suggestion that I visit Joe and Susie Haynes, who live in the hollow behind the hills. They, in turn, guided me to Aunt Katherine. One life was threaded to another, and so tenuously...

It was a young housewife in a small Indiana town who led me to the strip miner, with whom she had some words, though recognizing his inner conflicts. She told me, too, of the stonemason, who, at the moment, was nursing a beer at the tavern near the river. And of the farmer having his trials in the era of agribusiness. And of the three newsboys, who might have a postscript or two to offer readers of Horatio Alger.

There were questions, of course. But they were casual in nature—at the beginning: the kind you would ask while having a drink with someone; the kind he would ask you. The talk was idiomatic rather than academic. In short, it was conversation. In time, the sluice gates of dammed up hurts and dreams were opened.

Choices were in many instances arbitrary. People are engaged in thousands of jobs. Whom to visit? Whom to pass by? In talking to the washroom attendant, would I be remiss in neglecting the elevator operator? One felt his job "obsolete." Wouldn't the other, too? In visiting the Chicago bookbinder, I missed the old Massachusetts basket weaver. I had been told about the New Englander, who found delight in his work. So did my Chicago acquaintance. Need I have investigated the lot of an assembler at the electronics plant, having spent time with spot-welders at Ford? An assembly line is a line is a line.

"The evil genius of our time is the car," Barry Byrne, an elderly architect, observed several years ago. "We must conquer the automobile or become enslaved by it." (He was a disciple of Frank Lloyd Wright, who spoke of the *organic* nature of things. "It was his favorite word. When you look at a tree, it is a magnificent example of an organic whole. All parts belong together, as fingers belong to one's hands. The car today is a horrible example of something not belonging to man.") Less than a year after our conversation, Mr. Byrne, on his way to Sunday mass, was run down by a car and killed.

As for the men and women involved in its manufacture, a UAW local officer has his say: Every time I see an automobile going down the street, I wonder whether the person driving it realizes the kind of human sacrifice that has to go in the building of that car. There's no question there's a better way. And they can build fewer cars and resolve many of the human problems..."

But it provides millions with jobs. So does ordnance work (another euphemism called upon; "war" has only one syllable).

As some occupations become obsolete, others come into being. More people are being paid to watch other people than ever before. A cargo inspector says, "I watch the watchman." He neglected to tell who watches *him*. A young department head in a bank finds it amusing. "Just like Big Brother's watching you. Everybody's watching somebody. It's quite funny when you turn and start watching them. I do that quite a bit. They know I'm watching them. They become uneasy."

Here, too, grievances come into play. The most profound complaint, aside from non-recognition and the nature of the job, is "being spied on." There's the foreman at the plant, the supervisor listening in at Ma Bell's, the checker who gives the bus driver a hard time, the "passenger" who gives the airline stewardess a gimlet eye...The indignation of those being watched is no longer offered in muted tones. Despite the occasional laugh, voices rise. Such humiliations, like fools, are suffered less gladly than before.

In the thirties (as rememberers of "Hard Times" remembered), not very many questioned their lot. Those rebels who found flaws in our society were few in number. This time around, "the system stinks" was a phrase almost as recurrent as "more or less."

Even the "company girl" had a few unexpected things to say. I was looking for an airline stewardess, who might tell me what it was really like. Pressed for time, I did what would ordinarily horrify me. I called a major airline's public relations department. They were most cooperative. They suggested Terry Mason (that's not her name). I assumed it would be a difficult experience for me—to find out what it was really like, under these circumstances. I underestimated Miss Mason's spunkiness. And her sense of self.

So, apparently, did the PR department. She concluded, "The younger girls don't take that guff any more. When the passenger is giving you a bad time, you talk back to him." Her name may be Terry, but obviously nobody can "fly her."

Not that being young makes one rebellious. Another well-nurtured myth we live by. This may be "The Age of Charlie Blossom," but Ralph Werner, twenty, is far more amenable to the status quo and certainly more job-conscious than Bud Freeman, sixty-seven. And Ken Brown, a tycoon at twenty-six, respects the "work ethic" far, far more than Walter Lundquist, forty-eight. It isn't the calendar age that determines a man's restlessness. It is daily circumstance, an *awareness* of being hurt, and an inordinate hunger for "another way." As Lundquist, who gave up a "safe" job for "sanity" puts it: "Once you wake up the human animal you can't put it back to sleep again."

Perhaps it is time the "work ethic" was redefined and its idea reclaimed from the banal men who invoke it. In a world of cybernetics, of an almost runaway technology, things are increasingly making things. It is for our species, it would seem, to go on to other matters. Human matters. Freud put it one way. Ralph Helstein puts it another. He is president emeritus of the United Packinghouse Workers of America. "Learning is work. Caring for children is work. Community action is work. Once we accept the concept of work as something meaningful—not just as the source of a buck— you don't have to worry about finding enough jobs. There's no excuse for mules any more. Society does not need them. There's no question about our ability to feed and clothe and house everybody. The problem is going to come in finding enough ways for man to keep occupied, so he's in touch with reality." Our imaginations have obviously not yet been challenged.

"It isn't that the average working guy is dumb. He's tired, that's all." Mike LeFevre, the steelworker, asks rhetorically, "Who you gonna sock? You can't sock General Motors...you can't sock a system." So, at the neighborhood tavern, he socks the patron sitting next to him, the average working guy. And look out below! It's predetermined, his work being what it is.

> Even a writer as astringent and seemingly unromantic as Orwell never quite lost the habit of seeing working classes through the cozy fug of an Edwardian music hall. There is a wide range of similar attitudes running down through the folksy ballyhoo of the Sunday columnists, the journalists who always remember with admiration the latest bon mot of their pub pal, 'Alf.'*

Similarly, on our shores, the myth dies hard. The most perdurable and certainly the most dreary is that of the cabdriver-philosopher. Our columnists still insist on citing him as the perceptive "diamond in the rough" social observer. Lucky Miller, a young cabdriver, has his say in this matter. "A lot of drivers, they'll agree to almost anything the passenger will say, no matter how absurd. They're angling for that tip." Barbers and bartenders are probably not far behind as being eminently quotable. They are also tippable. This in no way reflects on the nature of their work so much as on the slothfulness of journalists, and the phenomenon of tipping. "Usually I do not disagree with a customer," says a barber. "That's gonna hurt business." It's predetermined, his business—or work—being what it is.

Simultaneously, as our "Alf," called "Archie" or "Joe," is romanticized, he is caricatured. He is the clod, put down by others. The others, who call themselves middle-class, are in turn put down by still others, impersonal in nature—The Organization, The Institution, The Bureaucracy. "Who you gonna sock? You can't sock General Motors…" Thus the dumbness (or numbness or tiredness) of both classes is encouraged and exploited in a society more conspicuously manipulative than Orwell's. A perverse alchemy is at work: the gold that may be found in their unexamined lives is transmuted

---

* Richard Hoggart, *The Uses of Literacy.*

into the dross of banal being. This put-down and its acceptance have been made possible by a perverted "work ethic."

But there are stirrings, a nascent flailing about. Though "Smile" buttons appear, the bearers are deadpan because nobody smiles back. What with the computer and all manner of automation, new heroes and anti-heroes have been added to Walt Whitman's old work anthem. The sound is no longer melodious. The desperation is unquiet.

Nora Watson may have said it most succinctly. "I think most of us are looking for a calling, not a job. Most of us, like the assembly line worker, have jobs that are too small for our spirit. Jobs are not big enough for people."

During my three years of prospecting, I may have, on more occasions than I had imagined, struck gold. I was constantly astonished by the extraordinary dreams of ordinary people. No matter how bewildering the times, no matter how dissembling the official language, those we call ordinary are aware of a sense of personal worth—or more often a lack of it—in the work they do. Tom Patrick, the Brooklyn fireman, brings this essay to a close:

"The fuckin' world's so fucked up, the country's fucked up. But the firemen, you actually see them produce. You see them put out a fire. You see them come out with babies in their hands. You see them give mouth-to-mouth when a guy's dying. You can't get around that shit. That's real. To me, that's what I want to be.

"I worked in a bank. You know, it's just paper. It's not real. Nine to five and it's shit. You're lookin' at numbers. But I can look back and say, 'I helped put out a fire. I helped save somebody.' It shows something I did on this earth."

MIKE LEFEVRE

It is a two-flat dwelling, somewhere in Cicero, on the outskirts of Chicago. He is thirty-seven. He works in a steel mill. On occasion, his wife Carol works as a waitress in a neighborhood restaurant; otherwise, she is at home, caring for their two small children, a girl and a boy.

At the time of my first visit, a sculpted statuette of Mother and Child was on the floor, head severed from body. He laughed softly as he indicated his three-year-old daughter: "She Doctor Spock'd it."

I'm a dying breed. A laborer. Strictly muscle work...pick it up, put it down, pick it up, put it down. We handle between forty and fifty thousand pounds of steel a day. [Laughs.] I know this is hard to believe—from four hundred pounds to three- and four-pound pieces. It's dying.

You can't take pride any more. You remember when a guy could point to a house he built, how many logs he stacked. He built it and he was proud of it. I don't really think I could be proud if a contractor built a home for me. I would be tempted to get in there and kick the carpenter in the ass [laughs], and take the saw away from him. 'Cause I would have to be part of it, you know.

It's hard to take pride in a bridge you're never gonna cross, in a door you're never gonna open. You're mass-producing things and you never see the end result of it. [Muses.] I worked for a trucker one time. And I got this tiny satisfaction when I loaded a truck. At least I could see the truck depart loaded. In a steel mill, forget it. You don't see where nothing goes.

I got chewed out by my foreman once. He said, "Mike, you're a good worker but you have a bad attitude." My attitude is that I don't get excited about my job. I do my work but I don't say whoopee-doo. The day I get excited about my job is the day I go to a head shrinker.

How are you gonna get excited about pullin' steel? How are you gonna get excited when you're tired and want to sit down?

It's not just the work. Somebody built the pyramids. Somebody's going to build something. Pyramids, Empire State Building—these things just don't happen. There's hard work behind it. I would like to see a building, say, the Empire State, I would like to see on one side of it a foot-wide strip from top to bottom with the name of every bricklayer, the name of every electrician, with all the names. So when a guy walked by, he could take his son and say, "See, that's me over there on the forty-fifth floor. I put the steel beam in." Picasso can point to a painting. What can I point to? A writer can point to a book. Everybody should have something to point to.

It's the not-recognition by other people. To say a woman is *just* a housewife is degrading, right? Okay. *Just* a housewife. It's also degrading to say *just* a laborer. The difference is that a man goes out and maybe gets smashed.

When I was single, I could quit, just split. I wandered all over the country. You worked just enough to get a poke, money in your pocket. Now I'm married and I got two kids...[trails off]. I worked on a truck dock one time and I was single. The foreman came over and he grabbed my shoulder, kind of gave me a shove. I punched him and knocked him off the dock. I said, "Leave me alone. I'm doing my work, just stay away from me, just don't give me the with-the-hands business."

Hell, if you whip a damn mule he might kick you. Stay out of my way, that's all. Working is bad enough, don't bug me. I would rather work my ass off for eight hours a day with nobody watching me than five minutes with a guy watching me. Who you gonna sock? You can't sock General Motors, you can't sock anybody in Washington, you can't sock a system.

A mule, an old mule, that's the way I feel. Oh yeah. See. [Shows black and blue marks on arms and legs, burns.] You know what I heard from more than one guy at work? "If my kid wants to work in a factory, I am going to kick the hell out of him." I want my kid to be an effete snob. Yeah, mm-hmm. [Laughs.] I want him to be able to quote Walt Whitman, to be proud of it.

If you can't improve yourself, you improve your posterity. Otherwise life isn't worth nothing. You might as well go back to the cave and stay there. I'm sure the first caveman who went over the hill to see what was on the other side—I don't think he went there wholly out of curiosity. He went there because he wanted to get his son out of the cave. Just the same way I want to send my kid to college.

I work so damn hard and want to come home and sit down and lay around. *But I gotta get it out.* I want to be able to turn around to somebody and say, "Hey, fuck you." You know? [Laughs.] The guy sitting next to me on the bus too. 'Cause all day I wanted to tell my foreman to go fuck himself, but I can't.

So I find a guy in a tavern. To tell him that. And he tells me too. I've been in brawls. He's punching me and I'm punching him, because we actually want to punch somebody else. The most that'll happen is the bartender will bar us from the tavern. But at work, you lose your job.

This one foreman I've got, he's a kid. He's a college graduate. He thinks he's better than everybody else. He was chewing me out and I was saying, "Yeah, yeah, yeah." He said, "What do you mean, yeah, yeah, yeah. Yes, *sir.*" I told him, "Who the hell are you, Hitler? What is this *"Yes, sir"* bullshit? I came here to work, I didn't come here to crawl. There's a fuckin' difference." One word led to another and I lost.

I got broke down to a lower grade and lost twenty-five cents an hour, which is a hell of a lot. It amounts to about ten dollars a week. He came over—after breaking me down. The guy comes over and smiles at me. I blew up. He didn't know it, but he was about two seconds and two feet away from a hospital. I said, "Stay the fuck away from me." He was just about to say something and was pointing his finger. I just reached my hand up and just grabbed his finger and I just put it back in his pocket. He walked away. I grabbed his finger because I'm married. If I'd a been single, I'd a grabbed his head. That's the difference.

You're doing this manual labor and you know that technology can do it. [Laughs.] Let's face it, a machine can do the work of a man; otherwise they wouldn't have space probes. Why can we send a rocket ship that's unmanned and yet send a man in a steel mill to do a mule's work?

Automation? Depends how it's applied. It frightens me if it puts me out on the street. It doesn't frighten me if it shortens my work-week. You read that little thing: what are you going to do when this computer replaces you? Blow up computers. [Laughs.] Really. Blow up computers. I'll be goddamned if a computer is gonna eat before I do! I want milk for my kids and beer for me. Machines can either liberate man or enslave 'im, because they're pretty neutral. It's man who has the bias to put the thing one place or another.

If I had a twenty-hour workweek, I'd get to know my kids better, my wife better. Some kid invited me to go on a college campus. On a Saturday. It was summertime. Hell, if I had a choice of taking my wife and kids to a picnic or going to a college campus, it's gonna be the picnic. But if I worked a twenty-hour week, I could go do both. Don't you think with that extra twenty hours people could really expand? Who's to say? There are some people in factories just by force of circumstance. I'm just like the colored people. Potential Einsteins don't have to be white. They could be in cotton fields, they could be in factories.

The twenty-hour week is a possibility today. The intellectuals, they always say there are potential Lord Byrons, Walt Whitmans, Roosevelts, Picassos working in construction or steel mills or fac-tories. But I don't think they believe it. I think what they're afraid of is the potential Hitlers and Stalins that are there too. The people in power fear the leisure man. Not just the United States. Russia's the same way.

What do you think would happen in this country if, for one year, they experimented and gave everybody a twenty-hour week? How do they know that the guy who digs Wallace today doesn't try to resurrect Hitler tomorrow? Or the guy who is mildly disturbed at pollution doesn't decide to go to General Motors and shit on the guy's desk? You can become a fanatic if you had the time. The whole thing is time. That is, I think, one reason rich kids tend to be fanatic about politics: they have time. Time, that's the important thing.

It isn't that the average working guy is dumb. He's tired, that's all. I picked up a book on chess one time. That thing laid in the drawer for two or three weeks, you're too tired. During the weekends you want to take your kids out. You don't want to sit there and the kid comes up: "Daddy, can I go to the park?" You got your nose in a book? Forget it.

I know a guy fifty-seven years old. Know what he tells me? "Mike, I'm old and tired *all* the time." The first thing happens at work: When the arms start moving, the brain stops. I punch in about ten minutes to seven in the morning. I say hello to a couple of guys I like, I kid around with them. One guy says good morning to you and you say good morning. To another guy you say fuck you. The guy you say fuck you to is your friend.

I put on my hard hat, change into my safety shoes, put on my safety glasses, go to the bonderizer. It's the thing I work on. They rake the metal, they wash it, they dip it in a paint solution, and we take it off. Put it on, take it off, put it on, take it off, put it on, take it off…

I say hello to everybody but my boss. At seven it starts. My arms get tired about the first half-hour. After that, they don't get tired any more until maybe the last half-hour at the end of the day. I work from seven to three thirty. My arms are tired at seven thirty and they're tired at three o'clock. I hope to God I never get broke in, because I always want my arms to be tired at seven thirty and three o'clock. [Laughs.] 'Cause that's when I know that there's a beginning and there's an end. That I'm not brainwashed. In between, I don't even try to think.

If I were to put you in front of a dock and I pulled up a skid in front of you with fifty hundred-pound sacks of potatoes and there are fifty more skids just like it, and this is what you're gonna do all day, what would you think about—potatoes? Unless a guy's a nut, he never thinks about work or talks about it. Maybe about baseball or about getting drunk the other night or he got laid or he didn't get laid. I'd say one out of a hundred will actually get excited about work.

Why is it that the communists always say they're for the workingman, and as soon as they set up a country, you got guys singing to tractors? They're singing about how they love the factory. That's where I couldn't buy communism. It's the intellectuals' utopia, not mine. I cannot picture myself singing to a tractor, I just can't. [Laughs.] Or singing to steel. [Singsongs.] Oh whoop-dee-doo, I'm at the bonderizer, oh how I love this heavy steel. No thanks. Never hoppen.

Oh yeah, I daydream. I fantasize about a sexy blonde in Miami who's got my union dues. [Laughs.] I think of the head of the union the way I think of the head of my company. Living it up. I think of February in Miami. Warm weather, a place to lay in. When I hear a college kid say, "I'm oppressed," I don't believe him. You know what I'd like to do for one year? Live like a college kid. Just for one year. I'd love to. Wow! [Whispers] Wow! Sports car! Marijuana! [Laughs.] Wild, sexy broads. I'd love that, hell yes, I would.

Somebody has to do this work. If my kid ever goes to college, I just want him to have a little respect, to realize that his dad is one of those somebodies. This is why even on—[muses] yeah, I guess, sure—on the black thing... [Sighs heavily.] I can't really hate the colored fella that's working with me all day. The black intellectual I got no respect for. The white intellectual I got no use for. I got no use for the black militant who's gonna scream three hundred years of slavery to me while I'm busting my ass. You know what I mean? [Laughs.] I have one answer for that guy: go see Rockefeller. See Harriman. Don't bother me. We're in the same cotton field. So just don't bug me. [Laughs.]

After work I usually stop off at a tavern. Cold beer. Cold beer right away. When I was single, I used to go into hillbilly bars, get in a lot of brawls. Just to explode. I got a thing on my arm here [indicates scar]. I got slapped with a bicycle chain. Oh, wow! [Softly.] Mmm. I'm getting older. [Laughs.] I don't explode as much. You might say I'm broken in. [Quickly.] No, I'll never be broken in. [Sighs.] When you get a little older, you exchange the words. When you're younger, you exchange the blows.

When I get home, I argue with my wife a little bit. Turn on TV, get mad at the news. [Laughs.] I don't even watch the news that much. I watch Jackie Gleason. I look for any alternative to the ten o'clock news. I don't want to go to bed angry. Don't hit a man with anything heavy at five o'clock. He just can't be bothered. This is his time to relax. The heaviest thing he wants is what his wife has to tell him.

When I come home, know what I do for the first twenty minutes? Fake it. I put on a smile. I got a kid three years old. Sometimes she says, "Daddy, where've you been?" I say, "Work." I could have told her I'd been in Disneyland. What's work to a three-year-old kid? If I feel bad, I can't take it out on the kids. Kids are born innocent of everything but birth. You can't take it out on your wife either. This is why you go to a tavern. You want to release it there rather than do it at home. What does an actor do when he's got a bad movie? I got a bad movie every day.

I don't even need the alarm clock to get up in the morning. I can go out drinking all night, fall asleep at four, and bam! I'm up at six—no matter what I do. [Laughs.] It's a pseudo-death, more or less. Your whole system is paralyzed and you give all the appearance of death. It's an ingrown clock. It's a thing you just get used to. The hours differ. It depends. Sometimes my wife wants to do something crazy like play five hundred rummy or put a puzzle together. It could be midnight, could be ten o clock, could be nine thirty.

What do you do weekends?

Drink beer, read a book. See that one? *Violence in America.* It's one of them studies from Washington. One of them committees they're always appointing. A thing like that I read on a weekend. But during the weekdays gee...I just thought about it. I don't do that much reading from Monday through Friday. Unless it's a horny book. I'll read it at work and go home and do my homework. [Laughs.] That's what the guys at the plant call it—homework. [Laughs.] Sometimes my wife works on Saturday and I drink beer at the tavern.

I went out drinking with one guy, oh, a long time ago. A college boy. He was working where I work now. Always preaching to me about how you need violence to change the system and all that garbage. We went into a hillbilly joint. Some guy there, I didn't know him from Adam, he said, "You think you're smart" I said, "What's your pleasure?" [Laughs.] He said, "My pleasure's to kick your ass." I told him I really can't be bothered. He said, "What're you, chicken?" I said, "No, I just don't want to be bothered." He came over and said something to me again. I said, "I don't beat women, drunks, or fools. Now leave me alone."

The guy called his brother over. This college boy that was with me, he came nudging my arm, "Mike, let's get out of here." I said, "What are you worried about?" [Laughs.] This isn't unusual. People will bug you. You fend it off as much as you can with your mouth and when you can't, you punch the guy out.

It was close to closing time and we stayed. We could have left, but when you go into a place to have a beer and a guy challenges you—if you expect to go in that place again, you don't leave. If you have to fight the guy, you fight.

I got just outside the door and one of these guys jumped on me and grabbed me around the neck. I grabbed his arm and flung him against the wall. I grabbed him here [indicates throat], and jiggled his head against the wall quite a few times. He kind of slid down a little bit. This guy who said he was his brother took a swing at me with a garrison belt. He just missed and hit the wall. I'm looking around for my junior Stalin [laughs], who loves violence and everything. He's gone. Split. [Laughs.] Next day I see him at work. I couldn't get mad at him, he's a baby.

He saw a book in my back pocket one time and he was amazed. He walked up to me and he said, "You read?" I said, "What do you mean, I read?" He said, "All these dummies read the sports pages around here. What are you doing with a book?" I got pissed off at the kid right away. I said, "What do you mean, all these dummies? Don't knock a man who's paying somebody else's way through college." He was a nineteen-year-old effete snob.

Yet you want your kid to be an effete snob?

Yes. I want my kid to look at me and say, "Dad, you're a nice guy, but you're a fuckin' dummy." Hell yes, I want my kid to tell me that he's not gonna be like me...

If I were hiring people to work, I'd try naturally to pay them a decent wage. I'd try to find out their first names, their last names, keep the company as small as possible, so I could personalize the whole thing. All I would ask a man is a handshake, see you in the morning. No applications, nothing. I wouldn't be interested in the guy's past. Nobody ever checks the pedigree on a mule, do they? But they do on a man. Can you picture walking up to a mule and saying, "I'd like to know who his granddaddy was?"

I'd like to run a combination bookstore and tavern. [Laughs.] I would like to have a place where college kids came and a steelworker could sit down and talk. Where a workingman could not be

ashamed of Walt Whitman and where a college professor could not
be ashamed that he painted his house over the weekend.

If a carpenter built a cabin for poets, I think the least the poets
owe the carpenter is just three or four one-liners on the wall. A
little plaque: Though we labor with our minds, this place we can
relax in was built by someone who can work with his hands. And his
work is as noble as ours. I think the poet owes something to the guy
who builds the cabin for him.

I don't think of Monday. You know what I'm thinking about on
Sunday night? Next Sunday. If you work real hard, you think of a
perpetual vacation. Not perpetual sleep...What do I think of on a
Sunday night? Lord, I wish the fuck I could do something else for
a living.

I don't know who the guy is who said there is nothing sweeter
than an unfinished symphony. Like an unfinished painting and an
unfinished poem. If he creates this thing one day—let's say,
Michelangelo's Sistine Chapel. It took him a long time to do this,
this beautiful work of art. But what if he had to create this Sistine
Chapel a thousand times a year? Don't you think that would even
dull Michelangelo's mind? Or if da Vinci had to draw his anatomi-
cal charts thirty, forty, fifty, sixty, eighty, ninety, a hundred times a
day? Don't you think that would even bore da Vinci?

*Way back, you spoke of the guys who built the pyramids, not the
pharaohs, the unknowns. You put yourself in their category?*

Yes. I want my signature on 'em, too. Sometimes, out of pure
meanness, when I make something, I put a little dent in it. I like to
do something to make it really unique. Hit it with a hammer. I
deliberately fuck it up to see if it'll get by, just so I can say I did it.
It could be anything. Let me put it this way: I think God invented
the dodo bird so when we get up there we could tell Him, "Don't
you ever make mistakes?" and He'd say, "Sure, look." [Laughs.]

I'd like to make my imprint. My dodo bird. A mistake, *mine*. Let's say the whole building is nothing but red bricks. I'd like to have just the black one or the white one or the purple one. Deliberately fuck up.

This is gonna sound square, but my kid is my imprint. He's my freedom. There's a line in one of Hemingway's books. I think it's from *For Whom the Bell Tolls*. They're behind the enemy lines, somewhere in Spain, and she's pregnant. She wants to stay with him. He tells her no. He says, "if you die, I die," knowing he's gonna die. But if you go, I go. Know what I mean? The mystics call it the brass bowl. Continuum. You know what I mean? This is why I work. Every time I see a young guy walk by with a shirt and tie and dressed up real sharp, I'm lookin' at my kid, you know? That's it.

DOLORES DANTE

She has been a waitress in the same restaurant for twenty-three years. Many of its patrons are credit card carriers on an expense account—conventioneers, politicians, labor leaders, agency people. Her hours are from 5:00 P.M. to 2:00 A.M. six days a week. She arrives earlier "to get things ready, the silverware, the butter. When people come in and ask for you, you would like to be in a position to handle them all, because that means more money for you."

I became a waitress because I needed money fast and you don't get it in an office. My husband and I broke up and he left me with debts and three children. My baby was six months. The fast buck, your tips. The first ten-dollar bill that I got as a tip, a Viking guy gave to me. He was a very robust, terrific atheist. Made very good conversation for us, 'cause I am too.

Everyone says all waitresses have broken homes. What they

don't realize is when people have broken homes they need to make money fast, and do this work. They don't have broken homes because they're waitresses.

I have to be a waitress. How else can I learn about people? How else does the world come to me? I can't go to everyone. So they have to come to me. Everyone wants to eat, everyone has hunger. And I serve them. If they've had a bad day, I nurse them, cajole them. Maybe with coffee I give them a little philosophy. They have cocktails, I give them political science.

I'll say things that bug me. If they manufacture soap, I say what I think about pollution. If it's automobiles, I say what I think about them. If I pour water I'll say, "Would you like your quota of mercury today?" If I serve cream, I say, "Here is your substitute. I think you're drinking plastic." I just can't keep quiet. I have an opinion on every single subject there is. In the beginning it was theology, and my bosses didn't like it. Now I am a political and my bosses don't like it. I speak *sotto voce*. But if I get heated, then I don't give a damn. I speak like an Italian speaks. I can't be servile. I give service. There is a difference.

I'm called by my first name. I like my name. I hate to be called Miss. Even when I serve a lady, a strange woman, I will not say madam. I hate ma'am. I always say milady. In the American language there is no word to address a woman, to indicate whether she's married or unmarried. So I say milady. And sometimes I playfully say to the man milord.

It would be very tiring if I had to say, "Would you like a cocktail?" and say that over and over. So I come out different for my own enjoyment. I would say, "What's exciting at the bar that I can offer?" I can't say, "Do you want coffee?" Maybe I'll say, "Are you in the mood for coffee?" Or, "The coffee sounds exciting." Just rephrase it enough to make it interesting for me. That would make them take an interest. It becomes theatrical and I feel like Mata Hari and it intoxicates me.

People imagine a waitress couldn't possibly think or have any kind of aspiration other than to serve food. When somebody says to me, "You're great, how come you're *just* a waitress?" *Just* a waitress. I'd say, "Why, don't you think you deserve to be served by me?" It's implying that he's not worthy, not that I'm not worthy. It makes me irate. I don't feel lowly at all. I myself feel sure. I don't want to change the job. I love it.

Tips? I feel like Carmen. It's like a gypsy holding out a tambourine and they throw the coin. [Laughs.] If you like people, you're not thinking of the tips. I never count my money at night. I always wait till morning. If I thought about my tips I'd be uptight. I never look at a tip. You pick it up fast. I would do my bookkeeping in the morning. It would be very dull for me to know I was making so much and no more. I do like challenge. And it isn't demeaning, not for me.

There might be occasions when the customers might intend to make it demeaning—the man about town, the conventioneer. When the time comes to pay the check, he would do little things, "How much should I give you?" He might make an issue about it. I did say to one, "Don't play God with me. Do what you want." Then it really didn't matter whether I got a tip or not. I would spit it out, my resentment—that he dares make me feel I'm operating only for a tip.

He'd ask for his check. Maybe he's going to sign it. He'd take a very long time and he'd make me stand there, "Let's see now, what do you think I ought to give you?" He would not let go of that moment. And you knew it. You know he meant to demean you. He's holding the change in his hand, or if he'd sign, he'd flourish the pen and wait. These are the times I really get angry. I'm not reticent. Something would come out. Then I really didn't care. "Goddamn, keep your money!"

There are conventioneers, who leave their lovely wives or their bad wives. They approach you and say, "Are there any hot spots?"

"Where can I find girls?" It is, of course, first directed at you. I don't mean that as a compliment, 'cause all they're looking for is females. They're not looking for companionship or conversation. I am quite adept at understanding this. I think I'm interesting enough that someone may just want to talk to me. But I would philosophize that way. After all, what is left after you talk? The hours have gone by and I could be home resting or reading or studying guitar, which I do on occasion. I would say, "What are you going to offer me? Drinks?" And I'd point to the bar, "I have it all here." He'd look blank and then I'd say, "A man? If I need a man, wouldn't you think I'd have one of my own? Must I wait for you?'

Life doesn't frighten me any more. There are only two things that relegate us—the bathroom and the grave. Either I'm gonna have to go to the bathroom now or I'm gonna die now. I go to the bathroom.

And I don't have a high opinion of bosses. The more popular you are, the more the boss holds it over your head. You're bringing them business, but he knows you're getting good tips and you won't leave. You have to worry not to overplay it, because the boss becomes resentful and he uses this as a club over your head.

If you become too good a waitress, there's jealousy. They don't come in and say, "Where's the boss?" They'll ask for Dolores. It doesn't make a hit. That makes it rough. Sometimes you say, Aw hell, why am I trying so hard? I did get an ulcer. Maybe the things I kept to myself were twisting me.

It's not the customers, never the customers. It's injustice. My dad came from Italy and I think of his broken English—*injoost*. He hated injustice. If you hate injustice for the world, you hate more than anything injustice toward you. Loyalty is never appreciated, particularly if you're the type who doesn't like small talk and are not the type who makes reports on your fellow worker. The boss wants to find out what is going on surreptitiously. In our society today you have informers everywhere. They've informed on cooks, on coworkers. "Oh, someone wasted this." They would say I'm talking to all the customers. "I saw her carry such-and-such out. See if she wrote that on her check." "The salad looked like it was a double salad." I don't give anything away. I just give myself. Informers will manufacture things in order to make their job worthwhile. They're not sure of themselves as workers. There's always someone who wants your station, who would be pretender to the crown. In life there is always someone who wants somebody's job.

I'd get intoxicated with giving service. People would ask for me and I didn't have enough tables. Some of the girls are standing and don't have customers. There is resentment. I feel self-conscious. I feel a sense of guilt. It cramps my style. I would like to say to the customer, "Go to so-and-so." But you can't do that, because you feel a sense of loyalty. So you would rush, get to your customers quickly. Some don't care to drink and still they wait for you. That's a compliment.

There is plenty of tension. If the cook isn't good, you fight to see that the customers get what you know they like. You have to use diplomacy with cooks, who are always dangerous. [Laughs.] They're madmen. [Laughs.] You have to be their friend. They better like you. And your bartender better like you too, because he may do something to the drink. If your bartender doesn't like you, your cook doesn't like you, your boss doesn't like you, the other girls don't like you, you're in trouble.

And there will be customers who are hypochondriacs, who feel they can't eat, and I coax them. Then I hope I can get it just the right way from the cook. I may mix the salad myself, just the way they want it.

Maybe there's a party of ten. Big shots, and they'd say, "Dolores, I have special clients, do your best tonight." You just hope you have the right cook behind the broiler. You really want to pleasure your guests. He's selling something, he wants things right, too. You're giving your all. How does the steak look?

If you cut his steak, you look at it surreptitiously. How's it going?"

Carrying dishes is a problem. We do have accidents. I spilled a tray once with steaks for seven on it. It was a big, gigantic T-bone, all sliced. But when that tray fell, I went with it, and never made a sound, dish and all [softly] never made a sound. It took about an hour and a half to cook that steak. How would I explain this thing? That steak was salvaged. [Laughs.]

Some don't care. When the plate is down you can hear the sound. I try not to have that sound. I want my hands to be right when I serve. I pick up a glass, I want it to be just right. I get to be almost Oriental in the serving. I like it to look nice all the way. To be a waitress, it's an art. I feel like a ballerina, too. I have to go between those tables, between those chairs…Maybe that's the reason I always stayed slim. It is a certain way I can go through a chair no one else can do. I do it with an air. If I drop a fork, there is a certain way I pick it up. I know they can see how delicately I do it. I'm on stage.

I tell everyone I'm a waitress and I'm proud. If a nurse gives service, I say, "You're a professional." Whatever you do, be professional. I always compliment people.

I like to have my station looking nice. I like to see there's enough ash trays when they're having their coffee and cigarettes. I don't like ash trays so loaded that people are not enjoying the moment. It offends me. I don't do it because I think that's gonna make a better tip. It offends me as a person.

People say, "No one does good work any more." I don't believe it. You know who's saying that? The man at the top, who says the people beneath him are not doing a good job. He's the one who always said, "You're nothing." The housewife who has all the money, she believed housework was demeaning, 'cause she hired someone else to do it. If it weren't so demeaning, why didn't *she* do it? So anyone who did her housework was a person to be demeaned. The maid who did all the housework said, "Well, hell, if this is the way you feel about it, I won't do your housework. You tell me I'm no

good, I'm nobody. Well, maybe I'll go out and be somebody."
They're only mad because they can't find someone to do it now. The
fault is not in the people who did the—quote—lowly work.

Just a waitress. At the end of the night I feel drained. I think a
lot of waitresses become alcoholics because of that. In most cases,
a waiter or a waitress doesn't eat. They handle food, they don't
have time. You'll pick at something in the kitchen, maybe a piece of
bread. You'll have a cracker, a litle bit of soup. You go back and
take a teaspoonful of something. Then maybe sit down afterwards
and have a drink, maybe three, four, five. And bartenders, too,
most of them are alcoholics. They'd go out in a group. There are
after-hour places. You've got to go release your tension. So they go
out before they go to bed. Some of them stay out all night.

It's tiring, it's nerve-racking. We don't ever sit down. We're on
stage and the bosses are watching. If you get the wrong shoes and
you get the wrong stitch in that shoe, that does bother you. Your feet
hurt, your body aches. If you come out in anger at things that were
done to you, it would only make you feel cheapened. Really I've been
keeping it to myself. But of late, I'm beginning to spew it out. It's
almost as though I sensed my body and soul had had quite enough.

It builds and builds and builds in your guts. Near crying. I can
think about it…[She cries softly.] 'Cause you're tired. When the
night is done, you're tired. You've had so much, there's so much
going…You had to get it done. The dread that something wouldn't
be right, because you want to please. You hope everyone is satisfied. The night's done, you've done your act. The curtains close.

The next morning is pleasant again. I take out my budget book,
write down how much I made, what my bills are. I'm managing. I
won't give up this job as long as I'm able to do it. I feel out of contact if I just sit at home. At work they all consider me a kook.
[Laughs.] That's okay. No matter where I'd be, I would make a
rough road for me. It's just me, and I can't keep still. It hurts, and
what hurts has to come out.

POSTSCRIPT

"After sixteen years—that was seven years ago—I took a trip to Hawaii and the Caribbean for two weeks. Went with a lover. The kids saw it—they're all married now. [Laughs.] One of my daughters said, "Act your age." I said, "Honey, if I were acting my age, I wouldn't be walking. My bones would ache. You don't want to hear about my arthritis. Aren't you glad I'm happy."

ROBERTO ACUNA

I walked out of the fields two years ago. I saw the need to change the California feudal system, to change the lives of farm workers, to make these huge corporations feel they're not above anybody. I am thirty-four years old and I try to organize for the United Farm Workers of America.

His hands are calloused and each of his thumbnails is singularly cut. "If you're picking lettuce, the thumbnails fall off 'cause they're banged on the box. Your hands get swollen. You can't slow down because the foreman sees you're so many boxes behind and you'd better get on. But people would help each other. If you're feeling bad that day, somebody who's feeling pretty good would help. Any people that are suffering have to stick together, whether they like it or not, whether they are black, brown, or pink."

According to Mom, I was born on a cotton sack out in the fields, 'cause she had no money to go to the hospital. When I was a child, we used to migrate from California to Arizona and back and forth. The things I saw shaped my life. I remember when we used to go out and pick carrots and onions, the whole family. We tried to scratch a livin' out of the ground. I saw my parents cry out in despair, even though we had the whole family working. At the time, they were paying sixty-two and a half cents an hour. The average income must have been fifteen hundred dollars, maybe two thousand.*

This was supplemented by child labor. During those years, the growers used to have a Pick-Your-Harvest Week. They would get all the migrant kids out of school and have 'em out there pickin' the crops at peak harvest time. A child was off that week and when he went back to school he got a little gold star. They would make it seem like something civic to do.

We'd pick everything: lettuce, carrots, onions, cucumbers, cauliflower, broccoli, tomatoes—all the salads you could make out of vegetables, we picked 'em. Citrus fruits watermelons—you name it. We'd be in Salinas about four months. From there we'd go down into the Imperial Valley. From there we'd go to picking citrus. It was like a cycle. We'd follow the seasons.

After my dad died, my mom would come home and she'd go into her tent and I would go into ours. We'd roughhouse and everything and then we'd go into the tent where Mom was sleeping and I'd see her crying. When I asked her why she was crying she never gave me an answer. All she said was things would get better. She retired a beaten old lady with a lot of dignity. That day she thought would be better never came for her.

One time, my mom was in bad need of money, so she got a part-time evening job in a restaurant. I'd be helping her. All the growers would come in and they'd be laughing, making nasty remarks, and make passes at her. I used to go out there and kick 'em and my mom told me to leave 'em alone, she could handle 'em. But they would embarrass her and she would cry.

---

* "Today, because of our struggles, the pay is up to two dollars an hour. Yet we know that is not enough."

My mom was a very proud woman. She brought us up without any help from nobody. She kept the family strong. They say that a family that prays together stays together. I say that a family that works together stays together—because of the suffering. My mom couldn't speak English too good. Or much Spanish, for that matter. She wasn't educated. But she knew some prayers and she used to make us say them. That's another thing, when I see the many things in this world and this country, I could tear the churches apart. I never saw a priest out in the fields trying to help people. Maybe in these later years they're doing it. But it's always the church taking from the people.

We were once asked by the church to bring vegetables to make it a successful bazaar. After we got the stuff there, the only people havin' a good time were the rich people because they were the only ones that were buyin' the stuff...

I'd go barefoot to school. The bad thing was they used to laugh at us, the Anglo kids. They would laugh because we'd bring tortillas and frijoles to lunch. They would have their nice little compact lunch boxes with cold milk in their thermos and they'd laugh at us because all we had was dried tortillas. Not only would they laugh at us, but the kids would pick fights. My older brother used to do most of the fighting for us and he'd come home with black eyes all the time.

What really hurt is when we had to go on welfare. Nobody knows the erosion of man's dignity. They used to have a label of canned goods that said, "U. S. Commodities. Not to be sold or exchanged." Nobody knows how proud it is to feel when you bought canned goods with your own money.

I wanted to be accepted. It must have been in sixth grade. It was just before the Fourth of July. They were trying out students for this patriotic play. I wanted to do Abe Lincoln, so I learned the Gettysburg Address inside and out. I'd be out in the fields pickin' the crops and I'd be memorizin'. I was the only one who didn't have to read the part, 'cause I learned it. The part was given to a girl who was a grower's daughter. She had to read it out of a book, but they said she had better diction. I was very disappointed. I quit about eighth grade.

Any time anybody'd talk to me about politics, about civil rights, I would ignore it. It's a very degrading thing because you can't express yourself. They wanted us to speak English in the school classes. We'd put out a real effort. I would get into a lot of fights because I spoke Spanish and they couldn't understand it. I was punished. I was kept after school for not speaking English.

We used to have our own tents on the truck. Most migrants would live in the tents that were already there in the fields, put up by the company. We got one for ourselves, secondhand, but it was ours. Anglos used to laugh at us. "Here comes the carnival," they'd say. We couldn't keep our clothes clean, we couldn't keep nothing clean, because we'd go by the dirt roads and the dust. We'd stay outside the town.

I never did want to go to town because it was a very bad thing for me. We used to go to the small stores, even though we got clipped more. If we went to the other stores, they would laugh at us. They would always point at us with a finger. We'd go to town maybe every two weeks to get what we needed. Everybody would walk in a bunch. We were afraid. [Laughs.] We sang to keep our spirits up. We joked about our poverty. This one guy would say, "When I get to be rich, I'm gonna marry an Anglo woman, so I can be accepted into society." The other guys would say, "When I get rich I'm gonna marry a Mexican woman, so I can go to that Anglo society of yours and see them hang you for marrying an Anglo." Our world was around the fields.

I started picking crops when I was eight. I couldn't do much, but every little bit counts. Every time I would get behind on my chores, I would get a carrot thrown at me by my parents. I would day-dream: If I were a millionaire, I would buy all these ranches and give them back to the people. I would picture my mom living in one area all the time and being admired by all the people in the community. All of a sudden I'd be rudely awaken by a broken carrot in my back. That would bust your whole dream apart and you'd work for a while and come back to daydreaming.

We used to work early, about four o'clock in the morning. We'd pick the harvest until about six. Then we'd run home and get into our supposedly clean clothes and run all the way to school because we'd be late. By the time we got to school, we'd be all tuckered out. Around maybe eleven o'clock, we'd be dozing off. Our teachers would send notes to the house telling Mom that we were inattentive. The only thing I'd make fairly good grades on was spelling. I couldn't do anything else. Many times we never did our homework, because we were out in the fields. The teachers couldn't understand that. I would get whacked there also.

School would end maybe four o'clock. We'd rush home again, change clothes, go back to work until seven, seven thirty at night. That's not counting the weekends. On Saturday and Sunday, we'd be there from four thirty in the morning until about seven thirty in the evening. This is where we made the money, those two days. We all worked.

I would carry boxes for my mom to pack the carrots in. I would pull the carrots out and she would sort them into different sizes. I would get water for her to drink. When you're picking tomatoes, the boxes are heavy. They weigh about thirty pounds. They're dropped very hard on the trucks so they have to be sturdy.

The hardest work would be thinning and hoeing with a short-handled hoe. The fields would be about a half a mile long. You would be bending and stooping all day. Sometimes you would have hard ground and by the time you got home, your hands would be full of calluses. And you'd have a backache. Sometimes I wouldn't have dinner or anything. I'd just go home and fall asleep and wake up just in time to go out to the fields again.

I remember when we just got into California from Arizona to pick up the carrot harvest. It was very cold and very windy out in the fields. We just had a little old blanket for the four of us kids in the tent. We were freezin' our tail off. So I stole two brand-new blankets that belonged to a grower. When we got under those blankets it was nice and comfortable. Somebody saw me. The next morning the grower told my mom he'd turn us in unless we gave him back his blankets—sterilized. So my mom and I and my kid brother went to the river and cut some wood and made a fire and boiled the water and she scrubbed the blankets. She hung them out to dry, ironed them, and sent them back to the grower. We got a spanking for that.

I remember this labor camp that was run by the city. It was a POW camp for German soldiers. They put families in there and it would have barbed wire all around it. If you were out after ten o'clock at night, you couldn't get back in until the next day at four in the morning. We didn't know the rules. Nobody told us. We went to visit some relatives. We got back at about ten thirty and they wouldn't let us in. So we slept in the pickup outside the gate. In the morning, they let us in, we had a fast breakfast and went back to work in the fields.*

The grower would keep the families apart, hoping they'd fight against each other. He'd have three or four camps and he'd have the people over here pitted against the people over there. For jobs. He'd give the best crops to the people he thought were the fastest workers. This way he kept us going harder and harder, competing.

When I was sixteen, I had my first taste as a foreman. Handling braceros, aliens, that came from Mexico to work. They'd bring these people to work over here and then send them back to Mexico after the season was over. My job was to make sure they did a good job and pushin' 'em ever harder. I was a company man, yes. My

---

* "Since we started organizing, this camp has been destroyed. They started building housing on it."

parents needed money and I wanted to make sure they were proud of me. A foreman is recognized. I was very naïve. Even though I was pushing the workers, I knew their problems. They didn't know how to write, so I would write letters home for them. I would take 'em to town, buy their clothes, outside of the company stores. They had paid me $1.10 an hour. The farm workers' wage was raised to eighty-two and a half cents. But even the braceros were making more money than me, because they were working piecework. I asked for more money. The manager said, "If you don't like it you can quit." I quit and joined the Marine Corps.

I joined the Marine Corps at seventeen. I was very mixed up. I wanted to become a first-class citizen. I wanted to be accepted and I was very proud of my uniform. My mom didn't want to sign the papers, but she knew I had to better myself and maybe I'd get an education in the services.

I did many jobs. I took a civil service exam and was very proud when I passed. Most of the others were college kids. There were only three Chicanos in the group of sixty. I got a job as a correctional officer in a state prison. I quit after eight months because I couldn't take the misery I saw. They wanted me to use a rubber hose on some of the prisoners—mostly Chicanos and blacks. I couldn't do it. They called me chicken-livered because I didn't want to hit nobody. They constantly harassed me after that. I didn't quit because I was afraid of them but because they were trying to make me into a mean man. I couldn't see it. This was Soledad State Prison.

I began to see how everything was so wrong. When growers can have an intricate watering system to irrigate their crops but they can't have running water inside the houses of workers. Veterinarians tend to the needs of domestic animals but they can't have medical care for the workers. They can have land subsidies for the growers but they can't have adequate unemployment compensation for the workers. They treat him like a farm implement. In fact, they treat their implements better and their domestic animals better. They have heat and insulated barns for the animals but the workers live in beat-up shacks with no heat at all.

Illness in the fields is 120 percent higher than the average rate for industry. It's mostly back trouble, rheumatism and arthritis, because of the damp weather and the cold. Stoop labor is very hard on a person. Tuberculosis is high. And now because of the pesticides, we have many respiratory diseases.

The University of California at Davis has government experiments with pesticides and chemicals. To get a bigger crop each year. They haven't any regard as to what safety precautions are needed. In 1964 or '65, an airplane was spraying these chemicals on the fields. Spraying rigs they're called. Flying low, the wheels got tangled on the fence wire. The pilot got up, dusted himself off, and got a drink of water. He died of convulsions. The ambulance attendants got violently sick because of the pesticides he had on his person. A little girl was playing around a sprayer. She stuck her tongue on it. She died instantly.

These pesticides affect the farm worker through the lungs. He breathes it in. He gets no compensation. All they do is say he's sick. They don't investigate the cause.

There were times when I felt I couldn't take it any more. It was 105 in the shade and I'd see endless rows of lettuce and I felt my back hurting...I felt the frustration of not being able to get out of the fields. I was getting ready to jump any foreman who looked at me cross-eyed. But until two years ago, my world was still very small.

I would read all these things in the papers about Cesar Chavez and I would denounce him because I still had that thing about becoming a first-class patriotic citizen. In Mexicali they would pass out leaflets and I would throw 'em away. I never participated. The grape boycott didn't affect me much because I was in lettuce. It wasn't until Chavez came to Salinas, where I was working in the fields, that I saw what a beautiful man he was. I went to this rally, I still intended to stay with the company. But something—I don't know—I was close to the workers. They couldn't speak English and wanted me to be their spokesman in favor of going on strike. I don't know—I just got caught up with it all, the beautiful feeling of solidarity.

You'd see the people on the picket lines at four in the morning, at the camp fires, heating up beans and coffee and tortillas. It gave me a sense of belonging. These were my own people and they wanted change. I knew this is what I was looking for. I just didn't know it before.

My mom had always wanted me to better myself. I wanted to better myself because of her. Now when the strikes started, I told her I was going to join the union and the whole movement. I told her I was going to work without pay. She said she was proud of me. [His eyes glisten. A long, long pause.] See, I told her I wanted to be with my people. If I were a company man, nobody would like me any more. I had to belong to somebody and this was it right here. She said, "I pushed you in your early years to try to better yourself and get a social position. But I see that's not the answer. I know I'll be proud of you."

All kinds of people are farm workers, not just Chicanos. Filipinos started the strike. We have Puerto Ricans and Appalachians too, Arabs, some Japanese, some Chinese. At one time they used us against each other. But now they can't and they're scared, the growers. They can organize conglomerates. Yet when we try organization to better our lives, they are afraid. Suffering people never dream it could be different. Ceasar Chavez tells them this and they grasp the idea—and this is what scares the growers.

Now the machines are coming in. It takes skill to operate them. But anybody can be taught. We feel migrant workers should be given the chance. They got one for grapes. They got one for lettuce. They have cotton machines that took jobs away from thousands of farm workers. The people wind up in the ghettos of the city, their culture, their families, their unity destroyed.

We're trying to stipulate it in our contract that the company will not use any machinery without the consent of the farm workers. So we can make sure the people being replaced by the machines will know how to operate the machines.

Working in the fields is not in itself a degrading job. It's hard, but if you're given regular hours, better pay, decent housing, unemployment and medical compensation, pension plans—we have a very relaxed way of living. But the growers don't recognize us as persons. That's the worst thing, the way they treat you. Like we have no brains. Now we see they have no brains. They have only a wallet in their head. The more you squeeze it, the more they cry out.

If we had proper compensation we wouldn't have to be working seventeen hours a day and following the crops. We could stay in one area and it would give us roots. Being a migrant, it tears the family apart. You get in debt. You leave the area penniless. The children are the ones hurt the most. They go to school three months in one place and then on to another. No sooner do they make friends, they are uprooted again. Right here, your childhood is taken away. So when they grow up, they're looking for this childhood they have lost.

If people could see—in the winter, ice on the fields. We'd be on our knees all day long. We'd build fires and warm up real fast and go back onto the ice. We'd be picking watermelons in 105 degrees all day long. When people have melons or cucumber or carrots or lettuce, they don't know how they got on their table and the consequences to the people who picked it. If I had enough money, I would take busloads of people out to the fields and into the labor camps. Then they'd know how that fine salad got on their table.

ERIC NESTERENKO

He has been a professional hockey player for twenty years, as a member of the Toronto Maple Leafs and the Chicago Black Hawks. He is thirty-eight. He has a wife and three small children.

I lived in a small mining town in Canada, a God-forsaken place called Flinflan. In the middle of nowhere, four hundred miles north of Winnipeg. It was a good life, beautiful winters. I remember the Northern Lights. Dark would come around three o'clock. Thirty below zero, but dry and clean.

I lived across the street from the rink. That's how I got started, when I was four or five. We never had any gear. I used to wrap *Life* magazines around my legs. We didn't have organized hockey like they have now. All our games were pickup, a never-ending game. Maybe there would be three kids to a team, then there would be fifteen, and the game would go on. Nobody would keep score. It was pure kind of play. The play you see here, outside the stadium, outside at the edge of the ghetto. I see 'em in the schoolyards. It's that same kind of play around the basket. Pure play.

My father bought me a pair of skates, but that was it. He never took part. I played the game for my own sake, not for him. He wasn't even really around to watch. I was playing for the joy of it, with my own peers. Very few adults around. We organized everything.

I see parents at kids' sporting events. It's all highly organized. It's very formal. They have referees and so on. The parents are spectators. The kids are playing for their parents. The old man rewards him for playing well and doesn't reward him for not doing so well. [Laughs.] The father puts too much pressure on the kid. A boy then is soft material. If you want a kid to do something, it's got to be fun.

I was a skinny, ratty kid with a terrible case of acne. I could move pretty well, but I never really looked like much. [Laughs.] Nobody ever really noticed me. But I could play the game. In Canada it is part of the culture. If you can play the game, you are recognized. I was good almost from the beginning. The game became a passion with me. I was looking to be somebody and the game was my way. It was my life.

At sixteen, while in high school, he was playing with semi-pro teams, earning two hundred dollars a week. At eighteen, he joined the Toronto Maple Leafs.

There's an irony that one gets paid for playing, that play should bring in money. When you sell play, that makes it hard for pure, recreational play, for play as an art, to exist. It's corrupted, it's made harder, perhaps it's brutalized, but it's still there. Once you learn how to play and are accepted in the group, there is a rapport. All you are as an athlete is honed and made sharper. You learn to survive in a very tough world. It has its own rewards.

The pro game is a kind of a stage. People can see who we are. Our personalities come through in our bodies. It's exciting. I can remember games with twenty thousand people and the place going crazy with sound and action and color. The enormous energy the crowd produces all coming in on the ice, all focusing in on you. It's pretty hard to resist that. [Laughs.]

I was really recognized then. I remember one game: it was in the semi-finals, the year we won the Stanley Cup. I was with Chicago. It was the sixth game against Montreal. They were the big club and we were the Cinderella team. It was three to nothing, for us, with five minutes left to go. As a spontaneous gesture twenty thousand people stood up. I was on the ice. I remember seeing that whole stadium, just solid, row on row, from the balcony to the boxes, standing up. These people were turned on by us. [Sighs.] We came off, three feet off the ice...[Softly.] Spring of '61.

When Toronto dropped me I said, "I'm a failure." Twenty-two, what the hell does one know? You're the boy of the moment or nothing. What we show is energy and young bodies. We know our time is fleeting. If we don't get a chance to go, it makes us antsy. Our values are instant, it's really hard to bide your time.

Violence is taken to a greater degree. There is always the specter of being hurt. A good player, just come into his prime, cracks a skull, breaks a leg, he's finished. If you get hit, you get hit—with impersonal force. The guy'll hit you as hard as he can. If you get hurt, the other players switch off. Nobody's sympathetic. When you get hurt they don't look at you, even players on your own team. The curtain comes down—'cause it could have been me. One is afraid of being hurt himself. You don't want to think too much about it. I saw my teammate lying there—I knew him pretty well—they put forty stitches in his face. I saw him lying on the table and the doctors working on him. I said, "Better him than me." [Laughs.] We conditioned ourselves to think like that. I think it's a defense mechanism and it's brutalizing.

The professional recognizes this and risks himself less and less, so the percentage is in his favor. This takes a bit of experience. Invariably it's the younger player who gets hurt. Veterans learn to be calculating about their vulnerability. [Laughs.] This takes a little bit away from the play. When I was young, I used to take all sorts of chances just for the hell of it. Today, instead of trying to push through it, I ease up. It takes something off the risk. The older professional often plays a waiting game, waits for the other person to commit himself in the arena.

The younger player, with great natural skill, say Bobby Orr, will actually force the play. He'll push. Sometimes they're good enough to get away with it. Orr got hurt pretty badly the first couple of years he played. He had operations on both knees. Now he's a little smarter, a little more careful, and a little more cynical. [Laughs.]

Cynicism is a tool for survival. I began to grow up quickly. I became disillusioned with the game not being the pure thing it was earlier in my life. I began to see the exploitation of the players by the owners. You realize owners don't really care for you. You're a piece of property. They try to get as much out of you as they can. I remember once I had a torn shoulder. It was well in the process of healing. But I knew it wasn't right yet. They brought their doctor in. He said, "You can play." I played and ripped it completely. I was laid up. So I look at the owner. He shrugs his shoulders, walks away. He doesn't really hate me. He's impersonal.

Among players, while we're playing we're very close. Some of the best clubs I've played with have this intimacy—an intimacy modern man hardly ever achieves. We can see each other naked, emotionally, physically. We're plugged into each other, because we need each other. There have been times when I knew what the other guy was thinking without him ever talking to me. When that happens, we can do anything together.

It can't be just a job. It's not worth playing just for money. It's a way of life. When we were kids there was the release in playing, the sweetness in being able to move and control your body. This is what play is. Beating somebody is secondary. When I was a kid, to really *move* was my delight. I felt released because I could move around anybody. I was free.

That exists on the pro level, but there's the money aspect. You know they're making an awful lot of money off you. You know you're just a piece of property. When an older player's gone, it's not just his body. With modern training methods you can play a long time. But you just get fed up with the whole business. It becomes a job, just a shitty job. [Laughs.]

I'm not wild about living in hotels, coming in late at night, and having to spend time in a room waiting for a game. You've got a day to kill and the game's in back of your mind. It's hard to relax. It's hard to read a good book. I'll read an easy book or go to a movie to kill the time. I didn't mind killing time when I was younger, but I resent killing time now. [Laughs.] I don't want to *kill* time. I want to *do* something with my time.

Traveling in the big jets and going to and from hotels is very tough. We're in New York on a Wednesday, Philadelphia on a Thursday, Buffalo on a Saturday, Pittsburgh on a Sunday, and Detroit on a Tuesday. That's just a terrible way to live. [Laughs.] After the game on Sunday, I am tired—not only with my body, which is not a bad kind of tiredness, I'm tired emotionally, tired mentally. I'm not a very good companion after those games.

It's a lot tougher when things are going badly. It's more gritty and you don't feel very good about yourself. The whole object of a pro game is to win. That is what we sell. We sell it to a lot of people who don't win at all in their regular lives. They involve themselves with *their* team, a winning team. I'm not cynical about this. When we win, there's also a carry-over in us. Life is a little easier. But in the last two or three years fatigue has been there. I'm sucked out. But that's okay. I'd sooner live like that than be bored. If I get a decent sleep, a bit of food that's good and strong, I'm revived. I'm alive again.

The fans touch us, particularly when we've won. You can feel the pat of hands all over. On the back, on the shoulder, they want to shake your hand. When I'm feeling good about myself, I really respond to this. But if I don't feel so good, I play out the role. You have to act it out. It has nothing to do with pure joy. It has nothing to do with the feeling I had when I was a kid.

'Cause hell, nobody recognized me. I didn't have a role to play. Many of us are looking for some kind of role to play. The role of the professional athlete is one that I've learned to play very well. Laughing with strangers. It doesn't take much. It has its built-in moves, responses. There is status for the fans, but there's not a whole lot of status for me. [Laughs.] Not now. I know it doesn't mean very much. I shy away from it more and more. When I'm not feeling good and somebody comes up—"Hello, Eric"—I'm at times a bit cold and abrupt. I can see them withdrawing from me, hurt. They want to be plugged into something and they're not. They may make a slurring remark. I can't do anything about it.

I'm fighting the cynicism. What I'd like to do is find an alter-life and play a little more. I don't have another vocation. I have a feeling unless I find one, my life might be a big anticlimax. I could get a job, but I don't want a job. I never had a job in the sense that I had to earn a living just for the sake of earning a living. I may have to do that, but I sure hope I don't.

I have doubts about what I do. I'm not that sure of myself. It doesn't seem clear to me at times. I'm a man playing a boy's game. Is this a valid reason for making money? Then I turn around and think of a job. I've tried to be a stockbroker. I say to a guy, "I got a good stock, you want to buy it?' He says, "No." I say, "Okay." You don't want to buy, don't buy. [Laughs.] I'm not good at persuading people to buy things they don't want to buy. I'm just not interested in the power of money. I found that out. That's the way one keeps score—the amount of money you earned. I found myself bored with that.

I've worked on construction and I liked that best of all. [Laughs.] I'd been working as a stockbroker and I couldn't stand it any more. I got drunk one Friday night and while I was careening around town I ran into this guy I knew from the past. He said for the hell of it, "Why don't you come and work on the Hancock Building with me?" He was a super on the job. The next Monday I showed up. I stayed for a week. I was interested in seeing how a big building goes up—and working with my hands.

A stockbroker has more status. He surrounds himself with things of status. But the stockbroker comes to see me play, I don't go to see him be a stockbroker. [Laughs.]

The real status is what my peers think of me and what I think of myself. The players have careful self-doubts at times. We talk about our sagging egos. Are we really that famous? Are we really that good? We have terrible doubts. [Laughs.] Actors may have something of this. Did I do well? Am I worth this applause? Is pushing the puck around really that meaningful? [Laughs.] When I'm not pushing that puck well, how come the fans don't like me? [Laughs.] Then there's the reverse reaction—a real brashness. They're always rationalizing to each other. That's probably necessary. It's not a bad way to handle things when you have no control over them. Players who are really put together, who have few doubts, are usually much more in control. If you're recognized by your peers, you're all right.

I still like the physicality, the sensuality of life. I still like to use my body. But the things I like now are more soft. I don't want to beat people. I don't want to prove anything. I have a friend who used to play pro football, but who shares my philosophy. We get into the country that is stark and cold and harsh, but there's a great aesthetic feedback. It's soft and comforting and sweet. We come out of there with such enormous energy and so fit. We often go into town like a couple of fools and get mildly drunk and laugh a lot.

Being a physical man in the modern world is becoming obsolete. The machines have taken the place of that. We work in offices, we fight rules and corporations, but we hardly ever hit anybody. Not that hitting anybody is a solution. But to survive in the world at one time, one had to stand up and fight—fight the weather, fight the land, or fight the rocks. I think there is a real desire for man to do that. Today he has evolved into being more passive, conforming...

I think that is why the professional game, with its terrific physicality—men getting together on a cooperative basis—this is appealing to the middle-class man. He's the one who supports professional sports.

I think it's a reflection of the North American way of life. This is one of the ways you are somebody—you beat somebody. [Laughs.]

You're better than they are. Somebody has to be less than you in order for you to be somebody. I don't know if that's right any more. I don't have that drive any more. If I function hard, it's against a hard environment. That's preferable to knocking somebody down.

I come up against a hard young stud now, and he wants the puck very badly, I'm inclined to give it to him. [Laughs.] When you start thinking like that you're in trouble, as far as being a pro athlete is involved. But I don't want to be anybody any more in those terms. I've had some money, I've had some big fat times, I've been on the stage.

It's been a good life. Maybe I could have done better, have a better record or something like that. But I've really had very few regrets over the past twenty years. I can enjoy some of the arts that I had shut myself off from as a kid. Perhaps that is my only regret. The passion for the game was so all-consuming when I was a kid that I blocked myself from music. I cut myself off from a certain broadness of experience. Maybe one has to do that to fully explore what they want to do the most passionately.

I know a lot of pro athletes who have a capacity for a wider experience. But they wanted to become champions. They had to focus themselves on their one thing completely. His primary force when he becomes champion is his ego trip, his desire to excel, to be somebody special. To some degree, he must dehumanize himself. I look forward to a lower key way of living. But it must be physical. I'm sure I would die without it, become a drunk or something.

I still like to skate. One day last year on a cold, clear, crisp afternoon, I saw this huge sheet of ice in the street. Goddamn, if I didn't drive out there and put on my skates. I took off my camel-hair coat. I was just in a sort of jacket, on my skates. And I flew. Nobody was there. I was free as a bird. I was really happy. That goes back to when I was a kid. I'll do that until I die, I hope. Oh, I was free!

The wind was blowing from the north. With the wind behind you, you're in motion, you can wheel and dive and turn, you can lay yourself into impossible angles that you never could walking or running. You lay yourself at a forty-five degree angle, your elbows virtually touching the ice as you're in a turn. Incredible! It's beautiful! You're breaking the bounds of gravity. I have a feeling this is the innate desire of man.

[His eyes are glowing.] I haven't kept many photographs of myself, but I found one where I'm in full flight. I'm leaning into a turn. You pick up the centrifugal forces and you lay in it. For a few seconds, like a gyroscope, they support you. I'm in full flight and my head is turned. I'm concentrating on something and I'm grinning. That's the way I like to picture myself. I'm something else there. I'm on another level of existence, just being in pure motion. Going wherever I want to go, whenever I want to go. That's nice, you know. [Laughs softly.]

PHIL STALLINGS

He is a spot welder at the Ford assembly plant on the far South Side of Chicago. He is twenty-seven years old; recently married. He works the third shift: 3:30 P.M. to midnight.

I start the automobile, the first welds. From there it goes to another line, where the floor's put on, the roof, the trunk hood, the doors. Then it's put on a frame. There is hundreds of lines.

The welding gun's got a square handle, with a button on the top for high voltage and a button on the button for low. The first is to clamp the metal together. The second is to fuse it.

The gun hangs from a ceiling, over tables that ride on a track. It travels in a circle, oblong, like an egg. You stand on a cement platform, maybe six inches from the ground.

I stand in one spot, about two- or three-feet area, all night. The only time a person stops is when the line stops. We do about thirty-two jobs per car, per unit. Forty-eight units an hour, eight hours a day. Thirty-two times forty-eight times eight. Figure it out. That's how many times I push that button.

The noise, oh it's tremendous. You open your mouth and you're liable to get a mouthful of sparks. [Shows his arms] That's a burn, these are burns. You don't compete against the noise. You go to yell and at the same time you're straining to maneuver the gun to where you have to weld.

You got some guys that are uptight, and they're not sociable. It's too rough. You pretty much stay to yourself. You get involved with yourself. You dream, you think of things you've done. I drift back continuously to when I was a kid and what me and my brothers did. The things you love most are the things you drift back into.

Lots of times I worked from the time I started to the time of the break and I never realized I had even worked. When you dream, you reduce the chances of friction with the foreman or with the next guy.

It don't stop. It just goes and goes and goes. I bet there's men who have lived and died out there, never seen the end of that line. And they never will—because it's endless. It's like a serpent. It's just all body, no tail. It can do things to you…[Laughs.]

Repetition is such that if you were to think about the job itself, you'd slowly go out of your mind. You'd let your problems build up, you'd get to a point where you'd be at the fellow next to you—his throat. Every time the foreman came by and looked at you, you'd have something to say. You just strike out at anything you can. So if you involve yourself by yourself, you overcome this.

I don't like the pressure, the intimidation. How would you like to go up to someone and say, "I would like to go to the bathroom?" If the foreman doesn't like you, he'll make you hold it, just ignore you. Should I leave this job to go to the bathroom I risk being fired. The line moves all the time.

I work next to Jim Grayson and he's preoccupied. The guy on

my left, he's a Mexican, speaking Spanish, so it's pretty hard to understand him. You just avoid him. Brophy, he's a young fella, he's going to college. He works catty-corner from me. Him and I talk from time to time. If he ain't in the mood, I don't talk. If I ain't in the mood, he knows it.

Oh sure, there's tension here. It's not always obvious, but the whites stay with the whites and the coloreds stay with the coloreds. When you go into Ford, Ford says, "Can you work with other men?" This stops a lot of trouble, 'cause when you're working side by side with a guy, they can't afford to have guys fighting. When two men don't socialize, that means two guys are gonna do more work, know what I mean?

I don't understand how come more guys don't flip. Because you're nothing more than a machine when you hit this type of thing. They give better care to that machine than they will to you. They'll have more respect, give more attention to that machine. And you *know* this. Somehow you get the feeling that the machine is better than you are. [Laughs.]

You really begin to wonder. What price do they put on me? Look at the price they put on the machine. If that machine breaks down, there's somebody out there to fix it right away. If I break down, I'm just pushed over to the other side till another man takes my place. The only thing they have on their mind is to keep that line running.

I'll do the best I can. I believe in an eight-hour pay for an eight-hour day. But I will not try to outreach my limits. If I can't cut it, I just don't do it. I've been there three years and I keep my nose pretty clean. I never cussed anybody or anything like that. But I've had some real brushes with foremen.

What happened was my job was overloaded. I got cut and it got infected. I got blood poisoning. The drill broke. I took it to the foreman's desk. I says "Change this as soon as you can." We were running specials for XL hoods. I told him I wasn't a repair man.

That's how the conflict began. I says, "If you want, take me to the Green House." Which is a superintendent's office—disciplinary station. This is when he says, "Guys like you I'd like to see in the parking lot."

One foreman I know, he's about the youngest out here, he has this idea: I'm it and if you don't like it, you know what you can do. Anything this other foreman says, he usually overrides. Even in some cases, the foremen don't get along. They're pretty hard to live with, even with each other.

Oh yeah, the foreman's got somebody knuckling down on him, putting the screws to him. But a foreman is still free to go to the bathroom, go get a cup of coffee. He doesn't face the penalties. When I first went in there, I kind of envied foremen. Now, I wouldn't have a foreman's job. I wouldn't give 'em the time of the day.

When a man becomes a foreman, he has to forget about even being human, as far as feelings are concerned. You see a guy there bleeding to death. So what, buddy? That line's gotta keep goin'. I can't live like that. To me, if a man gets hurt, first thing you do is get him some attention.

About the blood poisoning. It came from the inside of a hood rubbin' against me. It caused quite a bit of pain. I went down to the medics. They said it was a boil. Got to my doctor that night. He said blood poisoning. Running fever and all this. Now I've smartened up.

They have a department of medics. It's basically first aid. There's no doctor on our shift, just two or three nurses, that's it. They've got a door with a sign on it that says Lab. Another door with a sign on it: Major Surgery. But my own personal opinion, I'm afraid of 'em. I'm afraid if I were to get hurt, I'd get nothin' but back talk. I got hit square in the chest one day with a bar from a rack and it cut me down this side. They didn't take x-rays or nothing. Sent me back on the job. I missed three and a half days two weeks ago. I had bronchitis. They told me I was all right. I didn't have a fever. I went home and my doctor told me I couldn't go back to work for two weeks. I really needed the money, so I had to go back the next day. I woke up still sick, so I took off the rest of the week.

I pulled a muscle on my neck, straining. This gun, when you grab this thing from the ceiling, cable, weight, I mean you're pulling everything. Your neck, your shoulders, and your back. I'm very surprised more accidents don't happen. You have to lean over, at the same time holding down the gun. This whole edge here is sharp. I go through a shirt every two weeks, it just goes right through. My coveralls catch on fire. I've had gloves catch on fire. [Indicates arms.] See them little holes? That's what sparks do. I've got burns across here from last night.

I know I could find better places to work. But where could I get the money I'm making? Let's face it, $4.32 an hour. That's real good money now. Funny thing is, I don't mind working at body construction. To a great degree, I enjoy it. I love using my hands—more than I do my mind. I love to be able to put things together and see something in the long run. I'll be the first to admit I've got the easiest job on the line. But I'm against this thing where I'm being held back. I'll work like a dog until I get what I want. The job I really want is utility.

It's where I can stand and say I can do any job in this department, and nobody has to worry about me. As it is now, out of say, sixty jobs, I can do almost half of 'em. I want to get away from standing in one spot. Utility can do a different job every day. Instead of working right there for eight hours I could work over there for eight, I could work the other place for eight. Every day it would change. I would be around more people. I go out on my lunch break and work on the fork truck for a half-hour—to get the experience. As soon as I got it down pretty good, the foreman in charge says he'll take me. I don't want the other guys to see me. When I hit that fork lift, you just stop your thinking and you concentrate. Something right there in front of you, not in the past, not in the future. This is real healthy.

I don't eat lunch at work. I may grab a candy bar, that's enough. I wouldn't be able to hold it down. The tension your body is put under by the speed of the line…When you hit them brakes, you just can't stop. There's a certain momentum that carries you forward. I could hold the food, but it wouldn't set right.

Proud of my work? How can I feel pride in a job where I call a foreman's attention to a mistake, a bad piece of equipment, and he'll ignore it. Pretty soon you get the idea they don't care. You keep doing this and finally you're titled a troublemaker. So you just go about your work. You *have* to have pride. So you throw it off to something else. And that's my stamp collection.

I'd break both my legs to get into social work. I see all over so many kids really gettin' a raw deal. I think I'd go into juvenile. I tell kids on the line, "Man, go out there and get that college." Because it's too late for me now.

When you go into Ford, first thing they try to do is break your spirit. I seen them bring a tall guy where they needed a short guy. I seen them bring a short guy where you have to stand on two guys' backs to do something. Last night, they brought a fifty-eight-year-old man to do the job I was on. That man's my father's age. I know damn well my father couldn't do it. To me, this is humanely wrong. A job should be a job, not a death sentence.

The younger worker, when he gets uptight, he talks back. But you take an old fellow, he's got a year, two years, maybe three years to go. If it was me, I wouldn't say a word, I wouldn't care what they did. 'Cause, baby, for another two years I can stick it out. I can't blame this man. I respect him because he had enough will power to stick it out for thirty years.

It's gonna change. There's a trend. We're getting younger and younger men. We got this new Thirty and Out. Thirty years seniority and out. The whole idea is to give a man more time, more time to slow down and live. While he's still in his fifties, he can settle down in a camper and go out and fish. I've sat down and thought about it. I've got twenty-seven years to go. [Laughs.] That's why I don't go around causin' trouble or lookin' for a cause.

The only time I get involved is when it affects me or it affects a man on the line in a condition that could be me. I don't believe in lost causes, but when it all happened…[He pauses, appears bewildered.]

The foreman was riding the guy. The guy either told him to go away or pushed him, grabbed him…You can't blame the guy—Jim Grayson. I don't want nobody stickin' their finger in my face. I'd've probably hit him beside the head. The whole thing was: Damn it, it's about time we took a stand. Let's stick up for the guy. We stopped the line. [He pauses, grins.] Ford lost about twenty units. I'd figure about five grand a unit—whattaya got? [Laughs.]

I said, "Let's all go home." When the line's down like that, you can go up to one man and say, "You gonna work?" If he says no, they can fire him. See what I mean? But if nobody was there, who the hell were they gonna walk up to and say, "Are you gonna work?" Man, there woulda been nobody there! If it were up to me, we'd gone home.

Jim Grayson, the guy I work next to, he's colored. Absolutely. That's the first time I've seen unity on that line. Now it's happened once, it'll happen again. Because everybody just sat down. Believe you me. [Laughs.] It stopped at eight and it didn't start till twenty after eight. Everybody and his brother were down there. It was really nice to see, it really was.

TOM PATRICK

He has been a city fireman for two years. During the preceding four years he had been a member of the city's police force. He is thirty-two, married. "It's terrific for a guy that just got out of high school with a general diploma. I don't even know English. My wife is Spanish, she knows syllables, verbs, where to put the period…I wish I was a lawyer. Shit, I wish I was a doctor. But I just didn't have it. You gotta have the smarts.

There was seven of us. Three brothers, myself and my sister, mother and father. It was a railroad flat. Me and my brother used to sleep in bunk beds until we were twenty-seven years old. And they're supposed to be for kids, right?

He owns his own house and can't get over the wonder of it, mortgage or not. A back yard, "it's like a piece of country back there. It smells like Jersey. We have barbecues, drink beer, the neighbors are good.

Twenty years ago it was all Irish, Italian, Polish. I went in the army in '62 and everybody was moving out to Long Island. There's a lot of Puerto Ricans now. They say the spics are movin' in, the black are movin' in. They're good people. They don't bother me and I don't bother them. I think I'm worse than them. Sometimes I come home four in the morning, piss in the street. I think they might sign a petition to get me out.

The guys in this thing were prejudiced. I'm probably prejudiced too. It's a very conservative neighborhood. A lot of the cops are here. Up to the fifties, these guys were my heroes, these guys in the bar. You hear this guy was in the Second World War…I was a kid and a lot of these guys are dead now. Forty-eight, fifty years old, they died young, from drinking and shit. You just grow up into this prejudice—guy's a spic, a nigger. When I was in the army I didn't think I was prejudiced, until the colored guy told me to clean the floor five, six times, and I was calling him nigger. You express yourself, get the frustration out.

One o'clock in the morning, in August, we had a block party. They were dancing on the fire escapes. People were drinking. We had three, four hundred people there. We had a barricade up on the corner and the cops never came around. The fuckin' cops never came around. We don't need 'em. I think when you see a cop everybody gets tense. Instead of concentrating on the music and drinkin' beer, you keep lookin' over your shoulder: Where's the cop? You know.

I got out of the army in '64. I took the test for transit police, housing police, and city police. It's the same test. It was in March '66 when I got called. I got called for the housing police. For the first six months you just bounce around different housing projects.

I was engaged to this other girl and her father was mad that I didn't take the city police, because I could make more money on the side. He said I was a dope. He said, "What are you gonna get in the housing projects? The people there don't pay you off." Because they were poor people. I said, "The money they give me as a cop is good enough." Most of the people around here don't go on to be doctors or lawyers. The thing to get is a city job, because it's security.

I worked in Harlem and East Harlem for three years. There was ten, eleven cops and they were all black guys. I was the only white cop. When they saw me come into the office they started laughin'. "What the fuck are they sendin' you here for? You're fuckin' dead." They told me to get a helmet and hide on the roof.

This one project, there were five percenters. That's a hate gang. They believed that seventy percent of the black population are Uncle Toms, twenty-five percent are alcoholics, and five percent are the elite. These fuckin' guys'll kill ya in a minute.

This project was twenty-five buildings, thirteen stories each. Covered maybe twenty acres. It was like a city. I remember the first night I got there, July fourth. It was 105 degrees out. I had come in for the midnight to eight tour. I had an uncle that was a regular city cop. He called me up the night before and he said they expected a riot in this project. He said the cops had helicopters going around above the people and a lot of cops in plain clothes and cars. He was worried about me: "Be careful."

Working

This one black guy said, "You stay with me." That night we went on the roof and we're lookin' down and people are walkin' around and drinkin' on the benches. This colored guy was drinkin' and I went down there seven in the morning. I told him to move. "Somebody's gonna rob you." He said, "Man, I ain't got a penny on me. The most they could do is give me somethin'." And he went back to sleep.

The thing is you gotta like people. If you like people, you have a good time with 'em. But if you have the attitude that people are the cause of what's wrong with this country, they're gonna fuckin' get you upset and you're gonna start to hate 'em, and when you hate, you get a shitty feeling in your stomach that can destroy you, right?

When I went to the housing project, I said, There's a lot of people around here and you meet 'em and the older people want you to come in and have a beer with 'em. I used to go to some great parties. I'd go up there nine o'clock at night and I'm in uniform with my gun on and you'd be in the kitchen, drinking Scotch, rye, beer, talking to these beautiful Spanish girls. These are people, right? Poor people. My family's poor. They talk about the same thing and the kids come over to me and they'd pet you or they'd touch the gun.

I made an arrest. Some kid came over and told me a guy across the street had robbed his camera. So I ran over and grabbed the guy. It was petty larceny. The colored cop said I broke my cherry. So he took me to the basement that night and they had a party. A portable bar, record player, girls come down, they were dancin'.

I couldn't wait to go to work, because I felt at ease with these people. Sometimes I'd look in the mirror and I'd see this hat and I couldn't believe it was me in this uniform. Somebody'd say, "Officer, officer." I'd have to think, Oh yeah, that's me. I wouldn't really know I was a cop. To me, it was standin' on the corner in my own neighborhood. Poor. I'd see drunks that are like my father. A black drunk with a long beard and his eyes…He'd bring back memories of my father. I'd be able to talk to the kids. They'd be on the roof, fuckin', and I'd say, "I'll give you ten minutes." It took me two minutes to come. "Ten minutes is enough for you right?"

One project I worked out of I made nineteen arrests in one year, which was tops. I didn't go out lookin' to make 'em, I ran into shit. If you run into a person that's robbin' another person, man, that's wrong! My mind was easy. I just figured if a guy was drunk or a guy's makin' out with a girl, it shouldn't be a crime. I was with this one cop, he used to sneak up on cars and look in and see people gettin' laid or blow jobs. I used to be embarrassed. I don't like that shit.

I made all these arrests and they transferred me out. I didn't want to leave, 'cause I knew the people and I thought I could be an asset. It was Peurto Rican, black, I had like a rapport. Jesus Christ, I loved it. They're sending me to Harlem because I'm so good. Bullshit! That jerked me off. I wanted East Harlem because you had every thing there. You had Italians, still. I used to go up the block and drink beer. I used to listen to Spanish music. And the girls are beautiful. Jesus! Unbelievable! Spanish girls. My wife's from Colombia. She's beautiful. I love it when her hair's down. I think that's where I got the idea of marrying a Spanish girl. In East Harlem.

I wasn't against Harlem, but there was no people. It was a new project. I was just there to watch the Frigidaires. I was a watchman. Sewers open, the ground wasn't fixed, no grass, holes. We used to stand in lobbies of an empty building. I want to be where people are. So I got pissed off and put a transfer in. After six months people started moving in—and I liked it. But they transferred me to Canarsie. Middle-income white. And all these bullshit complaints. "Somebody's on my grass." "I hear a noise in the elevator." Up in Harlem they'll complain maybe they saw a dead guy in the elevator.

I never felt my life threatened. I never felt like I had to look over my shoulder. I was the only white cop in that project. The kids'd be playin', come over and talk to me. Beautiful. But sometimes they just hate you. I'm in uniform and they just go around and say, "You motherfucker," and stuff like that. I can't say, "Wait, just get to know me, I'm not that bad." You haven't got time. If you start explainin', it's a sign of weakness. Most people, if you try to be nice, they're nice. But you get some of these guys that got hurt, they really got fucked, they got arrested for not doing anything.

I was with a cop who arrested a guy for starin' at him! Starin' at him! The cop I was with, Vince, he had a baby face and the guy on the bus stop kept lookin' at him because this cop never shaved. He said, "Motherfucker, what're you lookin' at?" The guy said, "I'm just lookin'. I said, "The guy probably thinks you're not a cop 'cause you got a pretty face." Vince puts the night stick under the guy's chin. Naturally when a guy puts a night stick under your chin, you push it away. As soon as you do that, you got an assault. He arrested the guy. The guy was waitin' for a bus!

With this same Vince, another kid came around, a Puerto Rican seventeen years old. They all knew me. He says, "Hi, baby," and he slapped my hand like that. "How you doin', man?" Vince said, What're ya lettin' the kid talk to you like that for?" I said, "This is the way they talk, this is their language. They ain't meanin' to be offensive." He says, "Hey fucko, come over here." He grabbed him by the shirt. He said, "You fucker, talk mister, sir, to this cop." He flung the kid down the ramp. We had a little police room. His girl started crying. I went down after this Vince, I said, "What're you doin'? You lock that fuckin' kid up, I'm against you. That fuckin' kid's a good friend of mine, you're fuckin' wrong." He said, "I'm not gonna lock him up, I'm just gonna scare him. You gotta teach people. You gotta keep 'em down."

Just about that time twenty kids start poundin' on the door. The kid's brother was there and his friends. We're gonna get a riot.

And the kid didn't do anything. He was just walkin' with his girl.

I was in the riots in '67 in Harlem. I saw a gang of kids throwin' rocks and they hit this policeman. The cops inside the car couldn't see where the rocks was comin' from. When they all piled out, the kids was gone. They thought the rocks was comin' from the roof. So these guys come out shootin' to the blues. One big white guy got out, he says, "Come out, you motherfuckin' black bastard." I was with five black cops and one said to me, "Get that fucker away from me or I'll kill him."

City cops, they got clubs, they think they're the elite. Housing is H.A.—they call us ha-ha cops. Transit cops are called cave cops because they're in the subway. These are little ribs they give. Who's better, who's New York's Finest?...I was in the park three years ago with a transit cop. We're with these two nice lookin' girls—I was still single. It's about one o'clock in the morning. We had a couple of six-packs and a pizza pie. We're tryin' to make out, right? Cops pull up, city cops, and they shine the light on us. So my friend shows the cop his badge. The cop says, "That's more reason you shouldnt' be here. You're fuckin' on the job, just get the fuck outa the park." 'Cause he was a transit cop they gave him a hard time. My friend was goin' after this cop and this cop was goin' after him. I grabbed him and the driver in the police car grabbed his buddy and they were yelling, "Keep outa the park." And the other guy's yellin', "Don't come down in the subways." I coulda turned around and said, "Don't ever come in the housing projects." It was stupid shit, right? A guy'll pull out a gun and get killed.

You can't laugh at a gun. I had a gun put to my head in a bar, over the Pueblo incident. A cop. I got a load on and argue with these guys about shit in Vietnam. I said, "Saigon's got a million-dollar police station and my brother's got a station a hundred years old. Where's the money come from? The cops and firemen are paying taxes and they're not fixin' up their stations." This guy, Jim, who's a city cop for twenty-four years, is everything you want a cop to be. When I was eighteen he was thirty-eight, he was a supercop. But the hate just fucked him up, and the war.

I was in the bar and Jim had his load on, too. He's got personal problems, he's married twice, divorced. He said, "We should invade Korea, bomb it." I said, "You're ready to drop a bomb on a country with civilians." He said, "Ah, you fuckin' commie." So I turn my back. I feel this thing on my temple, he had a gun to my head. Two guys next to me dived for the ground. With my left hand I came towards his fuckin' left wrist. The gun went to the ground and I grabbed him in a headlock. Three other cops in civilian clothes broke it up. You gotta watch that gun.

I coulda been like Jim or Vince. I started seein' the problems of people. Ten people in an apartment and there's no place to go except sit out on the street drinkin' beer. I guess I got this feeling from my father.

My father's a great man. I see what he went through and the shit and hard times. I don't see how he lived through it. I used to lay awake when I was drinkin' and listen to him talk all right. And I used to cry. He talked about the shittin' war, all the money goin' for war. And the workers' sons are the ones that fight these wars, right? And people that got nothin' to eat…I tell ya, if I didn't have an income comin' in…These kids hangin' around here, Irish kids, Italian kids, twenty-five years old, alcoholics, winos. One guy died of exposure. He went out with my kid sister and he's dead now.

I was in a four-man detail in Harlem for about six months, just before my transfer to Canarsie. It's four thirty-story buildings, and the people'd be movin' in there. Every day I have a list of names of people that are movin' in. One black family came with eight kids. They had seven rooms on the twentieth floor. The mother, this big, fat woman, asked could I show her the apartment. The kids just wanted to see it. Beautiful painting, real clean. The kids started crying, little kids. I could cry when I think of it. They ran into the bedrooms and they laid on the floor. They said, "This is mine! this is mine!" The kids said, "Look at the bedroom, it's clean." These little black kids with sneakers and holes in their pants, crying. It was empty, but they wouldn't leave that room. The woman asked me could they stay over night. Their furniture was gettin' delivered the next day. You get people a job or decent housing, you won't have no trouble.

What led me to be a cop? I'm not that smart to be a lawyer. I failed in Spanish. I'm lucky I can talk English. A good day in school for me was when the teacher didn't call on me. I used to sit in the back of the room and slide down into the seat so she didn't call on me.

When I got pimples on my face, that made it worse. I was shy with girls. One thing I told my father, "I'm gonna kill myself, I got pimples." He said—I'll never forget it—"The world's bigger than the pimples on your face." At that time I didn't think it was. I used to pile Noxzema on my face and I was with a girl makin' out and she'd say, "I smell Noxzema." It used to be in my hair, up my nose...

I liked mathematics. I could add like a bastard. I started gettin' to algebra, but then I got lost. I didn't want to raise my hand because I had this skin problem. It's crazy, right? I sunk down and the teacher never called on me for two years.

The more arrests you make, they got the assumption you're a better cop, which is not right. They put pressure on me to make arrests. You gotta get out and you gotta shanghai people because you got the sergeant on your back. It comes down to either you or the next guy. You got a family and you got everybody fuckin' everybody...It's crazy, know what I mean?"

The project I worked in in East Harlem, you grab a kid doin' wrong. "Come here, you fuck." That's it. He don't argue. But the middle-income, the kid'll lie to you. He won't tell you his right name. His name is a fireman or a cop. He tells his son, "Don't fuckin' give any information." They know the law better.

Like the last project I was on, white middle-income. They were all kids with long hair, right? This cop, he'd be seein' me talkin' to the kids, playing guitars. I'd be talkin' about records. He'd call me, "Hey, what're ya talkin' to those fags?" I'd say, "They're all right." One of the kids with long hair, his father's a cop. He said, "Aw fuck that, they're all commies."

A couple of times the kids burned me. I saw five kids smokin' pot. They're passin' around the pipe. I grabbed them and threw the shit on the ground. I didn't want to arrest them. I let 'em all go. The next day one of the kids told this cop. "That Tommy's a good cop, he let us go." It got back to the sergeant and he says, "You're gonna be hung." So a few times I got charges brought up on me.

I didn't want to be a cop. Money comes into it. I was twenty-six and I worked in the post office and I wasn't makin' money, $2.18 an hour. I was young and I wanted to go out with the girls, and I wanted to go down to the Jersey shore. I wanted to buy a car, I just got out of the army. That's why I took it.

When I became a cop I thought I was going against my father. Cops are tools of the shittin' Rockefeller. Cops can't understand when they built a new office building in Harlem the people in that community want a hospital or a school. Rockefeller built that office building, right? Built by white construction workers. And these people demonstrate. Suppose they built in this neighborhood a state office building and black people built it and black people work in it. The cops go in there and break up the demonstrations and who gets it? The cops. Rockefeller's a million miles away. Cops are working guys, they don't understand.

You got cops that are fuckin' great cops, they're great people. Your supercops. The man in the front line, the patrolman, they do all the work. The sergeants aren't in with the people. They'd be doin' paper work. That's what got me mad.

I know a lot of cops that even liked people more than me. And some were fucks. You got black cops in the projects who were harder on their own people than a white guy. They think the poor people are holdin' them back. But a lot of them are supercops. Maybe if it was the other way around, if the whites were down and the blacks were top dog, you'd get better white cops.

Know why I switched to fireman? I liked people, but sometimes I'd feel hate comin' into me. I hated it, to get me like that. I caught these three guys drinkin' wine, three young Spanish guys. I said, "Fellas, if you're gonna drink, do it in some apartment." 'Cause they were spillin' the wine and they'd piss right in front of the house, in the lobby. I came back in a half-hour and they had another bottle out. They were pissin' around. I'm sayin' to myself, I'm tryin' to be nice. I walked over. There was two guys facin' me and one guy had his back to me. So he says, "What the fuck's the mick breakin' our balls for?" He's callin' me a mick. He's changing roles, you know? He's acting like they say a cop does. So I said, "You fuckin' spic." So I took the night stick and I swung it hard to hit him in the head. He ducked and it hit the pillar. He turned white and they all took off. It scared me that I could get this hatred so fast. I was fuckin' shakin'.

A few times I pulled my gun on guys. One time I went to the roof of this project and there's this big black guy about six seven on top of the stairs. He had his back to me, I said. "Hey fella, turn around." He said, "Yeah, wait a minute, man." His elbows were movin' around his belt. I was half-way up. I said "Turn around, put your hands up against the wall." He said, "Yeah, yeah, wait a minute." It dawned on me he had a gun caught in his belt and he was tryin' to take it out. I said, "Holy shit." So I took my gun out and said, "You fucker, I'm gonna shoot." He threw his hands against the wall. He had his dick out and he was tryin' to zip up his fly, and there was a girl standin' in the corner, which I couldn't see. So here was a guy gettin' a hand job and maybe a lot of guys might have killed him. I said, "Holy shit, I coulda killed ya." He started shaking and my gun in my hand was shaking like a bastard. I said—

I musta been cryin'—I said, "Just get the hell outa here, don't..."

I took the fire department test in '68 and got called in '70. I always wanted to be a fireman. My other brother was a fireman eleven years. He had a fire and the floor gave way, he was tellin' me the story. He thought it was just a one-floor drop. But the guys grabbed him by the arms. They said, "If you go, we all go." He couldn't believe this kind of comradeship. They pulled him out. He went down to get his helmet and it was two floors down. He really woulda got busted up.

I like everybody workin' together. You chip in for a meal together. One guy goes to the store, one guy cooks, one guy washes the dishes. A common goal. We got a lieutenant there, he says the fire department is the closest thing to socialism there is.

The officer is the first one into the fire. When you get to captain or lieutenant, you get more work not less. That's why I look up to these guys. We go to a fire, the lieutenant is the first one in. If he leaves, he takes you out. One lieutenant I know got heart trouble. When he takes a beatin' at a fire he should go down to the hospital and get oxygen or go on sick. He don't want to go on sick. I used to go into a fire, it was dark and I'd feel a leg and I'd look up and see the lieutenant standing there in the fire and smoke takin' beatings.

When I was in the army I didn't respect the officers, because the men did all the work. That goes for the police department, too. Cops get killed. You never see a lieutenant get shot. Ten battalion chiefs got killed in fires in the last ten years in the city. The last three guys in the fire department were lieutenants that got killed. 'Cause they're the first ones in there. I respect that. I want to respect an officer. I want to see somebody higher up that I can follow.

You go to some firehouses, these fuckin' guys are supermen. I'm not a superman, I want to live. These guys are not gonna live. Every day orders come down, guys are dyin', retirement. I don't think these guys get their pensions too long. I never heard a fire-man livin' to sixty-five.

When you get smoke in your lungs, these guys are spittin' out this shit for two days. A fireman's life is nine years shorter than the average workingman because of the beating they take on their lungs and their heart. More hazardous than a coal miner. The guy don't think nothing's wrong with him. You don't think until you get an x-ray and your name's on it. We got this lieutenant and when he takes a beating he can't go to a hospital because they'll find some-thing wrong with him. He was trapped in a room and he jumped out of the second-story window. He broke both his ankles, ran back into the building, and he collapsed.

There's more firemen get killed than cops, five to one. Yet there's only one-third of the amount of men on the job. We get the same pay as policemen. These politicians start to put a split between the departments. I'd like to take some of these politicians right into the fuckin' fire and put their head in the smoke and hold it there. They wouldn't believe it. They don't give a shit for the people. Just because they wave the flag they think they're the greatest.

The first fire I went to was a ship fire. I jumped off the engine, my legs got weak. I nearly fell to the ground, shakin', right? It was the first and only time I got nerves. But we have to go in there. It's thrilling and its scary. Like three o'clock in the morning. I was in the ladder company, it's one of the busiest in the city, like six thou-sand runs a year.* The sky is lit up with an orange. You get back to the firehouse, you're up there, talkin', talkin' about it.

I was in a fire one night, we had all-hands. An all-hands is you

* "You go on false alarms, especially two or three in the afternoon, kids comin' home from school. And four in the morning when the bars are closed. Drunks. Sometimes I get mad. It's ten, eleven at night and you see ten, twenty teenagers on the corner and there's a false alarm on that corner, you know one of 'em pulled it. The kids say, 'What's the matter, man? What're ya doin' here?' and they laugh. You wanna say, 'You stupid fuck, you might have a fire in your house and it could be your mother.' "

➔ 372 ⬅

got a workin' fire and you're the first in there, and the first guy in there is gonna take the worst beatin'. You got the nozzle, the hose, you're takin' a beating. If another company comes up behind you, you don't give up that nozzle. It's pride. To put out the fire. We go over this with oxygen and tell the guy, "Get out, get oxygen." They won't leave. I think guys want to be heroes. You can't be a hero on Wall Street.

There's guys with black shit comin' out of their ears. You got smoke in your hair. You take a shower, you put water on your hair, and you can still smell the smoke. It never leaves you. You're coughin' up this black shit. But you go back and you have coffee, maybe a couple of beers, you're psyched up.

You get a fire at two, three in the morning. The lights go on, you get up. I yelled, "Jesus, whatsa matter?" It dawned on me: Where else could we be goin'? All the lights goin' on and it's dark. It's fuckin' exciting. Guys are tellin', "Come on, we go. First Due." That means you gotta be the first engine company there. You really gotta move. It's a pride. You gotta show you're the best. But what they're fightin' over is good. What they're fightin' over is savin' lives.

You go in there and it's dark. All of a sudden smoke's pourin' outa the goddamn building. It's really fast. Everybody's got their assignments. A guy hooks up a hydrant. A guy on the nozzle, I'm on the nozzle. A guy's up to back me up. A guy's puttin' a Scott Air Pack on. It's a breathing apparatus. It lasts twenty minutes.

Two weeks ago we pulled up to this housing project. On the eighth floor the flames were leaping out the window. We jumped out, your fuckin' heart jumps. We ran into the elevator. Four of us, we rolled up the hose, each guy had fifty feet. We got off on the seventh floor, the floor below the fire. We got on the staircase and hook into the standpipe. The guys were screamin' for water and smoke was backin' up. You're supposed to have a wheel to turn on the water and the wheel was missin'! Someone stole it in the project.

You get these junkies, they steal brass, anything. They steal the shittin' life. A guy with a truck company came with a claw tool and the water came shootin' out.

They started yellin' for a Scott. It weighs about thirty pounds, got the face mask and cylinder. I couldn't get the damn thing tight. There's three straps, I tied one. They need me upstairs. They push you into the room. [Laughs.] This is it. One guy's layin' on the floor and I'm crawlin', feeling along the hose. The second company comes in with Scotts on. One guys got his face piece knocked to the side, so he's gotta get out because the smoke is gettin' him. The other guy yells, "Give me the nozzle." It started whippin' around, fifty, sixty pounds of pressure. Knocked my helmet off. I grabbed the nozzle. I looked up and saw this orange glow. I start hittin' it. The damn thing wouldn't go out. It was a fuckin' light bulb. [Laughs.] A bulb in the bathroom.

I felt this tremendous heat to my left. I turn around and this whole fuckin' room was orange, yellow. You can't see clear through the plastic face piece. You can just see orange and feel the heat. So I open up with this shittin' nozzle to bank back the smoke. The guys come in and ventilated, knocked out the windows. A seven-room apartment, with six beds and a crib. That's how many kids were living there. Nobody was hurt, they all got out.

There was a lot of smoke. When you have two minutes left on the Scott, a bell starts ringin'. It means get out, you got no oxygen. The thing I don't like about it, with the piece on your face, you feel confined. But as I went to more fires, I loved the thing because I know that thing's life. Ninety percent of the people die from smoke inhalation, not from burns.

You got oxygen, it's beautiful, but you can't see. It's a shitty feeling when you can't see. Sometimes a Scott's bad because it gives you a false sense of security. You go into a room where you're not supposed to be. You'd be walkin' into a pizzeria oven and you wouldn't know it. You can't see, you feel your way with the hose.

You straddle the hose as you get out. You gotta talk to yourself. Your mind's actually talkin'. I'm sayin' things like: It's beautiful, I can breathe, the fire's over.

In 1958 there was a fire across the street from where I live. It was about one o'clock in the morning. There's flames on the second floor. I ran up the stairs and grabbed this little girl. She was burnt on the arm. I ran down the street and yelled to the firemen, "I got a girl here got burnt." They went right past me. I hated the bastards. Now I understand. You gotta put the fire out. There's more life up there you gotta save. This girl's outside…It's real…

When you're with the police, it wasn't real. I heard guys makin' arrests, they found a gun in the apartment. In the paper they say the guy fought with the guy over the gun. When you know the truth, the story's bullshit. But in the fire department there's no bullshit. You gotta get into that fire—to be able to save some-body's life.

About two years ago a young girl ran to the firehouse. She's yellin' that her father had a heart attack. The guy was layin' in the kitchen, right? He pissed in his pants. That's a sign of death. The fella was layin' there with his eyes open. Angie pushes the guy three times in the chest, 'cause you gotta shock his heart. The son was standin' in the room, just starin' down. I got down on his mouth. You keep goin' and goin' and the guy threw up. You clean out his mouth. I was on a few minutes and then Ed Corrigan jumped on the guy's mouth. The captain bent down and said, "The guy's dead. Keep goin' for the family. We took over for ten minutes, but it was a dead man. The son looked down at me and I looked up. He said, "Man, you tried everything. You tried." You know what I mean? I was proud of myself. I would get on a stranger, on his mouth. It's a great feeling.

We had this fire down the block. A Puerto Rican social club. The captain, the lieutenant, and the other firemen took the ladder up and saved two people. But downstairs there was a guy tryin' to get out the door. They had bolts on the door. He was burnt dead. Know what the lieutenant said? "We lost a guy, we lost a guy." I said "You saved two people. How would you know at six in the morning a guy's in the social club sleeping on a pool table?" He said, "Yeah, but we lost a guy." And the lieutenant's a conservative guy.

You get guys that talk about niggers, spics, and they're the first guys into the fire to save 'em. Of course we got guys with long hair and beards. One guy's an artist. His brother got killed in Vietnam, that's why he's against the war. And these guys are all super firemen. It's you that takes the beating and you won't give up. Everybody dies…

My wife sees television, guys get killed. She tells me, "Be careful." Sometimes she'll call up the firehouse. I tell her we had a bad job, sometimes I don't…They got a saying in the firehouse. "Tonight could be the night." But nobody thinks of dying. You can't take it seriously, because you'd get sick. We had some fires, I said, "We're not gettin' out of this." Like I say, everybody dies.

A lotta guys wanna be firemen. It's like kids. Guys forty years old are kids. They try to be a hard guy. There's no big thing when you leave boyhood for manhood. It seems like I talked the same at fifteen as I talk now. Everybody's still a kid. They just lose their hair or they don't fuck that much.

When I was a kid I was scared of heights. In the fire department you gotta go up a five-story building with a rope around you. You gotta jump off a building. You know the rope can hold sixteen hundred pounds. As long as you got confidence in your body and you know the guy's holding you, you got nothing to be scared of. I think you perform with people lookin' at you. You're in the limelight. You're out there with the people and kids. Kids wave at you. When I was a kid we waved at firemen. It's like a place in the sun.

Last month there was a second alarm. I was off duty. I ran over there. I'm a bystander. I see these firemen on the roof, with the smoke pouring out around them, and the flames, and they go in. It fascinated me. Jesus Christ, that's what *I* do! I was fascinated by the people's faces. You could see the pride that they were seein'. The fuckin' world's so fucked up, the country's fucked up. But the firemen, you actually see them produce. You see them put out a fire. You see them come out with babies in their hands. You see them give mouth-to-mouth when a guy's dying. You can't get around that shit. That's real. To me, that's what I want to be.

I worked in a bank. You know, it's just paper. It's not real. Nine to five and it's shit. You're lookin' at numbers. But I can look back and say, "I helped put out a fire. I helped save somebody." It shows something I did on this earth.

Part III

The Divide

The Great Divide
(1988)

INTRODUCTION

In the making of this book (and even while considering it), I was burdened with doubts far more disturbing than any I had ever experienced earlier. In undertaking this self-assigned and at times perverse task, I was aware of an attribute lacking in the 1980s that had been throbbingly present in the earlier decades, even in the silent 1950s: memory.

It isn't that the gift of remembering was any richer then than it is now. I encountered in survivors of the Great Depression and World War Two egregious lapses, blockages, and forgetteries. Nonetheless, they remembered core truths about themselves and the world around them. They remembered enough of their yesterdays to tell us what it was like to live in those times. Today, amnesia is much easier to come by.

As technology has become more hyperactive, we, the people have become more laid-back; as the deposits in its memory banks have become more fat, the deposits in man's memory bank have become more lean. Like Harold Pinter's servant, the machine has assumed the responsibilities that were once the master's. The latter has become the shell of a once thoughtful, though indolent, being. It is the Law of Diminishing Enlightenment at work.

Ironically enough, Jacob Bronowski observed, the average person today knows far more facts about the world than Isaac Newton ever did, though considerably less truth. Certainly we know more facts, overwhelmingly trivial though they be, than any of our antecedents. But as for knowing the truth about ourselves and others...

A TV wunderkind explains: "In the last ten years we've shifted to faster communication. We depend on these little bursts, these little sound bites. All good politicians as well as good advertisers lay out their programs in something that will play in ten to twelve seconds on the nightly news." In an old burlesque skit, the second banana, a Dutch comic in baggy pants, challenges the first: "Qvick, vat's your philosophy of life in fife seconds?" The bald-heads, potbellies, and pimply faces in the audience (I was one) roar at the randy though succinct riposte. Today's TV anchorperson asks the same thing of the expert (fifteen seconds is the usual allotment). It is deadly solemn in the asking, equally so in the response, and duly acknowledged by the audience. Nobody's laughing.

Still, in my prowlings and stalkings during these past three years, I've come across individuals, surprising in number though diffident in demeanor, who are challenging the doctrine of the official idea.

Repeated often enough and authoritatively enough, on televised Sunday mornings, by pundits of familiar face and equally familiar cabinet members and the even more familiar elder statesman, Doctor K. (who evokes startling memories of the Dutch comic), the announced idea becomes official. Yet something unofficial is happening "out there."

Consider the market research man, the up-and-coming father, the archetypal Middle American. He had been foreman of a jury that acquitted four odd birds (including a Catholic nun) who had in the spirit of Isaiah committed an act of civil disobedience. He, a fervent believer in law and order, experienced something of a small epiphany.

> "We are quiet people," he said, "quiet in our disturbance. But once confronted with facts, they're really hard to let go of. You start asking yourself, What can I begin to do?
>
> "We see on the news today something happened. A week later, something else is presented just as important. It's got the same kind

of emphasis in the speaker's voice. All of a sudden, last week is gone behind us. A year ago is even further gone. How we blow up things that aren't important and never talk about things that are important."

In dealing with time past, whether it concerns the Great Depression, its lessons apparently forgotten, or World War Two, often misremembered,* the storyteller's memory is tapped and recollections pour forth as through a ruptured floodgate.

In dealing with time present, memory is absent, stunningly so, among the young. "I am struck by the basic absence of historical memory in this year's—or any year's—college freshmen. These young students are not the children but rather the grandchildren of the atomic age, born almost a quarter of a century after Hiroshima and Nagasaki. They have never known a time when nuclear weapons did not exist. As my freshmen might ask: 'Why bother?' "†

An elderly maverick I ran into whimsically asked a college assembly, "Why should the FBI investigate a man who had once been chairman of Young Republicans for Herbert Hoover?" There was a dead silence. When he had explained that Herbert Hoover had been president during the Depression, there was a roar of laughter.

Could Henry Ford have been right after all? "History is bunk," he declared.

Despite such bleak communiqués from the academic front, a subtle change of climate may be detected as we approach the 1990s. Courses on Vietnam and its history are among the most popular in a surprising number of colleges. A professor of Russian

---

* About half of the hundred or so college graduates I encountered thought the Soviet Union was our enemy in World War Two. Several were astonished to learn that the Russians had taken any part in it at all. For the record, most had majored in business administration and engineering.

† Joe Patrick Dean, assistant professor of history at Concordia Lutheran College, Austin, Texas (*New York Times,* op-ed page, September 13, 1986).

history and literature at a large Midwestern university tells me that his classes are standing room only. John Kenneth Galbraith maintains that his students today are the brightest he's ever had.

Although I've come across depressingly many eighteen-year-olds who admire J. R. Ewing because "he kicks butts," a young instructor in journalism discovers that his students insist on asking about professional ethics: "This year nobody in class asked me what I make." The majority of recent graduates at a college in the Northwest accepted a pledge "to take into account the social and environmental consequences of any job opportunity I consider."

Don't bet the farm on it (if there is any farm left to bet), but there does appear to be a new kid on the block. This one is not a sixties remainder nor an eighties automaton; not as stormy as the first nor as air-conditioned as the second. He or she is more ambivalent perhaps, yet possibly more reflective.

I encountered a couple of these new ones. He's fifteen, she's nineteen. Their family backgrounds are planets apart: his, middle-class; hers, blue-collar. Each is unaware of the other's existence. He, a short Holden Caulfield, muses: "It's amazing how cynical you can get by age fifteen. Yet sometimes you really get a surge of idealism and want to go out and participate." She, born in the year of the tempest, 1968, appears tranquil in nature, yet a spirited independence manifests itself. "My parents tend to go along with things as they are. But I began to wonder why are these things happening today. You look back in history and see what caused these things..."

To intimate that they are the future would, unfortunately, be far off the mark. They are a baby-faced Gideon's army, considerably outnumbered by their peers who cheer on Rambo and disparage wimps. Yet the two may reflect something in the others, something unfashionable for the moment and thus hidden away, something "fearful": compassion. Or something even more to abjure: hope.

At an extension college in Little Rock, the students damned the victims of AIDS—"They deserve to die." Yet on seeing a documentary film about those they damned, they wept softly. Their teacher attributed the overt absence of generous heart to their thoughts of eventual Armageddon: "With absence of hope, I found absence of generosity. Why bother?" But why did they weep?

Of all my experiences during the past three years, it is this image that most haunts me. These young, who wept for those they damned, may offer the challenge as yet unrecognized. In a wholly different context, Tom Paine remarked on it: the nature of infidelity to oneself, professing to believe what one does not believe. Could this be "our dirty little secret"?

There was no absence of hope in those early 1920s. Certainly it was a time of great expectations. Was I eight or nine that Saturday matinee when I saw the silent film *Get Rich Quick Wallingford?* It was a forgettable movie with an unforgettable theme: making it. Fast. The market was bellowingly bullish, the goose hung higher than high, and all things on the Street looked handsome. And who was more handsome than our president, Warren Gamaliel Harding?

With the Crash of '29, another eight-year-old boy, Johnny, had the curtain line of a play: "I'm not mentioning any names, pa, but something's wrong somewhere." William Saroyan's *My Heart's in the Highlands* had an unforgettable theme, too: the Great Depression.

There's no point in mentioning any names, though Herbert Hoover's was most frequently invoked. "Most people cussed him up one side and down the other," recalls an Appalachian survivor. "I'm not saying he's blameless, but I'm not saying either it was all his fault. Our system doesn't run by just one man and it doesn't fall by one man either."

Some fifty-eight years after that Black October day, while a new generation of Wallingfords was making it fast, came another black October day, the nineteenth. Again from the temple of wisdom came an explanation: "It's a correction."

Correction of what? I hadn't the heart to ask anybody.

If April is the cruelest month, October may be the most revelatory. It may provide a metaphor for the eighties and, hopefully, for this book.

> The poorest one-tenth of Americans will pay 20 percent more of their earnings in federal taxes next year than they did in 1977 and the richest will pay almost 20 percent less, the Congressional Budget Office said Tuesday.*

> Just before the stock market crashed, *Forbes* magazine announced that the number of billionaires in America had doubled in the past year. Just before the stock market crashed, Shasta County, California, closed its entire library system for lack of money.
> Is there any question that something has gone wrong in America?†

After half a century, eight-year-old Johnny's question still reverberates. Something is indubitably wrong somewhere. Then, a president was 'buked and scorned and sudden acres of shacks bore his name: Hoovervilles. Today, the most popular president since FDR is faulted only by odd birds. Since the Irangate scandal and Black Monday, there has been a diminishing of delight in his incumbency; yet, unlike the Great Engineer, he is not personally held responsible. Nor, despite homeless millions, is there any record of a tent city named Reaganville.

Circumstances in much of our land are the same as in the thirties: ghost towns, where smokestacks once belched forth; family farms going, going, gone; and the homeless.

Two young journalists of the *Sacramento Bee* hit the road to find out for themselves.‡ They rode the freights; they walked the highways; they hitchhiked; they hunkered down in big cities and

---

* A sidebar on one of the back pages of the *Chicago Sun-Times,* November 11, 1987. The front-page headline concerned the Chicago Bears.

† Lead editorial, *Los Angeles Times,* October 25, 1987.

‡ Dale Maharidge and Michael Williamson, in *Journey to Nowhere: The Saga of the New Underclass* (New York: Doubleday, 1985).

small towns; they spent nights in missions; they saw as much of our country's underside as Woody Guthrie Bound For Glory in the thirties.

In boxcars, old-time hoboes complained bitterly of the green-horns who in the last few years have taken over. Talk about over-crowding. Fifteen years ago, there were four to a boxcar; now there are thirty, thirty-five. A new class of bums; an old class of Middle Americans.

Of the 22 million hungry reported by the Harvard School of Public Health (an old figure by now), the sources were churches, social agencies, soup kitchens, and sallies.* "Half the people we met on the road don't go near those places," said the two hard travelers. Double the Harvard figures and you've got yourself a pretty safe bet.

They had studied the photographs of the thirties, of Dorothea Lange, Walker Evans, Margaret Bourke-White. They saw the same faces. "When people are down and out, they always look the same."

The new nomads have come from the Rust Belt, the abandoned farms, the small failed businesses. Many of them had voted for Reagan because "he made us feel good." They resent being called losers, though that *is* what they are called. In the thirties (at least in retrospect), they were called victims. If there is a core difference between Then and Now, it is in language. It is more than semantics; it is attitude. Then, the words of the winners reflected discomfort in the presence of the more unlucky. Now, they reflect a mild contempt. And fear.

"It scares me sometimes thinkin' people are never goin' to learn," says the West Virginia truckdriver. "There's no trust in anybody. Used to be hitchhikin', you'd get a ride. Now they're afraid to pick you up. They're afraid they'll be robbed, but people has always been robbed all their life."

---

*Salvation Army missions.

In 1934, Sherwood Anderson took a trip across much of the country. *Puzzled America,* he called his book. Yet the hitchhikers he picked up in his jalopy were less puzzled than their nomadic descendants. At least, they made a stab at unraveling it.* Anderson found "a hunger for belief, a determination to believe in one another, in the leadership we're likely to get out of democracy."

A hunger for belief is certainly no less today than it was then. It is the nature of belief that may have changed. In the time lapse, new phenomena have taken over our lives and psyches: the cold war, the sanctity of the military, union-busting beyond precedent (encouraged by the cravenness of labor's pooh-bahs), along with televised sound bites† offered with the regularity of a cuckoo clock and a press that has assiduously followed the dictum of Sam Rayburn: To get along, go along. As a result, reflective conversations concerning these matters have become suspect, or at best, the avocation of odd birds, vestigial remainders of a long-gone past.

A daughter of Appalachia may have put her finger on it. "We've gotten away from our imaginations. The reason we're image-struck is because we don't like who we are. The more we get over this fake stuff, the more chance we've got to keep our sanity and self-respect."

LONG LIVE IMAGINATION. It was a banner carried by the students of Paris during the tempestuous year 1968. It was an idea that crossed the waters, undoubtedly misused and abused in some quarters. Nonetheless, it was a banner of strange and exhilarating device, not unlike the one borne by Longfellow's youth: EXCELSIOR.

With all passion spent in the twenty years that followed, we've

---

* *Sherwood Anderson,* by Kim Townsend (Boston: Houghton Mifflin, 1987).

† Some months ago, a Cincinnati TV anchorman suggested, "How about a bite?" I immediately accepted his invitation. I envisioned roast duck and red cabbage in one of the city's celebrated German restaurants. To my grievous disappointment, he had something else in mind: a sound bite in a TV studio.

experienced 1987's best-selling work of nonfiction upbrading the young of that epoch as a barbaric lot.* Written by an academician, it may have more closely approached in temper William Claude Dukenfield† than Alfred North Whitehead.

Another sort of banner appeared on national television in 1987. During the football players' strike, at a game played by strike-breakers, a bare-chested band of youths unfurled a flag: WE LOVE OUR SCABS. What's even worse, the game was awful.

Never in all the bitter history of labor-management battles has strikebreaking been so unashamedly espoused. Always, in the past, scabs were shadows who entered the workplace through back doors. Just as the letter A was Hester Prynne's mark of shame, so was the letter S for those who crossed the picket line. Until now.

"I'm a professional strikebreaker," said a genial acquaintance. I thought he was kidding until I came across his profile in the *Wall Street Journal*. He's not a club-wielding goon; he's a prep school and Ivy League alumnus. "It's exciting." His pride is manifest in these pages.

With Reagan's breaking of the air controllers' strike during his first year in office, to the thunderous applause of most Americans, including union members, things changed. (Mystery: For all the worried headlines of air crashes and near misses, with more than occasional references to understaffed, overworked, and unseasoned air controllers, hardly any mention has ever been made of the non-persons: 11,000 blacklisted *seasoned* air controllers. It appears that even our priorities have taken a necrophilic turn.)

The pert file clerk across the hall lets me know of her disdain for unions. Her immediate boss, a young accountant, who describes himself as "management," nods solemnly. They put in eight hours

---

* *The Closing of the American Mind,* by Allan Bloom (New York: Simon & Schuster, 1987).

† A.k.a. W. C. Fields.

a day. When I ask them how their eight-hour day came to be, their fresh faces are pure Mondrian: the absence of any human detail—the furrowed brow, the thoughtful squint.

It was unfair of me. After all, the Haymarket Affair took place in 1886, a good hundred years before I asked the impertinent question. I hadn't the heart to ask them about life before the minimum wage—and that came about a good fifty years ago. Labor unions, along with Big Guv'ment, which my two young friends also abhor, may have brought it forth, but that's ancient history. And we know what Henry Ford said about history.

The old-timer understands why so many of the bright-eyed band feel that way. "Notice something about the media? They always refer to labor as a special interest. Unions, minorities, women. Ever hear of corporations referred to as special interests? How many papers have reporters that cover the labor beat? Or TV stations? What the hell, they've got whole sections on business and finance. Is it any wonder that the young are so ignorant?"

The locked-out steelworker in the country's biggest ghost town, Youngstown (although Gary could give it a run for its money), says with a newly honed sense of irony, "My son is listed among the newly employed. He lost his $13-an-hour job and is now pumping gas at $3.50."

At the day of this writing, the headline in the local paper reads: Jobless Rate Lowest in 8 Years. It is also the lead on the six o'clock news.

His son, an ex-marine who served time in Vietnam, says, "This is the first time in four generations that I have it worse than my father." He stares at his two small boys. "How will it be for them?"

As we pass over the Monongahela River, the defrocked Lutheran pastor points toward the dark waters. "A twenty-three-year-old guy drowned this week, after drinking heavily. Where should he have been Tuesday morning? He should have been at work. At Christmastime, we had one weekend of fourteen suicides. All laid-off steelworkers. I guess they'll never make government statistics, will they?"

The old-timer is in a constant state of disbelief. "For the first time in the history of the country, a new generation is coming of age that will have a lower standard of living than their parents. Before, they could anticipate going beyond. What happened to the American dream?"

The compass is broken.

In the old badman song, Duncan hollers a challenge: Brady, where is you at?* That's the question we ask one another: Where are we at? What had presumably been our God-anointed patch of green appears to be, for millions of us, a frozen tundra. We race higgledy-piggledy, first one way, and a thirty-second commercial later we're headed elsewhere: all for a piece of the afternoon sun.

In De Sica's post–World War Two Italian movie *Miracle in Milan,* there is an indelible moment. The wretched homeless of the jungle camp shove, push, elbow one another out of the way for a sliver of the sun that comes and goes. An instant later, as the North Italian cold overcomes, all is forgotten save a bruise or two, the legacy of an equally miserable peer. Nothing has been learned, other than it is good to have sharp elbows. It is the lesson we have been taught, especially during this past decade. In authoritative quarters, it has been called entrepreneurialism. Ivan Boesky had his own word for it and may have been much closer to the truth.

Yet something is happening out there, across the Divide, often in unexpected quarters; something of an old American tradition, with new twists. Grass-roots movements, with techniques learned from the sixties, have never been more flourishing. Most of their foot soldiers had nothing to do with anti–Vietnam War protests, yet now challenge the Big Boys.

---

* "Duncan and Brady" was, in time past, a favorite barroom ballad of baritones and basses.

A bantam housewife in Chicago leads her blue-collar neighbors in a challenge to the Waste Management Corporation, a powerful multinational. She beats the outfit: there will be no toxic-waste dump in the neighborhood. A local, Bob Bagley, let Congress know about Somebody's spray trucks hauling dioxin through his forgotten town in the Ozark foothills. He won the battle. Name a place, a big-city block or a village square, and you'll find corporate dumpers with tigers by the tails. "Ordinary people, quiet in our disturbance" are the first bubbles in what has most of this decade been a tepid kettle.

The movements, remarkably disparate in issue, ranging from local grievances—utility hikes, tax inequities, developers' trans-gressions—to matters more encompassing—Sanctuary, Pentagon spending, threats to Social Security—have been both secular and sacred in impulse. (A young computer wizard has determined there are more than six thousand peace groups in business.) In most of these instances, the participants are unaware of the others' works. They are a movement awaiting coalescence.

It is what my two young acquaintances, the fifteen-year-old middle-class boy and the nineteen-year-old blue-collar girl, were intimating earlier in this essay. And reaching out for. It is what the newer students in that journalism class were curious about. It is what the old South Dakota Swede was awaiting in those bleak days of the Great Depression: something trickling up.

In spite of these hopeful signs, it's still clear that things can go either way. There may be a shaft of awareness sifting through. There are such signs. Or there may be a sharpening of elbows. There are such signs. There was a phrase in vogue during World War Two, shortly before the Normandy invasion: Situation Fluid. It is so now as it was then.

Nowhere has the Great Divide been as deep as in our religious conflicts today. It is in this sphere that the issues have been most dramatically joined.

Consider the case of Gary C. and his father. Both are Christian evangelicals. Both interpret Scripture literally. The son, who had done missionary work in El Salvador, reads the Bible "the same way the *campesinos* do. The Bible tells them of today, oppressors and oppressed, word for word. My father also believes in it, word for word. But he doesn't read it the same way they do. Or the way I do. He believes in this administration's Central American policy wholeheartedly. The same Book we both love is on the table we sit at, yet we're worlds apart."

CARROLL NEARMYER

A farm in Iowa, twenty-four miles southeast of Des Moines.

Instantly, you sense hard times. It isn't that the place is neglected; it's precisely the other way around: the farm's well-kept appearance evokes the image of the proud working poor, tatteredly neat and clean. It is the old house itself that gives away what is now an open secret: the desperate circumstances of the farmer.

It is an especially soft and easy twilight in May. His wife Carolyn is preparing a meal: not a farm supper of tradition and legend, but a bit of this, a dab of that, and more of something else. Thanks to her skill and care, it turns out to be wholly satisfying and filling—hunger, of course, being the best sauce. It will be ready by the time their son Chris gets home from his factory job in Des Moines. Eight-year-old Cary, a good talker, is ready any time.

This kitchen is part of the old house. My great-grandparents bought the place around 1895 or somewhere in there. I'm fourth-generation. Chris is not about to be the fifth. Just like all kids that lived on the farm, he followed me around quite a bit and was driving a tractor at, oh gosh, what age? Eight or nine, just old enough to touch the brakes and the clutch. The reason he's not working at that, I could not help him get started in farming.

It does look like the beginning of the end. I can go up and down the road and point you out the neighbors that is in the same predicament that their sons won't farm and that means the end of the family farm.

Dad was always telling me about it, and I didn't listen to him. The older I get now, the smarter my dad gets, even after he has passed away. "Don't trust a bank." He says they'll do anything when things are going good, but the minute it turns around and starts going bad, they'll jerk the rug from out under you.

The particular bank I dealt with was in Newton, Iowa. The Prairie City Bank, right by here, closed just eleven months ago. It went belly-up. I believe about three hundred here in the state of Iowa that has went down.

Oh, the bigger banks are getting bigger. You want to go in there and borrow $50,000, they won't talk to you. But if you wanted to borrow 2 or 3 million, then they'll talk to you.

When problems started coming up, I went to talk to my banker. I knew him personally and he knew me. But he had pressure from up above and so he was putting the pressure on me. He was trying to convince me I was a bad manager and for me to come home and write up a sale bill, list everything, and sell out. If I did that, I could pay them off and they, therefore, would not have had the pressure from up above. Being's as I'm a fourth-generation farmer, I wasn't about to just come home and sell out.

They come at us with, You gotta have a cash flow, you gotta do a better job on your bookkeeping, a better job on your farming. But still when you sell that bushel of corn for less money than you produce it, you can only cut so far. Our taxes kept going up, interests kept going up on us. At one time, I was paying eighteen percent interest on my farm notes. I came up more short on payments. If I don't make a go of it now, the Newton National Bank will take it.

They'll turn around and sell it to someone else. It will probably be a corporation. We call 'em vultures.

I've been involved in farm activism for three years. There is less people now than there were then, involved. They just gradually fall by the way. It's just like a cancer. Pretty soon one goes, then there's another one gone. I would say in three years' time, we lost somewhere around forty percent of them. Some of them don't have the money to come. It takes gas to go somewhere. If it comes to the choice of feeding your family and buying gas, you're going to feed the family.

Jerry Streit, a farmer from West Bend, Iowa: "We had a son playing baseball. We quit going to his away games because we didn't have gas for the car. I told him it wasn't because I didn't want to see him play. I loved it, but we just couldn't afford the gas."

When I was really down and out, I couldn't find a job. You talk about prime of life, I'm forty-six years old. That went against me. I was already too old. If we're forced off the farms, we'll have to take jobs like ridin' on the outside of the garbage truck. Carrying garbage for a minimum wage. What we'll really become is white slaves and just barely livin'. When they're coming down here after ya, you really feel what happens to a person on the inside. When you realize you're losing everything and be forced out of your home, you get mad. Damn mad.

I kept the whole problem to myself. She didn't know and the kids didn't know that I was having problems. There was times that I got suicidal. I would be driving and didn't know how I got there. There was several times that I had the gun to my head and she didn't know that. And then I got damn mad. I got to thinkin' about it and I got madder. These people don't have the right to do this to me! I have worked, I have sweated, and I have bled. I have tried out there to keep this place goin'. And then they tried to take it away from me! I worked out there to keep food on the table for the people over this whole nation. Nobody has the right to keep me from doin' that! I got so damn mad that I would have picked up arms to protect myself and the family. I would have shot somebody.

Then I got involved with this farm group, and there is people just like me. They get tagged as radicals right away. 'Cause we're supposed to be civilized now. It's all right for some S.O.B. in a white shirt and tie to come along and take our farms away from us on paper. But it's not all right for us to try to keep him from doin' that. The minute we say we're not gonna let him do that, we become radicals.

We have went to farm sales and helped farmers that was being sold out, to keep their machinery and stop the sale. Again we get tagged as radicals. I've helped organize farm sales to stop the sheriff's sale. Most of the time it's in winter. He stands out in the cold, the farmer being sold out. Sheriff comes. If you shout him down he still knocks off the farm to the bank. The farmer's sold out and they they try to put the guilt on you.

My banker even suggested, "You don't want to let your neighbors know that you're having financial trouble, 'cause you're the only one that's having trouble." I know several other farmers he's told that to. There's a neighbor down here two miles, we was meetin' each other on the road, we'd wave at each other but we wouldn't stop to talk to each other. He thought I was doin' all right and he was wonderin' how come, and I was wonderin' the same thing about him.

There is a neighbor across the road. He's a lot bigger than I am, but last summer when the Prairie City Bank foreclosed, they took his son down, too. The only thing his son saved was his wife and his kids. But they won't come and speak out. I don't know why they don't.

The next neighbor down the road is just a young guy. Him and his wife both work in town. He farms evenings, after he gets home. Just to survive.

There's another neighbor down the road, he was borrowing money from FHA. They turned him every which way but loose and he still hasn't said anything. There's one here last winter, wasn't able to put any food on the table, and he still hasn't ever said anything.

I've had some farmers argue with you that they have the right to go broke. When our administration is ruling out what we can get for our product, then we don't have that right. There ain't one farmer in the state of Iowa that says he voted for Reagan. They just won't admit it!

FHA was supposed to loan you money and stretch it out to ten or fifteen years or however long it took. When people started having trouble, first thing we heard from FHA was that they were running out of funds. They accelerated some notes on farmers, even if they was keeping up on their payments. Demanded payment in full. They would call it high-risk, so they would raise the interest two percent each time.

There's a big bunch of money the Pentagon has, unspent, unobligated. All they'd have to do is transfer just a very small percentage of it to FHA, and it would save thousands of small farmers.

I've got a reputation of talking. I'm trying to get them to understand. They will listen a little better than they did six months ago. I have been called crazy: "You don't know what the hell you're talking about." I've even been told if I get to talking about Reagan or the Federal Reserve, I am not an American any more. Yes, I'm a troublemaker.

A year ago last winter the governor of Iowa was to give his state speech. We wasn't allowed to go in there and listen to him, but we could be in the rotunda. We decided to do a demonstration there, 250 of us farmers. As he come off the legislative floor, I stopped him. I asked him to listen to us and we would tell him the real state of the state. He refused, of course.

Slowly, real slowly, we got the American Ag Movement started in Iowa. You will get people that will say, "I'm supportin' what you're doing, but I can't afford to join." It costs one hundred dollars a year to be a member. To a lot of people, it is a difference between putting food on the table and spending money for something like that.

I can see support coming faster and faster. Knowing what the administration has planned for us, we're going to see more people finally stand up and say, Enough is enough. Let's change this thing.

How much can a man take? I've seen it cause a lot of divorces. I can name you family after family that have split up. It has caused problems between me and my wife. Sometimes I take off and travel from one state to the other and she accuses me, and rightly so, of putting this ahead of the family. I've got an older daughter—is she twenty?—that no longer lives with us. She couldn't stand the stress. As soon as she was out of school, she moved to Des Moines. Me and my son have at times exchanged words. I know fathers and sons where the son has took off on account of the stress. You bet it affects families.

Our youngest, who is eight—when they had the sheriff looking for me to give me a repossession notice on the machinery—she stood out there on the deck as a lookout. He come down on me after dark, we started moving and hiding the machinery. Anytime she saw car lights, she told us and we scattered. We caught her one time hiding her tricycle. She said she didn't want the sheriff to find it. That's the kind of stuff families go through.

Take this situation here in Iowa, with a banker shot by a farmer. I knew this man. This particular farmer had two days before deposited money into his checking account. His wife told me that day they didn't have groceries in the house. He was going to write a check at the bank for sixty dollars so they could have food on the table. You understand, if a guy is going to bounce a check, he doesn't go into the bank to write a check. He handed the check to the teller and she told him she couldn't cash it. There wasn't any money in the account. He said he just deposited two days ago. She told him it had been seized by the banker—the guy that he shot—put on the note that "you owed here at the bank." That was the straw that broke the camel's back. That story has not been told publicly. How come?

If we don't stand up as citizens and as farmers, we're going to become second-class citizens. We're going to be fighting over jobs. At the same time, prices in the grocery store are going to skyrocket as soon as the corporations take over. Even the people that's got good jobs now are going to be struggling just to keep food on the table. It's not only what's gonna happen to us farmers, it's gonna happen to us as a nation and a world.

I see labor coming together with the farmers. For a long time they kept us separated. Whenever a farmer complained about a high-priced tractor, they say the labor man is the cause of all that. We come to find out, you take a $100,000 combine, the labor man got eleven percent of that. That includes his benefits, even his parking-lot cost. So it wasn't him that was causing it. They was trying to keep us split, but we have got ourselves educated. We're coming more and more together.

I went to the line a lot of times on different things. We was picketing the Board of Trade in Chicago. They are the ones that control our prices. They can sell one bushel of beans that we grow fifteen times on paper. We was trying to get them to change that policy.

We had a tractorcade to Omaha, Nebraska, last September. That's about 130 miles. It took four days to get there. We tractorcaded from four different directions. There was some four hundred tractors when we all got there. My tractor and our bunch barricaded the main street downtown to keep the traffic out. We was kickin' off the Harkin-Gephardt bill to give us parity. During the 130 miles, we got horns and waves supportin' us and some was givin' us the finger. Those was thirty-year-old people.

The young guy that lives on his mother-in-law's farm over there doesn't speak out. But he privately supports us. He donated fifteen dollars for diesel oil for the tractorcade. The older guy right by here won't publicly back us. But I've talked to him in his shed. He got so mad, he was takin' the wrench and beatin' it on the corn picker. He was almost in tears as he was doin' this. His son just went through a foreclosure. When we protested the Board of Trade in Chicago, he said we should have drove a loaded gas tanker through the front door.

It takes a lot of time and a lot of studying to get insight into what is going on. And that's another thing. Time. A farmer is just like a bird. When it comes spring, a bird flies north, and a farmer is the same way. When it comes spring, he's gonna go out and plant his corn. He don't care if he's gonna lose money. It's born in him, it's a natural instinct.

When it comes time to go to the field, I throw away whatever I'm reading to educate myself, and go out there. Even at times when I should be someplace screaming and hollering, I'll still be in the field. Every one of us is like that.

REX WINSHIP

He deals in futures. In fact, he deals in just about anything: grains, metals, livestock, bonds, bills, currencies, interest rates. "Anything you can buy, we can trade."

His offices run to two floors in a skyscraper near the New York Stock Exchange. There is a plenitude of art work, courtesy of his personal collection. He is one of the Forbes 400 richest Americans. His estimated net worth is more than $400,000,000.

Adjacent to his private office, the size of a small gym, is an enormous trading room, where forty young commodities brokers are single-mindedly studying the quote machines, one on each desk. They are among his 470 employees in this city. His payroll, in cities throughout the world, runs to 1,500.

Imagine Robert Duvall, to whom he bears a remarkable resemblance, in shirtsleeves, handling a continuous flow of messages, the phone constantly ringing. His feet are, of course, on the desk. He is, it is plain to see, a take-charge guy. One of his young traders said it all: "When he says jump, you ask, How high?"

In his private dining room, a chef-attendant serves lunch. "This is all macrobiotic, no fast food." The talk, though, is a fast flow, free-associative.

I'm just a poor old country boy, a fella who likes to work. Some people enjoy tennis, I enjoy work. I only put in about sixty, seventy hours a week. I enjoy being a leader. I enjoy being the guy everybody looks to. I like the responsibility of having thousands of people working for me.

I started out as a runner twenty years ago. Eighty-two bucks a week. When I got out of the army in '66. In 1968, I bought a membership; 1969, my uncle and I started the company. In '74, I bought him out. A whole bunch of people from the grain industry came with me. In those years, I was probably the largest commodities trader in the world. I had a vision I was in the right place at the right time. I also have a high energy level.

It was a robber-baron period for the commodity business. LBJ. Guns and butter. The Shah of Iran. Decontrolling of railroads, of airplanes. Gold-market window closed. Floating foreign-exchange rates. All taking place at the same time, okay? As that happened, we expanded the money supply.

We had every fruitcake as president, but they made you make money. We had oil at three dollars a barrel. We had interest rates at five percent maximum yield. We had everything pushed down. When they released it all, the budget doubled, inflation took off.

I was dealing in cattle, grains, gold, everything. You had a tax roll, so you could defer your taxes. If any dummy cannot make success out of that—The robber barons made a lot of money. They didn't have to pay any tax. The rules of the game in 1975 were very loose. The robber barons had everything going for them. We did, too. We were coming out of control prices, out of control exchange rates, out of control currencies. All of a sudden they were let go. I was in the business where you could trade it. I knew it was a unique period in history and it wouldn't go on forever.

If you were in real estate in Houston, up until five years ago, you were considered a business genius, right? If in the same twenty years, you were in some real estate business in Sioux City, you were considered a schmuck. You're in the wrong place, okay?

In '66, what if I had gone into the stock business instead of futures? The only thing I knew that was smart was being able to sell short. Having the flexibility of being short easily was a big advantage.

What if General Motors could hedge their auto production for a year out? What if every pension fund could hedge? What if U.S. Steel could sell futures forward and lock up their margins? I saw the concept of futures as a winner.

Now in our world of money, money management has become the sexiest topic there is. We're risk managers.

I'm sure we're close to another change. I don't know if it'll come next week or ten years from now. I'm not sure if we're going to have inflation or deflation. Deflation takes money out of the country into the city. New York's a gold mine. Inflation moves it away from cities back to the country. So all you have to do in life is figure which way the money flow is gonna go.

Nothing is forever. You always have to stay flexible, so you can change. That means education. Five years ago, we were in the commodity business. You bought and sold. The customer was a farmer in Iowa. Today he is a major New York bank. That kid who talked to the farmer can't talk to a New York City bank. The kid isn't educated enough. Either I fire him and hire one of those guys at $500,000 a year. Or I have to re-educate him. I re-educate him.

There's a business we should go into: training people to be in the service business. Give them basic skills: math, speaking, diction. Right now, we give diction courses here. I take 'em. You can't be in the business world and not be able to communicate. It wasn't as important when you had a screwdriver in your hand. Now there's satellite communications all over the place. The globalization of the communication market is going to be dramatic. You're going to be able to sit in your office in Chicago, look up at the wall. The conversation will be about interest rates and taxation.

It'll mean you'll have longer days. It'll be a young man's game, which it is already. Back in the fifties, when you went in for a job, the guy said, How old are you? Twenty-six. Married? You bet. Boy, that's good. What a guy, you're married. Stabilizing force, right? Today, you don't want the kid married.

You want to be able to move. You want to be able to send him to Singapore for two years, Sydney, Australia, for a year, and then back to Chicago. Two, he's gotta go to school nights. He's gotta learn math, statistics, he's gotta learn Fed policy. When he goes to school from seven o'clock till nine three days a week, and he's newly married, and he gets to work at six, gets out at six, has to be at school at seven, gets home at nine-thirty, what's his new wife gonna say to him?

How can you compete when the Japanese come over here, without their wives? They get to work at eight o'clock in the morning, get home ten o'clock at night. The average work week of the American executive is fifty-four hours. It's probably sixty-some hours in Japan. It's a question of time before the guy who works sixty hours will have all the marbles. Everybody must adjust to the marketplace.

What happens to that most solid of citizens and family men, the American farmer?

Why is he a solid citizen? That's a myth. The myth is that land is good, right? Farmers work hard, right? That's also a myth. The guy that runs the local dry-cleaner store works longer hours, right? He's in a fixed location. He can't move. He's got his plant and equipment tied up in his building, right? Except no one sends him a check and says, You're entitled to $3\frac{1}{4}$ for your corn. What business in the world says you gotta make money? Why should you make a profit? Without loss, no one can win. Unless you have losers, you cannot have winners.

Just because, forty years ago, half the population lived on the farm, and people thought, Wasn't that a great life? Today nobody lives on the farm. The American government ruined the American farmer. Three embargoes: '73, '76, and 1980. There probably aren't as many Third World countries that have defaulted as much as we have. An embargo's defaulting tells you that your contract's no good, rip it up. That's why we have to spend 35 billion a year to support the farmers. Australia, Canada, Argentina, Brazil expanded. We made them all rich.

Cargill takes half their money outside the United States. When you go spend a billion in Brazil to build railroads and trucks and terminals, it doesn't come back very easy here. Harley-Davidson never got it back from Honda, did it?

Ten years from now, there will be less farmers. We don't need them. We've imported food. We import more meat than any other country in the world: more chicken, more beef, more pork. When the government gets out, the people that are left will produce what we want. Some farms will collapse, some won't.

And unions. As you change society, unions are not set up for the change. They're designed to keep people out. They're designed to lock prices. Isn't that how you raise prices? They're built for inflexibility. They have to go the way of the fixed exchange rate. Why should the most talented electrician make the same as the biggest dummy? The union is unfair to its own people.

Why aren't there any more craftsmen today? What happened to all those ethnic craftsmen? I believe kids work harder today than ever before. Maybe they don't want to go into these crafts because the pay wasn't right. Maybe the greatest carpenter didn't make enough money because the guy at the low end made as much as he did. Unions.

They stop the top guy from becoming great. Why shouldn't the greatest carpenter become a multimillionaire? The greatest basketball player does. Why shouldn't the greatest stonecutter? Why? Why? Because the union says, You gotta stay here because we gotta pull this other guy up.

Unions are less and less important. The trend's already in place. It's gonna keep goin'. The market will take care of it.

We need accountability. You can't fire the union guy, so the boss has an unaccountable work force. What if the girl types up your manuscript backwards? I couldn't fire her because she's gonna go to the grievance committee. No accountability, you have no business. Another obstacle to free progress: government regulations. The government caused the Depression in the first place. The Federal Reserve didn't know what it was doing. It kept tightening the money supply. Today, if our Fed was not expanding our money supply, we'd have a depression, too. To say controls took us out of the Depression, that's another myth. Like the farmer's good, and the land's good. Myths.

We have Social Security, right? Japan doesn't have it. You got to save your money to protect yourself in old age. Does anyone ever think maybe there's a correlation between Social Security and non-saving? The Japanese weren't born savers and we weren't born spenders. My uncles and aunts and grandma and grandpa saved string and butter wrappers and everything else. They were savers. Now, with Social Security, why save? Everybody consumes.

Reagan had a chance to change the Social Security laws and didn't have the guts to do it. So that will be a tremendous debt in the future. Reagan is a good president and could have done something. He could have gotten rid of the COLAs, cost of living adjustments. He could have changed America forever.

Jimmy Carter's administration was a trader's dream. Made more money with him than either Nixon or Reagan. Because he made distortions. Wage and price controls, no wage and price controls. Credit controls, no credit controls. Embargo, no embargo. Wonderful for me.

It's very hard to make a profit in a free market. Look at the airlines decontrolled. It's hard to make a profit since Jimmy Carter. With controls, you're simply smarter than the controllers. You just outsmart the regulators. Knowing how to get in and get out, you make a profit. It's easy. Christ, if you can't outsmart one little government staff, you shouldn't get to work in the morning.

If you're called a freebooter—

A free what?

A pirate, a robber baron. Is that a put-down?

It's a compliment. Absolutely. I wish I had their money. Who developed America? The regulator? The President? Or was it Mellon, Rockefeller? I mean, *tell* me what they did bad? Seriously, what did they do bad?

Rockefeller shot down some workers in the copper fields. Some say he exploited them...

Absolutely. And who's benefitted? There's still Standard Oil, isn't there? Mellon's bank's still around. Chase Manhattan's still around. Listen, how many charities were started by these people? How many national parks were preserved by these robber barons?

We look at them, we say they didn't play fair. Absolutely not.

Kid Pharaoh, a minor syndicate tiger in Chicago, caught in a reflective moment:

"I might have been a success at the turn of the century. If I was born fifty years ago, I believe I would have been a multimillionaire. I shoot the same shot that Rockefeller shot while somebody was tapping an oil well that was competitive to him. He put guys in trick bags. Got 'em in jail. There's a history written about these guys. John Jacob Astor, with his trapping, with his furs. Hitting guys. This is the way the system works. What else is there? These new laws are holding them back, destroying incentive.

"These were the giants who built the cities. These are the guys who built our country. They elect presidents. All these guys came up the hard way...shoeshine guys and bust-out crapshooters...shoot a shot against blackjack. These are the guys we need in our country. Who needs educated mooches?"*

The robber barons made it because the marketplace wasn't fluid enough. The Rothschilds had carrier pigeons. H. L. Hunt had the guy drunk in the room and had his friend out on the pay phone. Today this could never happen. You'd have nine hundred reporters there. And it's all on the news the same night. Instant communications. Our robber-baron period lasted from '73 to '80. What killed it was [slaps hands] instant communications. Now it's shifted to securities. The market'll take care of it.

The rules of the New York Stock Exchange on insider trading make more profits for the rich arbitrager. If they had no laws against insider trading, these risk-arbitrage guys couldn't make any money, 'cause the market's broader and they don't have the edge. The law makes it easier for them because they outwit

* *Division Street: America* (New York: Pantheon Books, 1967).

the regulators. I'm saying the marketplace knows more than the regulators.

Here's another kind of flow: mergers and acquisitions. Everybody's merging, right? Big conglomerate, right? What's the next thing's gonna happen? They're gonna take 'em all apart.

Small, independent companies? Good, right?

Wrong. Terrible. Very, very scary to me. A lotta competition. I can move quicker against the big inflexible ones.

The only way you can keep everybody upwardly mobile is to have the GNP get bigger and grow. If it grows, you don't have to have have-nots. If it doesn't grow, you have to have have-nots.

Like the frontier was. Space mining, space technology, space health. How far can we grow? Forever. We're only limited by our imaginations.

In the trading room, where his scores of young brokers are intently studying their quote machines, his public relations person, in the manner of a gracious hostess, guides me. "We are young and energetic. It's fast, intense. But it offers a lot of money. At a certain age, that's what you're interested in, making money.

"The turnover is tremendous. Two to five years with one firm and then out. The business just changes so fast. Lots of stress, so if you make a lot of money, you get out early [laughs.]

"We affectionately call it the war room. You feel like you're going to battle [laughs]. Yeah."

POSTSCRIPT

Another visit, another macrobiotic lunch. It is precisely one month after Black Monday, October 19, 1987.

A five-year bull market had a correction. As long as there is greed, you'll have days like October 19. Interest rates and lack of leadership were the cause. It will probably take two years for us to get back in shape again—'89 and '90 will be bad.

It will not be like 1929. The bear market can be over in a day. Isn't it better to have a down in one day than for four years? Bonds went up twelve points in twenty-four hours. In my business, futures, it was pretty good. I picked up a few bucks.

If the stock market went back to 1,200 tomorrow, it will be all right. It's high-volatile. There's a scare and a correction. People will take less risks in the future, which is what they should have done in the first place. It probably won't happen again in the next ten years.

In 1929, you didn't have world trade in cash, futures, and options. If Germany makes a decision, it affects America, because of telecommunications, the computer. You have a decision to make quickly. But no matter what policies are made, the market is gonna adjust to it. So it's a much safer world. The reason for the thirties Depression was the government not allowing the free market economy to work its way out. The Depression wouldn't have lasted that long.

In contrast to 1929, there is far less playing the stock market. The big traders are now in pension funds. They have made so much money that in the long run, they'll be okay.

October 19 has changed our policy. Now we are addressing our budget deficit. The market will discipline the politicians. People will tighten their belts in some spending. They'll buy less VCRs, less Sonys, less Mercedes. But they won't be stinting on U.S. clothing, U.S. food, services.

If we lowered the taxes and cut down on government spending, the business sector will explode. The first thing I'd cut would be the military spending. Blowing up bombs in practice doesn't help the economy.

I wouldn't cut welfare payments. When you give money to some-body on welfare, she spends it to buy food and clothing. Jobs are created. I would change the way the government gives them the money. I wouldn't spend a buck and a half to give her a buck. I would just mail her the check. I would always give poor people money because they spend it.

I see a couple of years sideways and then we'll adjust. We'll pull out better than 1929.

SAM TALBERT

He is a member of Teamsters for a Democratic Union (TDU). It is a maverick group of truckdrivers, who are challenging the administra-tion of Jackie Presser and the Teamsters hierarchy.

He lives in Charleston, West Virginia. He is fifty-five, divorced. "I raised my own two children": a son, thirty-one, and a daughter, twenty-eight. He lives by himself.

I drove a truck all my life, ever since I was fifteen. What little edu-cation I have isn't formal. It's all from behind the barn. For years, I didn't know much about labor, but here and there, I've picked up a few things.

I know more about farmers than anything else. My dad and mom lived on a farm all their lives.

Most people around here voted for Reagan. I visualized him as being something like American apple pie. He just said things that I had always, since I was a kid, thought was right. Now I feel I've learned a little.

Some people are advancing and others is backtracking. It's just like in our unions, I think we're going backwards. Everybody's just tending to their own business, meantimes the ones that are gettin' the profits from all this is banding together and controlling the majority. You have young people that come on the job, started out with decent wages, that takes it for granted. They think the company is giving this to them out of the goodness of their hearts. They don't know that down the line somebody had to fight to get this.

I've seen these young fellows as soon as they get there jump in and buy 'em a new house. They get married, they have two or three kids. Well, the company come along and ask for concessions. These fellows that thought this company was giving this money to start with, say, Okay, I'll do it, because I've got to meet these payments. They just give to the company and give and now the company has a hold on everybody. The younger people is the majority that hadn't had to fight for what the older people had to do.

They're tryin' to get the right-to-work law passed in this state. People thinks if they get this law passed, some of the companies moved out of the valley, shut down, will come back. They seem to think the high cost of labor is what's makin' all these people move out. So they've a tendency to lean against the unions, ordinary working people. They get it from what they read in the papers and what their bosses tell 'em.

I learnt that things I dreamed of when I was a kid just wasn't there, because we live in a land of plenty and there just isn't plenty for everybody. Just like the poor old farmer, for instance. I'd see him feedin' the country and just havin' nothin'. I used to wonder about these things. I'd think, well, what in the heck. They talk about workin' hard all your life and the American dream. Here's old Sanford down the road. He's worked hard all his life and the poor old fellow can't make it. Things just didn't fit together.

They give me the Silver Star in Korea. Yes sir. But I'll tell you what, if I had to do it all over, I don't think I could do the same things that I done then. We had no business there, because some fellow wanted to make war materials, is the way I see it. They brainwashed me into believin' those people were my enemy and they wasn't.

Those people didn't want to fight and I didn't want to fight. Just for instance, they promoted me to staff sergeant. I wouldn't sew my chevrons on. They said, "You won't get this extra pay if you don't put 'em on." I put 'em on because I was poor and I'd send my money home to my mom.

They said, "Well, what do you think of this war over here?" I said, "I oughta be home and the fellows that start it, come over here and let them fight it. 'Cause I don't want to be here. I don't want to wade this mud, I don't want to be here in this heat in the summer. I want to go home, I don't care about your war."

This instance, it sticks with me, inside of me, and I think of it quite often. This ROK* soldier, he was a good friend of mine. He was attached to our unit. We were sitting eating one day, we was backing up this hill so we could go in to attack, and they brought us up some hot food. Boy by the name of Sneed from Alabama said, "Yong, if it wasn't for us over here, you wouldn't be eatin' this food." So Yong, he looked at us and said, "You're all my friends and I don't wanna hurt your feelin's. I like your good food. But those people over there's my people. I just wish all of you would go home." [Deep sigh.] It sticketh in my heart like I don't know what.

I didn't pay much attention to Vietnam. I was like a lot of people in our tribe. It didn't affect me directly. I was working, I was getting a paycheck, business was good, was hauling plenty of chemicals out. I was getting overtime. I didn't really pay much attention.

I really started paying attention when these younger fellows starting runnin' to Canada. At first I thought, those terrible people. But after a while, I thought, well, now, if I had to go back, what would I do, knowing what I know? I started puttin' those two things together. Now those fellows that went was educated people. They knew what was happenin'. I knew what was happenin', too,

* Republic of Korea.

because of my experience. I thought, well, hell, I'd go to Canada, too, before I'd go back.

Mostly people worry about what's gonna happen tomorrow. If you belong to a union for twenty years, you never asked for nothin' and you file a card against your company that's right, they subject to tell you that you're a troublemaker, you're liable to put this company out of business.

First time it happened to me, I thought what the heck is this thing? Then the TDU started fillin' me full of knowledge of my rights, and what's wrong and what's right. And they mentioned some books to read.

Things out here is gettin' tougher. The Volkswagen plant just moved out, it went to Mexico. True Temper Corporation, they just sold out, operating someplace else under another name. Another plant sold out to a Swedish company. People who worked in those plants are in service places, like hamburger joints. They get far, far less money. Poverty wages, I guess you'd call it.

My daughter and my son are both workin' for Carbide. They're doin' okay. I try to talk to them, it's like tryin' to talk religion to some people. They don't want to hear it. They're livin' high on the hog. They work long hours and it's rarely we discuss anything. They're both very generous. They're people that would help their neighbors. They'd loan you their automobile or money or buy food for you or anything—but they're just not involved in anything.

They've asked me a few times why I'm doin' it. Passin' out literature, writin' letters to the papers. I get some write-ups. They read about me. I had one in the paper today about Jackie Presser. I called him a dirty dog. Every advantage I get to put out word on him, I do it.

I have had threats. I was goin' to have my windows knocked out. I better stay in the house at night. I had a threat from the local president that I'd lose everything I'd worked for, that I'd lose my pension.

Oh, they tried to intimidate me. But they don't know, the more they try, that just gives me the juices to keep goin'. That makes me not want to quit.

I don't hunt, I don't fish. I wouldn't catch a little fish and tear its mouth up, or I wouldn't shoot a deer. On the other hand, I'd like to go up there and shoot some of those union officials.

I get tired, I get aggravated, I quit sometimes, for two or three days, but, then, I can't quit. I feel there's a principle, they's morals involved, they's human lives involved. I feel like I'm doin' a little somethin' that's contributin' to the cause of the workin' class of people.

One time, I wasn't gettin' enough contributions to keep our newsletter goin'. I said, Hell, I'm tired of fightin', I'm gonna quit. The word got around.

One Saturday mornin', I heard a knock on the door. This big red-headed fellow said, "Sam, we wanna talk to you. There's five fellows with me." They had three hundred dollars among them, said, "We want to give you this. We heard the rumor that you were disgusted and wanted to quit. We come out to ask you not to quit. You keep on doin' what you're doin'."

It's been my dream to find a young fellow interested. Now we have a lot of educated people in our union, as truckdrivers. We have people that are good talkers and I'd love to get one of them that can talk, can talk with compassion, to where he can lay his feelings out, to work with me. And let me work with him and try to build him up to be the leader in our local.

I'm one of those fellows that can get a whole lot inside of me. I can have this feeling, that I don't know how to get it out into words how I feel.

I think things is going to continue to be bad until the majority of the people gets pushed down to where they're all equal. Am I making any sense? It'll have to be like when I was a kid. We was all poor and we had to stick together and look out for each other.

Everybody's afraid, everybody's holding on tight to what little they have, but when you're pushed down to where you don't have nothing you don't have any choice but to band together.

It scares me sometimes thinkin' people are never goin' to learn. I sometimes get to thinkin' people's gettin' too hard-hearted. There's no trust in anybody. Used to be hitchhiking, you'd get a ride. Now they're afraid they'll be robbed, but people has always been robbed all their life. So it's hard for me to pass up a hitchhiker.

One day last week, I was in the grocery store. This fellow come in, he's pretty well dressed, nice, tall, handsomelike fellow. He said, "I was told from the register to come back here, that you-all might cash a check for me. I'm hungry, I don't have a nickel in my pocket and I'd like to get a five-dollar check cashed." She said, "No, there's no way we can do that."

I said, "I'm goin' to give you five dollars." He said," You gotta be kiddin'." He wrote me a five-dollar check and said it's good. He asked me, "Why did you do that? Here they won't cash my check and you, an individual, you will." I said, "Buddy, I've hitchhiked, I've come from a poor family, I've been all over the country, and I have been fed by people. I have not had a penny in the pocket and people say here's fifty cents." He said, "I hope I can repay you, this generosity." I said, "Don't give it back to me. Give it to somebody else along the road."

POSTSCRIPT

Since his conversation took place, the Teamsters Union had the first rank and file election in its history and the old guard was ousted by the reform slate, with the help of the TDU (Teamsters for a Democratic Union).

LARRY HEINEMANN

His demeanor, at first glance, is a cool customer's. As he recounts the Chicago moment of nineteen years ago, a feverishness sets in.

His family background is blue-collar. He is married and has two small children.

He has written two novels, based upon his experience in Vietnam. His second, Paco's Story, *won the 1987 National Book Award.*

I'm forty-three, close enough to be called a boom baby.

I was in college for the same reason everybody else was: to stay out of the draft. Ran out of money. Got drafted in May of '66. I was twenty-two. My younger brother and I were drafted at the same time. He couldn't adjust. He came back from Germany with a discharge in his hand on the same day I left for San Francisco. We had two hours in the kitchen to sit and talk. He was home and I got a year overseas. Vietnam. I was in combat from March of '67 to March of '68, a couple of months after the Tet offensive began.

I left Vietnam on a Sunday afternoon at four o'clock and was home in my own bedroom Monday night at two. Half the people in my platoon were either dead or in the hospital. It was disorienting, I must say.

In my household, there was never any political discussion. We were raised to just submit to the draft, stiffly and strict. I went there scared and came back bitter. Everybody knows it was a waste.

I wasn't willing to go to jail. Nobody told me I could go to Canada. Out of four brothers, three of us served in the armed forces. My youngest brother, a two-time marine, was wounded, sent back, and has had a very hard time of it since.

It was clear from the first day that it was a bunch of bullshit. We were there to shoot off a bunch of ammo and kill a bunch of people.

We were really indifferent. The whole country was indifferent: Why are we fighting in Vietnam?

When I got back here, I was scared and grateful and ashamed that I had lived, 'cause I started getting letters: So-and-so got hit, So-and-so burned to death. My good friend flipped a truck over an embankment and it hit him in the head. I had been given my life back, I felt a tremendous energy. At the same time, I felt like shit.

Right after I got back, I was in Kentucky where my wife was going to school. Martin Luther King was shot dead—was it April 4, 1968? I was gettin' a haircut for my wedding. These guys in the barber shop were talking, I remember: Somebody finally got that nigger.

Black cities were just going up in flames. And then Bobby Kennedy was shot. It was almost as if I had brought the war home myself. I didn't want any part of it whatever.

I didn't get involved with any antiwar movement. I felt I would be breaking faith with my friends who were still overseas. Now I'm sorry I didn't.

Some guys are bemoaning that they didn't share the rite of passage, fighting in Vietnam. They regret they have no war stories to tell. I would trade them my stories for my grief any time.

The summer of '68, I got a job driving a CTA bus.* It was the worst decision I ever made. I had come from a place where I drove a fifteen-ton armored personnel carrier, and we didn't take shit from anybody. I had a .45 and a shotgun while I drove. We had the road to ourselves. I was living every eighteen-year-old's fantasy about having a big ugly-sounding car and being able to drive anywhere we wanted. The whorehouses were all in a row and it was one car wash after another. I didn't wanna take shit from anybody.

The one thing they teach about bus driving is that you're a

---

* Chicago Transit Authority.

public servant, okay? Any asshole with a fare can give you shit and you have to sit there and take it. Anyone gave me an argument, I threw 'em off the bus. This transfer's no good—woooshh!—get out! I was never that way before Vietnam.

Halfway through that Chicago summer in '68, the streets were just crazy. I was driving a bus. The drivers were all tense. There were still reverberations of the King assassination. A week before the convention, the black drivers called a wildcat strike. Anywhere you went, there was this undercurrent. I was at the end of my rope.

That night, I'm driving down Clark Street, past Lincoln Park. I look out under the trees to see what's happening. You could see the silhouettes of cops, cop cars, and kids. I heard there was tear gas and cops beating up kids. When I was in Vietnam, we used tear gas to flush people out of tunnels.

You know that somebody's in a spider hole and you'll just go *Lah-dee, lah-dee.* I don't know how it's spelled, it means come out. If they didn't, you'd pop tear gas. It would make you extraordinarily sick. It has a very distinctive smell. Like the one this night.

Near Lincoln Park, I could see the cop cars and the kids. As we came closer, I pulled the brake and said, "I'm sorry, we're not goin' anywhere. I'm not gonna get mixed up in this at all." I waited until the whole carbony smell died down.

The passengers hollered go on, go on. I said no, no, no, no. "You don't want to get a snort of that tear gas, it'll make you sick." I stayed at that corner maybe fifteen, twenty minutes. Guys behind me were pissed off, but passed me up. The supervisor argued with me. I fully expected people were gonna get killed.

I think the police riot was the next night. I came to this light, through the south end of the Loop. All four curbs were bumper-to-bumper buses, which held maybe sixty guys. They were just filled with cops and all the lights were off. All I could see was riot gear: helmets and billy clubs. One guy looks through the window as if I'm a hippie who has stolen the bus. It was the look on his face:

Who are you? What are you doing here? I just showed him my CTA badge. If I didn't—[laughs].

I knew exactly what was gonna happen. These guys were gonna do the same thing I had done overseas. They were gonna go wherever they were gonna go and they were just gonna smash people. I just turned my bus around, the hell with it.

I was not one of those GIs who came back and didn't say boo about it. I was vocal. Anybody asked me, I told them it was a lot of evil bullshit. We did mean things to people. It made you into a mean person. I stayed away from the other vets. It was self-imposed isolation. I was going through the classic symptoms of what is now called delayed stress. Luckily some people started putting books in my hand.

I knew something was wrong when I saw the Vietnam Veterans' Parade in Chicago. There were an awful lot of K-Mart cammies marching in it. Camouflage fatigues. Overseas everybody wore these jungle fatigues, just plain faded jade green. Now the fashion is these K-Mart cammies, which are like costumes. Nobody in his right mind would have worn them overseas.

When I heard General Westmoreland was going to be the parade marshal, I said, No way. I'm not marchin' in that fuckin' parade. I wouldn't get in line behind him if he was goin' to the shithouse.

I had ambivalent feelings about the parade. There were good things and bad things about it. You weren't allowed to have any banners expressing any political opinion. There was this celebration of the war being a good thing and why didn't we do more? At the same time, we were together for the first time in twenty years as brothers.

Now there's a kind of amnesia. But a tremendous curiosity. There are college courses on it. I'm lecturing at Lindblom* next week in the history class. It is beginning to happen. My daughter who is nine wants to know. The war is in our house.

---

* A Chicago Public High School.

Vietnam veterans took a lot of shit from World War Two people. They said we lost the war. I was never in a firefight and lost. We killed plenty of people. I mean me, me, me. A soldier is a soldier and the process is the same. We're simply sons of bitches, just as mean as anybody else.

I think the kids today want to do the right thing and get on with their lives. I see a lot of energy used pointlessly. I don't think Americans understand exactly the way the rest of the world sees us. We don't understand what people respect about us and envy or despise us for. They just wish we'd go home. We feel everything has to go our way, no matter what. I think this attitude is gonna get us into big trouble.

I haven't seen my oldest brother since 1970. My next younger brother loves Reagan. He and I never talk politics. My youngest brother, the two-time marine, hasn't talked to me for ten years. He thought we did the right thing. He despised me because I went to our old family lawyer and asked him how I could get my kid brother from going over the second time. He wanted to go. When he left, I couldn't bring myself to write to him. Our friendship ended with a bitter argument. My little brother, I haven't seen him since 1982. I don't know what he's doing.

I don't think the country's learned anything from the war. The guys who organized the Vietnam Veterans' Parade wanted it to be remembered as a nostalgic positive experience. They wanted so hard for it to be all right. It's not. It's going to be an evil thing in our lives and nothing's gonna change it.

JEAN GUMP

A grandmother; mother of twelve, ranging in age from twenty-two to thirty-five. She and her family have lived in a middle-class western suburb of Chicago for thirty-two years.

She has, all her adult life, been active in church and community work: Christian Family Movement; president of the high school PTA; League of Women Voters; executive secretary of the township's Human Relations Council. She was a delegate to the 1972 Democratic Convention. A neighbor recalls: "I'd come into her kitchen, she'd have the phone on one ear, as she'd be mixing a pot of spaghetti and talking to me all at the same time."

For something she did on Good Friday, 1986, she was arrested. Along with her, four other Catholics, young enough to be her children, have been sentenced to different terms in prison. Their group is called Silo Plowshares. This conversation took place shortly after her arrest. It had hardly made the news.

We commemorated the crucifixion of Christ by entering a missile silo near Holden, Missouri. We hung a banner on the outside of the chain-link fence that read: SWORDS INTO PLOWSHARES, AN ACT OF HEALING. Isaiah 2, from Scriptures: We will pound our swords into plowshares and we will study war no more.

It's a Minuteman II silo, a first-strike weapon. There are 150 of these missiles. If one of these missiles were to leave the ground, it would decimate an area of seventy-two miles. And all the children and others. We wanted to make this weapon inoperable. We succeeded.

We carried three hammers, a wire clipper, three baby bottles with our blood, papers with an indictment against the United States and against the Christian church for its complicity. Ken Ripito, who is twenty-three, and Ken Moreland, who is twenty-five, went with me. The other two went to another silo about five miles away.

It is going to be the citizens that will have to eliminate these weapons. They were built by human hands. People are frightened of them, yet view them as our Gods of Metal. It is a chain-link fence with barbed wire on top. We have become so accustomed to these monstrosities that there are no guards. It is nondescript. If you were passing it on the road, you would see this fence. The silo itself is maybe a foot or two out of the earth. It looks like a great concrete patio. It's very innocuous.

To get through the fence, we used a wire clipper. We had practiced in the park the day before. Once we were in, I proceeded to use the blood and I made a cross on top of the silo. Underneath, I wrote the words, in black spray paint: DISARM AND LIVE.

We sat down and waited in prayer. We thanked God, first of all, that we were alive. We expected a helicopter to come over and kill us terrorists. We thanked God for our successful dismantling, more or less, of this weapon. We assumed the responsibility for our actions and we waited to be apprehended.

About forty minutes later, the soldiers arrived in an armored vehicle. There was a machine-gun turret at the top. The commander used a megaphone and said, "Will all the personnel on top of the silo please leave the premises with your hands raised?" So all of us personnel [laughs] left the silo. I was concerned because it would be difficult getting out of that little hole in the fence with our hands up. We made it fine.

They put the men up against the fence in a spread-eagle position. They asked the female—myself—to "take ten steps and stand with your hands raised." I did it for a few minutes and my fingers were beginning to tingle. I put my hands down. The soldier said, "You must put your hands up." I said, "No, I have a little funny circulation." He said, "You must put your hands up." I said, "Shoot me." He chose not to, which I thought was good.

I said, "I'll compromise with you. I will raise my hands for five minutes and I will put them down for five minutes." He said, "You can't put them down." I said. "But I will." It was hysterical.

I wanted to turn around to see if my friends were being maltreated. The soldier who had his gun aimed at me said, "You can't turn around." I did. I was watching them try to put handcuffs on the two men. I have been arrested in Chicago. I've seen an efficient police force put handcuffs on people in two seconds. It must have taken these soldiers fifteen minutes. I had to tell them they were doing it wrong. With my suggestions, they finally did it right.

There was a big discussion about what to do with the female suspect. Apparently they weren't allowed to frisk a female suspect. I was kind of wondering what they were going to do with me. They asked me to remove my coat, which I did. He said, "Throw it ten feet over here." I said. "I'll never make it, but I'll do the best I can."

They took things out of my pocket and put them on the ground. One of the items was a handkerchief. I said, "It's getting a little chilly. I think I'm getting a cold and a runny nose. I will have to get my handkerchief." It was about three feet away. The soldier said. "Don't you dare move." I said, "I'm going to get this handkerchief and I'm going to blow my nose." I did that and put the handkerchief in my pocket. The soldier said, "You have to leave your handkerchief over here." I said, "All right. But if my nose should run again, I'll go over there and I will get my handkerchief and I will blow my nose." At this point, the poor soldier looked sort of crestfallen. He was about the age of my youngest child.

By this time, the area was filled with about eight automobiles. FBI, local sheriffs, and so on. They took us into this armored vehicle. On its right-hand side was a big sign: PEACEKEEPER. I said, "Young man, have an opportunity to read Orwell's *1984*." He said, "I'm not allowed to talk to you." I said, "I'll talk to you, then." He said, "If I had my uniform off, we could talk." I said, "Maybe we'll meet and have coffee someday."

At the police station, we were treated rather deferentially. Someone from the sheriff's office asked if we wanted coffee. There had been no charges made. We were very, very tired. We were allowed to make one phone call. We'd been given the name of a young lawyer, who had worked with a previous group, the Silo Pruning Hooks.

One of the jail guards was handing our tray through a slot in the door. She said, "Mrs. Gump, I want to thank you for what you did." I said, "You're welcome." Then when I saw her lined up with all the other guards, she had a wholly different demeanor.

The FBI came to interview us. I find them very funny. They come in like yuppies, all immaculately dressed. Probably six or eight. The five of us are now together. The gentleman behind the desk wanted to read me the Miranda rights. "You have a right to remain silent." I said, "You're right. I do and I am."

At the Federal Building in Kansas City, where we were taken, I was asleep on the bench. A nice young man joined me: "We might be able to negotiate something to get you out on bail." I said, "Young man, there's no way I'd pay a nickel for bail money. You're wasting your time." Darla, my co-cellmate, she's twenty-two, agreed also not to answer.

The judge said he'd like to let us out on a $5,000 bond, with our signature. We'd not commit any crimes between now and the arraignment date. John Volpe said, "I don't really know if I can, because there are a lot of silos out there."

My children knew nothing about this. Mother's doing her thing, is what they always say. As I leave the house, they often say, "Don't get arrested, ma." I'd been arrested five other times for civil disobedience.

I felt peace marching was fine, but what we needed was a freeze group. After campaigning in Morton Grove, we had a referendum. Five thousand voted for the freeze, two thousand against.

When I came back from Kansas City on Easter Sunday morning, the children had learned about it. There were tears between times of much laughter. They were supportive, though it's an imposition on their lives.

My one daughter graduates from the University of California. I will not be there. My other daughter is getting married. I will not be there. I want more than anything in the world to be there. These are my children and I love them. But if they're going to have a world, we have to stop this madness. I think they understand that as much as I want to be with them and with my loving husband—He wasn't with me on this at first, but now he's all the way.

About three weeks ago, I had asked for certain things to be done. I wanted the power of attorney for all our property to be in his hands. As he was going out the door, he said, "Jean, you're planning to die, aren't you?" It startled me because I'd been thinking about that. I thought it was something that could happen. Hearing him say it made it very real. I said, "Yeah, Joe." So we took up our lives again and our love affair has never been nicer.

My mother was a person that believed, I mean really believed, in justice. Maybe it came from her. When the kids were little, I always said, "Don't ever look to the next guy to affect change. Do it yourself."

I remember one day, golly, it was 1967. I was watching television. This was the time when the people came over the bridge with Martin Luther King and with the hoses. My little son turned to me and said, "Mother, what are you going to do about this?" What could I say? I went down to Selma.

I suppose my neighbors out here think I'm kind of a kook. I'm pretty ordinary [laughs]. When I'm not doing these things, I'm a good cook and I have swell parties. A sense of humor helps. They don't know yet about what happened in Missouri. There is a suspicion. If somebody has cancer, you don't say, How's your cancer today? If I meet somebody on the street, it's, "Hi, Jean, how are things going?" "Swell, how are things going with you?"

Shortly before she entered the federal prison, she and two other members spoke at her church: St. Martha's. Four people attended. They had come to tell her they disapproved of her actions.

Joe Gump: "At a gathering in our church two weeks after Jean's arrest, not a single person came up to me to ask how she was doing. At another gathering, they seemed shocked that anyone they had known would do something like this."

The Gumps had been regular parishioners of the church for thirty-two years.

"Now and then, there's an encouraging word," says Joe. "I dropped something off at a repair shop and the salesclerk whispered, 'Mr. Gump, God bless your wife.' "

Their son, Joe, Jr., has occasional encounters: "Once in a while, a person who knows about the case comes up to me, holds my hand, and says, 'God bless your mother.' "

There's a ripple effect from what we're doing. That's quite exciting. You never know where it's going to hit. You just know you must do what you must do and let the chips fall where they may.

All I wanted to do when I was young is to be like everybody else. The same thing all nice little Catholic girls want. Periodically, I found I had to separate myself. I tried not to do that, because who wants to be different?

When I started dating my husband, right after World War Two, my aunt said, "Jean is going to marry a Hun." I thought, What the hell is a Hun? My husband's of German descent. We had just gotten through a war and we had to hate Germans. They were bad people. We certainly had to hate the Japanese. They were bad people. Through these years, I found out there's a lot of people that I have to hate.

We have to hate the Iranians, 'cause we have to go over there and kill 'em. I had to hate the Vietnamese people. I have to hate the commies. Everybody has to hate the commies. There is no end to my nation's enemies. But I don't think they're my enemies. I think, God help me, these are people.

What I did on Good Friday in Holden, Missouri, is only the expression of my Christianity. This is God's world, okay? We are stewards of the earth. I think we're rather bad stewards.

You know, I have never been so hopeful. If I can change my way of thinking, anybody can. I don't want to be singled out as anybody special, because I'm not. We have got to have a future for our children and we've got to make some sacrifices for it, okay?

Call it a legacy, if you want to. What else is there? My grandchild, I want to offer him a life, that's all. We all had a crack at it, so I think it's fair that this generation should.

POSTSCRIPT

Jean Gump was sentenced to eight years at a federal penitentiary on the charge of conspiracy and destroying public property. The presiding judge, at Christmastime, reduced her sentence to six.

For the past eleven months, she has been number 03789-045 at the Correctional Institution for Women, Alderson, West Virginia.

POST POSTSCRIPT

Since then, she and her husband, Joe (who had himself committed an act of civil disobedience and was sent to a Minnesota Federal Penetentiary), were freed. Neither recanted nor paid any fine. They are still at it.

Race:
How Blacks and Whites Think and Feel About the American Obsession
(1992)

INTRODUCTION

Obsession, n. 1 (archaic) The state of beset or actuated by the devil or an evil spirit. 2. a. Compulsive preoccupation with a fixed idea or unwanted feeling or emotion, often with symptoms of anxiety. b. A compulsive, often unreasonable, idea or emotion causing such pre-occupation.

—*American Heritage Dictionary of the English Language*

Obsession,...The action of any influence, notion or fixed idea, so as to discompose the mind.

—*Oxford English Dictionary*

"It obsesses everybody," declaimed my impassioned friend, "even those who think they are not obsessed. My wife was driving down the street in a black neighborhood. The people at the corners were all gesticulating at her. She was very frightened, turned up the windows, and drove determinedly. She discovered, after several blocks, she was going the wrong way on a one-way street and they were trying to help her. Her assumption was they were blacks and were out to get her. Mind you, she's a very enlightened person. You'd never associate her with racism, yet her first reaction was that they were dangerous.

It was a slow day. The waitress and I were engaged in idle talk: weather, arthritis, and a whisper of local scandal. She was large, genial, motherly. The neighborhood was an admixture of middle-class and blue-collar. On its periphery was an enclave of black families. As I was leaving, she said. "Of course, we're moving. You know why." It was an offhand remark, as casual as "See ya around."

You know why.

During the Boston school crisis, some twenty years ago, the leader of the fight against court-ordered busing proclaimed, "You know where I stand."

You know where I stand.

In Chicago, during the black mayor's first campaign, his white opponent's slogan was "Before It's Too Late."

Before it's too late.

Why were these people speaking in code? Why didn't the waitress tell me why? Where did the Boston mother stand? Why didn't the Chicago candidate tell us what it might be too late for? There was really no need. All of us, black and white, know what it's about. Yet, why the veiled language?

It is the speech of a beleaguered people, or those who see themselves as such. A tribe, besieged, has always been possessed of a *laager* mind-set. Every Afrikaner schoolchild has been taught the history of the Great Trek and the covered wagons drawn into a circle, holding off the half-naked Zulus. On late TV, we still see John Wayne and his gallant frontier-comrades holding off the half-naked Sioux. In neither of these instances was the language veiled. A savage was a savage was a savage. Yet, contemporary white America is somewhat diffident in language, if not in behavior. Therein is the exquisite irony.

Before Emancipation, black slaves, dreaming of escape and freedom, were forever talking and singing in code. Regard the spirituals. Jordan River, though heavenly in Biblical lore, was, in earthly truth, the swampland separating slave from free state. Pharaoh's army was not Egyptian: it was, in flesh and blood, the slaveowner. Daniel's deliverance was not from the lion's den but from pursuing bloodhounds. The Sweet Chariot was not driven by a Roman paladin but by underground-railway captains. There is no need to explain the veiled language in these instances. It was a matter of survival: life and death.

What is it, though, that impelled the waitress, the Boston woman, and the Chicago candidate to desist from direct reference to African-Americans? It certainly was not a matter of survival, though the *laager* fright was indubitably there. Had they been less euphemistic, they'd have suffered no public scorn. (Al Campanis and Jimmy the Greek faced the red eye of the TV camera; here, pretense must be maintained. Their punishment was manifestly unfair. After all, George Bush, in effect, employed Willie Horton as his campaign manager and was rewarded with the presidency.) It had to be something else that restrained the others; something that, perverse though it seems, offers a slender reed of hope.

Diane Romano, a mother of five, reflected on black depredations and her low opinion of most. "Maybe it's not really *me* saying this. I don't want to be that type of person. It makes me less a good human being. A good human being is rational, sensible, and kind. Maybe layers and layers of prejudice has finally got to me." She sighs. "I have such a mixed bag of feelings. I'm always fighting myself. One part of my brain sees all these things and is fighting the other part, which is my real deep, deep-down feeling."

A young schoolteacher, who had encounters with black school-mates at college and black parents at her job, says, "Though I was brought up not to be prejudiced, I hate to admit that I am. I don't like my thoughts and feelings. It is not a Christian feeling."

A case *in extremis:* A small-time collector for the syndicate casu-ally refers to "shines," "spades," "jigs," "loads of coal." When asked whether he considers himself a racist, he is indignant: "Hell, no! Did you hear me say 'nigger'? Never!"

The young construction worker, after offering a litany of griev-ances, especially in the matter of affirmative action, assures me that the stereotypes of African-Americans are true. "I seen 'em.

They live like low-lifes. Don't like to work. Let their homes run down." He quickly adds, "Oh, the black guys I work with are okay." He speaks of his black friend whom he'd defend against all comers. "Racism" is a word that disturbs him. Like Oscar Wilde's forbidden love, it dare not speak its name.

(A caveat: Since the election of Ronald Reagan in 1980, racial pejoratives have been more openly, more unashamedly expressed. His hostility toward civil rights legislation was interpreted as something of a friendly wink toward those whose language may be more gamey than civil. John Hope Franklin, the American historian, is "astounded at the amount of rancor in some quarters. The feelings that once were covert because people were ashamed of them are now expressed overtly. This crude and barbaric outburst of racism that we've seen in the last several years has been encouraged somewhere." It has, in fact, become *à la mode* not only among tavern troopers, but in the most respected quarters.

(A visiting Afrikaner journalist was astonished. "Being from South Africa, I am obsessed with race. Any chance remark registers with me. Click. I just sense the whole *zeitgeist* has changed ever since Ronald Reagan was elected. In 1979, I ran into very few who expressed antagonism to black claims for restitution. Now you hear it at dinner parties, without any embarrassment. I met country-club patricians who were as outspoken in their racism as their blue-collar counterparts. You hear the litany, wholly uninvited."

(During a visit to South Africa in 1963, I was stunned by the preponderance of racial news in the *Rand Daily Mail*. In reading our local papers twenty-eight years later, I have come to accept the obsession here as a matter of course. Have I become an easy-going Afrikaner?)

"Our worst selves are being appealed to," says a black dowager in North Carolina. "The signals flashed by Mr. Bush are the same as those of Mr. Reagan."

A weary cabdriver at the end of a twelve-hour day squints as he sips his coffee: "When traffic's beginning to close in on me and I'm behind in my money, I'm really uptight. There's a black driver in front of me, the word "nigger" will come into my head. No matter how much education you may have had, the prejudices you were taught come out. These sinister forces are buried deep inside you."

Much more may be buried deep, interred within the bones of all of us. Including myself.

As I stepped onto the bus one early morning, the driver, a young black man, said I was a dime short. I was positive I had deposited the proper fare. I did a slight burn, though concealed. To avoid an unpleasant exchange, I fished out another dime and dropped it into the box. My annoyance, trivial though the matter was, stayed with me for the rest of the trip. Oh, I understood the man. Of course, I know the history of his people's bondage. It was his turn—a show of power, if only in a small way. If that's how it is, that's how it is. Oh, well.

As I was about to disembark, I saw a dime on the floor. My dime. I held it up to him. "You were right." He was too busy driving to respond. In alighting, I waved: "Take it easy." "You, too," he replied. I've a hunch he'd been through something like this before.

In this one man, I had seen the whole race. In his behavior (especially before my discovery of the dime), I saw all African-Americans. During the trips I had conducted a silent seminar on ontogeny recapitulating philogeny.

A favorite modern-day parable of Martin Luther King concerned ten drunks. One was black, the other nine, white. "Look at that black drunk," says the indignant observer.

Several years ago, an old friend and I were in a car. He was regarded with great affection by his black colleagues. They knew his track record. He had been in the middle of civil rights battles in the early days when very few whites participated. Anti–Jim Crow, that was the phrase. A black teen-ager rode by on a bike. "I wonder if he stole that," murmured my friend. To my stunned silence, he responded, "He's poorly dressed. I'd have said the same thing about a poorly dressed white kid." I wonder. About myself as well. As the cabbie said, it's deep, these sinister forces.

The paramedic, who has worked in the black ghetto, who understands cause and effect, was driving along with his nine-year-old son. "There's a black guy crossing the street. He breaks into a fast run to make the traffic. My kid says, 'Looks like he's running from the police.' I hit the ceiling. 'Where the hell did you get a racist comment like that?' "

Where? Everywhere, it seems. Consider our media.

A TV station chartered a plane to fly a black journalist and a crew to cover a routine speech by Louis Farrakhan. "We had to put it on the air that night. It was the usual stuff, nothing extraordinary. I know why they sent me down there. They were hoping he'd say something outrageous."

During the Continental Airlines strike several years ago, an unusual picket line had formed in Chicago's Loop. It was led by a handsome pilot and an attractive flight attendant. A sort of Mr. and Miss America. TV crews had assembled from all three major channels. I assumed this would be the lead story on the six-o'clock news. It was a natural. Seldom before had flight attendants hit the bricks. Suddenly all the crews took off. They had not yet begun shooting. They had received word from their respective news directors that a shooting (of another kind) had occurred at a black high school. One student had wounded another. That evening, all three channels featured the black high-school incident. The picket line didn't make it.

The petite, gentle mother of two, an accountant, softly offers her opinion of television and the press. "We usually see the young black men in a gang. They can't talk. They have leather coats and are trying to conquer the world by being *bad*. What do you see first? A black person killed another black person or killed a policeman or stabbed someone. Of course, you're going to be scared of black people. You can't help but think they're all that way. That's not really what black people are about."

"My father is the kindest, sweetest man you ever wanted to know," says another young black woman. She writes for a trade journal. "He's very dark-skinned. It infuriates me to think that some little white woman would get on the elevator with my father and assume, just by the color of his skin, that he's going to harm her, and clutch her purse tighter. To think that my father, who's worked hard all his life, put us through school, loves us, took care of us—to think that she would clutch her purse because he's there. The thought of it makes me so angry."

Visibility is high these days for African-Americans, especially in matters of street crime.

Mayor Daley, surrounded by bodyguards, aldermen, photographers, video cameramen, and print, radio, and television reporters, toured the gang-plagued Englewood neighborhood, site of the summer's worst violence.

The purpose of the visit: to motivate the community to help police fight gangbangers.... Residents peered through windows and watched from porch steps and viewed the mayor's visit with cynical eyes.

One thirty-nine-year-old man shared a cigarette with some streetcorner buddies. "His face ain't good enough. You got to have some action behind it. If they give us some jobs cleaning up and taking care of the neighborhood, maybe there wouldn't be so much crime. We're tired of being out here broke: we got family to take care of. We get up and have to look at each other every day. We got nowhere to go."*

Yet in our daily run of the course, the black is still the invisible man. Consider the case of the senior editor of *Ebony*. He, elegant in dress, manner, and speech, lives in an expensive high-rise. As he waited at the curb, a matronly white handed him her car keys. I would not trade places with him on a rainy night were we hailing the same cab. Nor would a shabbily dressed white.

When Mayor Richard J. Daley died, many Chicagoans were in a state of trauma: What will happen to our city? When the news of Mayor Harold Washington's death broke, the first question asked by a prominent elder citizen seated next to me was: "What will Eddie do?" He was referring to an alderman who was unremitting in his hostility to Washington's programs. In the minds of our makers and shakers, the five historic years of a black mayor's administration never happened. He was the invisible man. Or, at most, an aberration.

Is it any wonder that I came so close to being run down by a crazy black driver?

I am a professional pedestrian. I am also nearsighted. I have never driven a car. Often, as I cross the street, I hold up my hand in the manner of a traffic cop. One day, as the light was changing, a cab did not stop and came within inches of knocking me down. I shouted. The cab screeched to a stop. The driver, a black man, leaped out. His words sprang forth, feverishly, uncontrollably. "You did it because I was black." Though I was equally furious, my attempt to explain my raised arm was in vain.

Was my arm, raised in the manner of a policeman, the fuse that

---

* Frank Burgos, writing about Richard A. Daley, son of the more famous former Mayor Daley, in the *Chicago Sun-Times*, September 19, 1991.

set off the explosive? In his stream of consciousness, was I, a white, giving him the official finger? Was he, once again, as I've a hunch he had so often been, 'buked and scorned?

The eleven-year-old black kid, with his comrade-in-mischief, a twelve-year-old white boy, cracked the window of an elderly neighbor. It was a small stone, sprung from a slingshot. When the woman confronted them, he was an indignant counsel for the defense. "You're accusing me just because I'm black." Why do I think he had heard this somewhere before?

"When I was young, I used to get a lot of grief from the cops." The musician remembers a bike ride through the park, somewhat roughly interrupted. "They thought I stole it. Cops still hassle me sometimes. I don't know one black person who has never had an encounter with cops."

The elderly ex–social-worker recalls a ride to Wisconsin with her black colleagues. "I was the only white in the car. Just as we were leaving the city, we were stopped by a cop. I don't know why. Our driver, the husband of my friend, was himself a cop. He got out, came back quickly, and said it was all right. I felt very uncomfortable. I remember saying, 'This is ridiculous.' Why were we stopped? I doubt this would have happened to white people. Nobody in the car said anything about it. We talked about something else. On reflection, I think this has happened to black people so often, they didn't think it was worth discussing."

Langston Hughes's dangling question is more pertinent today than ever: "Does it sag like a heavy load? Or does it explode?"

When I heard Big Bill Broonzy, the nonpareil of country-blues singers, moan the lyric, "Laughin' to keep from cryin'," I had to remember he died in 1958. He didn't live to experience the sixties, the civil rights movement, and the Second Betrayal. Bill knew all about the First Betrayal in the 1870s. His mother, born a slave, had told him about the promise to every freed man: forty acres and a mule. It was in the nature of a check that bounced. A hundred and twenty years later, with a couple of winking presidents canceling one check after another, Bill's sons and daughters are "laughin' to keep from ragin'." The laughter is no longer that frequent.

"Is race always on a black person's mind from the time he wakes up to the time he goes asleep? Wouldn't that drive a person crazy?" The middle-aged insurance man is repeating the question I had asked on a black call-in radio program. "Remember my answer? We are already crazy.

"Being black in America is like being forced to wear ill-fitting shoes. Some people adjust to it. It's always uncomfortable on your feet, but you've got to wear it because it's the only shoe you've got. Some people can bear the uncomfort more than others. Some people can block it from their minds, some can't. When you see some acting docile and some acting militant, they have one thing in common: the shoe is uncomfortable.

"Unless you go back to the roots and begin to tell the truth about the past, we'll get nowhere. If someone would rape my daughter in front of my eyes and sold my daughter and I'd never see her again, sure I'd go crazy. And if I didn't get any help to raise another child, with my insanity, I'd pass that along. The brutality that the next generations went through, it was enough to drive them mad. So our foreparents have been driven mad. It reflects itself in black hatred, too."

(In the late forties, *Destination Freedom* was a Peabody Award–winning radio series on NBC. Satchel Paige, the hero of one episode, asked Richard Durham, the writer, "Is colored folks in charge of this?" "Yes." "Ain't gonna be no good."

(Vernon Jarrett, a black Chicago columnist, says, "If I'm feeling good and want to have my morale lowered, all I have to do is drive out Madison Street and look at the throngs of unemployed youngsters in their weird dress, trying to hang on to some individuality. Can't read or write, looking mean at each other. You see kids hanging around, hating themselves as much as they hate others. This is one thing that contributes to the ease with which gangs kill each other. Another nigger ain't nothin'.")

The insurance man concludes: "I don't know where the story will end, but we are all kind of messed up."

It may be true, muses Lerone Bennett, Jr., a black historian. "But I still have hope. Know why? Given the way we were forced to live in this society, the miracle is not that so many families are broken, but that so many are still together. That so many black fathers are still at home. That so many black women are still raising good children. It is the incredible toughness and resilience in people that gives me hope."

"We live with hope. Otherwise we couldn't go on," says Professor Franklin. "But blind hope is not realistic. A strong sense of self had developed during the sixties, during the civil rights movement. When there is no longer that kind of hope, the response is frustration, anger."

When I was seventy-five, I was mugged by a skinny young black man. Was his name Willie? My loss: a Timex watch, net worth $19.95. When I was twenty-three, I was jackrolled by a burly young white man. Was his name Bruno? My loss: $1.25. It was during the Great Depression.

It was Bruno whom Nelson Algren celebrated in his novel *Never Come Morning*. "This was the sleepless city where a street-corner nineteen-year-old replied to a judge, who sentenced him to the electric chair, 'I knew I'd never get to be twenty-one anyhow'—and snapped his bubble gum."

Was it Willie's little sister I ran into a few years ago, as she was skipping rope outside the Robert Taylor Homes? In response to my banal question, she sounded eminently sensible, considering the circumstances: "I might not live to be grown up. My life wasn't promised to me." She was ten.

The difference between Bruno and Willie lay in their legacies. Their forbears were horses of a different color and their arrivals in the New World were of a different nature.

Maggie Holmes, a retired domestic, had little patience with the centennial celebration of the Statue of Liberty in 1984. She had followed its extensive TV coverage. "When you had your hundred years of that Statue of Liberty, I got damned mad. It was sickening to me. That wasn't made for me. We didn't come through Ellis Island. Do you understand what I'm sayin'? You came here in chains, in the bottom of ships and half-dead and beaten. What are you doin' to help them celebrate. A hundred years of what?"

Professor Franklin was interviewed during the centennial celebration. "I was reminded of Frederick Douglass's comment on the Fourth of July, 1852. 'This holiday is yours, not mine.' The same can be said of the Statue of Liberty celebration, 1984."

Dr. Kenneth B. Clark, with a sense of irony close to despair, reflects. "One thing white immigrant groups could do in America was to believe they were moving upward because the blacks were always there: down below.

"What I found fascinating is the tragically humorous condition of northern whites. The civil-rights movement made the white ethnic groups more democratic. The Poles, Jews, Italians, and Irish could all get together in their hostility to the blacks. It has become another aspect of the democratic creed.

"Being white in America made them feel equal to all other whites, as long as the black man was down below. They voted this way. Consider the blue-collar vote for Reagan. He may not have been their friend, but they felt equal to him."

The poor southern white had earlier teachings in this matter. Lillian Smith, in her short story "Two Men and a Bargain," writes of the rich white who persuaded the poor white to work for fifty cents an hour and, when the other complained, said, "I can get a nigger for two bits an hour. You're better than him, ain't you? We're the same color, ain't we?" Martin Luther King was more succinct in his 1965 Montgomery speech: The poor white was fed Jim Crow instead of bread.

Little Dovie Thurman had never met poor white people before her arrival in Chicago. "I thought all whites were rich. I began to understand there's somebody in control that I couldn't get to. It wasn't the person I could see. If white people hate black people so much, how come there's so many poor whites? Why are they doin' this to their own people, callin' them white trash?"

The maverick southern preacher, Will Campbell, dislikes the word "redneck." Remember the Edwin Markham poem? 'Bowed by the weight of centuries/ He leans upon the hoe/ And gazes on the ground.' As he so leans and so gazes, this parching, searing midday sun turns his neck red. We've equated that with racism."

"I began to seek knowledge about power," says Little Dovie. "Who's got it? Who's benefiting from keeping people separated? If you keep us divided, we will continue to fight each other, while the one has all the pie for themselves and we will scuffle over the crumbs. He can't eat it all by himself.

"As long as you holler 'Black Power' or 'White Power,' that's fine with them because you're never coming together. Dr. King was knocking a dent because he was pointing a finger not at race, but at who was really in control. He was gettin' at *it*."

Peggy Terry, her "hillbilly" friend from Kentucky, quit school after fifth grade, but she and Kenneth Clark share the same thoughts. "When a wave of immigrants came here, there was always some just above them. There has to be a top crust and a bottom crust in our society. Somebody has to be on the bottom.

"I think you become an adult when you reach a point where you don't need anyone underneath you. When you can look at yourself and say, 'I'm okay the way I am.' One of the things that keeps my class of people from having any vision is race hatred. You're so busy hating somebody else, you're not gonna realize how beautiful you are and how much you destroy all that's good in the world."

Leona Brady is vice-principal of a black high school. She was seeing "good signs when things opened up a bit after the sixties. We had a smart group of students. They had IQs, good study habits, and marched for their inalienable rights. Then a more docile group of students came along. It was right after the rash of assassinations and the Vietnam War. We ran into the Reagan years. They stopped asking questions.

"The white American is not innately racist. I sense innate docility. He will follow the law if the leadership tells him to do that. He would not rebel if he thought he'd be punished. But if the laws are flouted and winked at, he'll wink, too. We should have a beautiful country by now. We have no business having to go back and remake this wheel."

During the sixties, the dream, so long deferred, was by way of becoming the awakening. Marches, gatherings, voices from below, and a stirring of national conscience led to the passage of civil-rights laws. It appeared that this nation, white and black, was on the threshold of overcoming. It seemed prepared, though stubbornly resisted in some quarters, to make the playing field more even. After all, the law was the law, and we prided ourselves on being a law-abiding society.

It was a difficult moment, a strange one, for many white working people, let alone the middle class, accustomed to old "comfortable" ways. It was a discomfort to make room for those whom they had been taught most of their lives to regard as invisible or, at best, below them. Some considered it an assault on their family-taught virtues.

"I went through a bad time," recalls a fireman's wife. "I felt like being white middle-class had a stigma to it. Everything was our fault. Every time I turned on the TV, it would be constant trying to send me on a guilt trip because I had a decent life. I was sick of people making the connotation that because I was raising a good family, I was responsible for the ills of the world. The white middle class was getting a bum rap. Even when I went to church, I was really getting angry."

She was ready for someone to calm her condition, to assuage her hurts: someone with simple answers. Along came Ronald Reagan in the fall of 1980, with anecdotes of welfare queens and Cadillacs. In winning the presidency, the Gipper reversed the field and made the eighties the decade unashamed. "I liked the things Reagan did," said the woman, absolved of sin and imbued with a newfound innocence.

Yet, a still, small voice disturbs the fireman's wife. "People's expectations are too high. You can't expect us to like black people without knowing them. I'm very Christian, but not overly Christian. There's only a couple of people I dislike and they're white. I don't know black people well enough to hate them. Those I know, I like."

The embittered black man, sensing the dream once again deferred, responds in metaphors. "I'm not coming back to your house anymore, because you made it obvious you don't want me. I think we'd best be getting on, separating from these people. When Moses led the people out of Egypt, they didn't say, 'Let's integrate.' They said, 'Let's get the heck out of here.' " He sighs. "But I guess I still believe in integration. My daughter goes to the Eastman School of Music."

During the eighties, "the races have drifted apart in so many ways, have fallen out," observes Douglas Massey, Professor of Sociology, University of Chicago. "Even in language. Black English is farther than ever from standard American English. Increasingly, blacks isolated in ghetto poverty are speaking a different language with its own rules of grammar. It may not be inferior, but if speaking standard English is the minimum requirement for a good job, an increasingly large share of our population is frozen out.

"I don't think most whites understand what it is to be black in the United States today. They don't even have a clue."

"They don't like to work, the blacks," the young construction worker said. Yet why was that long line of job-seekers, mostly young blacks, snaking all the way around the block? In the building where I work, there's the hiring office of a large hotel chain. There were at least three hundred hopefuls, patiently waiting. I asked the personnel director how many jobs were available. "About thirty," she replied.

Even though it was cold, even though only one in twenty could make it, even though the pay isn't so hot, about 5,000 people waited up to six hours outside the Cook County Building in the Loop Monday, hoping for a job.

They were responding to an ad placed Sunday for 270 guard jobs that will open next year with the expansion of the Cook County Jail.

"We had people waiting in line since three in the morning, and by nine, we had thousands of people out there," said William Cunningham, spokesman for Sheriff Michael F. Sheahan.

The line, four abreast, circled the Cook County–City Hall Building at Clark and Randolph. About 4,600 single-page applications were distributed for the $21,000-a-year job of jail correctional officer.*

A ghetto schoolteacher tells of the new fast-food chain in the neighborhood. "They were gonna hire about twenty kids. Four hundred showed up for the interviews. This is common. They don't want to

---

* Ray Hanania, *Chicago Sun-Times,* front page, October 29, 1991. The applicants were overwhelmingly black.

work in a job that pays below minimum wage and never get out of it. But they're as hardworking people as you'd find anywhere. I'm talking about full employment."

"Affirmative action" has become an explosive phrase as well as an idea. The president vetoes a civil rights bill because he's against "quotas." Respected journals sound the righteous battle cry: "Reverse racism." Ben Hensley makes no public pronouncements on the subject. He's from Harlan County, Kentucky. He's driven buses and trucks, and is now a chauffeur for big-time executives.

"When I worked in Nashville as a helper on a delivery truck for Fred Harvey, a black fellow was working with me. He was older and had been there more years than me. They gave me the job driving and I became his boss. He knew the area better than I did, had to tell me where to go. I don't know how many guys he trained for that job. I always wondered about it, but never mentioned it. He didn't either. This was 1954.

"I never owned any slaves but I profited at that black fellow's expense. I think it's very fair to have affirmative action. For hundreds of years, the black people have had negative action. So they're not starting even."

Big Bill Broonzy laughs as he remembers his work-days at the foundry in the thirties. "I trained this white guy for three months. They kept him and fired me." Black laughter swells forth in the recounting of a hurting experience. It is both a survival mechanism and a saving grace. Else you go crazy. Or sing the blues:

> Me and a man was workin' side by side
> Here is what it meant:
> They were payin' him a dollar an hour
> They was payin' me fifty cents
> Sayin': If you're white, you're right
> If you're brown, stick aroun'
> But as you black, oh brother,
> Get back, get back, get back.

Frank Lumpkin, a retired steelworker, has seen it all, from the Great Depression to our current troubles. "This whole business of affirmative action was no problem at all till the jobs run out. It's no big thing when you're on the job. If the lion and the deer is both full, nobody attacks. It's only when the lion gets hungry, he really fights for the thing.

"At the mill, the Latinos said if the blacks gonna get up, we wanna get up. I says, 'Look, you got twenty white foremen and one black foreman and you arguing about the one black that come up!' It seems that we're just fighting against each other."

Howard Clement, a conservative black executive in North Carolina, favors affirmative action, "though there's a bit of unfairness to it. I see it as a way to level the playing field. There must be some other way, but what it is, I don't know. I do believe self-help is going to be the order of the day. We shouldn't go with our hands out, depending on white society to help us."

"When I found out I was an affirmative action case, I was devastated," remembers a black teacher of music. "I was not that hot spit I thought I was. I understood the historical reasons for it, but I found it tough to take."

Charles Johnson, winner of the 1990 National Book Award for fiction, teaches literature at a university in the Northwest. "On one hand affirmative action is justifiable. You need a structural solution to a problem that is centuries old. On the other hand, it's humiliating. A person, otherwise deserving, may be perceived as something special, having gotten a degree of help he didn't need. But without affirmative action, the first step toward hiring blacks would never have been taken.

"I suspect when I was hired at this university, it was an affirmative-action decision. It was in 1976 and there was only one other black in the English department. One out of fifty. Now there are two. So it's not that big a change."

What is to be made of Scholastic Aptitude Tests? The findings are, of course, devastating. As expected, black students fare poorly, in contrast to whites and Asiatics. Very poorly.

The irreverent Reverend Campbell has his own ideas. "What does it mean if the tests are written by white values? If the question has to do with pheasants under glass, white and black ghetto people will flunk. If you ask them about the breeding habits of cockroaches, they'll make a good score. You ask a black ghetto kid why his grandmother had iron beds, he'll know: to keep the rats from crawling up. A kid from Scarsdale will flunk. He'd say, I don't know. I guess she just liked iron beds.' "

A couple of years ago, I asked a black street boy about his grandmother. His "auntie," he called her. For the next forty-five minutes, there flowed forth tales, some apocryphal, some true, some hilarious, some poignant, all enthralling. He was Garrison Keillor, all five feet two of him. Others, freshmen members of a gang, danced around, eager to get in their two-cents' worth. They had gran'ma stories, too. I was an hour late for dinner.

A week or so later, I asked a little white girl, attending a posh private school, about her grandmother, who was living in a retirement community in St. Petersburg, Florida. "Oh, she visits us every Christmas and brings me nice presents. She's very nice." That was it. She undoubtedly scored much higher in the IQ tests than the black storyteller. They were approximately the same age.

A high-school teacher, who has had trouble with black students, remembers an especially difficult one. "The girl can barely read, can barely comprehend what we're doing. Odd thing with this girl. We did *Romeo and Juliet*. We'd listen to a recording, chunks at a time. She was the first to go up and interpret what she had just heard. She just had that innate way. I can't understand it."

Hank de Zutter feels he understands it. He teaches at a black urban college. "There may be a literacy problem in terms of the written word. But there is no literacy problem when it comes to reading people.

"If I come into class not feeling good, my students will know it immediately. They'll say, 'What's wrong?' They'll want to know if I had a fight with my wife. They'll want to know my feelings first. Then they're ready for teaching.

"I think this amazing ability to read people must be able to translate itself into riches in the job world. How many jobs rely on the written word, anyway? They can wire computers to change every 'he don't' to 'he doesn't.' The highest-placed executives don't write their own letters. Why aren't my students, who have this unique ability to read people, working where this quality is so important? They're experts and could be marvelous at managing people."

In order to read other people, knowing them is the *sine qua non*. "We know more about you than you know about us," the invisible folk had been saying long before James Baldwin so informed white America. "Look at me!" cried Richard Wright's Bigger Thomas. We didn't, until he killed somebody. Somebody white. He was quite visible then, as the young gang member is when a white is his victim. Otherwise, the shades are drawn. And he's still invisible.

As I walk down the street, mumbling to myself, I see an elderly black woman, toting two heavy bags. She's finished a day's work at the white lady's house. She is weary, frowning. I say, as a matter of course, "How's it goin'?" She looks up. Her face brightens. "Fine. And you?"

Three young black kids are swaggering along. As they come toward me, I say, "How's it goin'?" The tall one in the middle is startled. "Fine. And you?"

A presence was acknowledged. That was all.

I am not suggesting a twilight stroll through the walkways of a public housing project. The danger is not so much black hostility as a stray bullet fired by one black kid at another. What I am suggesting is something else: Affirmative Civility.

Mamie Mobley serves as the Prologue to this book. She is the mother of Emmett Till, the fourteen-year-old boy murdered in Mississippi by two white men. They were acquitted. It was 1955, one year after the *Brown vs. Board* decision, desegregating public schools. The Till case was regarded, along with the Supreme Court resolve, as a turning-point in black-white America. "Let justice be done, though the heavens fall." Or so it seemed.

Those of a certain age, both black and white, remember the boy's name and the circumstances. Neither this knowledge nor its significance has been passed on to today's young. To an astonishing degree, when asked to identify Emmett Till, their usual response is in the form of a question: Who? It is not a commentary on them so much as on our sense of history. Or lack of it.

On remembering her sons battered face, Mrs. Mobley's grief is infused with awe. "I was reading in Scriptures where the Lord Jesus Christ was scarred. His face was marred beyond that of any other man, and I saw Emmett. Oh, my God! The spirit came to me and said: 'If Jesus Christ died for our sins, Emmett Till bore our prejudices,' so..."

The spirit that spoke to Mamie Mobley is the same one buried in Diane Romano. "One part of me is fighting the other part, which is my real deep, deep-down feeling." Have we the will as a nation to exorcise the one and evoke the other? In order for us, black and white, to disenthrall ourselves from the harshest slavemaster, racism, we must disinter our buried history. Only then can we cross the Slough of Despond. Though John Bunyan's stagnant bog was of the spirit, it is, in an earthly sense, the same patch of swamp that separates slave from free state. We are all the Pilgrim, setting out on this journey.

Lloyd King, who closes the book, envisions a somewhat more secular trip. "I have faith we can mature. Stranger things have happened. Maybe America, maybe the world is in its adolescence. Maybe we're driving home from the prom, drunk, and nobody knows whether we're going to survive or not.

"I am guardedly optimistic—definitely guardedly. If everything is going to hell, it would be hard for me to get up in the morning. But I can't honestly say, 'Sure, things will get better.' We might not make it home from the prom."

JOSEPH LATTIMORE

"I am a typical African-American."

He is fifty, an insurance broker with another small business. During my appearance as a guest on a black radio station, he, a listener, responded. We subsequently met.

I was born and raised in Mississippi and after a stint in the army, I came to Chicago to make my fame and fortune.

I grew up in a small community. Piney Woods. My mother was a music and math teacher: my father was blue-collar, a plasterer.

Piney Woods was founded by a black man at the turn of the century for underprivileged black boys and girls. We had a lot of northern white people who would donate their time. They were not your typical Southern whites. I played with their small children as equals. It had an integrated staff.

I didn't have any real southern experience, but I was well aware. If I went to Jackson, which was twenty-two miles away, I had to sit in the back of the bus, and there were the 'Colored Only' fountains and bathrooms.

Some things are better today and some things are worse. In

1954, when the Supreme Court outlawed school segregation, it felt like Christmas was coming. I was fourteen. A year later, Emmett Till was killed. It made me realize that going into Jackson, I could have gotten the same treatment. I was a pretty spirited kid. If I saw a pretty white girl, I might say something, go beyond the borderline of what a black kid could say. It was all in innocence, but it could get you killed.

When I was about five, I was making noise in the classroom. The principal, a white woman from the North, said, "Little Joe, will you be quiet?" I used some profanity that the big boys had put into my vocabulary. I think I call her "a white s.o.b." She was going to tell my mother, I said, "I don't care, 'cause mama don't like white folk anyhow." When I would hear my mother and father talking about the dirty things that had happened, not by someone like this woman, I didn't know one white from another. It was real embarrassing to my mother, and I couldn't sit down for a week. [Laughs.] In another environment, I might have been lynched.

We used to go to the black drugstore in Jackson. They were just ordinary people, but someone we could look up to. We didn't think about it as anything glorious. It was just a fact of life. The neighborhood I live in now, all black, still has no black businesses. You've got a few in the city, but not nearly enough where kids in the summertime could work at somebody's drugstore or cleaners.

We encouraged our children to go to college and become computer experts. We didn't encourage them to come back to the family business, help it grow, and become owners. We told them to go to IBM where, even if they were geniuses, they'd never be president. After they finished college, they bought houses in the suburbs or a middle-class community.

We have left the hard-core underprivileged poor, have moved away from them and, as a result, they don't see us, the professionals.

My idea of Chicago, pre-1962, was almost like going to heaven. It was coming to integration, where you could sit anywhere you wanted on the bus, anywhere you wanted in the theater. Utopia. After I got here, I began to realize there was not the integration I had envisioned.

I had just gotten out of the army. I used to hitchhike home across Highway 80, and go through Montgomery and Selma. I could hardly count the number of state police cars. I didn't know what the heck was going on. It was some Freedom Riders or somebody.

I never had any trouble with southern whites. They would give a person a ride if he knew "his place." I wasn't threatening them in any way. My soldier's uniform. Yet I began to realize the dangerous situation I was in.

Vietnam was heating up. We were talking about going over there to fight for freedom, and all these buses were getting bombed and people were getting their heads cracked. I began to wonder, "Why should I go and fight for something that I don't have on my own?" I began to take a closer look on the America that I love. Until that time, although I was aware of things, I would have jumped on a hand grenade. I loved the United States. I had seen all the John Wayne movies. [Laughs.]

Mama, who is going on eighty-nine, was in academia and living in a world few blacks knew. She just closed her eyes to everything. My father was pretty close to militant. Mama used to get scared that somebody would overhear him talking about this country. He would be talking about Russia in a favorable way. He wasn't political, but he just knew that we were the one meddling rather than them meddling us. And he'd talk about injustice in this country. I'd get a little ticked off, though I never said anything to him. Oh yeah, I was patriotic.

In Chicago I started out as a bus driver for the CTA. That ended in 1968, with me getting fired and put in jail. I was a so-called leader of the strike. We had a great number of black CTA employees, but nobody in the hierarchy. It was during the Martin Luther

King years. We were going to a union meeting one night. We had the numbers and were going to make changes. The president gaveled the meeting to a close as soon as it was opened. One of us jumped up and said, "If you don't bring your ass back here, ain't a bus that's going to move tomorrow morning."

It wasn't really planned. We went back to somebody's house and to our separate bus garages and didn't know what was happening at the other ones. The radio picked up the news. Other drivers on the way to work heard this. It helped us.

Finally it happened. We were babes in the wood up against the sharks in the water. We weren't going to budge until they gave us our demands. It's difficult to take a working person past payday and keep him loyal. [Laughs.] We had a negotiated settlement that was really in a forked tongue. We were outmaneuvered.

They fired us in the leadership positions. Some of us got five days for violating an injunction. We didn't spend but a couple of hours in jail.

During the turbulent sixties, I remember driving the Archer Avenue bus. I'd look back and see a bunch of white folks just reading their papers and feeling very comfortable. I was up there bored over whatever the hot issue of the day was and I said to myself, "Boy, I ought to run this bus right into Lake Michigan, fly it, and jump off." [Laughs.]

I'd driven a charter bus of policemen over to Marquette Park during one of Dr. King's marches. That was the first time I had seen him with my own eyes.

I saw the mob. I remember down South we used to say as soon as the old heads die out, things will be better. I didn't challenge it. But now I saw women with two- and three-year-old children hollering, "Niggers, get out of here!" I knew that a parent was as close to God as a child would encounter. If mama was doing this, it had to be the right thing to do. Now these kids are on their own and I'm sure they have these same attitudes. I know that just living will never end bigotry. There's a lot of things that got to be changed before these attitudes will be changed.

I was thinking about how we celebrate George Washington. If we do anything to knock him off his pedestal, we're really gonna run into opposition. But we got to start telling the truth. He owned other people. If they were good slaves, somebody made them good by beating them half to death or whatever you have to do to a person. It's kind of like the Jews being made to celebrate Hitler. That's the way black people have to celebrate slaveowners of our past.

Remember what you asked on the radio? Is race always on a black person's mind from the time he wakes up to the time he goes asleep? Wouldn't that drive a person crazy? Remember my answer? We are already crazy.

Being black in America is like being forced to wear ill-fitting shoes. Some people adjust to it. It's always uncomfortable on your foot, but you've got to wear it because it's the only shoe you've got. You don't necessarily like it. Some people can bear the uncomfort more than others. Some people can block it from their mind, some can't. When you see some acting docile and some acting militant, they have one thing in common: the shoe is uncomfortable. It always has been and always will be.

Unless you go back to the roots and begin to tell the truth: everybody who participated in slavery was dead wrong. Sure, black folk are probably a little insane. If a soldier back from Vietnam was captured when the war began and had been in a bamboo cage and beat half to death, first thing we'd do is rush him to a psychiatrist.

Same thing with black people in America. Some children were sold from their mothers. A mother seeing her teen-age daughter raped by the slavemaster—I could talk forever about that. If someone would rape my daughter in front of my eyes or sold my daughter and I'd never see her again, sure I'd go crazy.

And if I didn't get any help, for me to raise another child with my insanity, I'd have to pass some of that along. The segregation and discrimination that the next generations went through, it was enough to drive them mad. So our foreparents have been driven mad.

When you see a black like myself proud to call myself Joseph Lattimore, I don't even attempt to find out who my folks were: the African name that I would truly have. It doesn't cross my mind. Nor does it cross many blacks'. Some, like Malcolm X, yeah. But the vast majority of blacks, none of us are trying to find our way back after we have gotten out from under slavery. I don't know where the story will end, but we are all kind of messed up.

In the black community, we saw the same TV shows as everyone in America. So it is natural for me to want Liz Taylor more than I want Aunt Jemima. And it's normal for my sister to want Tony Curtis over Stepin Fetchit. How would you define madness? [Laughs.]

To get out from under this yoke, black people will try to be lighter if that's what it takes. It's like a mouse in a cage with a boa constrictor. The mouse will do everything he knows how to please the boa constrictor, but when the boa is ready to eat, the mouse is gone. [Laughs.] Same thing with us. I don't care what we do, if they want to rub out King, they rub out King.

A lot of us are still praying and trusting in God and hoping for a better day. I don't have a lot of faith in a better day coming. I think we'd best be getting on, separating from these people. When Moses led the people out of Egypt, they didn't say, "Let's integrate." They got the heck out of there.

When World War II was over, the Jews didn't break bread with the Germans and be brothers and all integrate. They said, "These people was trying to wipe us off the face of the map. Let's get the heck out of here."

The Indians, as meager as their reservations are, are not in the civil rights marches saying, "Let's integrate." They say, "Hey, I've still got this little piece of dust, but I will stay here because this man will annihilate you." I just don't have the faith in integration I used to.

I feel like I'm going over to someone's house and they mistreat me. They make me sleep on the floor, they just do me all ways. I say, "Hey, I'll go back home and anybody that visits me, I'll treat you fair. Anybody can come visit me and I will make them feel just as welcome as the flowers in spring. But I'm not coming back to your house anymore, because you made it obvious you don't want me."

You once believed in integration...?

I guess I still do. My daughter is going to the Eastman School of Music. [Laughs.] She got pissed off at me the other day. She said, "Dad, I was talking to someone and I sounded just like you." She had protested a tiny bit because Eastman was not respecting Martin Luther King's birthday.

I don't want to build up any hatred in my children, but I want them to know the truth. And the truth is not gonna be found in an American history book. We grew up with these false notions, with these rip-off things. Somebody cheated some Indians out of some land and today history books tell us what a great thing it was to get Manhattan. Taking advantage of another man...

As far as integrating with you—we have sang "We Shall Over-come," we have prayed at the courthouse steps, we have made all these gestures, and the door is not open. I'm just tired. Pretty soon I'll have grandkids and they will want to sing "We Shall Overcome." I will say, "No, we have sang that long enough." We should not make a lifetime of singing that song. I refuse to sing it anymore.

I respect Farrakhan. He's an honorable man. I don't go along one hundred percent with anything anybody says. I would question anyone who went along one hundred percent with me, as smart as I am. [Laughs.] But I thinks he's got a lot on the ball and he is scratching where it itches—on me and whole lot of other folk.

I don't think he wakes up in the morning and says, "Let me tell off Whitey." I think he tells the truth as he sees it. Whitey interprets that as being told off.

He's advocating starting black businesses and whatnot. I agree with him. Booker T. Washington hit the nail on the head with "Cast down your bucket where you are." It was shortly after slavery and he said, "Hey, let's build up a community."

I don't think college is a total solution. If a kid is gifted and intelligent, he should be encouraged to go. If after about ninth grade, you give him a bite of the apple and show him the way to the library, he will go and get it. And let him do something the neighborhood needs. But in the black community, we're all saying, "Let them be computer analysts." I don't think that will do it.

As for Farrakhan and anti-Semitism—In Mississippi, I didn't distinguish between Jew and white. They were all white people as far as I was concerned. Even today I feel that. Jews might be the step-children of the white race, but they are still white. Tomorrow, if he decided he was no longer religious, he is still white.

There was this thing about Jews having bad meat and inferior merchandise. I'm sure there is some truth in that. I think Jews got caught with their fingers on the scale, but I don't think they were born to do this. Anybody in this capitalistic society will try to get over.

I think Farrakhan is having a bigger and bigger influence. I don't think it's his religious doctrine. I don't think there is any shortage in the Baptist churches of black people. His social ideas are what is scratching where the people itch.

It's like the black community has been hit in the jaw in a prizefight and they have been stung. If there are two fighters in the ring and one doesn't know he's in a boxing match, this other guy is going to hit him mercilessly. Black folk are still courting white folk, and white folk don't have it anywhere on their mind.

We went out for integration and it hasn't happened. We put our eggs in that basket and they're cracked. You can march, you can shout, you can do anything you want to, but I think we have to cast down the buckets where we are.

I did really believe there would be a harmonious getting along. I was all for Dr. King's March on Washington in '63. But I wouldn't take part in that now. I understand a little more now than I did then. I thought all we had to do was march and let them know we weren't going to bomb them. And put on nice clothes and let them know we bathed and everything. And they would accept this...[Laughs.]

I never really thought much whether I would be living next door to whites; that wasn't a burning desire. When I'm in an elevator with all whites, I have said, "Hey, they feel uncomfortable." I have always felt it. But I am not going to let their problem be my problem. I know the problem is there for them. I'm trying to get over mine: wearing an ill-fitting shoe every day of your life. I'm a practical joker. Sometimes I want to say, "Boo!" [Laughs.]

I have no desire to make anyone uncomfortable. I pity misinformed white people. Here we are, a nice, gentle race that has a great desire to be friends. I imagine if I had raped your sister and cut your mother's neck off and castrated your father and you came and told me you wanted to be buddies with me and live next door to me, I would feel awfully uncomfortable. I think white folk, deep down inside, do have that uncomfortable feeling. He feels that if he, the white, was treated the way he treated the black, he'd want to get even. That isn't the case, but he thinks it is.

DIANE ROMANO

1965

She is thirty-five. A mother of six children, she is separated from her husband. A devout Catholic, she is awaiting Vatican approval for a chance at remarriage, though it is out of the question for the immediate future. She provides for her family with a county job as "babysitter" for jurors. She reads law books, listens to hearings in courtrooms, and hopes one day to go back to school and become a lawyer, "even if I'm sixty."

She has lived in the same neighborhood on Chicago's Near West Side all her life. It is predominantly Italian, with some Mexican families nearby. Much of the community has been "renewed out" to make way for the Chicago campus of the University of Illinois. The area has the feel of an island surrounded by cement.

I'm in sympathy with Negroes. I'll go march with them, if it's something big. I don't use the term "nigger" in the house, and I never allow it. I don't know if the oldest is testing my authority; I know he has to conform to the rest of his group. Their parents are not really anti-Negro. It's just fear of the unknown. People here are afraid of the new. I know changes are coming and it's not all bad. I feel just as sorry for the white people who are scared as I am for the poor colored people who don't have much of a chance in the city.

A Negro girl is a good friend of mine. I've invited her to the house four or five times. Definite dates. "I'll expect you Sunday, three o'clock, and you'll have dinner with me." She always said the same thing. You see she was concerned for my welfare. "Now what do you want me to do, come up your front stairs, and stay half an hour and have your windows busted before I leave?" I don't know what my neighbors will do. I believe I am well liked and respected by the majority of the community. Now she's married so I'll have to invite her husband, too. But I want my children to see these people are no different from any other people, that they talk and they have manners and they eat like we eat, and they think and they have feelings, and they're sensitive and they're artistic, and some of them are strange and some of them are dumb—they are just like we are. And I think I'll do that before the summer's out. So that everybody will be sitting outside and they're gonna see these people come in. This is the step that's gotta be taken. Somebody's gotta take it.

1 9 9 0

She now lives in a high-rise condominium on Chicago's North Side.

"I went back to school and earned a college degree. I took a law-enforcement exam that lasted six to eight hours and I got a terribly high score." She works for a large federal agency, investigating violations of the law: "felonies, impersonations, extortion, embezzlement, thefts." Her job requires her to carry a gun.

Back in the sixties, I was very concerned with being a good mother and raising them in a proper way, not letting them have prejudices that I thought were unfounded.

Today I have mixed feelings. I don't know if it's because I'm getting older. I don't know if I've become a colder, harder person within myself. I still know all the things that the poor, that the black people have to go through. You notice the new term. I haven't yet got into the "African-American" thing. It was easier for me to go from "colored" to "black." But the new African-American thing, that's a little bit of a mouthful.

My feelings are really mixed today and I don't know why. Maybe it's because I've been out in the world now a heck of a lot more. I have seen things outside that don't please me. We're talking here about the race of black people. I have to be honest with you. Twenty-five years ago I was very sympathetic. Today I'm still sympathetic but I'm not a hundred percent sympathetic. That sounds terrible.

It probably has to do with the kind of work I do. I'm out looking for crooks and criminals. They're the people I deal with. It's a shame to say it, but quite a few of these are black people. They *seem* like they're all involved with the negative part of living: cheating, lying, stealing, dope, that type of thing.

Maybe it's not really *me* saying this. At least I hope it's not really me. I don't want to be that type of person. I've given up with the kids, *my* kids. I'm more concerned with myself and how *I* feel.

I think I'm a changed person. I realize one of the big reasons is that I see *only the bad*. I do have wonderful occasions to see the good. I've got friends. I hate to say black friends because they're just friends. They're wonderful people, artistic, thinking, profound, sensitive. Everything that I would hope I am, they are. But for the ten black people that I know who are very sweet and very good, a pleasure for anybody to know, I've got a hundred that are just the opposite. Maybe that's what's weighing on me so much. Because the majority of them are not the decent type of person that I would like to meet.

Yes, I know all the reasons that they are in the predicament they are today. I know they've been held back. I know they don't have friends who can push them into certain places. When Harold Washington was here, I think he was trying to do that. Here in the city most people look askance at that: "He's putting all black people in City Hall." Never thinking that when other mayors were in, they were putting all white people in. [Laughs.]

The office I deal with has mostly black clerical help. It angers me that a secretary won't proofread what she's supposed to proofread. If I write a misspelled word, she will put the misspelled word in there *knowing* that it's spelled a different way. She won't change it because she figures that's your job. She's extremely efficient, but she refuses to do anything that is not "her work." She's very snippy. I have to tone down my voice when I speak to her. I talk very soft and have to be very careful in my choice of words. Instead of saying, "Type this for me, I need it immediately," I have to say, "Do you have time to type this for me?" With other secretaries, I don't have to do that. She'll put all kinds of roadblocks up. I've called it a defensive mode. I think it's primarily antiwhite.

I'll go to City Hall, I'll see a bunch of people standing around, not doing their jobs. You ask for a little attention and they'll act like they're doing *you* a big favor by waiting on you. These things are magnified so much in my job.

Do you remember how it was when the whites were there?

[Laughs.] It was the same way. You give a little power to a clerk or someone behind a desk and they *immediately* grow with the power.

Do you feel guilty because you have less sympathy for the black than you once did?

Yes. It makes me less a good human being. A good human being is rational, sensible, kind...Maybe layers and layers, years and years of prejudice have finally got to me. Is it that I'm getting older and have less patience? I don't really want to be considerate of other people. I want people to be more considerate of *me*. Maybe that's it. All I know is I feel a sense of...loss.

I read that book again this morning.* I sat there and cried over the innocence of Diane Romano in 1965, how naïve she was. I sat and cried because I remembered how I felt at that time, in the hopes—oh my goodness, the hopes that I had for my own children, for the world, for the city. It has not come to pass.

All my children I'm proud of, but they all have their prejudices. What I attempted to do with their growing up was not a complete success. [Laughs.] I think the outside world and the neighborhood

---

* *Division Street: America* (1967).

carried more weight with them than what I said. I brought them up to be honest, to classify people by what they really were, not by their color. Listening to them speak today—they're all adults, so I wouldn't *dare* tell them, "Why are you saying that?"—They use derogatory terms for black people. I feel guilty because I laugh and go along with them. I would never have done it before. I would have said, "Listen, how can you say that? That's not so."

What I'm doing is the sin of most people. They classify them *all* as a lump. They're all on welfare. They're all selling dope, they're all selling their bodies. I know it's not true, but it takes me longer today to say, "I know it's not true."

I overcame prejudices in my own family. Now I'm reverting back to my parents' thinking. Blacks are poor, blacks are crooks, blacks are ADC, watch out for blacks. You're getting on the bus, there's two blacks on the corner, watch out because they're going to rob your purse, stick a knife in you.

If somebody makes a derogatory remark about blacks, I laugh with them, ha, ha, ha. Later I feel guilty. Why did I do that? Twenty-five years ago I'd tell them, "I'm sorry, but I don't appreciate that remark." I was a stronger person then. These years have taken a toll on me.

We have a new boss, a black man. Everybody's saying the only reason he got the job is because he's black. I feel bad because I agree with them. Not verbally, but with a smile, a laugh, body language. I come home and I think: why am I doing this? Why did I not say: "He's qualified, *extremely* qualified"? I'll say it to my-self but not to the white people who are making the derogatory remarks. Years ago, I'd have said, "What the hell are you talking about?"

What is it with me? Is it fear? I want to be part of the group? I don't want to be an outsider. I *want* to be part of the group. I think that's what my children had to contend with.

You'll find people who are quite qualified to do their job, but they don't want to do anymore than they have to. The blacks are defensive and content with doing the least amount of work possible.

Your friends—?

They're exceptions. Absolutely. And all the people from my church. It's ninety-five percent black. Holy Name. I still go to the same church. It was once Italian. We're all Catholics and we all attend the same mass. I go to 8:30 mass on Sunday morning. I put the coffee pot on, I make the tea, I make the cool drinks for the children, etcetera. They know me and I know all of them. We're all different ages, from the very young to the very old.

We have two young women who have a shoehouse full of kids. Do you know how hard it is for these young women to get those kids up in the morning and get them to church by 8:30?

And some of your black colleagues at work—

—Are exceptions. Oh absolutely. [Laughs.] I know, I know. I feel the reason the civil rights thing has slowed down is because of the black people, most of them. They've had time since the sixties to solidify a position in life. Most have had the opportunity to advance themselves and have made it bad for the next people coming in because they've been dogging on the job. There *are* exceptions but it's not enough to overcome all the negativism made by the others in the workforce today.

I'm ashamed sometimes of the way I feel. I went into a building to see a person who wanted to speak with me. It was an apartment building, three stories high. I didn't see any lights on anywhere. The door of her apartment was falling over, looked like someone had broken it. I tried to move the door and couldn't.

As I started to turn, the next door opened. Out came five black youths with bands around their heads. My imagination was going wild. They were between me and the exit. Now what happens? So I pulled a Clint Eastwood. I made sure my elbow moved my jacket so that my firearm was visible. And I talked to them in a very gruff, tough way. I walked past them with my back to the exit. So I could get out. And I did. *They didn't do anything except say, "Mama, what you doin' here?"* All they probably wanted to do was help me. But I couldn't take a chance. Why? Because it's a perception I have.

[Sighs.] Yeah, but if they hadn't seen my weapon, if they didn't know I was armed, might they not have done something? If I hadn't used my very official voice? I feel quite certain it was because I was armed, that I showed no fear, that I acted like I knew what I was doing.

You don't have the fear when they are white kids. You feel like you could talk to them or you could yell at them. You feel you could do that and nothing would happen to you. Even if they slapped you, you'd get real angry, but you wouldn't be terror-stricken. If these black kids did it to you, you'd be terror-stricken.

Most people have mixed feelings about the advance of blacks. Most have the impression that blacks are getting ahead because of the need for tokenism. You've got to fill a slot, we've got to have a black person. Nobody gives the black person credit for being a competent, intelligent worker.

Oh, I'm definitely for affirmative action. If affirmative action goes by the wayside, we're not going to have that opportunity for minorities. So it has to stay. [Sighs.] I have such a mixed bag of feelings.

I'm always fighting myself. One part of my brain sees all these things and is fighting the other part, which is my real deep-down feeling. I will come after an altercation and I'll think to myself, "That dirty, stupid, cheatin' black person." No, I don't use the N-word, not even in my head.

I want to be considered a high-class person. So I don't do the things that would typecast me as a low-class person. I wouldn't swear in general company. I wouldn't say dirty words nor would I talk about other people's race as being beneath mine. Because I know it's not true. I also know that low-class people think it's true.

It's all a contradiction. I want to be part of the accepted group. I just want to go along nicey-nice now. I don't want to confront people. I don't want to have arguments. I don't want to have bad feelings with anybody. Leave me alone.

I think it's going to take another hundred years, maybe two hundred, before the feeling of white superiority goes—this feeling against blacks, against Mexicans, against Orientals. Because they're different than us. Isn't that the whole thing? You look down on those people whose culture is different than yours. Naturally, you can't be as good as me.

That is human nature. How do we change human nature? I don't think we can. I think we can suppress it. Just like swearing. I'm the world's worst swearer, but in social activities, I hold it down. I don't use the F-word. I temper the way I speak. Maybe one day it will disappear, this racism. It's not going to happen in my lifetime.

Do you ever see your old friend, the one you invited to your old house twenty-five years ago?

I seldom see her, but we're still friends. We've gotten older. I'm a grandmother, she's a grandmother. When we meet, we run and grab each other and hug each other. It's so good to see her again and talk to her.

[Sighs deeply.] What I see out in the field are *not* intelligent, hardworking, honest black people. The majority of hardworking good ones I don't see. What do I do now? Wait until I retire and only have things to do with the good people? And then I'll change again. [Laughs.] Come see me twenty-five years from now, if we're alive.

POSTSCRIPT

"My closest friend at work, Anita Herbert, is black. I can talk to her without worrying how she's going to take it. She's one of the most intelligent people I know. I have an idea she's going to tell you the same things I did."

LLOYD KING

He is the third child of Leo and Vera King. He is thirty-one.

After he learned that I had met with his parents, he wrote me a letter:

"It seems children are always talked about when the subject of interracial marriage is broached, but we are never addressed directly. Many of us have something to say, not only about how we are perceived in America, but how we ourselves perceive America and the racial tension that exists, that has always existed. I am a child of that tension.

"The real tragedy between blacks and whites in America is not that we hate each other. Hatred by itself is a pretty shallow force and can only cut so deep. The real tragedy is that we love and admire each other. American culture as we know it would not exist if this weren't so.

"The tragedy lies in the complex folds of this love and admiration, which is somehow twisted into intolerance. We're like a married couple that got started on the wrong foot, foolishly believing that the man was superior and subjugating the woman, and like an unhappily married couple, we're sick to death of one another, sick of tension and strife that may be soothed occasionally, but never seems to go away. Rather it builds and builds, making us want a divorce before one of us goes crazy and kills the other. Yet, we love each other. Like a Greek play, there would be no tragedy if it weren't for the love.

"Give me a soapbox and I'll stand on it."

I remember growing up in the household of Leo and Vera. It was really active. There were intense dinner conversations that would go on for hours and hours. The bulk of my education was at dinner with my parents.

Since our father was black and our mother was Jewish, we called ourselves Jewbros. Me and my brothers, the race of the future. Everybody's going to be brown in the future. The pure blacks and the pure whites are going to be bred out of the race. I used to read science fiction as a kid. The good writers had everyone in the future being chocolate-colored.

Being the son of Vera and Leo is from day one having race as an issue. I became conscious that I was black in the sixties. I was pretty young. We moved from an all-black suburb to an all-white suburb and I had to get coaching all the time from my parents about how to behave, who to be, and what to do if someone calls you a nigger. It's something I've been grappling with all my life. At times I was down in the dumps, now I'm much more comfortable with who I am. I figure the world's got a lot of problems; either we straighten them out or we die. I hope we straighten them out.

If you got one drop of black blood in this society, you're considered black. Isn't it called the lethal drop? I went back and forth about that a lot. Sometimes I would put down "Other" in that little box, when you had to put down your race. Sometimes I'd scratch them all out and put down "Human." I studied anthropology in college for a while. If you try to define race or an ethnic group, it's tough. There are so many gradients, so many grays.

I was about ten in the early 1960s when Black Power came out. I used to hang with the Black Panthers. My mother was working in a Black Panther clinic. So I grew up thinking a lot about revolution. I thought black was definitely superior to white. It took me a while to realize that being considered white wasn't that bad. I began to realize that I love white culture. One of my favorite writers is John Cheever, who's the super-WASP. I married a WASP. I may have got it from my father. He started growing up in this all-black town, but at a young age got interested in Tolstoy and stuff like that. He had one of these turnarounds. He kept saying that he hated whites, but he loves them. And the white culture. That's why he married a white woman.

Racial tension has existed from day one in this country. You can't talk about American music, American art, even American dance and literature without understanding the love of the different races that founded this country. A lot of animosity, of course. Like a married couple, we have to live together. Sometimes we don't want to. Sometimes we want to beat each other up. Maybe one of us wants to get out of the marriage, but we can't.

I'm a musician, so I see a lot of things in terms of music. I think about the way white people love black music. They just go nuts over it. First, the white slaveowners outlawed drums. It's just not Christian, you're communicating, it's a way for insurrection. But even though they got rid of the drums, they wanted blacks to come up to the big house and entertain them at parties. They dug the music from day one.

The inverse is true. Blacks love white music and the instruments that Europeans made. I play the flute. Africans had bamboo flutes but the silver flute is something else. It's amazing what you can do with it. It's amazing what Bach did in codifying this twelve-tone system and harmony. It's equally amazing that there's a counterpoint in the rhythms that come out of Africa that you can find nowhere in Europe. When the two meet, it's very exciting.

It's no accident that I got into jazz. It's where black meets white. And that's what happened to me. I'm a child of black meeting white and it's a perfect home for me.

Now, the other side of the coin. Yesterday was the anniversary of Fred Hampton's murder.* When I was a kid, I hung out with some-

---

* He was a leader of the Black Panthers in Chicago. In a midnight raid, he

body who was shot in that raid. Four times in the belly. I was scared. I was eleven or twelve.

Then I was into rock-and-roll. I was heavily into Jimi Hendrix. A lot of people I knew seemed to be dying of overdosing. I was experimenting with drugs myself. I would break into my mother's infirmary and steal drugs. Experimenting. Because that's what we did in the sixties. I thought I was going to die of that. There was a lot of fear. I began to retreat.

For a while, I wanted to be really political. I came from a politically charged past. My white grandfather spent time in a Czarist prison for teaching peasants how to read. I was born into it. I thought I'd continue this strain, so I studied economics. I figured it boils down to money. The Golden Rule: He who's got the gold makes the rule.

In the white suburb, you'd get chased around by the greasers. They'd throw rocks and call you nigger. To me, it was fun in a way. You could run away from them and thought you were part of the struggle. It was different in high school. I got pretty much caught up with an artsy crowd and with hippies.

I went to Marlboro College in Vermont. There was a lot of pressure from my father to get into the hard sciences. He comes out of the Depression and he feels you'll not survive unless you have the hard stuff. Up there, I realized what I really wanted to do, so I switched to music.

It was a period of disillusionment for me. I think I inherited from my mother this vision of the world as a Utopia, where everybody got along and the poor were fed. I was escaping from my parents and a legacy. It was also a denial that I was black.

---

and a colleague, Mark Clark, were killed by the State's Attorney's task force, while they were asleep. Several others were wounded. In 1990, the Chicago City Council voted to commemorate Fred Hampton Day. Subsequently, sixteen white aldermen objected, maintaining they had thought it was Dan Hampton, a Chicago Bears lineman, they were honoring.

I was at an all-white school. I was hanging with all white people. I was getting into a more European culture. I was attending to classical music. Bach, Beethoven, and Stravinsky were my new heroes. At the same time, I was still very much into jazz. I did a fifty-page paper on John Coltrane. It was the beginning of an awakening.

I was playing tenor sax in an R&B band. It's a salt-and-pepper group, black and white. This is 1981. We were playing a gig at a blues club in Joliet. We're well paid. There's a big urban-blues renaissance that didn't happen in the sixties. That whole blues thing is like jumping through the hoops for Whitey.

We played two tunes and the owner pays us off for all three nights. He says, "Please leave my club." The Ku Klux Klan was putting heat on him. We'd noticed KKK graffiti on the dressing-room wall. The good ol' boys didn't like the idea of a salt-and-pepper group and threatened to wreck the place. If we were all-black, it would have been okay. I remember racial problems as a little kid in Oak Park, but this was the first time since I'd been a teen-ager. Remember, I'd gotten away. Race wasn't an issue with me, I thought.

These blues clubs depress the hell out of me. It's packed with young white people, mostly from the suburbs. I call them Cub fans. It's more like slumming. Remember the white guy on the plantation calling to the black? "Sing something for us." They were entertainers like these guys hadn't seen before. They were cutting loose in a way the more repressed European culture couldn't. Today these Cub fans feel this old black blues singer is preaching some sort of wisdom they didn't know about. There's a void in their lives, and they think he's gonna fill it. That's debatable. It's also a time when they can jump up, get drunk, and act crazy. It's a big party-time for them.

At a South Side blues club, you might see twelve, fifteen middle-aged black guys. They got off work, come here for a beer and the blues. It's not a place for them to act up. For them, it's more like sustenance. "This is what I need to cool off after a hard day's work." The singer doesn't talk between songs. He just goes from one blues to another. It's like you're in their living room.

At this time, I was personally lost, insecure about my skills as a musician, deeply in debt. I got a job teaching college down in Tennessee in '86.

Teaching at a white college boosted my ego. When I found out I was an affirmative action case, I was devastated. I wasn't their first choice. In fact, I wonder if they'd have interviewed me if I weren't black. I was not the hot spit I thought I was. I understand the historical reasons for it, but I found it tough to take.

I was there to save the school from a lawsuit. I found out that my best friend on the faculty wanted his other friend to get the job. He was a great classical-flute player, much better than I was. They interviewed him, a white male, a white female and myself. I found out they hated the woman but liked Jim and me. They thought he was better, but the administration said they had to hire me. "If he's your second choice, he's it." My friend now thinks that I turned out to be a better teacher than Jim probably would have been. He wasn't upset at all. *I* was upset.

I feel like I infiltrate the white world. I bring some African roots with me. I get co-opted on the way. My mother is white, the first bit of being co-opted. I go to this white school and get a white degree. I get co-opted by the system. At the same time, I change the rules. The more black people you get in there, the more the rules change.

I started getting grants and being hired without affirmative action. When you're black, you cannot help but second-guess everything. Does this person like me because I'm black or because I'm me? Does this person hate me because I'm black or because I'm a jerk? You're always second-guessing, unless it's another black person. Why do you think black people only hang out with other black people? They don't know what's going on half the time. You're working at an incredible disadvantage.

I live on the North Side now and hang out mostly with white musicians. I see a lot of love between the races here because they're nuts about music and it cuts across racial lines. My wife manages my business. She gets the jobs at parties and hotels. She also manages an office downtown. She got her MBA from Kellogg.*

When I started going with her, she got some flak from her family, not much. They're upper-crust suburban Connecticut. It was *Guess Who's Coming to Dinner?* Her mom worried for a while. She didn't want to have brown grandchildren. She's over that now. We plan to have kids.

I can't get too mad at white people. Half my family is white. But I don't stand in judgment of people who get pissed off. Part of me says, "Yeah, go ahead, good." My father's not like that and he's as black as black can be. He abhors ignorance. He sees ignorance as a cause of a lot of anger. You can't deny the anger people feel and it's got to run its course. Black people have got to get upset. I think they're going to get more upset.

But it's going to get ugly sometimes and there are going to be people like Louis Farrakhan and they have to be there. It's a purging process, like going to a psychiatrist.

It wasn't until three, four years ago, I had the nerve to talk to anybody in a urinal of a white movie theater. Something about it just brought back bad feelings. Though I'm half-white, I know that there's a myth going around about the black man and sexuality.

One of the things a lot of white women have told me is when they look at musicians on stage, they look at the way they move. A lot of black people move pretty loosely. Sometimes they have fantasies about how this person is in bed. It drives the white males nuts.

There are similarities between the black poor and "white trash." A kid like Elvis Presley grew up and had a rhythmic freedom that lot of white upper-crust kids just didn't have. They went nuts for it.

---

* The Kellogg School of Business Administration, Northwestern University.

"White trash" listened to Grand Old Opry on the radio. Black people tuned into that. Then white people started listening to race records being played on the air. They had similar tastes. They were loose.

Cops hassle me, but I'm too educated now. When I was young, I used to get a lot of grief from the cops. In this white suburb, when I was riding my bike, I'd get stopped by the cops. They thought I stole the bike. I was scared of cops. I don't know one black person who has never had an encounter with cops.

One day, I'm running to catch the El. This is the third time I got stopped by cops that year, okay? Once they searched my laundry because they thought I stuffed a stereo in there. This time I'm running for an appointment with my barber. I realize I don't have any money. So I stop by my bank on the way. I take out sixty dollars. I take a short-cut through the alley, counting my money. A cop car pulls up. They slam me against the wall, throw me in the car, no *Miranda* rights or anything.

I had a book under my arm. I think it was Salinger. I'm well-dressed. He said, "You stole this woman's purse." I said I didn't steal any purse. They take me to this lady's apartment building a few blocks away. They parade me in front of her window. She's three stories up. I look up. "Don't look at her!" I try to explain. "Shut up, you got no rights, kid." They really let me have it the whole time. I happened to look up a second and saw an old woman in her seventies with glasses. The window was dirty. I'm this black kid, three stories down, and she's going to identify me. I can't believe this. They had me walking back and forth. Fortunately, I was wearing glasses, too. She said it wasn't me because the guy that robbed her wasn't wearing glasses. They gave me my book back and said, "Get out of here."

Did they apologize?

[Laughs incredulously.] *What?*

It was '83 or '84. I was sitting there very polite. This is the way I behave around policemen. I didn't want to be late for my haircut. I was yessirring and no-sirring my ass off. When he gave me back my book, I said, "Thank you. I understand you're just doing your job." And I was gone.

If that happened to me today, I would give them hell. I feel big and bad. I wish they would pick me up now, because I've got a big mouth on me now.

I look at older people now and I love them. My father is beautiful, though he gets stuck in a few gears now and then. He says things that I think are crazy, and a few years later I find out that it wasn't so crazy. That old guy knew what he was talking about. I always make the analogy between a person and the world at large. If somehow, somewhere, the world could get objectivity. If there were some big universal mirror...

I have faith we can mature. Stranger things have happened. Maybe America, maybe the world is in its adolescence. Maybe we're driving home from the prom, drunk, and nobody knows whether we're going to survive or not. Maybe we'll survive and maybe we'll be a pretty smart old person, well-adjusted and mellow.

I am guardedly optimistic—definitely guardedly. If everything is going to hell, it would be hard for me to get up in the morning. But I can't honestly say, "Sure, things will get better." We might not make it home from the prom.

Coming of Age:
The Story of Our Century By Those Who Have Lived It
(1995)

INTRODUCTION

I am of the opinion that my life belongs to the whole community and as long as I live, it is my privilege to do for it what I can. I want to be thoroughly used up when I die, for the harder I work, the more I live. I rejoice in life for its own sake. Life is no brief candle for me. It is sort of a splendid torch which I have got hold of for a moment and I want to make it burn as brightly as possible before handing it on to future generations.

Was George Bernard Shaw touching ninety when he wrote that? Or eighty? Or seventy? The odds are his red whiskers had already turned white. I know this was so with the seventy-five-year-old storekeeper whose domain had become the center of the ghost town, somewhere in the hills and hollers of eastern Kentucky. "There's no way a man can slow down. I owe it to the people of this community. There's no end to the battle. The last flicker of my life will be against something that I don't think has to be."

Astonishingly, though the town is still up against it, among the many wretched enclaves of the strip-mined region, it refuses to die. The ghost has assumed flesh and is once again alive and kicking. Thanks in no small way to this man's obdurate nature. He had never met Shaw, nor, I'm fairly certain, had he ever read any of his stuff, yet the two subscribe to the same tenet.

I have chosen him, along with sixty-nine other graying contemporaries of like nature as the protagonists of this work. A few will be found here of another bent, perhaps, who nonetheless share his life span and hang on as obstinately as he.

The choice—seventy as the minimum age for admission to this circle—is not an arbitrary one. In our century, the scriptural three score and ten as the allotted earthly portion has been considerably extended, thanks to advances in medicine and—mixed blessing—technology. There is a note of exquisite irony here.

It is not technology per se that the grayheads in these pages challenge, though there are a couple of Luddites in the crowd. It is the purpose toward which it has so often been put. Among the grievances aired: the promiscuous use of the machine; the loss of the personal touch; the vanishing skills of the hand; the competitive edge rather than the cooperative center; the corporate credo as all-encompassing truth; the sound bite as instant wisdom; trivia as substance; and the denigration of language. Wright Morris, some thirty years ago, pinpointed the dilemma: "We're in the world of communications more and more, though we're in communication less and less."

I talk into the telephone these days as hopefully, though uncertainly, as my brother once talked to horses. He was a small-time follower of the races, who, at the corner bookie shop, listening to the wire, desperately urged on his long shots. Of course, they also ran. It was a precious moment, Lord, when one of them delivered. (O rare Morvich!)*

So it is with me and the telephone: Will I reach my party? In the dear, dead days almost beyond recall, a human voice responded. Today, in metallic speech, seemingly human, you are offered a choice of numbers from one to, say, six. If you are lucky, or if God is with you, you might connect—that is, if you remember who it was you called.

---

* A runty little colt who won the Kentucky Derby in 1922. My brother had a two-dollar bet on him. It was one of his life's memorable moments.

The Atlanta airport is as modern as they come. As you leave the gate, there are trains that transport you to the concourse of your choice. As you enter one, the voice you hear, unlike the old-time train caller's, is robotic. It, rather than he or she, offers destinations. The blessed moment for me, as I and fellow passengers entered in dead silence, was when a late-arriving couple desperately parted the pneumatic doors and made it inside. The voice, without missing a beat, intoned: "Because of late entry, there is a thirty-second delay." So much for the tardy miscreants. All eyes turned toward the guilty two. They quailed. Having had a couple of drinks, I called out, "George Orwell, your time has come and gone." Silence. I quailed. As any fool can plainly see, we have made remarkable technological advances.

There was a moment of saving grace in the presence of a baby, seated in the lap of its Hispanic mother. Having overcome my momentary guilt, I addressed the infant: "What is your considered opinion of all this?" The child broke into a wide FDR grin. "There is still hope," I cried triumphantly, despite the ensuing silence. Then came sobriety and a cold morning.

Chalk this up as the crotchet of an octogenarian, singularly suspicious of machines of any sort. It may have been one of my kindred spirits at the turn of the century, who, spotting a stranded motorist, shouted gleefully, "Get yourself a horse!"

It may have been an old man's arrogance in interpreting a baby's smile. The baby, much as Buckminster Fuller's grandchild, may have been attuned to the sound of the 727 long before it heard the song of the lark. The one song, the machine's, has become natural; the other, the bird's, has become exotic. Perhaps that's why old environmentalists sound so querulous.

Yet it was a ninety-year-old composer, who, at a concert of Stockhausen's electronic works, shouted "Bravo!" He had, sixty years before, in Vienna, cheered the revolutionary music of Webern, as others threw eggs. As I remained seated, bewildered by what sounded like static, he called out, "You'll see, my friend, one day you'll see." A young couple, seated nearby, holding hands, murmured, "They're playing our song." At least, I so imagined.

It evoked the memory of another concert, at a London watering hole, attended by serious, hardly audible young people. A tape of John Cage's sounds and silences filled the room, wall-to-wall with listeners enraptured. Standing. My calves were killing me. Bad circulation.

Life certainly does not begin at seventy, God knows, what with the ineluctable infirmities ruefully cited by our heroes. "I'm on my third pacemaker," says the eighty-year-old invalid, "and it's often out of rhythm and I use only half my heart. It takes down my spirits considerably." Yet her spirits soar, as she, in her sick bed, recalls her twenty-three-year-old self as the firebrand of the 1937 Flint sitdown strike. She is atop that sound truck once more. "I can't become cynical. I still hope we'll see a decent society, for cryin' out loud." A deep sigh. "I better take that pill now."

The Mexican-American doyen of his community, is philosophical as he responds to his buddy, who grieves on seeing him hobble with his cane. "It beats not walking at all." The widow of our century's preeminent cultural critic laments her husband's last years. "He was living half the way, obstreperous, incontinent, who had lived with such dignity." She bangs her fist on her walker. "This glorification of old age is a great mistake." Yet none of them will accept the status of Beckett's gaffers and crones. No trash can finale for these embattled ones. Their sphere is still Out There.

This work is not so much a gathering of individuals, survivors leading passionate lives, as it is about enclaves, helter-skelter, with these singular beings as metaphor as well as flesh. "Maybe there are people talking and thinking as we are now," says the African-American painter. "I feel as long as there's one person or two aware of our capacity to feel, think, and remember, we're on pretty sound ground." He adds tentatively, "I hope so."

During my occasional appearances in small towns as well as large cities—Dallas among them—there is always an individual or a couple, or an eccentric or town troublemaker, or a small group of gentle folk, who hang around after the formalities to unburden themselves. There is a recurrent refrain: What's happened to history? What's happened to imagination? It is these people the painter had in mind.

In Edwardsville, Indiana, home of Wabash College and General Lew Wallace, author of *Ben Hur,* an elderly woman, scion of the town's pioneer family, speaks softly, almost in a whisper, during the wine-and-cheese reception: "It is lonely here, thinking as I do. Remembering." It is she the painter had in mind.

Remembrance is the attribute that most distinguishes them. They are, in a sense, living repositories of our past, our history. Unfortunately, life's attrition is rapidly diminishing them in number; thus, the underlying note of desperation in the making of this book. Five I had hoped to visit died within a month of one another. At least three who appear in this book have since died. For that matter, I shall be eighty-three, if my luck holds out, at the time of this book's publication.

Naturally, the young are in the thoughts of these elders. Constantly. Though I had anticipated the touch of the curmudgeon, it was far less forthcoming than I had expected. There was sharp commentary, but the recurrent refrain was one of mourning. "I feel sorry for my grandchildren," says a pioneer public relations man. He adds, "I have no faith in my contemporaries." A West Coast philanthropist, a once-upon-a-time southern belle, provides a coda: "We must do something to merit their respect."

What is inescapable, a reflection offered by all the protagonists, is the innocence of the youngbloods when it comes to the past. And their lack of interest. There are the usual exceptions: the raggle-taggle marching kids so often maligned and ridiculed. "Most kids are frighteningly ignorant. They have no sense of history. What's worse, they don't think it matters." This from a woman who herself had been so much a part of our unwritten history.

The storekeeper remembers "the young lady student, she never heard of Roosevelt." Yet others saunter into his place seeking out his knowledge. The embattled old environmentalist counters, "Their history has been stolen from them." Among his most devoted colleagues are the young.

The actress regards her student-aspirants with guarded optimism. "Until five years ago, I thought they were all slobs. There was a kind of cynicism, an arrogance. In the last few years, I've sensed a change. There seems to be a new purpose in young people. Maybe, I don't know…"

The sparrow of a woman, touching ninety-four, says, "I think the young today are much more honest than we were. They see things as they are. I would not want to be young now. They're having a hell of a time. Often, they annoy me, almost knocking me down with their bikes and roller skates. Yet they help me across the street. They always come through, every single one."

A retired admiral who founded a whistle-blowing contingent of ex-officers which monitors the Pentagon is disturbed. "I lecture in colleges and high schools, the pick of the crop. It's obvious their attention is not on anything except their personal lives. I don't want to be an old curmudgeon who suggests that us older guys had a better world. We didn't. But this is unlike anything when I was in school." The elderly Jesuit suggests, "What they need is a national cause."

There appeared to be a couple of national causes in the '60s: civil rights and the Vietnam War. For all its excesses, well advertised by the media, many of the young engaged themselves in matters outside their personal lives. The ensuing decades of two conservative presidents succeeded in revising, rather than conserving, the story of that tumultuous time.

On a popular Sunday morning round-table program, two of its

regular participants savaged a guest who, we were told, was an emblem of the '60s. The two, one labeled conservative, the other, liberal (an egregious case of lingo-promiscuity), had a high old time with the hapless visitor. They were somewhat more self-righteous than the Katzenjammer Kids, but equaled them in lightheartedness and mischief. Joan Nestle put it succinctly. "The '60s is the favorite target of people who take delight in the failure of dreams." It is, I'm afraid, the sign of something else: a national Alzheimer's disease.

It is ironic that so many old ones in this book, though forgetful of many personal things, remember that decade as they had actually observed it. "I worry because I usually forget things, like where I put my shoes," says the Georgia widow who had been active in civil rights. "My daughter said, 'Mama, yes, deaf you are. Blind, yes, you are. But, Mama, you're not senile. You still think and remember important things.' "

The eighty-three-year-old woman, a stockbroker, laughs. "In some ways I'm better than I was thirty-five years ago when I broke in. My memory isn't so good on unimportant things: Where did I put my glasses? Where did I leave my keys? But if a customer asks me, 'Do you remember what I paid for my IBM stock?' I remember right off the bat. I remember the birth dates of people I love." In the remembrance of these elders may be a slender reed of hope. It is not upon them that a lobotomy has been performed, though you may find, especially among the golf-cart set, a self-imposed amnesia.

More than in any other sphere, it is the young's attitude toward the world of labor that most alarms the old trade union veteran. "The younger generation's outlook is shaped by the media, which draws a blank on labor matters. It's a rare newspaper that has a labor reporter these days."

At the very moment of this writing, a bitter strike is being waged in Decatur, Illinois, against a company owned by a British conglomerate. Most of the men and women on strike have lived in this town all their lives. Five minutes ago, I reran a homemade videotape: The city's police, helmeted, in full riot gear, are spraying the seated strikers with pepper gas. As the screams are heard, almost to a breaking point, I hold a stopwatch: ten and a half minutes.

I scanned both our local papers and several of our most respected journals: not one reference to the encounter. In 1937, when Chicago police attacked a gathering of steel workers, it made national headlines.

Each day, I sort out parts of the newspaper. I come across the Business section. Of course. I read about markets, mergers, LBOs, dividends, downsizing (read: *layoffs*) and related money matters. In an occasional spirit of whimsy, I look for the Labor section. It's my private joke. There ain't no such animal.

No wonder I had that contretemps with the young couple as we waited for our morning bus: I, with my haphazard bundle of papers; he, with the *Wall Street Journal* neatly under arm; she, with the latest *Vanity Fair*. We nodded toward one another, as we've done daily for at least a year. This time, I spoke. "I see where Labor Day is approaching." (It was a few days before that once-celebrated holiday.) The response was a cool, dead-blank stare. They turned away. I was hurt. Perversity got the best of me.

"That's the day," I insisted, "working people paraded down State Street by the thousands, honoring their unions." I was unable to stop; a soap box speech was in the making. With a clipped response worthy of Noel Coward, he cut off the old bum. "We *loathe* unions." Apparently, he spoke for both.

Instantly, I was the Ancient Mariner, fixing him with glittering eye. (Fortuitously, the bus was late.) "How many hours a day do you work?" It was something of a non sequitur. Caught off guard, he replied "Eight hours." I had him. "How come you don't work fourteen hours? Your great-grandfather did." He was pinned against the mail box. He looked about, as for a passing patrol car. The devil had me on the hip. "Know why you work eight hours instead of fourteen? Some guys got hanged in 1886. Fighting for the eight-hour day— for *you*." It was a reference to the Haymarket Affair in Chicago, so long, long, long ago. "They were union men." The young woman tugged at the sleeve of her stricken young man and, as the bus finally came, they scurried onto it. I never saw them again.

Often I think of them and feel ashamed of myself. How could I thus abuse them, this sweet-looking, all-American young pair? They had never done me any harm. Yet why do I, like Huck Finn on the raft feel so good when I think about it?

The labor advocate is even more critical of his peers: several, comrades in old battles. "Some of my generation has been elevated into the middle class, thanks to our fights to improve living standards. They have forgotten."

The economist, on the sunny side of eighty-six, sees further irony. "One of the reasons liberals have been marginalized is that government, through Social Security, through one benefit and another, has made many people comfortable, contented, and conservative. Where would Bob Dole be today were it not for the farm program and agricultural price supports?"

In the neatest trick of the century, big government the benefactor has been transmogrified into Big Guv'ment the bête noire. An old dissenter adds his touch to the tale: "Government today is most hated by those it's most helped." The old, old woman is less burdened by her Parkinson's than by her impotent rage: "They tell us what to think, the big ones up there. Don't they own everything— the TV, the radio, papers, the whatnot?" Her dark humor undiminished, she croaks: "Glory, glory, hallelujah, His truth goes marching on." Perhaps it's the mission of these old ones, vestigial remainders of a throbbing, embattled past, to question this chorus and remind us what the song was all about.

With our past become so irrelevant, with yesterday's fevered communiqué as archaic as a pharaonic news flash, is it any wonder that the young feel so disdainful of their elders? If it's a matter of competition (*competitive,* the fighting adjective that pervades all discourse on education, health, and business), it's "Out of my way, you old geezer. One side or a leg off!"

The retired CEO has seen it all. "There's a new breed now. In the old days, to become top man of a company, you had to be in your fifties and sixties. Today you've got twenty-nine-year-old CEOs. When I started out in the jungle, you were a baby at forty-five. Yet people are still vigorous at seventy, seventy-five. That's the catch."

The senior partner of one of Chicago's oldest and most prestigious law firms was retired after thirty-three years. It was mandatory: he was seventy-three. It was tradition. What was untraditional was his loss of pension. A disastrous merger had taken place without his consent or advice. He sued the partners and lost in federal court. The judge, a young alumnus of the law school the plaintiff had attended years before, said, in effect: "Those are the chances you take, Pops."

A pioneer television producer, a founder of the Chicago school,* is easy about it. "Naah, nobody wants lunch with me. Why should they? It's like spending time with your grandfather. You can't make a buck that way. Today's shows wouldn't have worked in our time. They're too hard, too cruel."

A successful comedy writer of the '60s and '70s has few offers of work these days. Though he is well-off in residuals, he's even richer in anecdotes. An agent was warned by a young executive: "Don't you dare send me any more over forty." A regular writer for Jack Benny pleaded with his daughter as they entered the office of a kid executive: "Please don't mention Jack Benny's name. He'll think I'm ninety years old."

---

* "TV, Chicago style" is a phrase coined by John Crosby, television's preeminent critic in the '50s. He was referring to a free and easy, improvisational approach.

The coming of age is regarded in some quarters as something of an affliction. For several years, a hand lotion commercial extolled its salubrious effect in freeing the elderly from "those ugly age freckles." A hair formula advertises, with considerable pride, the transforming of natural gray hair to ersatz black. The delighted wife, appraising her suddenly brunet spouse, announces to the world that he looks so much better. If further evidence were needed to prove that love is blind, this will do. The subtext is obvious: he may hold on to his job a bit longer.

Do schoolchildren still recite "John Anderson, My Jo John"? It was in all those *Most-Beloved Poems* readers: Robert Burns's endearing toast to gray locks, wrinkles, love, and beauty. How can they stifle their childish giggles, having been daily attuned to the message of Grecian Hair Formula?

George Bernard Shaw, as a drama critic, saw Europe's two most celebrated actresses at work, and aging: Sarah Bernhardt, mistress of makeup, and Eleanora Duse, who had no use for cosmetics. He said, "I prefer the Italian. Her wrinkles are her credentials of humanity."

Joe Matthews told me of his father's funeral. The old man was ninety. Joe, a minister, was asked by the family to say a few words. "I hadn't seen my father in years. I wanted one last look at him. In the funeral parlor, the night before, I looked into the casket and saw a kewpie doll! All rouged and powdered. I asked the undertaker for a basin of hot water, soap, and a towel. The guy was indignant. 'Your father looks perfectly wonderful.' I said, 'The hell he does. This is not my father.' Unless he gave me the stuff, I'd carry the body out myself. After two hours of washing off the guck, the old man's face caved in and all those wrinkles appeared. Those wrinkles we put there, my ten brothers, sisters, and mother. Those wrinkles told us that he had lived and so did we. At long last, I saw my father."

What most disturbs the painter is the young's obsession with the computer. "I am not averse to technology. But when a student can do a portrait by computer, without having laid a finger on brush, canvas, or paper, he's proud. 'My hand never touched it.' He can do that portrait in one day: no breathing felt, no blinking, no air around you, no space. Hammer? Chisel? They don't want to be accused of succumbing to this human thing: touch. Distance is a plus."

"The laying on of hands," says the doctor, "has been the most wonderful experience of my life. The house call, which may be coming back, became the hostage of high tech. Just as it's changed the nature of the practice, it has affected medical students. If you ask a doctor in training, 'How's Mrs. Smith doing?,' he'll instinctively go to the computer and punch out the latest lab test. 'Did she have a good night's sleep? Is that pain in her chest different?' 'Oh, I didn't check that.' Distant? You bet."

Yet the young scholar of avant-garde comic books points out the computer's liberating attributes: freeing us from drudge work for the more creative life. He's probably right, though I, a relic of another time, am somewhat bewildered by the new lingo. It is as arcane to me as Aramaic. "Hardware" does not concern hammer and nails and wrench, but something else. "Software" is altogether something apart from bedspread, pillowcases, and Turkish towels. My abysmal ignorance of the new technology has probably colored these introductory pages. I am, to put it baldly, a high-tech Philistine.

I envy the ninety-five-year-old sparrow who delights in her word processor and laser printer. "It's easy as pie," she says. I have just learned the mysteries of an electric *typewriter,* though it has in no way improved my hunt-and-peckery. It has, of this moment, gone on the blink. (Time out. It is a few hours later. The man has come and fixed it. "Nothing wrong with it. You pounded it too hard and bent the key slightly. There are some cigar ashes in the machine. The ribbon is stuck—I don't know how you did it." It was easy.)

After thirty-odd years with one tape recorder or another,

German Uher or Japanese Sony, I encounter trouble—court it, some would say. My ineptitude is ecumenical. Pressing the wrong button, I have lost (erased or failed to record) Michael Redgrave, Peter Hall, Martha Graham, Jacques Tati and almost succeeded in making Bertrand Russell disappear. You might say I'm a magician of sorts. Did Cagliostro ever make philosophers vanish?

These maladventures have nothing to do with age or oncoming dotage. It has been thus from the very beginning. My encounters with elevator doors need not be gone into. I have kicked at them on more than one occasion and there has always been a response. They close. Perhaps I'm a closet Luddite and my hostility, at times, bursts forth. So there is no point in my ever considering a computer or its next of kin.

The elderly lawyer finds his daily work far less demanding today than in pre-high-tech times. "We had to rely on the drudgery of recopying old documents. Today we photocopy. We have instant communication by fax. All of which makes the practice far more enjoyable than it used to be."

The investment banker remembers when "I used to sit with a spreadsheet, doing comparisons of statistics, ours and all the other companies. You'd be absolutely bleary-eyed. It was terrible work. Today it's easy: machines. I don't understand them. I don't want to. Too little time. The young ones know all about them. They're in, I'm out."

The carpenter agrees that technology has made his work easier, though he observes wistfully that "very few carpenters can file their own saws today. They don't need to. Hand saws are out." (It is the disappearance of the hand tool—and thus the loss of the human touch—that the painter mourned.)

There is a deeper grievance the carpenter feels. With technology putting so many skilled craftsmen out of work, why not a shorter workweek, say thirty hours? "More jobs and more time for creative leisure."

The retired printer says amen to that. "You can't stop progress, but don't tell me there's no way that replaced workers can't share in all these savings. It was their skills and muscle and pride that kept all this going all these years. Now our skills have been turned into binary numbers."

There is another matter that disturbs this voluble man: the disappearance of talk in the workplace. "Today the composing room is as silent as the editorial room. Have you been over at the city desk of any of the papers lately? It used to be so wild and romantic. Now it's dead. Like the composing room."

The irrepressible press agent, the last of his species, remembers his glory days as a familiar in the city room. "I'm in my shirt sleeves at the typewriter, flailing away with two fingers. I *belonged* there. If you tried that today, seven security guards would escort you out. Anyway, I couldn't work their computers."

On the desks of young reporters in the city room, as on the desks of young traders at the brokerage house, is the ubiquitous IT, through whose windows they stare, in the manner of voyeurs. Each is in a private world, close by colleagues, yet planets away. It is solipsism en masse.

Though silence pervades where once there was a human sound, conversely, noise overwhelms where once there was quiet. There was a time when a long-established Chicago restaurant had as its hallmark: No Orchestral Din. A quiet conversation could take place across the table and the patrons could actually hear one another. The place has long since been shuttered.

Several years ago, a friend of mine, a singer, concluded his concert. A half dozen of us adjourned to a nearby restaurant. It was about eleven at night. We were the only patrons. The canned Muzak was so loud we had difficulty hearing one another, though we shared the same table. We asked the hostess if she could turn it off or at least lower the volume. She declined. The simple truth: she could do nothing. It was remotely controlled.

When talk, where it matters, is discouraged, and quiet, where it matters, is also discouraged, is it any wonder that the speech of the young has been affected. "They talk in short, curt sentences," says the high-school teacher, "in phrases that are vague and often not to the point. It is their sound bite. And on the bus, with plugs in their ears, they're sitting next to you, but not near you."

The bus I take each morning affords me a window seat. The old ones are among the first to board. As we head downtown, it is no longer the Geriatric Special; the young ad people, traders, lawyers, secretaries crowd into it. For the most part, they are standing; the crones and gaffers, seated. My vantage point is a good one. I need hardly turn my head to see all my fellow passengers, especially the young standees.

Having nothing better to do, I study the young faces and, in passing, a wrinkled one or two. I stare almost to the point of rudeness; perhaps it's to attract their attention. I'm doing this more frequently than ever before—to make sure that I understand what is happening. I find what is happening somewhat troubling.

I am directly in their line of vision; they can't miss me. For a fleeting instant, Brooke looks down at me; Jason looks down at me. I, with the unblinking stare of a baby, await their recognition of my being—a something. Look, an old boy, a nut, a dirty old man, a retired lawyer, a landlord—a something. Not a flicker, not a millisecond blink of the eye. They look past the space I occupy and turn back to their casual, coded conversation. I am the invisible man, post-Ellison.

To make certain that my finding is not simply a matter of bruised ego, I peer several aisles forward and see the back of gray heads turned upward toward the standing young. I see the same piece of theater enacted; eyeless eyes passing through gray space, and becoming a touch alive as they turn languorously toward one another.

As for the old ones on the bus, they, having little else to do, sneak a peek, a squint at the young, in the manner of squirrels. They occasionally look at one another, too. They, in contrast to the new ones, recognize the presence of others, for better or worse.

Yet on the same bus, a doddering passenger is frequently offered a seat by a young one. "There is no rule of thumb," muses an old nonstop peace advocate. He passes out leaflets as frequently as he breathes; it's a matter of reflex. "The attitudes of the conductors on the trains I ride differ so much. Some were rough; some were wonderful. Same leaflets, same me, gray ponytail and everything."

The experience of a celebrated agitator is more personal. "My father was a right-winger, a real Horatio Alger hero. Yet he always defended people others looked down upon. When a waitress spilled something on my mother's new dress, he said it was his fault. Always. He was against almost every stand I took. But at his deathbed, I told him, 'Dad, you were my inspiration. I was following your example.' You simply can't prejudge people anymore."

So it is with retirement, too. When do you step down? Does the calendar decide when a person has had it? Is age of retirement a testament written in stone? To a spot welder at an auto plant, whose daily chore is mind-numbing, retirement after thirty years is devoutly to be wished. (Assuming, of course, an adequate pension.) To an old teacher in love with the job, it may be a disaster.

To me, at eighty-two, my job at the radio microphone, continuing or hanging up my gloves, is a matter of personal decision. Am I as skilled as I may have been when I began at the station forty-two years ago? I may be better in some ways, though not as adventurous as I once was. Do I enjoy the job as I once did, or is the law of diminishing delight taking effect? Energy or the loss of it may be the deciding actor. If only I had the wisdom and honesty of Lotte Lehmann.

One Sunday afternoon, at the end of her regular Town Hall concert, Mme. Lehmann, the nonpareil of our century's lieder singers, announced her retirement as of that moment. To her devoted, stunned audience crying out "No! No! No!" she gently responded, "Yes! Yes! Yes!" She graciously explained that, though her voice to others remained unblemished, *she* knew it was not so. She reminded them of her most celebrated role, the Marschallin in *Der Rosenkavalier.* "Remember the mirror scene? When she looked into the mirror and saw her first wrinkle, she decided to give up her young lover. I have learned from her, this wise, beautiful woman."

The aging CEO may see retirement as an end to power, yet the retired social worker may see her job-goodbye as the beginning of a new sort of power. He says: "When you suddenly leave the jungle, the phone stops ringing. You want to have lunch with old friends, but they're busy, working. I'm not in demand anymore. I'm seeking company rather than being sought." She says, "People who have had power, when they become powerless, are really tragic. We just allow ourselves to be conditioned by a society that tells us we've lost it, whether we really have or not. We accept premature death. When you inject something *live* into it, kick up your heels, you're exhilarated. You count."

Maggie Kuhn was recalling the moment she was declared redundant at sixty-five. She took to heart the lyric of Kris Kristofferson: "Freedom's just another word for nothin' left to lose"—and the Gray Panthers came into being. At eighty-eight, frail and faltering, she's still at it.

The Nebraska farmer, eighty, and the Kentucky storekeeper, seventy-five, still breathe fire, as keepers of the flame. Says the farmer: "If I could get ten active people, well organized, well informed, in each county, I could come pretty close to running this state." Says the storekeeper: "A handful in the beginning saved this country. They did the fightin'. While three quarters of 'em, by God, watched it. You never give up, because a handful can win."

Though the embattled spirit of the elderly suffuses this work, it is the sense of mortality, among the nonbelievers as well as the devout, that most colors their thoughts. As time is running out, their own and the century's, there is a consensus: We've had a pretty good run of it. Personally. As for their dreams of the world, there is a sense of loss. Their mourning is not so much for themselves as for those who follow. Their own passing is passed off casually, often with a touch of humor. "I would like to spend my day in a class at MIT, absorbing knowledge, says the eighty-five-year-old woman. "They can take me out in a body bag after that." (Among the Georgia Sea Islanders, the thought is put to song: "Throw me anywhere, Lord, in that old field...")

The printer, having a beer: "As time is running out, I want to win the lottery, buy three ships, man them with American Indians, and send them over to discover Italy."

The Iowa gadfly: "Mozart is my entrance into the sublime. At my service, let there be wine, cheese, and Mozart."

The radio bard, whose father lived to be 110, wants his obituary short: "At the age of 124, he was killed in a duel with a jealous lover. His gun jammed."

The sparrow sums up the light-hearted farewells: "Listen, since I got to be this age, I've got it made. No matter what happens next, I'm still ahead of the game."

Yet, the gay adieus do conceal a reluctance of these vital folk to cross the lonesome valley—not just yet. There are several, in despair, who would just as soon not greet the year 2000. Others insist on getting things in order before the long voyage, so, in the words of the venerable judge, "when I kick the bucket, I'll have everything filed." The ninety-nine-year-old child of slaves, considering her forthcoming hundredth birthday celebration: "I'd just as soon have a good dinner and let it go at that."

There are always second thoughts and regrets. The most frequent show of grief is toward the fate of their own children. The deaths, whether by auto accident, suicide, AIDS, war, or alcohol, they have, for much of their lives, taken unto themselves. Few are more rueful and moving than the dread of guilt felt by the Flint firebrand of '37, who gave so much of herself to the community. "Maybe I should have spent more time with the two wonderful kids I lost. Killed by a speeding taxi. Oh, my God, sometimes you think…they had such a short life." She offers a consoling coda: "Yet if I hadn't gone through all these experiences, I couldn't be the same person." Nor does she know how many others' children she may have saved from that dark and hollow bound.

It is she and her sixty-nine other colleagues in this work to whom the old battler pays tribute: "Think of what's stored in an eighty-, ninety-year-old mind. Just marvel at it. You see faces of people, places you've been to, images in your head. You've got a file nobody else has. *There'll be nobody like you ever again.* Make the most of every molecule you've got, as long as you've got a second to go. That's your charge."

BESSIE DOENGES, 93

We're in her apartment at a senior citizen's center in New York City. The electric fan gives forth a pleasant breeze on this hot day. She is relaxing on the divan, her tiny feet casually plopped onto the nearby end table. "Someone described me as petite. I can describe everybody else, but not myself. Maybe I don't want to look at myself. I'm just kidding."

She writes a regular column for a neighborhood weekly, The West-sider. *"I write about old age and how terrible it is."*

I can't seem to remember what happened yesterday, but I can remember what happened in 1912, things like that. I was eleven when the *Titanic* sank. They let the women and children into the lifeboats, as they themselves drowned. See, there is some goodness in people. I remember the suffragettes. And the writers, Galsworthy and H. G. Wells. We read him a great deal.

I was born in Canada, 1901. The Boer War was on, and there've been wars ever since. If we keep having them, we'll blow ourselves off the earth. Don't you think so? My mother and father were in church and the minister said, "All able-bodied men should go fight the Boers." My mother said she threw her arms around my father to keep him from going. She kept a diary. They all kept diaries. My ancestors were Tories who fled to Canada. They made the wrong turn. My great-great-grandfather's best friend was Benedict Arnold. Can you imagine?

What's my day like? I wake up in the morning and I think, "I'm glad to be alive." So I roll over on my stomach and feel just great. I look up to see what time it is and I go back to sleep. Finally, I get up and do a little dance on account of my arthritis. It helps. Then I stagger out to the kitchen and get this wonderful oatmeal. We used to call it porridge. I just pour hot water on the flakes. Get the coffee. Just pour water on that. I bring it back very carefully to this table. Then I get the *Times,* which a dear friend puts outside the door. And I read the obituaries. And I think things could be worse. In fact, it's damn good. I got through the night, by golly, and I'm likely to live through this day. One day is as good as a hundred days, when you reach this age.

I have a hundred things wrong with me. I could start at my head and go right on down. I smoked until 1958. When the doctor told me to stop, I said, "You're asking me to cut off my leg." He said, "Which leg?" So I stopped.

You're a salty one.

Oui, oui.

I take my time getting dressed, go downstairs and get my ticket for lunch. I've sat at the same table for eighteen years. We know each other thoroughly. Then I take my cane and try to get to the Strawberry Fields in Central Park. I ask someone to help me across the street and I've never been refused yet. They all come through, every single one. When you're ninety-two and five-sixths, you can get away with murder.

At the Strawberry Fields, I sit there. It's marvelous. It's like a beautiful picture: trees, a young man playing the violin. People have staked out claims. If I sit down at a certain place and the woman who always sits there comes along, I immediately get up, bow, and take another seat. You own that seat and it gives you a feeling of security, which you want very much when you're older.

Then I come home, take a little nap. Then I read and write this stuff for *The Westsider.* At six o'clock, the real evening starts. I have a scotch and soda and watch TV. I watch the news, and then *Jeopardy* comes on and *Wheel of Fortune.* Maybe you're too refined to watch it, but by this time I've had the drink and anything looks good to me.

Then it's eight o'clock and I fight sleep, damn it all. I fight it with everything I've got! I don't want to go to bed, life's too short. Actually, I sleep twelve hours or maybe fourteen. Sleep is my last lover. I don't want it, but there you have it. By nine o'clock, I've given in and fall into a delightful sleep. I accept it with grace. What else can I do? I wake up in the light of the morning. Yeah! Yah-hoo!

I always wanted to write when I came to New York. I used to get stuff in the *Times,* this was 1920. I wrote in the Hearst papers and got more money for verse than I get now. I never told anybody about it. I was writing brochures for a Protestant welfare group and got twenty-five dollars a month.

I grew up in a writing atmosphere. My father was a writer and a judge in New Brunswick. He had a story in the *Saturday Evening Post,* the same issue with Scott Fitzgerald. He wrote for Scribner's. High class. Then he suddenly stopped.

I came to New York to help my husband with his small printing business. I tried to write the great American novel. Well, I wrote it, but I couldn't sell it. I gave up writing and typed reports for a large insurance company. I was fifty-three and said I was forty-two. They were already funny about age.

About thirteen years ago, when I was eighty, I started writing again. A teacher at a senior club set me off. Almost at once, I began to sell to the "Metropolitan Diary" in the *Times*. At first, they only gave a bottle of champagne. Then the editor said, "We pay starving poets twenty dollars. Are you a starving poet?" I said, "I certainly am." So I got twenty bucks and my name in the papers. It's a family curse: we write and never get to the top. Then the great *New York Times* stopped paying. They didn't want any professionals for the section, they wanted sort of like "Letters to the Editor" stuff. I got something in Newsday's *Viewpoint* and they paid me 150 bucks. Wow!

I have something published in *The Westsider* every week. Fifty-two pieces a year when you're ninety-two and five-sixths—I've got scrapbooks here if you want to look through them. Verse, prose. I'm eight weeks ahead now.

What do I think of my contemporaries here? I like them. We have so much in common: surviving and trying to get something out of life. So we listen to each other's oft-told tales, because we probably do the same thing ourselves. We cannot help but like them, because we have common memories. They are really *us:* we're all one person.

I have a motto: "Judge not, lest ye be judged," and "Let him who is without sin cast the first stone." I believe that because man is prone to sin, and anyway, it's none of my business. I refuse to judge. My husband and I never judged each other. We were married forty-four years. He died in 1971 and I still wake up with his name on my lips. Writing about him makes me feel good.

I discovered things about him that I hadn't realized before. For instance, he had a way of thinking about animals and birds as if they're people. There was a swan up in Pelham Bay Park. He used to bring it food. Sometimes he even gave him our lunch. I didn't think much of that. I wrote about this: *The Wayward Swan.*

I think the young today are much more honest than we were. They see things as they are. I would not want to be young now. They're having a hell of a time. I feel I've been lucky in life. In the Depression, my husband's business, my goodness. Terrible. We slept in the park because we had no money for rent. He said, "I'm gonna sell the dump. I'm a burden to you." I wouldn't let him. I still had a job. We'd sleep in the park, what'd it matter? I let him do the worrying for both of us. No, I don't judge the young. They're having an unhappy time.

What are your thoughts as you read the news today?

Simply terrible. People starving to death. Do you have a right to be happy when you read about a Bosnian child as you have your morning toast? Do you know how many pills I take for everything? Six, seven times or so. One for emphysema; something I call "dipsydoodle," for circulation; for blood pressure; for my heart; for diverticulosis—which makes me sick. I cut it out.

Scientifically, the world has gone beautifully. It's very exciting. You see a young woman walk along the street with something in her ear. She's talking to someone on the telephone. It's exciting to be alive, but I don't have a great deal of hope for the world. I think we're going to blow ourselves up. We could have *everything,* everybody. We're going to make it so we don't have to do donkey work: press a button. We can enjoy music, art, gardening, all the fine things. And have time to be friends. But we're going to throw it all away. I think we're no damn good.

What is it about the human race?

Our jungle heritage. [Chuckles, self-deprecatingly.] I have the nerve to make any statement. It's such a complex, dark problem. A lot of stuff I write is about the supernatural. I don't know why that is.

Do you believe in the supernatural?

I don't know. I really don't care one way or the other. Yes, I do care. I don't want to die. How would I like to be remembered? I don't want to be celebrated, just forget it. Take all my writings that are left and make a big bonfire out of them. I'm going to be cremated, and I don't want to linger if there's something the matter with me. I've got a will to that effect.

I must be independent. I wouldn't want to live with relatives, have them boss me around and be a burden. That's why I went to my wonderful doctor of forty years. I told her my feet are going to sleep. She said, "Bang them on the floor."

Listen, I get out on the street with my cane and all of a sudden, I've lost my balance, I can't take a step, I holler, "Help, help." Immediately, a crowd will come and they'll want to help me home. But I get my balance back and I walk.

No one has ever failed to help you, yet you say these same people will blow themselves up—

There seems to be something in man, an altruistic something, away from the self, toward others. That is the hope of the world. But with all the wars I've seen, all the unhappiness, I don't think the world will survive. I sure *hope* it does.

I'm a Baptist and Methodist, but I haven't been to church for many years. I notice that people my age who have religion can face death better than the ones who don't. They'll say, "The Lord is watching over me and he'll take care of me. If he wants me to die, that'll be great. I'll die with His name on my lips. Oh, my blessed savior." I can't do that.

I envy them and I don't. They think they're going to heaven. I don't know about the hereafter. I think the soul survives, perhaps. Yeah, I think there's something in people that may survive. I just plain don't know. I don't laugh at people who believe in the supernatural. They may be right! I wouldn't say either way.

I'm an agnostic, I guess. Then again, maybe I'm not. I don't want to influence anybody one way or the other. I don't want to offend anybody, hurt them. 'Cause, listen, words can hurt. Oh, boy. I had a stepmother, a very beautiful woman of a very fine family. Somehow she hated us. I had a cancer on my nose when I was a baby. They had to cut through the nose to get it out. I was so sensitive about it as a child. They'd call out to me, "Split nose." My stepmother called me "an ugly little hussy," "a fiend out of hell." She said, "I hated you from the minute I set my eyes on you."

I used to run away a lot and was something of a problem child. Look at it from her point of view: she was a beautiful woman, thirty-one years old when she married my father. Here are these three kids dumped on her. She had been married to a planter from India, and there were all sorts of clippings about him and his lovely Canadian bride. You've got to think about that. I did judge her for years, but now I don't know.

Maybe that's why you're so lively. You don't carry that extra vengeance and self-righteousness.

I've got enough faults without that.

We look through her scrapbook. There are scores of her columns, "Bessie Writes" and some Times' *"Metropolitan Diary" pieces.*

Here's one I wrote in the '80s. [She reads.] "Entering the park, I stared at a chestnut tree that I fell into, or it fell into me, and I got to be it." I have a hundred things like that.

I wrote about my friend Jack. He sent me a note that's stuck on my Frigidaire. "Life, a hop, a skip, and a jump, and it's over." He died a week later.

Here's another: "My nephew said, 'Some birds just sing in the springtime. After that they only call.' I tried a little jig on my ninety-two-year-old feet. 'It's true all right,' I agreed. Everything sings in the springtime. The primal shout, when they all start singing at once. Aren't the birds telling us something? Something about survival, about hope, something about love, would you say? What else does it do? What else? It dares you not to believe in God."

T. S. Eliot was right when he wrote, "April is the cruelest month, breeding lilacs out of the dead land, mixing memory and desire." That's how I headed one of my things. "Imprisoned in the city on a rainy Sunday, in a fifth-floor walk-up. Hard for two to live in peace. You prefer the sanctuary of the empty streets. I didn't blame you, but you came back too soon, bringing me a bunch of purple lilacs, backyard lilacs, back home lilacs. Thrust them in my arms with love abundant, giving us a chance to start all over." I think I'll add another line. "Sixty years gone by, but I still see you standing there and smiling. With the lilacs in your arms. Yes, yes, April is the cruelest month."

In her office, the director of the center reads from a letter to the editor of The Westsider: *"In the last few issues, Bessie has become sublime. Her pieces have always been good, but suddenly they constrict the throat and make the breath catch. She's sharing herself in such an immediate and personal way now. She's offering herself with total unselfconsciousness and yet full consciousness. What a gift she's given us. Thank you, Bessie."*

In the manner of a tour guide, Bessie introduces me to some of her fellow residents as we pass through.

PORTLY MAN: *I'm blessed by the almighty, if there is such a thing. I* say to myself, "I don't know everything, therefore this is one of the things I don't know." I'm eighty-nine and I was in the clothing business. I'm interested in something I know nothing about. *The fact that I'm looking is the important thing. Seeking is more important than the end.*

WOMAN: *You've heard of my son. He translated* The Dead Sea Scrolls Uncovered.

PORTLY MAN: *I'm not interested in anything that's dead.*

THIN MAN: *Do you understand German? I'm a free thinker. Die Gedanken sind Frei.*

STUDS TERKEL: *I have to scram, but I enjoyed meeting you.*

PORTLY MAN: *That's what life is about, passing the time of the day.*

MUSCULAR MAN: *Not passing, filling. I'm a body builder, eighty-one years old. I've become known for that. I'm the oldest guy doing this.*

PORTLY WOMAN: *I sang Brunhilde in Germany, and I sang Kundry in Parsifal at La Scala. Without an agent. Are you interested in music? The story of my life is unbelievable.*

We're on the patio of a restaurant, watching the passing parade on the crowded city street.

I eat up their faces. They all look beautiful, and the reason is that they are alive. Everything alive is beautiful. Even murderers. Whatever good there is in them is still alive. The alive part, call it the soul, call it what you will. I choose not to see the other part. It's not my affair.

[She laughs at something she sees. Or is it something she thought?]

You've got to have humor to get through life. It's the one best thing, so help me. Maybe I'm laughing so I won't burst out crying. Who knows? Listen, I figure, since I got to be this age, I've got it made. No matter what terrible thing may happen, I'm still ahead of the game.

JACK CULBERG, 79

The corporation is a jungle. It's exciting. You're thrown in on your own and you're constantly battling to survive. When you learn to survive, the game is to become the conqueror, the leader.

—Larry Ross (pseudonym for Jack Culberg), *Working*, 1970

He is now a corporate consultant in Chicago. Over the years, he has served as CEO of several conglomerates.

We're a new generation. When we grew up anybody fifty or sixty was considered old. I remember as a young boy, thirteen, fourteen, attending the twenty-fifth wedding anniversary of my mother and father. Everybody was dancing and singing and having a wonderful time. I remember saying to myself: "What are they so happy about? They're on the verge of dying." They were maybe fifty-five.

There's a new breed now. I'm going to be seventy-nine in July and I don't for a second consider myself old. I still play a good game of golf, and I exercise and swim and am active in business. There are many corporations out there that feel you're old and should be out of it, no matter how you look or feel. You have to quit at sixty-five or seventy. You can't be on the board. I don't feel that way at all. I'm still involved. I don't feel any older than them in any way. I feel I have more vitality than those who call me an old man. You turn around and want to know who the hell they're talking about.

What I said about the corporate jungle twenty-five years ago still goes. I've been in it ever since 1942. When you suddenly leave it, life is pretty empty. I was sixty-five, the age people are supposed to retire. I started to miss it quite a bit. The phone stops ringing. The king is dead. You start wanting to have lunch with old friends. At the beginning, they're nice to you, but then you realize that they're busy, they're working. They've got a job to do and just don't have the time to talk to anybody where it doesn't involve their business. I could be nasty and say, "Unless they can make a buck out of it"—but I won't. [Chuckles.] You hesitate to call them.*

You get involved in so-called charity work. I did a lot of consulting for not-for-profit organizations. It was encouraging for a while, but the people who run that world are a different breed. They're social workers who've become managers. The great curse of business is amateurs running things. They can't make it. It's amazing how much money is foolishly wasted in charitable organizations.

But Jobs for Youth is something else. It's a sensational group. It takes dropouts from high school, ages seventeen to twenty-one. We train them, get them a diploma, counseling, and jobs. We place eight hundred to nine hundred a year. I'm still on the board.

As for the corporate jungle, it's even worse today. The circle of power is becoming smaller and smaller with fewer and fewer dominant people in control. IBM can lay off fifty thousand, or General

---

* It was Gaylord Freeman's last year as chairman of the board of the First National Bank of Chicago. A successor had already been chosen. "As soon as Bob was designated as my successor, it was inevitable that people say, 'Gale Freeman's a nice guy, but Bob's the fella we should be talking to.' I find now that every couple of weeks I have a free luncheon engagement. Where will I have lunch? I had a magnificent dining room here. I'll go to a club. I won't be in demand. I'll seeking company rather than being sought."

—From *American Dreams: Lost and Found,* 1980

Motors. They're not talking about blue-collar workers necessarily. They're talking about middle management who aspire to become CEOs. Today lots more people are fired or forced to retire before they reach the fifty percent mark on the way to the top. The jungle has become worse. You can smell the insecurity and fear all over the place. And the people who lose those jobs have nowhere else to go.

Most big corporations suggest early retirement. It isn't as much pension as you'd get if you lived out the entire thing. You take it. A genteel form of being fired.*

Of course, you're more afraid now than when we last met, twenty-five years ago. If you lost your job then, there were many more opportunities to find another. Today there are fewer companies. I'm talking about middle management and up. Let's say you're the manager of a company division and they're merged or bought out. They cut down on the bureaucrats and you're fired. Where do you go? A lot of them are taking lesser jobs.

Most of these people live on their investments or whatever they saved up. The interest rate is so low, they're having great difficulty. Let's say you have a million dollars saved. In the old days, it was an astronomical amount of money. If you're getting an interest of three percent, that's $30,000 a year. You can't live on that. So you have to go into the principal. It's very uneasy now. In the old days, it didn't mean a hell of a lot because nobody lived that long. The longer the life span, the more the insecurity—for the great majority.

I happen to be one of the lucky ones. When I retired at the age of sixty-five, I thought I had enough money to live comfortably. If things hadn't happened for me during my retirement, I'd have a rough time now. With retirement, I started doing some consulting.

---

* A neighbor of mine, an executive of a large consulting firm, had just touched fifty-five. It was suggested—astonishing him—that he accept early retirement. There had been no forewarning at all; he had been expecting a promotion. "They made me an offer I couldn't refuse," he deadpanned. "They had a younger guy in the wings, for about half my salary and none of my benefits…"

I wasn't satisfied just playing golf or spending winters in Florida. I was too involved in the business world because it was exciting. It had been my whole life.

So I started dabbling around. The LBO* swing came in. One of the top men in the business is someone I've known for years. I found some businesses for him. For at least nine years, I've been involved with these companies. I'm still the chairman of one. In the last seven, eight years, I've made myself an awful lot of money—I was able to work three to four days a week and have a ball. Now I spend maybe two days a month. I still have a hand in. I have a fax machine at home and daily reports, but I'm not in active management.

Because you're a top businessman, you don't stop being a human being. Human frailties exist in the corporate world as they do outside. The top executive is the loneliest guy in the world because he can't talk confidentially to the board of directors. They expect him to be strong and know everything. They don't want a guy that's doubtful or weak. He can't talk to the people working for him because he's got a guy who'll say yes to anything he says and the other guy wants his job. So he doesn't have anybody to talk to. So he becomes insecure and makes the decisions covering his ass.

The board of directors will never take the blame. They're heads of big corporations and don't have time to spend on this particular one. It's more or less a social thing.

With fewer companies, the tension is at its greatest in fifty years. There's a joke that someday there will be one manufacturing and one retailing concern. The retailer will say to the manufacturer, "I don't like your line." And the business dies. There used to be a business saying: "Eighty-twenty." Eighty percent of your volume comes from twenty percent of your customers. Eighty percent of the work is done by twenty percent of the workers. Today I think it's changed to ninety-five-five. Today, Wal-Mart, K-Mart, Target,

---

* Leveraged buy-out.

Service Merchandise. People aren't buying less. There are as many places to buy, but they're controlled by fewer people.

Youngsters are coming up now and want a crack at the big jobs. In the old days, to become president of a company, top man, you had to be in your fifties and sixties. Today, you've got CEOs that are thirty-seven years old, twenty-nine. When I started out in the jungle, you were considered a baby at forty-one.

Also, there's a new way of doing business. A lot of older people didn't keep up with the modern ways. It's difficult, too, because computers are running the world. Yet people are still vigorous at seventy, seventy-five.

Ageism is a tremendous problem today. Investment bankers will tell you they're very uncomfortable with old people running anything. Business analysts don't give a good rating if a seventy-five-year-old guy is running the company. What the hell, he's going to die any minute, a change in management, an upset. It starts getting dangerous at sixty, sixty-five.

A guy was saying the other day, "You people on Medicare are making it awful tough. The costs are unbelievable." There is that feeling: taxes wouldn't be so high if it weren't for the old geezers.

As for me, if I didn't work, I'd deteriorate and die. My doctor tells me to keep active, keep your brain going, keep your body going. Some people my age have hobbies—painting, gardening. That keeps them alive. Unfortunately, I'm not one of these. I love golf, I love swimming, but that doesn't stimulate the mind. I need something else.

Power, age, greed. These are human qualities. They don't disappear when you become a CEO. Having the telephone constantly ring, all the perks, people catering to you, asking your opinions, asking you on boards. It's very flattering and ego-building. Many of the top executives start to believe their publicity and think they walk on water. Many of the business failures today are the result of top executives feeling that they walk with God.

People of my age are a lost generation. What's left for him to do if he's not creating? Every businessman feels he's doing something creative. What the hell are you alive for? It's nice being a great father and a great grandfather—but they're a different generation, your kids, no matter how close you are to them. I don't know what's to be done.

We're living longer and we're cursed with such things as Alzheimer's, heart attacks, and strokes. That's the great fear with us. But if you're busy running a business, you don't sit around and think about your sicknesses. You have this big struggle not to deteriorate. When you create and contribute, you feel marvelous.

One of the nice things at this age is the luxurious morning. Before, you had to get up, get out, get going. Now, I can lay around, read the paper, *Wall Street Journal,* trade magazines, take my time with breakfast, go over the mail. Then I talk on the phone, spend time with my investment counselor. If it's a nice day, play golf or find someone to have lunch with. I'll take long walks, walk the treadmill, swim at about four o'clock, and then I'm ready for dinner. [Pauses.] It sounds pretty dull.

Yeah, I get a little bored. The pain of being unneeded and unwanted is uncomfortable at every stage. There are some guys who are unneeded 100 percent of the day. That would drive me absolutely insane. There are some guys who play golf in the morning, play cards in the afternoon, go out for dinner at night, spend the summers here and winters in Florida or Palm Springs, do the same things there. I don't know how they live.

When you're CEO, people are always after you. [Snaps his fingers.] What are we gonna do here? What are we gonna do there? What do you think about this guy? That guy? Mr. Culberg, so-and-so called and wants to have lunch with you at two o'clock. You're being wanted always. That ties in with being needed. That's a massive human desire.

When you're a CEO, my goodness, you're at the office at eight o'clock. You have meetings going on, correspondence, phone, this guy calls you, that guy calls you, planning for a board meeting, people problems, manufacturing problems. And they need somebody for a final decision.

Your social circle has diminished by the deaths. Mostly what's left of your social world are the widows. [Chuckles.] You read the obituaries by habit now.*

As for politics, I've become a cynical old man. I don't believe in miracles anymore. I don't believe anybody walks on water. It's kind of a hopeless feeling. There's a lot to be done, but I don't think it can ever be done because the people will never allow it. I don't think the human species has changed since it was created. The horrors of centuries ago are still happening today. What have we learned? The human failing. And the CEO is no different than the rest of us.

In my opinion, the world is in a worse mess than it's ever been. I know it's been said of every generation, but this time it's really true. I wasn't this cynical when I was younger. I thought we were helping save the world. I have no regrets for those feelings.

I envy the young their rage but not their future. I think they're in for some rough times. You see it in their daily lives. A small percentage of young executives will hit the top and make far more money than we did. But there will be far less opportunities for the majority. The great middle class is going to be less and less. There will be extreme wealth and extreme poverty. I hope I'm completely wrong. I'd be the happiest guy in the world, even if I'm not around. Personally, I look forward to some years of health, and when my time comes, to go immediately.

---

* "I wake up in the morning and dust off my wits,
I grab the newspaper and read the obits.
If I'm not there, I know I'm not dead,
So I have a good breakfast and go back to bed."
—From a turn-of-the-century parlor song

GENORA JOHNSON DOLLINGER, 80

Now living in Los Angeles, she became something of a legend during the first sit-down strike of 1937.

"I'd like very much to continue with the work I've done all my life, but my bad health pens me in as a prisoner. I'm not too generous about that. I chafe at the bit.

"My difficulties are mainly cardiac. I'm on my third pacemaker. It's often out of function, out of rhythm, and use only half of my heart. It takes down my spirits considerably.

"I would like to get out and participate in any effort, no matter how weak I may be. I've been active in the labor movement, the civil rights movement, the peace movement, all my life."

I was raised in Flint, Michigan. My family were pioneers in the city when Billy Durant was first experimenting in auto making. My father was a good, law-abiding citizen with all the prejudices of that day. He felt that women were not the equal of men. He was definitely middle class. He started out as a photographer for Buick, and made enough money to have a string of photographic shops throughout the state. He became very well-to-do. My mother, who was from a poor family, was always for the underdog, but she couldn't understand her daughter getting out, being a rebel.

While I was still in high school, a classmate invited me to her home, where I met her father and her brother. Her father was a very learned man who was something of a Eugene Debs socialist. He became my father-in-law, a man I always loved and admired very much. I called him Dad. I disliked my own father because he was so bigoted and narrow.

Things got so oppressive at home that I ran away and got married. I was seventeen. In my eyes, I was just escaping prison. My young husband got a job at Chevrolet and became an auto worker. Flint, aside from Ford's independent work, is where the auto industry began to grow. General Motors, DuPont, corporate power. Of course, there was no job security, no nothing.

By this time, I'd joined the Socialist Party and we were holding pretty large meetings in the center of the town. I was becoming very well known among the auto workers. I was not treated as just a woman but as someone who could join the battle.

By this time, I was pretty well known by the Flint police, too, and the company goons—and by some of the GM big shots. They tried to stop me through my father. My uncle was vice-president of General Motors, in charge of Chevrolet production. He had given jobs to some of my cousins. My father was closely connected to GM in many ways. They cut off all his transactions, all his photographic business, all his properties.

He tried to evict us from the apartment we had rented from him. We had two little boys at the time. My mother helped me get the children fed while I was at the union headquarters. My father and I never, never got along.

When the strike broke out in Fisher Tool, we were there. The big Chevrolet compound of factories was directly across the street and we were there, too. We were right in the middle of it from the very beginning. We sat down on the twenty-eighth and twenty-ninth of December, 1936, just before New Year's Day.

General Motors had complete control of all the means of communication in the city—the newspapers, the radio. They were putting out propaganda that the Communists were taking over Flint. The women were frightened to death because we'd gone through a long depression, a slim, hard existence. They believed much of what General Motors was saying. On New Year's Eve, I saw a contingent of women coming down to the plant threatening their husbands: "You get out of that plant and be with me on New Year's Eve or I'm starting divorce against you Monday morning."

There were a couple of divorces that were played up in the press. This was a big factor to weaken the resolve of the men who were just beginning the sit-down strike. Remember, we were just a handful against the biggest industrial corporation in the world. We knew we had to make some move. Well, I decided what my purpose was: to get the women organized, women talking to women.

We put out leaflets announcing that the women were organizing, to come down and join up—and bring other women. They didn't have cars and few had telephones at that time. You had to reach them door to door. For the first time in labor history, we organized a Women's Auxiliary. A lot of people thought the name wasn't very nice, that it should have been "Ladies Auxiliary" as the wives of craft union members were called.

We did everything. Mainly, it was to get women to understand why their husbands were taking the big chance. We visited their homes, organized a nursery for the children, a first aid station with a registered nurse. They organized the kitchen that fed the strikers hundreds of meals a day. We'd just walk across the street where the men were sitting in, they'd open the window and we'd push in cartons of food. We were protected by the picket lines that were there all the time.

General Motors would start rumors that somebody's mother or father was dying and that the man should come right home. We were losing a few people that way. But as soon as the wives understood what was being done, they'd send in messages that things were all right at home, to stick in there.

We had a few friendly merchants and farmer neighbors and auto workers who had farms. They'd send in bags of potatoes and sides of beef. We had a welfare committee going around soliciting everybody for food.*

The battle began when General Motors hired some goons and

---

* "They'd assign roles to you. When some of the guys at headquarters wanted

ordered the Flint police to throw the workers out of Fisher Tool. They were afraid that if the sit-down continued, it would spread to the fifteen other GM plants across the country. So they started tear-gassing. We formed a great big picket line in front of the plant and the men turned over their own cars to make a barricade.

The police were using buckshots and rifles and tear gas and everything against us. The men were throwing back whatever they could get their hands on: nuts and bolts and hinges. Any tear-gas bomb that came over unexploded, they'd throw back into the ranks of the police.

Whenever a woman appeared, the men would courteously escort them to safety. They wanted to escort me away and I said, "Hell, no. I have as many weapons as you have. I'm staying right here." So I stayed the whole night while the battle raged. When the fight was at its height, Victor Reuther, who had been on the sound truck, encouraging the people to keep on going, came over to us and said, "The batteries are running down. We may lose this battle, but we won't lose the war." I said, "How about my getting on that truck?" Women never were on the sound car. The men thought they had to win everything. He said, "We've got nothing to lose." So I got on and tried a new tactic—an appeal to the women.

On each side of these barricades there were thousands of men and women who had come to see what was going on. Naturally, the radio, controlled by GM, made it sound like the revolution had

---

to tell some of the guys in the plants what was cookin', I carried the message. I was a scavenger, too.

"The merchants cooperated. There'd be apples, bushels of potatoes, crates of oranges that was beginning to spoil. Some of our members were also little farmers, they'd come up with a couple of baskets of junk.

"The soup kitchen was outside the plant. The women handled all the cooking, outside of one chef who came from New York. Mostly stews, pretty good meals. They were put in containers and hoisted up through the window. The boys in there had their own plates and cups and saucers."

—Bob Stinson, *Hard Times: An Oral History of the Great Depression,* 1970

broken out. The sound car was reaching them. On the loudspeaker, on top of the truck, I directed my remarks to the women on both sides of the barricades. I said the cops were shooting into the bellies of unarmed men and the mothers of children. I made it sound as though there were an equal number of women down there. I begged the women to break through those lines of cops and come down here and join with us.

One woman started forward and a cop grabbed her coat. She pulled right out of it and marched down to join us. After that, other women came. The police didn't want to shoot them in the back. The women poured through and that ended the battle. I was smack dab in the middle.

But that wasn't the greatest moment. The biggest victory was the strategy that involved breaking the windows of one plant as a ruse, to make the corporation feel that that was the plant we were going to pull down on strike. This decoy was Chevrolet Plant No. 9. All the plant police and city cops rushed over there.

I had the women's emergency brigade marching up and down with clubs. When the company goons started attacking the men inside, one worker with a bloody face broke a window and shouted, "They're tear-gassing us inside." We flew at the windows and broke them out.

While this fight was going on at No. 9, and up until the time they carried the men out in ambulances and took them to the hospital, the men in Plant No. 4 were busy building barricades. This was the plant GM couldn't operate without. It produced all the motors of every Chevrolet car across the country. Their best seller.

My first husband, Kermit Johnson, was the only member of the strike committee working in that plant. It employed four thousand. He had a tiny piece of scrap paper that marked out all the exits, sliding doors, gondolas, and everything. The guys from all the other Chevrolet plants came pouring into Plant No. 4 and held it in a sit-down.

So while they were carrying the guys out in ambulances at the decoy plant, No. 9, I and four lieutenants strolled down to No. 4. We came to the gate and the guys inside were yelling, "For God's sake, don't let anyone through that gate." They were throwing out the scabs and all kinds of fighting was going on inside.

We five string ourselves across that iron gate entry. The Flint police came marching up to us: "All right, out of the way. We're going in." We said, "Over our dead bodies." One of the young women said, "My father and my brother work here and nobody is going in. If you were working here, your wife would do the same thing."

The five of us women held out, stalling the police. Beating an unarmed woman was a different story in those days. We looked up and here came the emergency brigade, the Red Berets. We called ourselves that because of our red berets, red arm bands with white letters: EB. They were carrying the American flag and singing "Solidarity Forever" and "Hold the Fort." The sound car came, I hopped on it, and we organized the big picket line at the gate.

That was the single biggest victory of the labor movement. Fifteen plants across the country were on strike, but No. 4 was the plant that settled the whole business. We shut this one down for fourteen days. It was part of the forty-four-day strike in the other two Fisher body plants. It was tougher here because we had no cushions or upholstery for sitting down.

We won. Our union was recognized. GM decided to sit down with us. John L. Lewis came in and they conducted negotiations in Detroit. The guys in the plant couldn't believe it. They were struck with astonishment.* Celebration? When the guys evacuated the plant, the whole town was reveling. I was smothered in the crowds

---

* "We finally got the word: THIS THING IS SETTLED. The guys in the plant didn't believe it. We had to send in three people, one after the other. When they did get it, they marched out of the plant with the flag flyin' and all that stuff.

"You'd see some guys comin' out of there with whiskers as long as Santa Claus. They made a rule they wasn't gonna shave until the strike was over.

➔ 516 ←

of people filling the streets, marching through the city, singing and dancing all night long. I was twenty-three.

That period was the high point of my life. It was the time of the Depression, when working people had a feeling for each other. We helped each other out in times of trouble. It was a time that most people never get a chance to live through. We started to organize against hunger, poverty, sickness, everything that's hard. We were just at the point where so many of us decided we'd rather die first before we'd ever go back to being nonunion scabs. A little different from today, I'm afraid.

I was blacklisted by every employer in Flint. They wouldn't touch me with a ten-foot pole. So we moved to Detroit. I got a job at Briggs. I was fired from the one before. They caught up with me before I got in my ninety days to be eligible for seniority.

At Briggs, I became one of the leaders of the most militant UAW local: 212. We were known as the Dead End Kids. This company still could not accept the union, so we went on strike frequently. I had taken a WPA training course in lathes and machinery, so they put me on a punch press. I thought I'd die because, by this time, I was left with one lung. I had tuberculosis at the time of the GM strike.

They offered me a job in the front office, hiring people. I said, "Of course not. The war is on and I want to do my part on the line." So I became head of the blueprint inspection department.

The girls were having a hard time with these macho foremen, who were saying horrible things to them, penalizing them at every chance. They didn't want women in the plant. In that new depart-

---

Oh, it was just like—you've gone through the Armistice delirium, haven't you? Everybody was runnin' around shakin' everybody by the hand, saying, 'Jesus, you look strange, you got a beard on, you know.' Wives kissin' their husbands. There was a lot of drunks on the street that night.

"When Mr. Knudson put his name to a piece of paper and says that General Motors recognizes UAW-CIO—until that moment we were non-people that didn't even exist. That was the big one."

—Bob Stinson, *Hard Times: An Oral History of the Great Depression,* 1970

ment, I didn't dare open my mouth for ninety days. About three days before the ninety days were up, the girls invited me to a union meeting. So I thought I'd sit in the back and not say a word.

The main speaker at the meeting was Emil Mazy, one of the original UAW organizers. Halfway through his speech, he looked out and recognized me. He said, "I don't know why you women are asking us for help. You've got one of the original UAW organizers sitting back there."

I said, "Emil, you just cooked my goose. I was just three days away from seniority." Emil said, "I want you and all these women to know that if they fire Genora, every Briggs plant in Detroit will go down." They did fire me, and eighteen thousand workers went on strike. Every Briggs plant went down. They took me back on the job.

I began to hold public speaking classes in the local, training people to get up and challenge contracts that were bad. Rank-and-file people. I became very active in our caucus. Our militant people were getting beaten up regularly. One of our best men suffered a brain concussion. Another was terribly beaten up while walking down the street with his wife. They were obviously professional jobs.

We formed an investigating committee to find out who was behind it. We suspected the Mafia and we were right. I was the only woman on that committee. When the Reuther brothers got shot and wounded—Vic lost an eye—the UAW hired a guy who had worked with the LaFollette Committee to work for them.*

Meanwhile, we're investigating on our own. One night, someone enters our bedroom with a lead pipe, clubs my husband and cracks me over the head. I wound up paralyzed down the whole side of my body. I was in the hospital for God knows how long.

We discovered that the son of the Mafia head in Detroit had a great big contract with Briggs for all the scrap metal. You see, we

---

* The committee, headed by Sen. Robert LaFollette, Jr., investigated violations of the Wagner Act, which allowed workers to join unions without employer interference.

were getting too close. That's when they came and did the job on us.

Now the war was over and the plants were being transferred back to civilian production. They laid off a great many women. The boys were back, you can now return to the kitchen.

Years later, in the '60s, I became active in the antiwar movement. I worked for the American Civil Liberties Union in Detroit. We had a very militant chapter. When they returned to California in 1966, I became interested in schools. I was organizing community advisory councils and appearing before boards. We played a big role in the first teachers' strike out here. There was the National Organization for Women, of course. I even signed up my granddaughter, when she was five months old.

I had to give all this up about three years ago, when my illness caught up with me. It's something you can't control. It's gotten worse and worse. I get so disgusted. At one point, my doctor suggested that I have a wheel chair. It's out in the garage. It belongs in a museum. I can't stand the thought of it. But I think that's where I'm heading, because only half my heart is functioning. I don't know anything that's okay with me right now! Oh, how I'd love to be back in action. It's been my whole life. But nature takes us all down.

It's not just *my* health, it's the health of our country that's so bad. Anybody who was at the birth of the CIO and went through all those upheavals must feel disillusioned, discouraged, and disgusted with present-day labor leadership. They think the back door to the White House is the way. Labor is in for some pretty dark days.

How can we reach the young? We've got to get a political party that addresses education, training, the needs of working people, and the four-day workweek. The first UAW meeting in Milwaukee called for a thirty-hour workweek with forty hours' pay. I'm pessimistic for the near future, but I think, someday, leaders will arise worthy of the American working class.

Old people, my generation, are being ripped off with a medical system that's stealing money out of their pockets left and right. The prescriptions alone, for me, run over three hundred dollars a month. How can people who receive only Social Security benefits pay for something like that? In a minute, I'll be taking one of those pills.

Any regrets? Second thoughts? Maybe I should have spent more time with the two young children I lost. Two wonderful kids, who were killed by a speeding taxi cab. One was ten, the other was fourteen. Sometimes you think, "Oh, my God, maybe I should have spent more time at home with them." They had such a short life. The kids in the classroom had new bikes and our kids didn't. I used to explain that we were doing it for everybody's children. They agreed with me, but they had to sacrifice a hell of a lot. Some things you can't help. I don't know. If I hadn't gone through all these experiences, I wouldn't be the same person. Other people helped make me what I am.

Sure, my body has slackened off, but my interest hasn't diminished. People who've lived through a great, great thing like that strike of 1937, people who called each other brother and sister and meant it, people who would give things to other families' kids because it was needed—when you saw that kind of loyalty to a person in the same boat as you, you can never forget, and I hope that feeling will come back one day.

I can't become cynical. I still hope we'll see a decent society, without greed, without plundering other nations, without war, and with the salvation of the earth, for crying out loud. [Slight pause, a sigh.] I better take that pill now.

She died a few months after this conversation.

JACOB LAWRENCE, 76

*We're in his studio on the second floor of his frame house in Seattle,
where he lives with his wife, Gwen, also a painter. On the walls are
some of his works in progress. On the tables are hand tools: hammer,
chisel, plane, brushes. There is an impromptu, easy touch here; not at
all precisely arranged. Everything he may need appears to be comfortably at hand.*

*He retired from teaching at the University of Washington nine
years ago.*

This is what my day is like. I sit here, I'm looking at my works, I'm
reading, I'll go back to my drawing table, do some drawing. That's
more or less it. Of course we go shopping because we have to eat.
But this is my place, this is where I work.

I work constantly. I look at my tools here. I'm not a cabinet-
maker, but I use them. I love to look at hand tools. They're beautiful to see, to feel. They're a symbol of working, of building. I use
them that way.

The tool is an extension of the hand. The hand is a very beautiful
instrument. Think of what we can do with the hand, its dexterity.
It's been with us hundreds of years. You look at works of art and
the tool hasn't changed. It maintains its beauty. It's like a work of
sculpture. I like to pick it up, look it, turn it. I use them in my
paintings as I would in a still life. To me, these tools are alive.

*About a year ago, his series of panels—moments in the lives of Har-
riet Tubman and Frederick Douglass—were on exhibition in a
number of American museums. At the Chicago Art Institute, he was
a gracious guide as we strolled past each painting. It was something
of a promenade: Mussorgsky's* Pictures at an Exhibition *came to my
mind's ear. "It is the spirit of our country. The largeness of spirits of*

our country. The largeness of spirits like Harriet Tubman, Frederick Douglass, John Brown, Abraham Lincoln is what made our country what it is."

How I became an artist? In elementary school, we were given crayons, poster paint, and were encouraged to put down color. In the great 1930s, I heard stories from older people. They'd talked about heros and heroines of an earlier day. They'd talk about Marcus Garvey, John Brown, Harriet Tubman, Frederick Douglass. I'd walk the streets of Harlem and hear corner orators talk about these people. It inspired me. I realized I couldn't tell their lives in one story, so I painted a series of their lives.

It is ironic that people like myself benefited from the Great Depression. The Roosevelt administration established programs where people of all ages could receive lessons in these art centers in whatever field attracted us: dance, music, theater, painting, sculpture. It lasted about five years, a wonderful, wonderful period.

I went into one of these federal art centers as a youngster. I was about sixteen. I didn't have the means of going to college, but at these centers I was encouraged and taught by elders. Librarians, teachers, the YMCA, the church—they all took an interest in us. There was a spirit of uplift. Too bad a depression had to come along to do this, but it was wonderful for people my age, some of them now renowned. Even today, in post offices, you'll see some of their murals.*

It's too bad we don't have more of that today—government support of the arts. In schools, the first programs cut back are music, dance, the arts. If we don't realize how much these things contribute to the quality of life, we'll lose it. I see these youngsters on

---

* On the walls of the cafeteria of Lane Technical High School in Chicago are such murals—Americans at work—courtesy of the WPA (Work Progress Administration).

the street, never exposed to this experience—they've lost it, their chance at that life.

When I was growing up, everybody took an interest in us kids. The neighborhood was very tight. You'd go out on the street, you'd know just about everybody around, even if you didn't know them by name. There was a great pride in that. We were poor, but we had so much in another way: the love of the community.

If it weren't for these federal programs, I probably would have been lost and drifting like so many young people were, without any sense of belonging. I dread to think what would have happened to me. Today I go out on the street and I look at these children, twelve, thirteen years old. Where will they be five years from now? Our society today doesn't recognize what potential may be in them.

What happened to me was a sense of appreciation of the human being. This feeling was developed in me, a sense of the worthiness of the person. This is what I try to get in my work. That's why I grasp the tools so much. What Walt Whitman put into words, I try to do with my tools as a painter.

I grew up in a big city, New York, with all those tall buildings. The spirit of the times encouraged an appreciation of color, of form, of texture, of just the beauty of looking at things. I heard hammering, people calling out to one another, people building. I became conscious of hearing the jackhammer, hearing a nail being driven in, hearing people walking the streets.*

---

* In 1965, Jessie Binford, ninety, a colleague of Jane Addams, was reflecting on her home town, Marshalltown, Iowa, to which she returned for her last years: "Nobody walks here anymore. He jumps into his car, of course. I walk more than anyone else in this town. I'm often the only one on the street. I'd much rather get out in the evening at sunset and walk here than get into a car, with probably all the windows closed. The commonest thing I hear in this town is fear, fear of the unknown."

—*Division Street: America,* 1967

In 1970, my wife and I were walking along the street of a small South

I was hearing and trying to visualize these sounds. The sense of being acute to these sounds has remained with me to this day.

I haven't changed. I'm afraid our society has. Today there seems to be a lack of communication. We don't touch. There is a coldness. I don't come in contact with you, you don't with me. I just don't know what it means.

In the 1930s, there was something going on, a human kind of communication. Words meant something. Today we're ashamed to express these feelings. A few years ago, the kids in school started a program called Touch. They were looking for something. That meant there was something lacking. We didn't have to think of such a program. It was just a natural kind of thing.

The young today are timid about expressing any kind of feeling. They're afraid to bare themselves. They're afraid they might be considered soft.

How can you explain why people have become the way they are? Maybe technology running wild has something to do with it. Everything has become so mechanical. It's frustrating, the telelphone. I hesitate. You don't hear a person. It's a machine. Maybe to a young person, it is natural—to me, it is not.† I'm not averse to technology, but not, if in developing it, we lose something else. We must become aware of this other thing we're sacrificing.

Some students feel good about not coming into contact with a canvas or with paper. It's done by machine. They say: "My hand never touched it." This is a plus, the way they think. They don't feel the paper, they don't feel the canvas. It's all machine. They plug something in and they can do a portrait by computer. A

Dakota town. It was about nine o'clock at night. We were the sole pedestrians. A police car slowed down; the officer solicitously inquired: "What are you doing out at this hour? Are you lost?"

† Buckminster Fuller reflected on his grandchild: "She heard the sound of the airplane before she heard the song of the nightingale. To her, the first sound was natural, the second, unnatural."

student can come back that same day and bring you a portrait of yourself, without his having laid a finger on the brush, canvas, or paper. He hasn't seen you breathing, blinking, nothing like that. The air all around you is not there. There's no space. Throughout our history, these have been important factors in making a work of art.

Hammer? Chisel? Feel of the hairs of a brush? They don't want to be accused by their peers of succumbing to this human thing: touch. They'd be ashamed. Distance has become a plus to their peers and to themselves.

Maybe one day we'll live in a world of robots, a world of mechanical devices. Fortunately, I won't be alive. I feel this way more now than I did a few years ago. I feel this drawing back.

I'm retired now. I retired from teaching at the University of Washington in 1984. I loved working with the students, but you get to the point where you leave it to the younger people. I didn't retire from painting. I never will.

In school, young students want young professors. They want someone closer to their own age. That the older person may offer so much in experience doesn't matter that much to them. I've heard my students say they don't want old professors. They mean somebody forty, fifty. They turn their backs to them.

If you get to be forty, fifty, you're old. The students show their disdain. It's not always meant to be cruel, it's not always absolute, but you get it. When they say they want someone closer to their own age, they mean someone two years older. You get it in all of our advertisements, too. Insurance companies don't want to insure you. You've outlived your time. It's the attitude that we're living too long—the resources can't support us. I definitely feel this generation gap. The irony is that we have worked and contributed to the young people all of our lives.

I feel there should be more emphasis on the humanities in the home as well as in the school. The importance of the church, too. I didn't just go to church on Sunday. I went to church two or three times a week. I was taught certain values which have remained with me to this day. You don't do certain things, even though you thought you could get away with it.

When I was a youngster growing up, a person would never attack an older person, a weaker person, because of the fear of God. Now the older person is vulnerable because of something lost, a sense of morality, of ethics. How can we have that in the streets if we don't have it in the higher places? Look at our leaders, committing all sorts of crimes, then going free. Roosevelt's people weren't all saints, but there was a quality there, a feeling we don't get today.

Are we about to give up that which we have as human beings? Are we losing it little by little. What price are we paying? Maybe there are people talking and thinking the way we are right now. Maybe we can prevent this. Maybe we can mantain the quality that we might be losing.

I'm not pessimistic. I think about these things. I talk about them. I feel as long as there's one person or two people who are aware of this quality, of our capacity to think and feel, we're on pretty sound ground. I hope so.

DAVID BROWER, 79

A leading apostle of the modern environmental movement. His fervor, as well as his vigor, is apparent. His young companions are obviously fond of him and get a kick out of his perorations and spirit of bonhomie. He lives in San Francisco.

What do I think about age? I think I've learned to accept it. I never expected to get this old. With no effort on my part, I'm now about to be eighty and an elder. I find a certain freedom in this.

I was in Prescott, Arizona, for the first day of the Dave Foreman* trial and I spoke out. The Earth Firsters were on the griddle. They'd been infiltrated by the FBI, some of them, and coaxed to do a certain act of violence on behalf of the earth—to try to knock down some power towers in Arizona. That was entrapment. I was at the trial with about two hundred others. Old as I was, I took on the FBI, who had infiltrated the audience. I said, "You should investigate those who are tearing the earth apart rather than those who are trying to save it. I invite the FBI to join our organization."

If I'm on the telephone and I know my line is tapped, I'll interrupt my conversation and say, "I have the following message for you eavesdroppers: For God's sake, we don't need you to entrap us. We need you to join us." There's never any response on the other end. [Laughs.]

At my age, they can't do much to hurt me. I have a new freedom. They can't change my career, I've got it made. If I go to jail or am executed, it doesn't matter—though I'd rather stick around. I'd rather be out of jail than in, but not at the expense of this newfound freedom.

Young people don't have this liberty. They've got years ahead of them, families, need for income. They can't alienate themselves too much from the system. I say to people my age, "You have this freedom. Please use it. You've had a role in whatever's happened to the earth, and it hasn't been that good. You now have a role in doing something about it. If you're going to die, make sure your boots are on. There are so many of us. More and more of us.

"You're not going to be around that much longer and you know it. Get into the fight, it gets your juices flowing. Maybe like me, you'll have a double martini because you're not sure you'll be around to order the next one. [He is, at this moment, having one.] Or maybe you hate phone mail and you're not sure you'll be around to answer all your calls.

---

* A founder of Earth First!

"You should be impatient with the slow pace of reform. You should resent having been put out to pasture, because no other species ever does that. You should fight against being put on the fringe of the herd. There is so much potential, you have so much to offer. There is so much information stored in you. At eighty, I've got this important file in my head. I'm not always able to find exactly what I want when I want it, but I can do so much better with my mind than with what's on—paper. I haven't reached for a single note, have I?

"Think of what's stored in an eighty- or a ninety-year-old mind. Just marvel at it. Think of these visual images stored in your head—your own videotapes. You can see the faces of people you've met throughout your life. You remember the places you've been to. If you're a concert pianist, where the hell did you store all those notes and in what order are they supposed to come, at what volume, at what pace? It's not going to be there much longer. Let's get with it.

"You've got to get out this information, this knowledge, because you've got something to pass on. You've got a file that nobody else has. *There'll be nobody like you ever again.* Make the most of every molecule you've got as long as you've got a second to go. That's the charge. That is your assignment."

I was forced out of the Sierra Club staff in 1969. I was just a kid of fifty-seven. Russell Train, who is the finest Republican conservationist—a contradiction in terms—we've ever had, said to John McPhee, "Thank God for David Brower because he makes it so easy for the rest of us to be reasonable." I enjoyed that. Eight years later, I retorted, "Thank God for Russ Train because he makes it so easy for the rest of us to be outrageous."

I don't like to reason with the people who are determined to get rid of what makes us possible: the realists. Richard Barnett says that we march toward annihilation under the banner of realism.

It's fun to rock the boat—particularly if you become unreasonable because within five years or so, your heresy becomes old hat. Maybe I started something that was worth starting. I've had a lot of delights. I didn't know where I was going, but I was going somewhere.

I wish that Earth Firsters were unnecessary, but they *are* necessary. After I left the Sierra Club, I founded Friends of the Earth to make the Sierra Club look reasonable. Now we need an organization that will make Dave Foreman look reasonable.

One night, as we were closing a bar in Ann Arbor, I said, "Hey, Dave, there's already an organization that makes you look reasonable: Earth Last. It's got a big membership—the Fortune 500. What they're doing to the earth makes what you're doing look more reasonable than anything else going on."

Everybody else says you're bad, you're getting in the way of everything, you're costing jobs, you're nasty, get lost. I've been called "cantankerous," "abrasive," a "troublemaker." All true. It all adds up to being really reasonable keeping the life support system alive. We all use it. We're trashing it and we should cut that out. This isn't what's getting across, so I say that the people who are trashing the earth's life support system are the unreasonables, the bad guys. We're trying to say, "The earth is not a bad place, people are not that bad, life is not that bad."

We have to have a sense of the future. The only thing that is real is Now. The Nows to come are going to be as real for the people living in the next year, the next century, the next millennium as the Now of this moment. The indigenous people were thinking seven generations ahead. They were too conservative. They didn't know the capability of the human species to damage their stamping ground the way we do. So we have to think further ahead. What is the earth going to be like a thousand years from now? What do we do with the nuclear stuff? What do we do for the new child or the new fawn or the new baby seal pup that's born a thousand years from now, so that it opens its eyes on a beautiful, livable planet? I don't know your answer. I have a pretty good idea of my answer.

This is no time to relax. They say you've reached the retirement age, but if you're this old, damn well, there's no real reason to retire and to be put on the shelf and forget what you've spent all this time learning. If you were in an indigenous culture, you would be an elder, and admitted, even required, to advise. And you'd be heeded. Don't demand that they pay that much attention to you. But just, hey, give us a little attention.

The old ones should try very hard not to be boring, not to talk endlessly, which I do constantly. In most other cultures—say, Native American—older women have a great deal of power. They determine who the chief will be. This is something we've got to learn again. It doesn't take very long to fertilize an egg, but it takes quite a while to mature that egg until it's ready to emerge and become an individual—and to help that individual into maturity. Decisions should be predominantly made by the people who do the nurturing, not by those who pass by quickly at the inception.

I'm leery of the feminists who say, "We cannot allow you to quote Robinson Jeffers's 'Man apart.'" It should be "person apart" or "people apart." The poet in him required one syllable. If they would worry less about nouns and pronouns and worry more about getting their rights back, we'd all be better off.

Of course, there are changes necessary in our vocabulary. When I went over some of my early writings, I was embarrassed. I was using "man," "his," "son," "father" all the way through. I can understand women being tired of that by now. Those changes were easy to make.

My wife appreciates the need. We were both editors at the University of California Press. She never forgot how abrupt I was with her. She was already working there. I passed her by and went to the guy instead. I was paid more than she was even though she'd been there for some time. That was fifty years ago, 1941, and she still remembers. Annoyed as she justifiably is, she says, "Feminists should be concentrating not on sisterhood but on being human beings, and maybe men will catch on." I'd like that as a goal, women's rights rather than watching the pronouns.

Women. Youth. Old age. All are connected in my mind. And memory. I remember when I was a battalion intelligence officer in World War II, in northern Italy. We were the mountain troops, the ski troops. Our first battle was in the Northern Apennines. The next, across the Po River valley. Our third took us into the Alps, as the war ended.

We were passing through these little old towns. The houses weren't big but all the generations were there. The old weren't put out to pasture. They were our best means of communication. They were what civilization is about: human history, work, generations. Old ones, grandparents, even great-grandparents, talked to the little ones, and fascinated them. It was the oral tradition, genera-tion after generation. Instead of watching television, the child lis-tened to the old one, learning his history of dreams and wonder.

Our young haven't lost their history, it was taken from them. We've stuffed them into a procrustean bed. Remember him? Pro-custes? If the guest didn't fit, he'd cut him or stretch him. That's what we're doing to our young, making them fit.

Here is a child, born with a sense of wonder, ready to admire and love what is seen and experienced. We say, "Watch it now, a little bit less, cool it, cool it," until this extraordinary sense of wonder is reduced to nothing.

I'm very fortunate to be working with young people. That's a big reason I haven't burned out. I keep getting recharged by these people. They're somebody to pass the torch on to. You don't hold on to it, that's no good. You have to pass it on.

In the Sierra Club, what bothered me was seeing the average age rising each year. There wasn't an influx of young ones. I work with a new group, Earth Island, which has a lot of younger people. You can't grow old as an organization without losing your effectiveness. You need that flow.

If the old person can't listen anymore, he perpetuates the errors of his ancestors. You don't need him. You need to say, "All right, Grandpa, when did you last change your mind about anything? When did you last get a new idea? Can I help you change your mind while you help me change mine? Considering that what has governed your behavior through your lifetime has gotten this world into one hell of a mess, have you got something new going on in your head?" That's what we need, your experience. That's what corporate boards should be about.

I like to collect rocks. The history of the earth is there. Finer forms are in the quarry than ever Michelangelo evoked. I think it's a quote from somewhere. As an old person, when I look at young people it charges me. Here, in effect, is a quarry. Something within this stone can be shaped. It's in somebody's imagination.

A student I once had at Stanford, where I taught for one quarter, told the class she had planted a garden, and one day they saw the seeds had sprouted and the first shoots were appearing and they applauded. They experienced a sense of wonder. It hadn't been squelched out of them yet. They were enjoying something that we all are forgetting how to enjoy: how the world works and the beauty of it. It still moves me. That's why I'm constantly challenging Operation Squelch.

My oldest son says I'm going through the "gee whiz" phase. But it is a sense of wonder. I know I'm not so young anymore, but I'm trying to get my damn knee to work better so I can get back to my rock climbing. I've got to lose some weight and get the right shoes. Listen, I'm not going to go very high.

For the next decade—what am I saying?—for the next century, we've got to put together what we so carelessly tore apart with so little concern for those who were gonna follow us. This sounds preachy and that's exactly what it is. I'm a preacher and I make no apologies. You've got to sound off. The older you are, the freer you are, as long as you last.

A NOTE ON THE TYPE

The text is set in DeVinne, a typeface classified
as Modern and named for the noted American printer
Theodore Low DeVinne (1828–1914).

The typography and binding designs are by

[sic]